AN EXPLORER'S GUIDE

The Berkshire Hills & Pioneer Valley of Western Massachusetts

Christina Tree

AN EXPLORER'S GUIDE

The Berkshire Hills & Pioneer Valley of Western Massachusetts

Christina Tree & William Davis

with photographs by the authors

THIRD EDITION

The Countryman Press * Woodstock, Vermont

To our family: Liam, Topher, Tim, Yuko, Aki, and Taiga

Third Edition

No entries or reviews in this book have been solicited or paid for.

The Berkshire Hills & Pioneer Valley of Western Massachusetts
ISBN: 978-0-88150-952-6

Cover and interior design by Bodenweber Design
Composition by PerfecType, Nashville, TN

Maps by Erin Greb Cartography, © The Countryman Press

Published by The Countryman Press, P.O. Box 748, Woodstock, Vermont 05091

Distributed by W. W. Norton & Company, Inc., 500 Fifth Avenue, New York, NY 10110

Printed in the United States of America

10 9 8 7 6 5 4 3 2 1

EXPLORE WITH US!

Welcome to the Berkshire Hills and Pioneer Valley of Western Massachusetts. In writing this guide, we have been increasingly selective in making recommendations based on years of conscientious research and personal experience. What makes us unique is that we describe the state by locally defined regions, giving you Western Massachusetts's communities, not simply its most popular destinations. With this guide you'll feel confident to venture beyond the tourist towns, along roads less traveled, to places of special hospitality and charm.

WHAT'S WHERE

In the beginning of the book you'll find an alphabetical listing of special highlights, with important information and advice on everything from antiques to weather reports.

LODGING

Prices: Please don't hold us or the respective innkeepers responsible for the rates listed, which were accurate as of press time in 2011. Some changes are inevitable. Massachusetts has a statewide 6.25 percent tax on both lodging and meals. Communities also have the option of levying an additional local tax of up to 6 percent, and many resort towns opt for the full amount.

Smoking: Massachusetts enforces a statewide ban on smoking in restaurants, bars, and nightclubs.

RESTAURANTS

Note the distinction between *Dining Out* and *Eating Out*. By their nature, restaurants listed in the *Eating Out* group are generally inexpensive.

KEY TO SYMBOLS

⚤ The wedding rings symbol appears beside facilities that frequently serve as venues for weddings and civil unions.

The special value symbol appears next to lodgings and restaurants that combine high quality and moderate prices.

The kids alert symbol appears next to lodgings, restaurants, activities, and shops of special appeal to youngsters.

The dog paw symbol appears next to lodgings that accept pets (usually with a reservation and deposit) as of press time.

♿ The wheelchair symbol appears next to lodgings, restaurants, and attractions that are partially or fully handicapped accessible.

The WiFi symbol appears next to inns, eateries, and other establishments that provide WiFi access for their guests.

We would appreciate your comments and corrections about places you visit or know well in the state. Please use the card enclosed in this book, or e-mail us directly at ctree@traveltree.net or bill@davistravels.com.

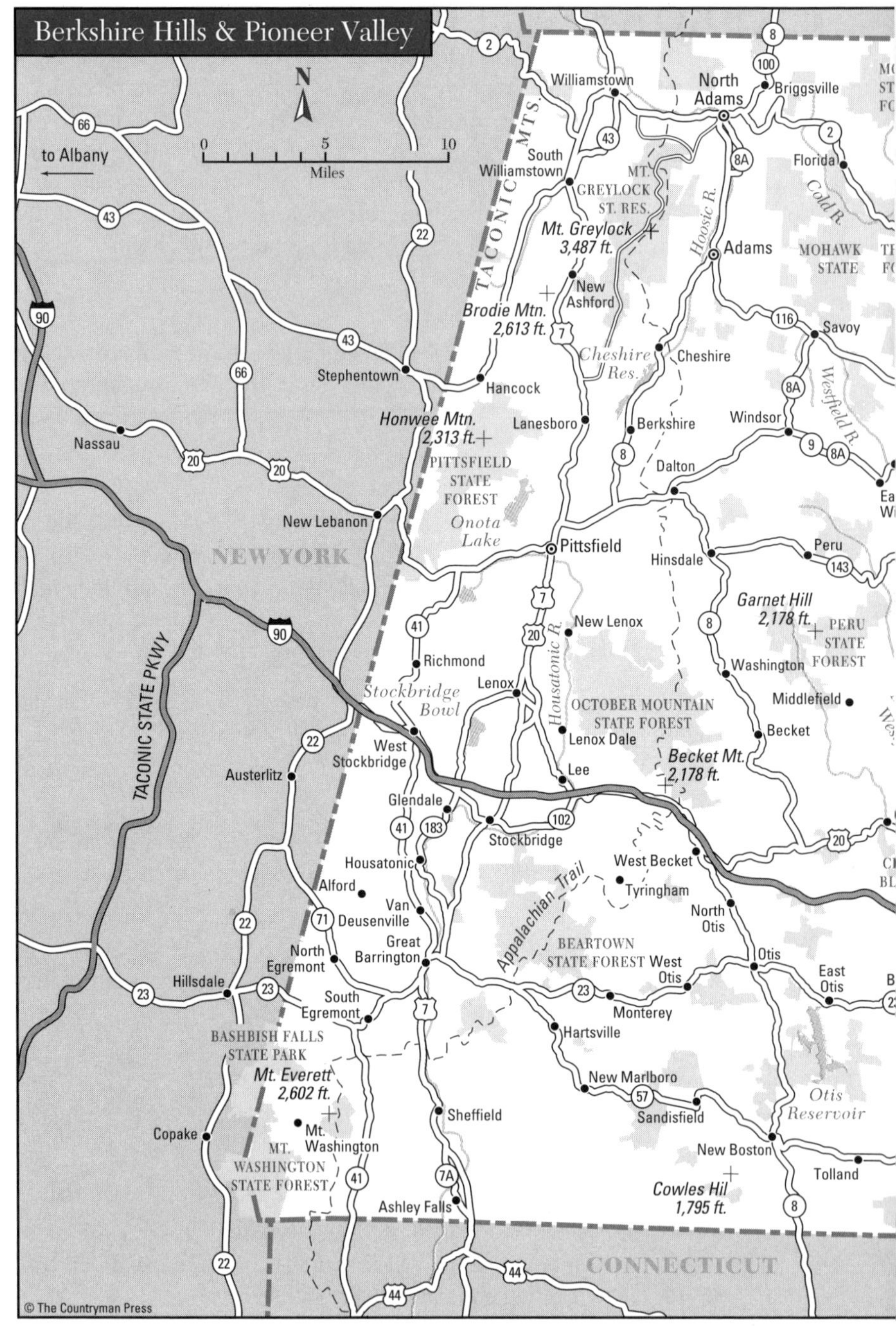
Berkshire Hills & Pioneer Valley
N
0
5
10
Miles
to Albany
NEW YORK
CONNECTICUT
TACONIC MTS.
TACONIC STATE PKWY
Williamstown
North Adams
Briggsville
South Williamstown
MT. GREYLOCK ST. RES.
Mt. Greylock 3,487 ft.
Hoosic R.
Florida
Cold R.
Adams
MOHAWK STATE
New Ashford
Brodie Mtn. 2,613 ft.
Savoy
Cheshire Res.
Cheshire
Westfield R.
Stephentown
Hancock
Honwee Mtn. 2,313 ft.
Lanesboro
Berkshire
Windsor
Nassau
PITTSFIELD STATE FOREST
Dalton
Onota Lake
New Lebanon
Pittsfield
Hinsdale
Peru
Garnet Hill 2,178 ft.
PERU STATE FOREST
New Lenox
Housatonic R.
Richmond
Washington
Lenox
Stockbridge Bowl
Middlefield
OCTOBER MOUNTAIN STATE FOREST
Lenox Dale
Becket
West Stockbridge
Austerlitz
Becket Mt. 2,178 ft.
Lee
Glendale
Stockbridge
West Becket
Housatonic
Appalachian Trail
Tyringham
Alford
Van Deusenville
North Otis
North Egremont
Great Barrington
BEARTOWN STATE FOREST
West Otis
Otis
East Otis
Hillsdale
South Egremont
Monterey
Hartsville
BASHBISH FALLS STATE PARK
Mt. Everett 2,602 ft.
New Marlboro
Sandisfield
Otis Reservoir
Mt. Washington
Sheffield
Copake
MT. WASHINGTON STATE FOREST
New Boston
Tolland
Cowles Hil 1,795 ft.
Ashley Falls
2
8
100
43
66
22
90
116
8A
9
20
143
7
41
183
102
71
23
57
7A
44
© The Countryman Press

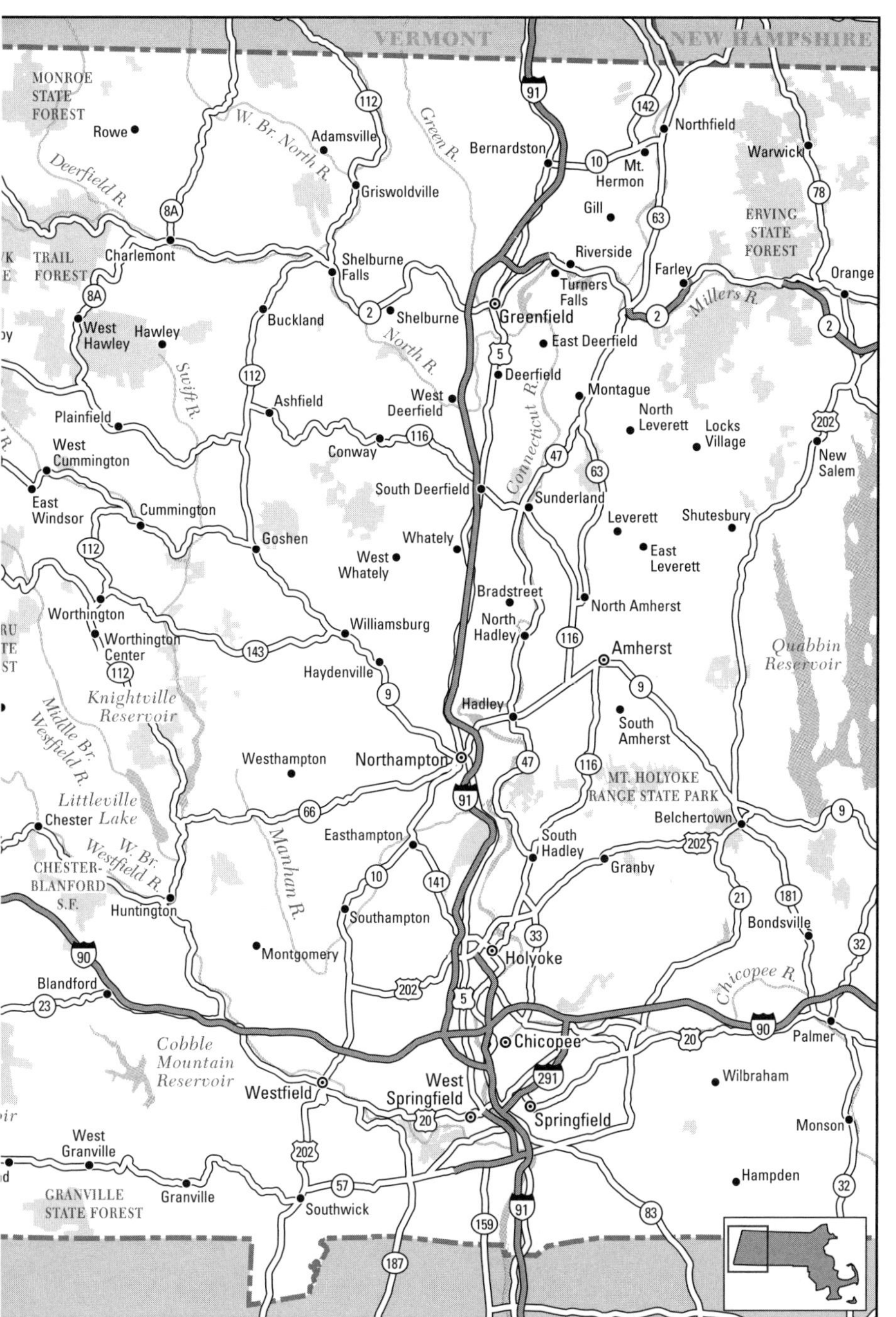
VERMONT
NEW HAMPSHIRE
MONROE STATE FOREST
Rowe
Adamsville
Griswoldville
Bernardston
Northfield
Mt. Hermon
Warwick
Gill
ERVING STATE FOREST
Charlemont
TRAIL FOREST
Shelburne Falls
Shelburne
Riverside
Turners Falls
Farley
Orange
Buckland
Greenfield
West Hawley
Hawley
East Deerfield
Deerfield
Montague
Ashfield
West Deerfield
North Leverett
Locks Village
Plainfield
West Cummington
Conway
New Salem
South Deerfield
Sunderland
East Windsor
Cummington
Leverett
Shutesbury
Goshen
Whately
East Leverett
West Whately
Bradstreet
North Amherst
Worthington
North Hadley
Williamsburg
Worthington Center
Amherst
Haydenville
Quabbin Reservoir
Knightville Reservoir
Hadley
South Amherst
Westhampton
Northampton
MT. HOLYOKE RANGE STATE PARK
Littleville Lake
Chester
Belchertown
Easthampton
South Hadley
Granby
CHESTER-BLANFORD S.F.
Huntington
Southampton
Bondsville
Montgomery
Holyoke
Blandford
Palmer
Chicopee
Cobble Mountain Reservoir
Wilbraham
Westfield
West Springfield
Springfield
Monson
West Granville
Hampden
Granville
Southwick
GRANVILLE STATE FOREST
Deerfield R.
W. Br. North R.
Green R.
Millers R.
North R.
Swift R.
Connecticut R.
Middle Br. Westfield R.
W. Br. Westfield R.
Manhan R.
Chicopee R.
91
142
112
10
8A
63
78
2
5
116
47
202
143
9
66
141
33
21
181
32
90
23
20
291
57
159
83
187

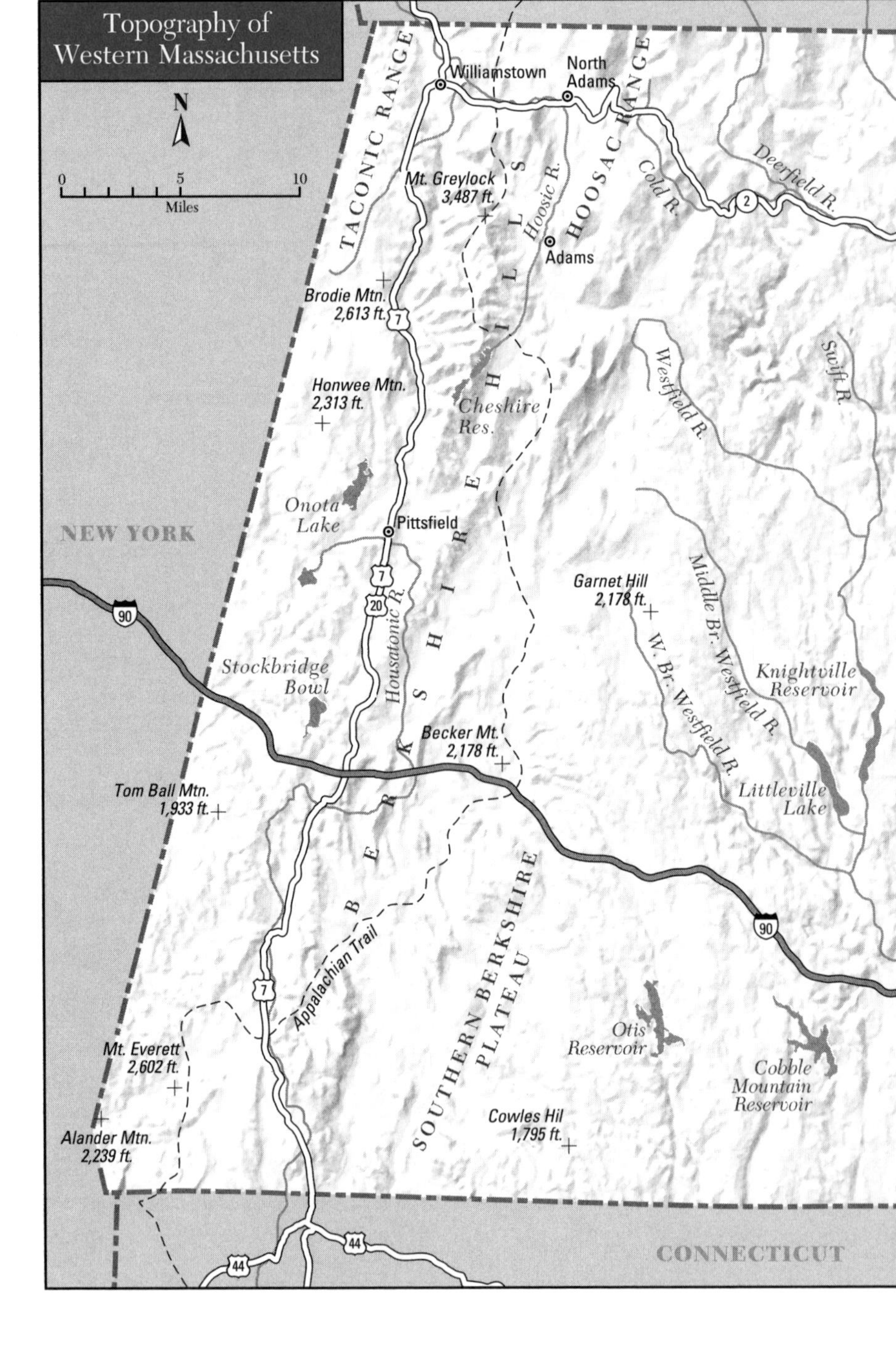
Topography of
Western Massachusetts
N
0
5
10
Miles
TACONIC RANGE
Williamstown
North
Adams
HOOSAC RANGE
Mt. Greylock
3,487 ft.
Hoosic R.
Cold R.
Deerfield R.
2
Adams
Brodie Mtn.
2,613 ft.
7
Honwee Mtn.
2,313 ft.
Cheshire
Res.
Westfield R.
Swift R.
Onota
Lake
Pittsfield
NEW YORK
7
20
90
Garnet Hill
2,178 ft.
Middle Br. Westfield R.
W. Br. Westfield R.
Housatonic R.
BERKSHIRE HILLS
Stockbridge
Bowl
Knightville
Reservoir
Becker Mt.
2,178 ft.
Tom Ball Mtn.
1,933 ft.
Littleville
Lake
90
SOUTHERN BERKSHIRE
PLATEAU
Appalachian Trail
7
Otis
Reservoir
Mt. Everett
2,602 ft.
Cobble
Mountain
Reservoir
Alander Mtn.
2,239 ft.
Cowles Hil
1,795 ft.
44
44
CONNECTICUT

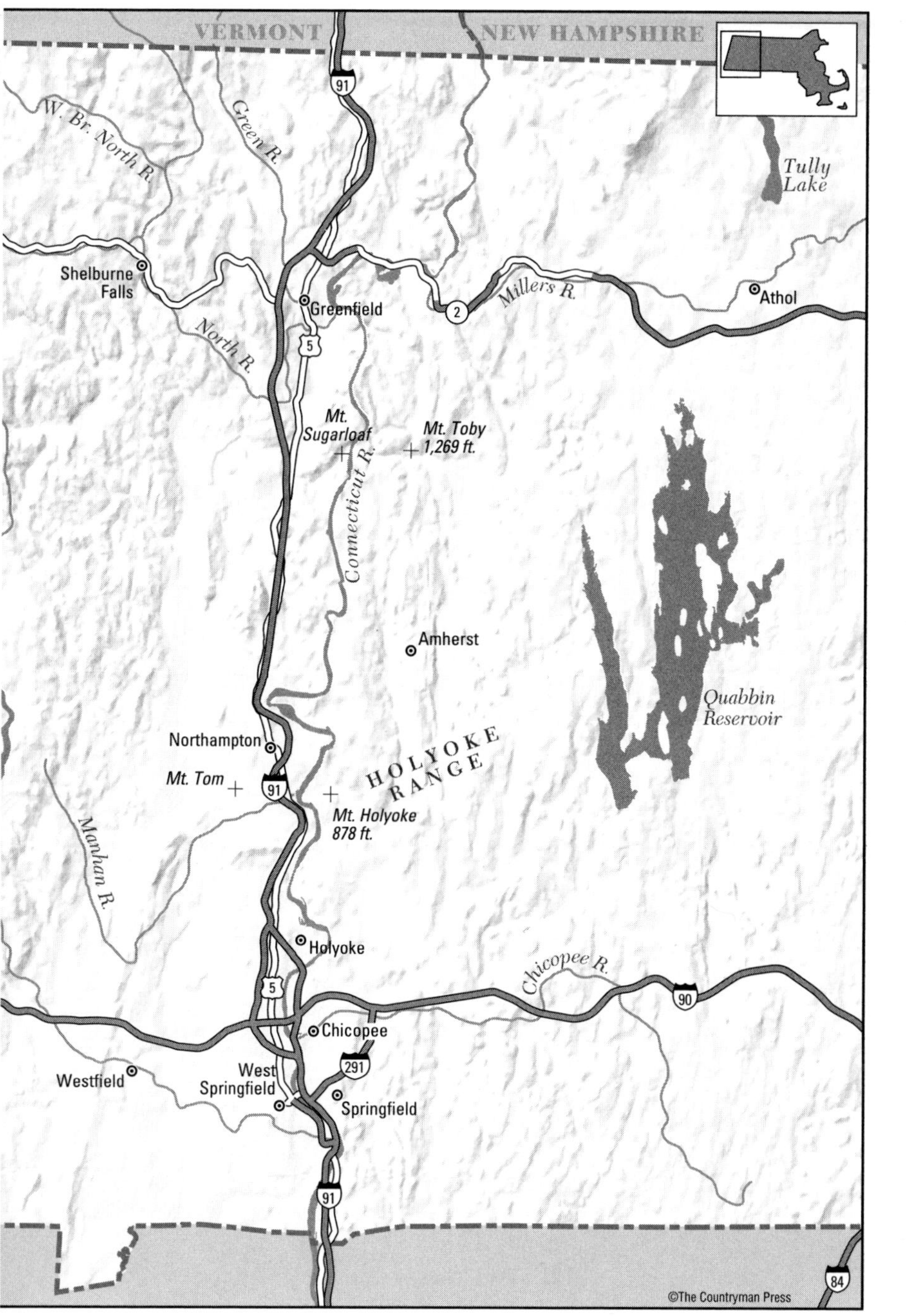

VERMONT
NEW HAMPSHIRE
91
W. Br. North R.
Green R.
Tully Lake
Shelburne Falls
Greenfield
2
Millers R.
Athol
North R.
5
Mt. Sugarloaf
Mt. Toby 1,269 ft.
Connecticut R.
Amherst
Quabbin Reservoir
Northampton
HOLYOKE RANGE
Mt. Tom
91
Mt. Holyoke 878 ft.
Manhan R.
Holyoke
Chicopee R.
5
90
Chicopee
291
Westfield
West Springfield
Springfield
91
84
©The Countryman Press

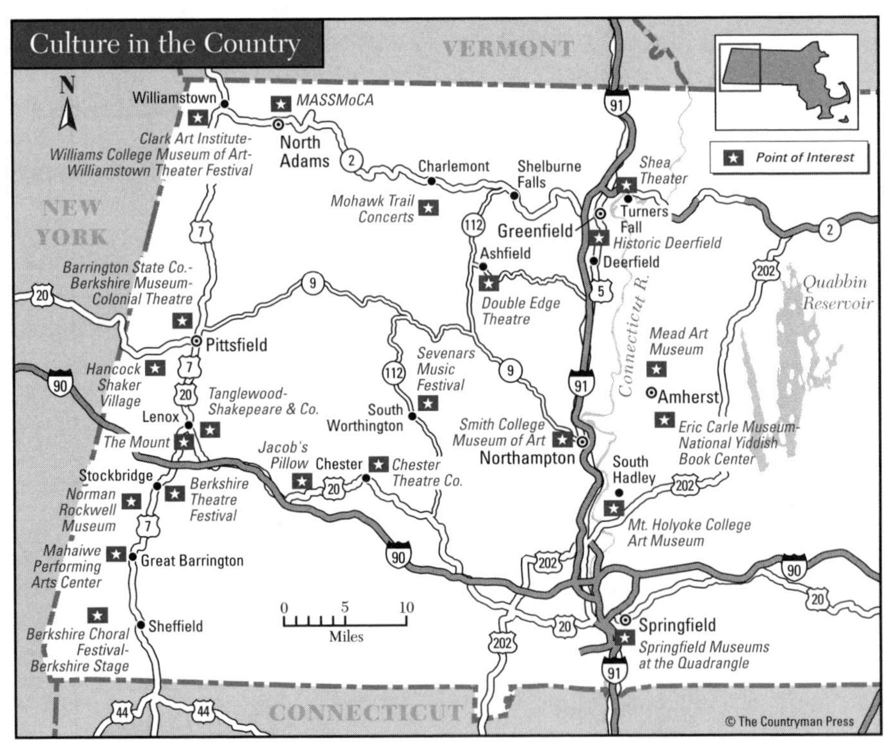
Culture in the Country
VERMONT
NEW YORK
CONNECTICUT
N
Point of Interest
Williamstown
Clark Art Institute-
Williams College Museum of Art-
Williamstown Theater Festival
MASSMoCA
North Adams
Charlemont
Shelburne Falls
Mohawk Trail Concerts
Shea Theater
Turners Fall
Greenfield
Historic Deerfield
Deerfield
Ashfield
Double Edge Theatre
Quabbin Reservoir
Barrington State Co.-
Berkshire Museum-
Colonial Theatre
Pittsfield
Hancock Shaker Village
Tanglewood-
Shakepeare & Co.
Sevenars Music Festival
South Worthington
Mead Art Museum
Amherst
Connecticut R.
Lenox
The Mount
Jacob's Pillow
Chester
Chester Theatre Co.
Smith College Museum of Art
Northampton
Eric Carle Museum-
National Yiddish
Book Center
South Hadley
Stockbridge
Norman Rockwell Museum
Berkshire Theatre Festival
Mt. Holyoke College Art Museum
Mahaiwe Performing Arts Center
Great Barrington
Berkshire Choral Festival-
Berkshire Stage
Sheffield
0 5 10
Miles
Springfield
Springfield Museums at the Quadrangle
2
7
9
112
5
20
90
91
202
44
© The Countryman Press

CONTENTS

MAPS

INTRODUCTION

Too often when we begin to enthuse about Western Massachusetts, we watch eyes glaze over, but when we mention "the Berkshires," people listen up. We talk about "the Pioneer Valley," however, and even Berkshire residents are puzzled. We rave about the "Hilltowns" and they are really confused. By bundling these three neighboring, variously known, and very different—but all culturally rich and scenic—areas into one book, we hope to suggest what an altogether amazing region Western Massachusetts is.

We make the case that "Culture in the Country"—a slogan coined for Berkshire County—applies to all of Western Massachusetts. Berkshire County is indeed the setting for internationally famous summer music, theater, and dance festivals, and the Pioneer Valley is home to a dozen colleges, an equal number of outstanding museums, and numerous concerts and performances, adding up to far more year-round "culture" within a small radius than can be found in many major cities.

The semantics of what's where in Western Massachusetts is, admittedly, confusing and unrelated to topography. Berkshire County posts WELCOME TO THE BERKSHIRES signs at its borders, while in fact the Berkshire Hills roll eastward, in places almost to the Connecticut River Valley—which of course needs a name other than *Connecticut,* because this is Massachusetts. Suggestions have included Asparagus Valley, Happy Valley, King Philip's Realm, and Knowledge Corridor, but *Pioneer Valley* is what has stuck since the 1940s. It refers to the 17th-century arrival of English colonists a century before they settled the flanking hills.

Politically, the Pioneer Valley encompasses three counties—Franklin, Hampshire, and Hampden—that extend far into those hills. Physically, the east–west Holyoke Range divides the Valley itself into the Springfield area to the south and the more rural Upper Valley to the north, and the Upper Valley in turn divides into the Five-College Area (with Amherst and Northampton as its dual hubs) and the Deerfield/Greenfield Area in the narrowest, northernmost end of the Valley. Technically part of the Pioneer Valley, the Hilltowns are salted through the roll of hills between Berkshire County and the Connecticut River Valley. They are the state's highest and most remote towns, with the kind of white-clapboard villages, orchards, sugarbushes, and farmscapes generally associated with Vermont.

Sandy Ward

ALONG THE NORWOTTUCK RAIL TRAIL.

Our definition of Western Massachusetts stops east of the Quabbin Reservoir and measures, based on the way the roads run, little more than 50 miles from east to west and less than 70 miles north to south. Divided as this small area is, however, by hills and mind-sets, it seems larger.

In 1910 Jacob's Ladder (the hilly stretch of US 20 east of Becket) was graded so that motorcars could access south Berkshire County from the east. In 1914 the more dramatic Mohawk Trail (MA 2 between Greenfield and North Adams), including a dramatic stretch over the higher Hoosac Range, was engineered and promoted as the country's first scenic auto route. Today both roads have been back-roaded by the Massachusetts Turnpike (I-90), as the river roads have been by north–south I-91 along the Connecticut. It's all about scenic roads once you're here.

Lodging includes the state's most elegant and expensive inns, resorts, and spas, as well as its most reasonably priced and rural B&Bs. Dining runs the same gamut—from exquisite gourmet to farm snack bars at which everything is home-grown as well as baked. With the exception of its most famous towns and attractions, little in this region is obvious. Few signs point the way to waterfalls and mountain summits, to bike trails, or even to world-class museums.

More so than other parts of New England, Western Massachusetts resembles European landscapes in the sense that the centuries have stamped it, leaving few corners untouched in a variety of ways, yet preserving things both natural and man-made that deserve to be preserved. It's a landscape that generously rewards those who explore it.

When the predecessor of this book, *Massachusetts: An Explorer's Guide*, was initially published in 1979, it was the first complete 20th-century guide to the state. This book has, however, been researched repeatedly from scratch. We have visited and otherwise checked out almost every place to stay we list and driven thousands of miles, much of it over unpaved roads. To our amazement, this book is actually almost as large as the original guide to the entire state, which included Boston and Cape Cod. Read on and you will see why.

We would like to thank, first and foremost, Ann Hamilton of Franklin County and Sandy Ward of Holyoke for their unfailing support and input. In the Berkshires, Linda Beach and Debbie Mossman of the Berkshire Visitors Bureau, Megan Whilden and Leslie Ferrin in Pittsfield, Rod Bunt of North Adams, and Joy Lyon and Claudia Leibert of Great Barrington were particularly helpful, as was Carol Bosco Baumann of Stockbridge and Frank Newton of Lenox. In the Hilltowns, heartfelt thanks go to Harry Dodson and Lucille Thibault of Ashfield, Susan Grader of Buckland, and Mary Vilbon of Shelburne Falls. In the Pioneer Valley, many thanks to Marion Noga of Greenfield, Joan Temkin of Amherst, Suzanne Beck of Northampton, Judy Loebel of Hadley, and Joan and Steve Stoia of Northfield. Thanks especially to Alexander Gilman of the Massachusetts Department of Conservation and Recreation, who went far beyond the call of duty to help us update our information on state forests and parks.

Thanks, too, to the many others who helped us along the way; to Lisa Sacks at The Countryman Press and to our competent copy editor, Kathryn Flynn, for keeping us precise and grammatical. We appreciate your comments and welcome your suggestions for the next edition of this guide. Feel free to contact us directly at ctree@traveltree.net or bill@davistravels.com.

A SUNDERLAND TOBACCO BARN.

Christina Tree

WHAT'S WHERE IN WESTERN MASSACHUSETTS

AGRICULTURAL FAIRS (mafa.org). The Berkshire Agricultural Society, incorporated February 15, 1811, was this country's first such society, and Elkanah Watson, its founder, is recognized as "the father of American fairs." The first was held in Pittsfield in 1814. By 1818 the state's agricultural societies included Northampton, which still holds its annual **Three County Fair** on Labor Day weekend. The **Franklin County Fair** at the Greenfield Fairgrounds is usually the following weekend. It's also worth checking out the colorful, old-fashioned fairs in small towns that feature pulling contests (by oxen, draft horses, and trucks), plenty of livestock, and live music. The **Littleville Fair** in Chester and the **Middlefield Fair** are early in August, and the **Cummington** and **Blandford Fairs** are in late August. In its 154th year, **Belchertown** continues to stage one of the few fairs in the state that does not have a gate fee. There are bands, hypnotists, and clowns, pumpkin carving, pedal tractor pulls, a baby contest, and much more, all free.

The **Eastern States Exposition** (thebige.com), held mid- to late September in West Springfield, is in a class by itself, a six-state event with thousands of animals competing for prizes, along with a midway, concession stands, big-name entertainment, and the Avenue of States with a pavilion for each New England state. Check the website for a year-round calendar of events at the fairgrounds.

Up-to-date lists of fairs are available from the **Massachusetts Agricultural Fairs Association** (mafa.org) and from the **Massachusetts Department of Agricultural Resources** (617-626-1700; mass.gov/agr).

AIRPORTS Contact the **Massachusetts Department of Transportation's** Aeronautics Division (massdot.state.ma.us/Aeronautics) in Boston for a database about the state's airports, big and small. **Bradley International Airport** (860-292-2000; bradleyairport.com) in Windsor Locks, Connecticut, is the region's major airport, served by 12 major airlines. With its centralized terminal and easy highway access (I-91, Exit 40), it's one of New England's more visitor-friendly gateways. **Albany International Airport** (518-242-2200; albanyairport.com) is served by nine carriers and is handy to much of Berkshire County.

AMTRAK (1-800-USA-RAIL; amtrak .com). On its way from New York to Burlington, Vermont, the *Vermonter* stops in Springfield and Amherst. Springfield is also a stop on some Boston-bound trains, but changes to this routing are in the works, so check. The *Lake Shore Limited* stops in Pittsfield en route to Chicago, and there is frequent service from New York to Albany, N.Y. *Note:* Canny Berkshire residents take reasonably priced **Metro-North** (mta.info) from Grand Central Station to **Wassaic Station,** N.Y. Taxis connect with Great Barrington. At this writing, plans call to reroute AMTRAK's *Vermonter*, bypassing Amherst and stopping instead in Holyoke, Northampton, and Greenfield. Stay tuned.

AMUSEMENT PARKS While all the state's other amusement parks (all founded in the late 19th century by trolley companies as an inducement to ride the cars out to the end of the line) have bitten the dust, Riverside Park in Agawam is now **Six Flags New England** (sixflags.com), the region's largest theme and water park, home to "Bizarro" and seven other thrill-inducing roller coasters.

ANIMALS **Forest Park** in Springfield (forestparkzoo.org) and the much smaller **Christenson Zoo** (native deer, peacocks, pheasants, and raccoons) in Northampton's Look Memorial Park are the area's only formal zoos. Check out our farm listings in each chapter for many more friendly animals to visit. At **Flayvors of Cook Farm** (413-584-2224; flayvors .com) in Hadley you can see the cows that supply your ice cream. **McCray's Farm** in South Hadley has both ice cream and an extensive barnyard menagerie. **Ioka Valley Farm** (413-738-5915; iokavalleyfarm.com) in Hancock features a Halloween-time maze as well as pigs, sheep, goats, calves, and rabbits. The most exotic collection of animals in Western Massachusetts is probably at **Tregellys Fiber Farm** (413-625-8618; tregellysworld.com) in Hawley, where animals include yaks, camels, and unusual heritage breeds.

Christina Tree

ANTIQUARIAN BOOKSELLERS For a descriptive listing of local dealers, check out the website of the **Massachusetts and Rhode Island Antiquarian Booksellers** (MARIAB; mariab.org) or pick up their booklet guide at one of the shops. Western Massachusetts is studded with antiquarian bookstores; you'll find them listed in each chapter. Many, like The **Motague Bookmill** (montaguebookmill.com) and **Meetinghouse Books** in South Deerfield (meetinghousebooks.com), are destinations in their own right.

ANTIQUES Berkshire County represents a major antiques center; the **Berkshire County Antiques & Art Dealer Association** (berkshireantiquesandart.com) publishes a pamphlet listing most of the shops, which we describe individually in each chapter under Selective Shopping. Sheffield alone has more than a dozen galleries. In the Pioneer Valley, auctions are frequent in Deerfield and Northfield.

APPALACHIAN TRAIL The AT runs 87.7 miles through the Berkshires, beginning near Sages Ravine in **Mount Everett State Reservation** in the town of Mount Washington in the very southwestern corner of Massachusetts. It leads up over **Mount Race** and Mount Everett, then turns east through Sheffield and continues on by **Benedict Pond** in **Beartown State Forest;** heads through Tyringham and on up through **October Mountain State Forest;** proceeds through Dalton and Cheshire, and along the eastern flank of **Mount Greylock** to the summit. Then it's down to MA 2 in **North Adams** and on up through **Clarksburg State Forest** to the Vermont state line. Access points, with and without parking, are far more frequent here than along the AT in northern New England, and many stretches are spectacularly beautiful.

APPLES The **Massachusetts Department of Agricultural Resources** (617-626-1700) offers a map of pick-your-own farms at mass.gov/agr/massgrown. The Berkshire Hilltowns represent one of the state's prime orchard areas. For apple wine lovers, **West County Winery** (413-624-3481; westcountycider.com) distributes throughout the East. Anything you want to know about apples can be found through the **New England Apple Association** (newenglandapples.org), headquartered in Hatfield. The first weekend in November is **CiderDays** (ciderday.org) in Franklin County, a collection of apple- and cider-oriented events including cider tastings and open houses at local orchards.

AREA CODE 413 applies to all of Western Massachusetts.

ART MUSEUMS Within Western Massachusetts, an area little more

Christina Tree

than 50 miles wide and less than 70 miles long, are several major art museums and some smaller museums with world-class pieces in their collections. The most famous is the **Sterling and Francine Clark Art Institute** (clarkart.edu) in Williamstown, drawing art lovers from throughout the world to see its collection of works by French impressionists and 19th-century American artists. Just around the corner is the **Williams College Museum of Art** (wcma.org), with its wealth of works by Maurice Prendergast and other choice American pieces donated by alumni. These museums in turn are complemented by **MASS MoCA** (Massachusetts Museum of Contemporary Art; massmoca.org), which opened in 1999 and is billed as one of the world's largest contemporary art centers. Continue east along the Mohawk Trail and down to Deerfield, site of **Historic Deerfield** (www.historic-deerfield.org) with its many portraits and decorative art pieces, then zip down I-91 to Northampton, where the recently expanded **Smith College Museum of Art** (smith.edu/artmuseum) showcases a superb collection of primarily 19th- and early 20th-century art as well as major contemporary exhibits. Drive east 9 miles to Amherst to see the **Mead Art Museum** (amherst.edu/mead) with its well-rounded permanent collection, much of it again contributed by alumni. In another corner of Amherst, The **Eric Carle Museum of Picture Book Art** (carlemuseum.org) shows work by the world's top children's book illustrators, recognizing this as an art form in its own right. The neighboring **Yiddish Book Center** (yiddishbookcenter.org) also frequently hosts art exhibits.

A short drive south on the scenic Notch Road (MA 116) over the Holyoke Range to South Hadley takes you to the **Mount Holyoke College Art Museum** (mtholyoke.edu/go/artmuseum), one of the country's oldest collegiate art collections, ranging from ancient Asian and Egyptian works through 19th-century landscapes and contemporary pieces. Another short ride to I-91 and into Springfield brings you to the **Quadrangle** (springfieldmuseums.org) of museums. This includes the **Museum of Fine Arts**—18th-century portraits and 20th-century works complemented by decorative arts—and the **George Walter Vincent Smith Art Museum,** with an outstanding collection of Japanese armor and cloisonné. For an overview of museums in the Valley, see museums10.org.

Hop on the Mass Pike (I-90) and in less than an hour you are back in Berkshire County at the **Norman Rockwell Museum** (nrm.org) in West Stockbridge, exhibiting not only works by its eminent namesake artist, but also changing exhibits by other noted illustrators. Finally, north on US 7 in Pittsfield are the **Berkshire Museum** (berkshiremuseum.org), a fine regional museum with a respectable collection of American paintings, and nearby **Hancock Shaker Village** (hancockshakervillage.org), which displays distinctive Shaker spirit paintings as well as furnishings.

Obviously no one should try to complete this marathon circuit in a day. It could easily make up a two- to five-day tour given the area's scenery, shopping, lodging, and dining. Art lovers will also find quality galleries along the way (listed in each chapter under *Selective Shopping*).

Sterling and Francine Clark Art Institute, Williamstown

BALLOONING **Worthington Ballooning** (worthingtonballooning.com) in Worthington offers hot air balloon flights year-round.

BASKETBALL The **Naismith Memorial Basketball Hall of Fame** (hoophall.com) in Springfield celebrates Dr. James Naismith's invention of basketball at a local YMCA college in 1891. The current $45 million Hall of Fame museum is Springfield's pride, its most visible landmark (it's shaped like a giant basketball and illuminated in different colors at night), and its biggest tourist attraction. A combination history museum, shrine, computer game arcade, and gymnasium—there's nothing else quite like it.

BED & BREAKFASTS B&Bs in this area range from country houses owned by longtime residents to mansions fit for a wedding. Many are off-the-beaten path and their hosts delight in orienting their guests. Our lodging focus here is on B&Bs, and we revisited almost every one in the process of updating this book. We do not charge for listings and limit them to those that we would stay in ourselves.

BICYCLING We have noted rentals and outstanding bike routes in most sections. The **Norwottuck Rail Trail** between Northampton and Amherst is a popular bike path, as is the 11-mile **Ashuwillticook Rail Trail** (berkshirebikepath.com), connecting Adams and Cheshire paralleling MA 8 but hugging the shores of Berkshire Pond and Cheshire Reservoir. The **Franklin County Bikeway** includes a bridge across the mouth of the Millers River, permitting a nice ride from Northfield Mountain down under the French King Bridge. The 4-mile **Canalside Rail Trail** runs south from the discovery center in Turners Falls to East Deerfield. A glossy *Massachusetts Bicycle Guide* available from the Massachusetts Office of Travel and Tourism (1-800-227-MASS; massvacation.com) lists state forests with bicycle facilities. Cyclists also find the *Rubel Western Massachusetts Bicycle and Road Map* (bikemaps.com) indispensable.

Serious mountain bikers should check out **River Road south from Chesterfield Gorge to the Knightville Dam** (see "The Hidden Hills"). **Northfield Mountain** (firstlightpower.com/northfield) and many state forests offer trails beloved by mountain bikers. Check out the **Department of Conservation and Recreation** website (mass.gov/dcr), as well as the **Massachusetts Bicycle Coalition** site (massbike.org).

BIRDING The **Massachusetts Audubon Society** (781-259-9500;

Christina Tree

massaudubon.org), founded in 1896 to discourage the use of wild bird plumage as hat decorations, also pioneered the idea of wildlife sanctuaries. Mass Audubon maintains two staffed sanctuaries in the **Pioneer Valley—Arcadia Wildlife Sanctuary** (413-584-3009) on the Oxbow of the Connecticut River in Easthampton/Northampton, and **Laughing Brook Wildlife Sanctuary** (413-584-3009) in Hampden. In Berkshire County the major wildlife sanctuaries are **Pleasant Valley** (413-637-0320) and **Canoe Meadows,** both in Lenox. In addition, numerous smaller sanctuaries are scattered throughout this area and described within individual chapters.

Hawkwatchers, we should add, converge on the Connecticut Valley in September, watching these birds ride the thermal highs; favorite lookout spots are Mount Tom and Mount Holyoke. The most famous birds in Western Massachusetts are, however, probably the **nesting eagles** in Barton Cove. TV cameras are trained on the nest and can be viewed at the discovery center in Turners Falls. *Birding Western Massachusetts* (New England Cartographics) by Robert Tougias describes more than two dozen birding sites.

BOAT EXCURSIONS Seasonal cruises of the Connecticut in the Five-College Area are offered aboard the ***Lady Bea*** in South Hadley (413-315-6342) and in the Greenfield area on the ***Quinnetukut II*** (1-800-859-2960), based at Northfield Mountain.

BOAT LAUNCHES Sites are detailed by the **Massachusetts Office of Fishing and Boating Access** (mass.gov/dfwele/pab). Also see *Boating* and *Fishing* entries in each chapter.

BUTTERFLIES Magic Wings (magicwings.com; 413-665-2805) in South Deerfield is a flowery, lush, year-round oasis filled with thousands of butterflies.

BUS SERVICE **Peter Pan-Bonanza** (1-800-556-3815) runs from New York City to Sheffield, South Egremont, Great Barrington, Lee, Lenox, and Pittsfield, with connections to Williamstown. **Peter Pan Bus–Trailways** (1-800-343-9999; peter panbus.com) connects Boston with Springfield, Holyoke, South Hadley, Northampton, Amherst, Deerfield, and Greenfield and with Lee, Lenox, and Pittsfield. From Albany, **Greyhound** (greyhound.com) also serves Pittsfield.

CAMPING At this writing, the **Department of Conservation and Recreation** (DCR) details information about camping in state forests in a brochure, as well as listing sites in a map and on its website (mass.gov /dcr). Campsites can be reserved online through reserveamerica.com or by calling 1-877-422-6762. Site occupancy is limited to four people or one family, and to 14 days. Rates vary with the park or site; many parks also offer log cabins.

Check out the **Beartown State Forest** in Monterey (413-528-0904); DAR State Forest in Goshen (413-268-7098); **Mohawk Trail State Forest** in Charlemont (413-339-5504); **Mount Greylock State Reservation** in Lanesborough (413-499-4262; mass.gov/dcr); **October Mountain State Forest** in Lee (413-243-1778); **Pittsfield State Forest** (413-442-8992); **Savoy Mountain State Forest** in Savoy (413-664-9567); and **Tolland State Forest** in East Otis (413-269-6002). A *Massachusetts Campground Directory* to commercial campgrounds is available from the Massachusetts Association of Campground Owners (774-284-1464; campmass.com). Seasonal camping is also available at wooded sites managed by Northfield Mountain at Barton Cove in Gill (1-800-859-2960).

CANALS The country's first canal is said to have been built in South Hadley in 1794 (scant remains). The Farmington Canal, which ran from Northampton through Westfield and Southwick on its way to New Haven, is still visible in parts. In **Holyoke** power canals still operate. You can stroll along the new Canalwalk and visit historic exhibits at the canalside Heritage State Park; in **Turners Falls,** near the new Great Falls Discovery Center, both power and transportation canals are still visible. Note the Canalside Rail Trail under *Bicycling*.

CANOEING AND KAYAKING The canoe is making a comeback, and kayaks demanding less skill are more popular than ever, increasing interest in paddling Western Massachusetts

Christina Tree

ponds, lakes, and rivers. Look for details in each chapter.

CAVING Seventy caves or caverns are known in Massachusetts, most in the Berkshires. A few caves are found in the Connecticut River Valley. Check with the caving group **Boston Grotto** (bostongrotto.org).

CHEESE Not only is **Monterey Chèvre** (413-528-2138) delicious, but buying it at the source—Rawson Brook Farm in Monterey—also makes a great excuse to visit with the goats that contribute their milk to its cause. While you're in Monterey, also check out **Gould Farm Cheddar** (gouldfarm.org), available at the roadside store and café. Never mind that **Granville Cheese** is made now in upstate New York; the cheddar is aged, as it has been since 1851, in the **Granville Country Store.** In South Williamstown find your way past Field Farm to **Cricket Creek Farm** (cricketcreekfarm.com), a glorious dairy farm with a self-serve shop selling the farmstead Tobasi, Maggie's Round, and fresh mozzarella.

CHILDREN, ESPECIALLY FOR Many Western Massachusetts attractions appeal to children, but those we note under *For Families* and with the ✎ sign highlight things of special interest to families with young children, as well as child-friendly lodging and restaurants. Such attractions include **The Eric Carle Museum of Picture Book Art** (carlemuseum.org) in Amherst and **Six Flags New England** (sixflags.com), the region's largest theme and water park. In Old Deerfield, the **Indian House Children's Museum** (old-deerfield.org) hosts activities geared to young visitors, and Holyoke offers a fine **Children's Museum** and adjacent merry-go-round in the Holyoke Heritage State Park. In Springfield there's the **Forest Park Zoo** (see *Animals*); the Quadrangle, with its Dr. Seuss figures (the father of the real Dr. Seuss ran the Forest Park Zoo); and the **Science Museum** (springfieldmuseums

Christina Tree

.org), with its many child-geared exhibits and dinosaurs. The **Amherst College Museum of Natural History** has an extraordinary exhibit of dinosaurs and the world's largest collection of dinosaur prints. The **Great Falls Discovery Center** at the Silvio O. Conte National Fish and Wildlife Refuge (greatfallsma.org) is now open regularly in Turners Falls, showcasing the flora and fauna of the Valley. We also describe where to find real dinosaur prints in the Pioneer Valley and the "Dino Dig" that's among the many interactive exhibits at the **Berkshire Museum** (berkshiremuseum .org) in Pittsfield. The nearby **Hancock Shaker Village** (hancock shakervillage.org) includes a great hands-on Discovery Room—and visitors younger than 18 are free.

CHRISTMAS TREES The **Massachusetts Christmas Tree Association** (978-365-5818; christmas-trees .org) lists Christmas tree farms by county on its website.

COVERED BRIDGES Covered bridges are found in Charlemont, Colrain, Conway, Greenfield, and Sheffield.

CRAFTS The country's largest concentration of craftspeople is reportedly in the Five-College Area and in West County. Northampton's Main Street showcases much of their work, as do several shops in Shelburne Falls. The region's outstanding craft fairs are the **Paradise City Arts Festivals** held on the Memorial Day and Columbus Day weekends at the Three-County Fairground in Northampton. The **Old Deerfield Craft Fairs** (deerfield-craft.org) showcase traditional crafts in April, June, September, and November at Memorial Hall in Old Deerfield. We list outstanding crafts galleries and studios in each chapter under *Selective Shopping*.

EVENTS This region generates several very different kinds of events. There are the seasonal happenings: **sugaring** sit-down breakfasts in the Upper Pioneer Valley and Berkshire Hilltowns in March, the **white-water races** on the Westfield and white-water sports on the Deerfield in April. May marks the beginning of most of this area's splendid **Farmers' Markets. Pick-Your Own** (PYO) season progresses as various fruits and veggies ripen (see *Farms, Farmers' Markets, and Farm Stands*). August is the season for small-town **agricultural fairs,** and September for the big ones. Early October is celebrated with fabulous **fall foliage festivals,** followed by November and early-December **craft fairs** combined with **holiday lighting festivals. Cultural happenings** staged for the general public (as opposed to the Five-College Area academic-year events and theater, music, and lecture offerings—which are almost all open to the public) begin in mid-June and end in August. The **Tanglewood Music Festival** in Lenox is the most famous of these, but there are many more, along with theater and dance staged primarily in south Berkshire County, but also found throughout the region. Many **town celebrations** are annual events, but some of the best are one-time celebrations. Check *Special Events* at the end of each chapter; area websites are also good sources of event information.

FACTORY OUTLETS The **Lee Premium Outlets** (premiumoutlets.com) are an attractive grouping of five dozen fairly upscale "outlets" just off Mass Pike Exit 2. Several old-fashioned outlets are found off the beaten path. In Greenfield, **The Textile Co., Inc.** (413-773-7516) is the last traditional outlet in this area of which we are aware, drawing patrons from far and wide for bargain-priced fabrics. In Shelburne Falls, **Lamson & Goodnow** (lamsonsharp.com), founded in 1837 and still housed in its 19th-century riverside mill buildings, has expanded its outlet to include a wide variety of kitchen gear and gadgets, and still offers its own cutlery at discount prices.

FALL FOLIAGE AND FOLIAGE FESTIVALS The most colorful small-town fall festivals in the state (ranking right of there with the most colorful in all of New England) are the **Conway Festival of the Hills** (festivalofthehills.com) the first weekend in October, and the **Fall Festival** in Ashfield on Columbus Day weekend. The **Northern Berkshire Fall Foliage Festival** in North Adams during the first weekend in October is a huge old event, and on Columbus Day weekend you can join residents of Adams who turn out in force to hike "their" side of the mountain.

Western Massachusetts is unquestionably as beautiful a region to explore in fall as any in New England, given its wealth of maple trees and back roads, many of them dirt. Be advised that color comes first to the higher reaches of Mount Greylock and spreads through the Berkshire Hills the first weeks of October, filling both the Berkshire and Pioneer Valleys a week or two later and lingering on there through October. We disapprove of the lodging practice of charging "foliage rates" throughout October. When it's over, it's really over.

Christina Tree

Christina Tree

FARMS, FARMERS' MARKETS, AND FARM STANDS "Agritourism" is big in Western Massachusetts. Several farms offer B&B and cottage rentals on their property. Many more farms have pick-your-own (PYO) apples, strawberries, and blueberries, for example, depending on the season; still others invite you in to see their animals. **Cook Farm** in Hadley makes fabulous ice cream from the cows grazing beside its shop, while farms in South Hadley, Hancock, and Hawley feature large collections of animals (see *Animals*).

A visit to a farm invariably gets you off the main drag and into beautiful countryside you might otherwise not find. The **Massachusetts Department of Agricultural Resources** (617-626-1700) maintains an extensive website (mass.gov/agr/massgrown) detailing information about farms that allow you to pick your own vegetables and fruit. Request or download the agritourism map of farms that welcome visitors with farm stands, PYO, B&B, or in other ways. The **Community Involved in Sustaining Agriculture,** or CISA (buylocalfood.com) publishes an annual guide to farmers in Franklin, Hampshire, and Hampden Counties who sell directly to the public. **Berkshire Grown** (berkshire grown.org) publishes an annual map/guide and performs a similar service for farmers in Berkshire County.

Look for asparagus in May in the Pioneer Valley (also known as Asparagus Valley); for strawberries in June throughout the area; for blueberries, raspberries, and sweet corn after July 4 and—through August—peaches, too. September is apple season, October is all about pumpkins, and in December it's time to cut Christmas trees. Also see *Maple Sugaring*.

FISHING Freshwater fishing options range from mountain streams in the Berkshires and Hilltowns to the wide Connecticut. For a listing of stocked fishing sites, best bets, and areas with handicapped access, call the Massachusetts Division of Fisheries and Wildlife (1-800-ASK-FISH or 1-800-275-3474; mass.gov/dfwele). Also check *Fishing* under each of the chapters in this guide.

FISH LADDERS Northfield Mountain naturalists staff fishways at the Holyoke and Turners Falls Dams when the fish are running upstream, late May to mid-June (1-800-859-2960).

GOLF We have listed golf courses under *To Do* in each chapter.

GUIDANCE At the beginning of each chapter we list the regional and local sources of information for that area. At the **Massachusetts Office of Travel and Tourism** (617-973-8500 or 1-800-227-6277; massvacation.com) website, updated seasonally, you can request a variety of printed brochures as well as find detailed online travel information. Phone queries are answered live during regular office hours.

HERITAGE STATE PARKS Conceived and executed by the state as a way of revitalizing old industrial areas, each "park" revolves around a visitors center in which multivisual exhibits dramatize what makes the community special. Though they have served as prototypes for similar parks throughout the country, the Heritage State Parks within the scope of this book have all suffered severe financial cutbacks under recent administrations. The **Holyoke** and **Western Gateway** (in North Adams) parks, however, are still operating as envisioned.

HIGHWAYS I-91 parallels the Connecticut River in its north–south passage through Western Massachusetts, and I-90—the Massachusetts Turn-

Christina Tree

pike—is a quick way across the southern tier of the state (see *Massachusetts Turnpike*). Much of the area described in this book is, however, blessedly far from any major highway—unless you want to count MA 2, which is four lanes, even six lanes in places, from Boston all the way to Wendell in the Pioneer Valley. From Boston, if you are heading west to the Amherst/Northampton area as well to most of the Berkshire Hilltowns and northern Berkshire County, MA 2 is actually quicker as well as more scenic and cheaper than the Mass Pike. For more on the westernmost stretch of MA 2, see *Mohawk Trail.*

HIKING AND WALKING The **Department of Conservation and Recreation** maintains hundreds of miles of hiking trails in the 47 state parks and forests in Western Massachusetts. The **Appalachian Trail** winds 87.7 miles through Berkshire County (see above). The **Taconic Crest Trail** offers many spectacular views along its 35-mile route, also in the Berkshires, including sections in New York and Vermont. Another dramatic but not easy hike follows the ridgeline of the east–west **Holyoke Range** (accessible from the state-run Notch Visitors Center in Granby). Elsewhere in the Five-College Area, the **Amherst Conservation Department** maintains some 45 miles of walking and hiking trails. Within this book several walks are suggested in each chapter (see *Hiking* and *Green Space*). The bible for hiking throughout the state is the Appalachian Mountain Club's *Massachusetts Trail Guide.*

HISTORY Within this book a fair amount of Massachusetts history is told through descriptions of many places that still commemorate or dramatize it.

The Connecticut River Valley was farmed by Native Americans for thousands of years before the first "pioneers" arrived, but today only place names recall their tribes: Woronoco (Westfield), Agawam (Springfield/West Springfield), Norwottuck (Hadley and Northampton), Pocumtuck (Deerfield area) and Squakheag (Northfield area). It's difficult to estimate how many people lived in this area before a smallpox epidemic, contracted through contact with English and Dutch traders, decimated these tribes in 1633. William Pynchon of Roxbury took advantage of this situation to establish a settlement at present-day Springfield in 1636, buying the land for 18 fathom of wampum, 18 coats, 18 hatchets, 18 hoes, and 18 knives. Settlers and Indians tentatively coexisted for several decades, but in 1675 the 24-year-old Wampanoag Indian chief Metacomet, better remembered as King Philip, attempted to unite all tribes east of the Hudson River to rise up against the colonists, who already outnumbered them. The uprising began in Plymouth Colony, but King Philip and more than 1,000 Wampanoags escaped to the Connecticut River Valley, killing 60 settlers at Deerfield. An obelisk in South Deerfield marks the site of this "Bloody Brook Massacre," and the nearby summit of Mount Sugarloaf, now a state reservation accessible by road and offering a spectacular view down the Valley, is still known as King Philip's Seat. Philip himself, however, barely escaped capture in a devastating ambush at Turners Falls (named for the English captain who directed it) and was slain soon after on the coast.

Local Indian tribes, understandably angry at being pushed off their land, began forming alliances with the French in Canada, then locked in a struggle with Britain for control of the continent. A series of conflicts known as the French and Indian Wars (1689–1763) devastated settlements over much of Western Massachusetts despite the efforts of the citizen soldiers of the colonial militia. During one campaign the song "Yankee Doodle" was reportedly written in Charlemont by a British army doctor to poke fun at the typical unmilitary-looking militiaman, whose idea of dressing up was to "stick a feather in his cap." Ignoring the doctor's sarcasm, Americans enthusiastically adopted the song, which became one of the marching tunes of the Revolution. Charlemont annually commemorates its composition with a festival called Yankee Doodle Days each July.

The most destructive and dramatic of all the French and Indian attacks occurred at Old Deerfield in February 1704. A large force of French soldiers and Indian allies from several tribes swarmed over the stockade just before dawn, catching the sleeping village completely by surprise. In the ensuing battle, 50 of the town's 291 inhabitants were killed and 112 were captured and carried away to Canada, while many of its houses were burned. Most of the captives were eventually ransomed and returned home, but some children, adopted by Indian or French families, remained in Canada. Serious settlement in the hills of the Connecticut River Valley commenced only after the end of the French and Indian Wars.

Deerfield was rebuilt and, although it was attacked twice more in the next 40 years, was never again captured. The stories (not just the settlers' side) of the 1704 attack are well told at Memorial Hall Museum and Indian House Children's Museum in Deerfield, which among other things display a door covered with gashes made by Indian tomahawks during the raid.

Native Americans in the southwestern corner of Massachusetts had been trading amicably with Dutch settlers along the Hudson for several decades before the English arrived in the 1730s. Families from the Connecticut River Valley settled Sheffield, and a young missionary, John Sergeant, was dispatched from Yale College to Stockbridge to propagate the Gospel to the Mahicans. The town's unusually wide street dates from its use as the site on which these friendly Indians built their wigwams, and Sergeant's Mission House survives, portraying how well a white family could survive in these backwoods in the early 18th century. But little about the Indians remains. Despite their service to Washington during the American Revolution, the Stockbridge Indians were forced west by the end of the 18th century, carrying their heavy, leather-bound Bible with them.

Pocumtuck Valley Memorial Association

Berkshire residents played a significant role in the Revolution. In 1773 Sheffield townspeople gathered in the Colonel Ashley House to draft the Sheffield Declaration, a petition against British tyranny, observing that "Americans are entitled to all the liberties, privileges and immunities of natural born British subjects." The following August a Berkshire Congress dedicated to taking practical action in defense of such rights met at Stockbridge, and when the British ministerial judges attempted to convene at the courthouse in Great Barrington, they found their way barred by angry locals. Tombstones of those who lost their lives in the Revolutionary War can be found throughout the area.

Boston merchants actually profited from filling war needs, but residents of rural towns in the west of the state found themselves hard hit in the years immediately following the war, especially when payment was required in hard currency, which farmers usually lacked. A farmer who could not pay was stripped of his lands and sent to prison.

In 1786, at the height of this rural depression, farmers held a three-day convention in Hatfield and decided to attack the county courthouse in Northampton. Led by Daniel Shays, a debt-ridden war hero from Pelham, they next attacked the Springfield Arsenal and failed miserably. A few little-noticed plaques tell the remaining story. A marker beside the Pelham Town Hall (just off US 202, the Daniel Shays Highway) commemorates the spot where the rebels camped for more than two winter weeks in their stand "against unjust laws." Another monument along the Sheffield–South Egremont Road records the finale of the uprising: HERE 100 REBELS WERE ROUTED AFTER PLUNDERING STOCKBRIDGE AND GREAT BARRINGTON. Shays himself escaped to Vermont, then not part of the United States, and a recorded 700 families from Western Massachusetts followed him.

The first decades of the 19th century were also the era of the quintessential New England village, with its steepled church and grouping of handsome houses around a common, a picture for which Greenfield architect Asher Benjamin is largely responsible. Aware of rural carpenters' need for a do-it-yourself guide, Benjamin in 1796 wrote *The Country Builder's Assistant,* then six more books that went through 44 editions and resulted in the Greenfield Public Library, Memorial Hall in Old Deerfield, and hundreds of handsome homes and churches in the area and throughout the region.

The Civil War fueled the state's industrial growth. At the Springfield Armory National Historic Site you learn that it also turned that city into a boomtown, the "Arsenal of the Union," which produced about half the rifled muskets used by Northern troops. The story of the region's first major planned mill city built from scratch in the 1840s is told in the Holyoke Heritage State Park, while that of the state's last industrial-era boom city—North Adams, spawned by the 25-year construction of the then world's longest railroad tunnel—is dramatized in the Western Gateway Heritage State Park. Such manufacturing cities continued to prosper, thanks to immigrant labor, until the 1920s, when the textile and other industries began moving out of the state. Innovative uses have been found for many old mill buildings, notably the Massachusetts Museum of Contemporary Art in North Adams, which occupies most of a sprawling industrial complex originally built as a textile plant.

What's generally forgotten is the flip side to this "industrial revolution." In the agricultural era farmers rarely left their land, but city dwellers who punched clocks also took vacations. Moneyed visitors from throughout the country flocked to summer hotels; to upward of 100 summer estates such as Naumkeag and Blantyre, Cranwell, Wheatleigh, Seven Hills, and Eastover in Lenox; and to more modest country houses like the William Cullen Bryant Homestead in Cummington. Many blue-collar workers and their families traveled the ubiquitous trolley lines to amusement parks, all now vanished except for Riverside in Agawam (currently Six Flags New England). Less affluent folks traveled the trolleys and rail lines to farms catering to guests throughout Western Massachusetts.

In 1910 Jacob's Ladder, a stretch of US 20 over the hills into south Berkshire County, was constructed to accommodate autos; in 1914 the Mohawk Trail (MA 2 West over higher and more dramatic Hoosac Mountain, then down into North Adams) was created specifically as one of the country's first scenic auto touring routes. The Hotel Northampton opened as a "motoring destination" in 1927, featuring a mini museum village of Americana, and at the same time Storrowton, a larger gathering of rural historic buildings, was assembled at the Eastern States Exposition. In ensuing decades, as train service atrophied and car travel increased, virtually all the old summer hotels disappeared, replaced by motels.

In the last few decades of the 20th century the settlement pattern of the 19th century was actually reversed, with people moving back to the country as urban refugees found ways to support themselves in rural places. Educational centers such as Northampton and Amherst became lively destinations in their own right, creating the need for lodging in surrounding hills.

Currently many of the state's true beauty spots are far more easily accessible than they were for most of the 20th century, thanks in large part to the state's enterprising Department of Conservation and Recreation (mass .gov/dcr) and to private land preservation groups like The Trustees of Reservations (thetrustees.org), the Massachusetts Audubon Society (see *Birding*), and many local conservation trusts. Lodging has also once more proliferated throughout the area.

HORSEBACK RIDING Over the past decade many Massachusetts livery stables have closed or limited themselves to lessons and clinics. In Lenox trail rides are offered at **Undermountain Farm** (413-637-3365) and **Berkshire Horseback Adventure** (413-623-5606); in Becket at **Sunny Banks Ranch** (413-623-5606; sunnybanksranch.com); and in Williamstown at **DeMayo's Bonnie Lea Farm** (413-458-3149). Trail rides are also available to guests at **High Pocket B&B** (413-624-8988; high pocket.com) in Colrain.

HUNTING The source for information about licenses, rules, and wildlife management areas is the Massachusetts Division of Fisheries and Wildlife (617-626-1590; mass.gov/dfwele), 251 Causeway St., Suite 400, Boston

Kim Grant

02114. To receive the division's newsletter, *MassWildlife News,* electronically, e-mail join-MassWildlife.news @listserve.state.ma.us.

LITERARY LANDMARKS In Amherst poet **Emily Dickinson** (1830–86) was born, lived virtually her entire life, and wrote most of her finest verse in an imposing mansion at 280 Main Street. Her second-floor bedroom has been restored to look much as it did when she was in residence. She is buried in West Cemetery on Triangle Street.

The **Jones Library** at 43 Amity Street has a collection of 8,000 items relating to Dickinson, including original handwritten poems. Seven panels in the research wing depict her life in Amherst. The library also has a collection devoted to poet Robert Frost, who lived in Amherst from 1931–38 and later taught at Amherst College.

Poet and editor **William Cullen Bryant** was born in Cummington in 1794. At the height of his fame, when he was editor and co-owner of the New York Post, he transformed the original humble family homestead off MA 112 into a graceful mansion, now owned by the Trustees of Reservations. Filled with memorabilia of Bryant and his era, the William Cullen Bryant Homestead also has an expansive view of a beautiful countryside.

The Mount, novelist **Edith Wharton's** home on Plunkett Street in Lenox, is a turn-of-the-20th-century copy of a 17th-century English mansion, but it incorporates a lot of her own ideas of gracious living (she was a wealthy New York socialite). It was here that she wrote Ethan Frome, which is set in the Berkshires. Edith Wharton Restoration, Inc. manages the property and conducts tours.

In 1850 **Herman Melville** bought Arrowhead, an 18th-century Pittsfield farmhouse, where he wrote his masterpiece, *Moby-Dick.* The house at 789 Holmes Road has a fine view of

Mount Greylock, the mass of which may have inspired his vision of a great whale. The house is now headquarters for the Berkshire Historical Society. The Berkshire Athenaeum on the Pittsfield common has a Melville Room with every book he ever wrote, and most of those written about him. Artifacts displayed include the desk at which he wrote *Billy Budd.*

At the time Melville moved to Pittsfield, **Nathaniel Hawthorne** was living in nearby Lenox, writing *Tanglewood Tales*, named for the estate (belonging to wealthy friends) on which he was living. The two became close friends after meeting on **Monument Mountain** in Great Barrington for a hike with Melville's neighbor, **Oliver Wendell Holmes,** in 1850. Tanglewood is now home to the state's most famous summer music festival, and Monument Mountain (thetrustees.org) is still a great place to picnic.

MAPLE SUGARING Native Americans reportedly taught this industry to early settlers in Tyringham (southern Berkshire County) in the early 18th century. Sugaring is thriving today, primarily in the Hilltowns, an area with more sugarhouses than the rest of the state put together. During sugaring season in March, visitors are welcome to watch producers "boil off" the sap, reducing it to the sweet liquid that is traditionally sampled on ice or snow, or savored on pancakes and waffles at sit-down seasonal restaurants. For a current map/guide to producers who welcome visitors, visit the Massachusetts **Maple Producers Association** website: massmaple.org.

MAPS Most of the Massachusetts this book explores has been backroaded by the limited-access highways—the Massachusetts Turnpike, MA 2, I-91, and I-3—and the free state road map available at this writing is of limited use. In this edition we have made a special effort to provide detailed maps to the areas that merit them, striving for accuracy both in the way back roads run and in the extensive amount of open space accessible to visitors (within each chapter, we detail it under *Green Space*). We recommend, however, that you secure copies of the DeLorme *Massachusetts Atlas and Gazeteer*, the detailed *Rubel Western Massachusetts Bicycle and Road Map* (see *Bicycling*), and the *Western Massachusetts Road Map published by Jimapco* (jimapco.com). Berkshire County, Franklin County, and the Hidden Hills also publish free detailed maps, available from the *Guidance* sources listed in those chapters.

MASSACHUSETTS TURNPIKE It's impossible to explore much of Massachusetts without encountering the "Mass Pike" (I-90). Completed in

1965, this superhighway cuts as straight as an arrow 135 miles across the state from Boston to the New York state line, with just 25 exits, 14 of them east of I-495. It was the first road in Massachusetts on which you could officially drive 65 miles per hour (between Auburn and Ludlow and again between Westfield and the New York line). Eleven service centers (most with fast-food restaurants) are scattered along the route.

MOHAWK TRAIL This westernmost stretch of MA 2 bears the name of the ancient footpath blazed through the hilly northwestern corner of the state by Native Americans on their way between the Connecticut and Hudson River Valleys. No one, however, believes that it's the exact same route. What's certain is the fact that on October 22, 1914, the 38-mile stretch of MA 2 between Greenfield and Williamstown was officially opened as New England's first "Scenic Road." At the time only a small percentage of roads in the region were paved, and this particularly hilly section was specifically designed to lure "tourists," touring in their first cars. In its namesake chapter we describe the Mohawk Trail's 1920s and 1930s viewing towers and trading posts, which are strategically spaced to permit those old autos to take on water after a steep climb. Thanks to white-water rafting and the dramatic renaissance of Shelburne Falls, visitors and residents alike are rediscovering this genuinely scenic road. The Mohawk Trail Highway has, incidentally, grown over the years and now extends a full 63 miles, beginning in Millers Falls. Website: mohawktrail.com.

MOUNTAINS **Mount Greylock** is the state's highest and deserves far more recognition than it gets from Berkshire visitors whizzing around its massive base. You can drive to a parking lot just below the 3,491-foot summit both from US 7 north of Pittsfield and from North Adams. The view from the summit is spectacular, and you can both dine and lodge at newly renovated **Bascomb Lodge** (bascom lodge.net). The Mount Greylock State

Christina Tree

Reservation Visitor Center (413-499-4262), 1.7 miles off US 7 in Lanesborough, is open year-round and offers winter camping, snowmobiling, snowshoeing and cross-country skiing. In the southwestern corner of the state, **Mount Everett,** the state's second-highest mountain, is accessible by a seasonal dirt road to a parking lot a mile below its 2,603-foot summit. In the Pioneer Valley you can also drive up Mount Sugarloaf in Deerfield, Mount Tom in Holyoke, and Mount Holyoke in Hadley. All these offer hiking trails as well.

MUSEUM VILLAGES Both **Hancock Shaker Village,** a restored Shaker community in central Berkshire County, and **Historic Deerfield,** a street lined with more than a dozen 18th- and 19th-century homes in the Upper Pioneer Valley, are composed of buildings still in their original locations. Both evoke an unusual sense of place as well as illustrating their respective stories. Both are also serious research centers. In East Springfield, the much smaller **Storrowton** represents one of the country's earliest re-created villages; **Greenfield Village,** just west of Greenfield on MA 2, is one man's collection, housed in a building he constructed himself.

MUSIC The area's best known music event is the **Tanglewood Music Festival** (bso.org) during July and August in Lenox. Other prestigious summer series of note include the **Aston Magna Festival** (astonmagna.org) in Great Barrington, the **Berkshire Choral Festival** (www.choralfest.org) in Sheffield, the **Sevenars** concerts in South Worthington, and the **Mohawk Trail Concerts** (mohawktrailconcerts.org) in Charlemont.

PETS, TRAVELING WITH The dog paw symbol 🐾 indicates lodgings that accept pets. Most require prior notice and a reservation; many also require an additional fee.

Stu Rosner

Zoar Outdoor

PUBLIC RADIO Albany-based WAMC-FM (90.3) enjoys a wide reception throughout Western Massachusetts thanks to a transmitter atop Mount Greylock. There's also Great Barrington–based WAMQ-FM (105.1) and Amherst-based WFCR-FM (88.5).

RAIL EXCURSIONS The **Berkshire Scenic Railway** (berkshiresscenicrailroad.org) offers seasonal 20-mile round-trips between Lenox, Stockbridge, and Lee. Also check out the **Chester Railway Station** (413-354-7878) in Chester.

ROCK CLIMBING Climbers seek out cliffs and boulders in Northfield, Ashfield, Erving, and Great Barrington. The **Appalachian Mountain Club** (amcberkshire.org) and **Zoar Outdoor** (zoaroutdoor.com) lead frequent trips.

ROOM TAX Unlike most states, which impose one state tax throughout, Massachusetts gives local communities the option of adding an extra levy of up to 6 percent—theoretically for local promotion—to the basic 5.7 percent room tax. Although resort towns tend to add the full 6 percent, there is no hard-and-fast rule. Alone among the communities covered by this guide, Springfield also levies an additional 2.75 percent convention center financing tax. It's also worth noting that B&Bs with only two or three rooms are exempt from room taxes.

SCENIC BYWAYS The most dramatic is the **Mount Greylock Scenic Byway,** the 16.3-mile-long, recently resurfaced road system: Rockwell Road winding up the western slope of Mount Greylock from Lanesboro, connecting at the 3,491-foot summit with the Notch Road from MA 2 in North Adams; also Reservoir Road, which connects with Notch Road beginning at the Western Gateway

Heritage State Park in North Adams. The most famous is the **Mohawk Trail**, to which we devote a chapter. **Jacob's Ladder Trail** (US 20) is described in *Scenic Drives* in the Southern Berkshire County chapter. The **Route 112 Scenic Byway** runs north/south through the Hilltowns from Colrain near the Vermont border on the north to Russell at US 20, and of course there is The **Connecticut River Byway** in the Pioneer Valley. We understand that MA 116 through Conway and Ashfield is also about to be officially christened "scenic." All these routes and many more are described in their respective chapters under *Scenic Drives*. For the official routes, see byways.org/explore/states/MA.

SHAKERS The Shakers are the oldest, and for a time were the most successful, of America's many 19th-century communal religions. Interest in Shaker furniture, clothing, drawings, and entire, architecturally distinctive Shaker villages runs wide and deep. So does fascination with the people who created these "visible prayers." The Shakers once numbered 6,000 celibate brethren and sisters scattered in 20 self-contained villages from Maine to Ohio. Today only eight villages survive in good enough shape to tell their story—and the Hancock Shaker Village in Central Berkshire is one of the best.

In the 1770s Ann Lee was the leader of England's small sect of the United Society of Believers in Christ's Second Appearing, known for their expressive style of worship as "Shaking Quakers." With her husband, brother, and six followers, Mother Ann settled in Watervliet, near Albany, New York, in 1776. These were years of religious revival as well as political revolution. Whole communities of New Light Baptists—those in New Lebanon, New York (just over the border from Hancock), and Hancock—embraced Mother Ann's dictates of celibacy, shared property, pacifism, equality of the sexes, and a firm belief that life could be perfected in this world.

This last philosophy bred not only fine workmanship, but also an astounding array of inventions: the flat broom, circular saw, clothespin, and seed packet, to name a few.

The Shaker Vatican, so to speak, was Mount Lebanon Shaker Village, straddling the Massachusetts–New York border just west of Hancock. Mount Lebanon elders and eldresses codified rules for all aspects of Shaker life. With 600 residents by the mid-19th century, this was the largest as well as most important Shaker community. On the Sabbath, brethren gathered to pray, sing, and dance in the theater-sized meetinghouse that had been ingeniously designed in 1824 without interior supports, and it was not unusual for more than 1,000 "World's People" (non-Shakers) to come for this "Sunday Show."

"They filed off in a double circle, one going one way, one the other—two or three abreast—laboring around this large hall with knees bent, hands paddling like fins and voices chanting weird airs," recorded Fanny Appleton Longfellow.

Most of Mount Lebanon's surviving Shaker buildings are now part of the Darrow School, which is also the venue for summer concerts at Tannery Pond. Hancock Shaker Village (hancockshakervillage.org), just east of New Lebanon in Hancock, is now a museum village—the area's prime

Christina Tree

showcase for all things Shaker. Another former Shaker village can be found in Tyringham, and yet another vanished community existed deep in Savoy State Forest.

SKIING, CROSS-COUNTRY, AND SNOWSHOEING Trails are noted throughout the book under *Cross-Country Skiing* and *Green Space.* The state's most dependable snow conditions are found in the Berkshire Hilltowns snowbelt, which runs north–south through **Stump Sprouts** (a lodge and touring center; stumpsprouts.com) in East Hawley; **Notchview Reservation** (thetrustees.org) in Windsor; and **Canterbury Farm** (canterbury-farms.com) in Becket. **Hilltop Orchards** (hilltoporchards.com) in Richmond straddles the New York–Massachusetts line and offers 20-mile views, while **Cranwell Resort** (cranwell.com) in Lenox offers trails with rentals and easy access to a full-service spa. In the southeastern corner of the Hilltowns, **Maple Corner Farm** (hidden-hills.com/maplecornerfarm) in Granville sits at an elevation of 1,400 feet with more than 12 miles of marked trails, easily accessed from I-91, as is **Northfield Mountain** with its extensive groomed-trail system in Northfield. The Western Massachusetts Ski Area Association maintains an excellent website: xcskimass.com. In addition, many state parks in Western Massachusetts offer cross-country trails (mass.gov/dcr/recreate/skiing.htm).

SKIING, DOWNHILL, BOARDING AND SNOW TUBING Within this book we have described each area. In Central and North Berkshire, **Jiminy Peak** (jiminypeak.com) is the big destination, while **Bousquet** (bousquets.com), founded in 1932, continues to offer beginner, intermediate, and night skiing. In South Berkshire, **Catamount** (catamountski.com) and

Butternut (skibutternut.com) both offer vertical drops of 1,000 feet and a variety of trails, while **Otis Ridge** (otisridge.com) is a small, family-geared area. With a 1,180-foot vertical drop and some challenging, steep trails, **Berkshire East** (berkshireeast.com) in Charlemont is affectionately known as "Berkshire Beast," and it's the first ski area in the nation to produce 100 percent of its electric power on-site from a wind-powered turbine. There is also **Blandford Ski Area** (skiblandford.org), a small, family-geared ski area established by the Springfield Ski Club in 1934.

SNOWMOBILING The **Snowmobiling Association of Massachusetts,** or SAM (413-369-8092; sledmass.com), P.O. Box 55, Heath 01346, coordinates local clubs and offers guidance for hundreds of miles of trails throughout the state. Conditions permitting, snowmobiles are permitted on the roads in **Mount Greylock State Reservation.** Check with the visitors center (413-499-4262).

SPAS Lenox is the state's spa capital, with **Canyon Ranch** (canyonranch.com), **Cranwell** (cranwell.com), and **Kripalu Center for Yoga and Health** (kripalu.org) drawing thousands of patrons seeking physical and mental renewal. The staff requirements at all these centers have drawn a large number of both New Age and traditional fitness practitioners to the area; several have opened small day spas catering to patrons of the many local inns, a situation worth noting, especially in winter and spring, when inn prices drop well below Tanglewood-season rates. **Mepal Manor & Spa** (mepalspa.com) in New Marlborough, the smallest of the region's full-service spas, is a gem in a beautiful setting.

STATE FORESTS AND PARKS
Would you believe that Massachusetts, the sixth-smallest state in the country, has the eighth-largest state park system? The **Department of Conservation and Recreation** (DCR) is responsible for more than 450,000 acres of public forests, parks, and watershed lands. It's the largest single landholder in the state. The system began in 1898 with the gift of 400 acres on Mount Greylock. Initially its mandate was to purchase logged-over, virtually abandoned land for $5 per acre, and during the Great Depression the Civilian Conservation Corps greatly expanded the facilities by building roads, trails, lakes, and campgrounds to accommodate recreation.

This book describes 47 forests and parks in their respective chapters under *Green Space,* suggesting opportunities for hiking, camping, boating, swimming, and skiing, both downhill and cross-country. The *Massachusetts Outdoor Recreation Map* (including state wildlife management areas) is an indispensable key to this vast system, along with the pamphlet guide *Universal Access* (detailing handicapped-accessible facilities), both available from the DCR (for the Berkshires, 413-442-8928; for the Pioneer Valley, 413-545-5993) during business hours, Mon.–Fri. 8–5. For specific state park information or trail maps, contact the individual facilities listed in this book or online at mass.gov/dcr.

THEATER The **Williamstown Theatre Festival** (wtfestival.org), held late June through August, is the premier summer theater festival of the

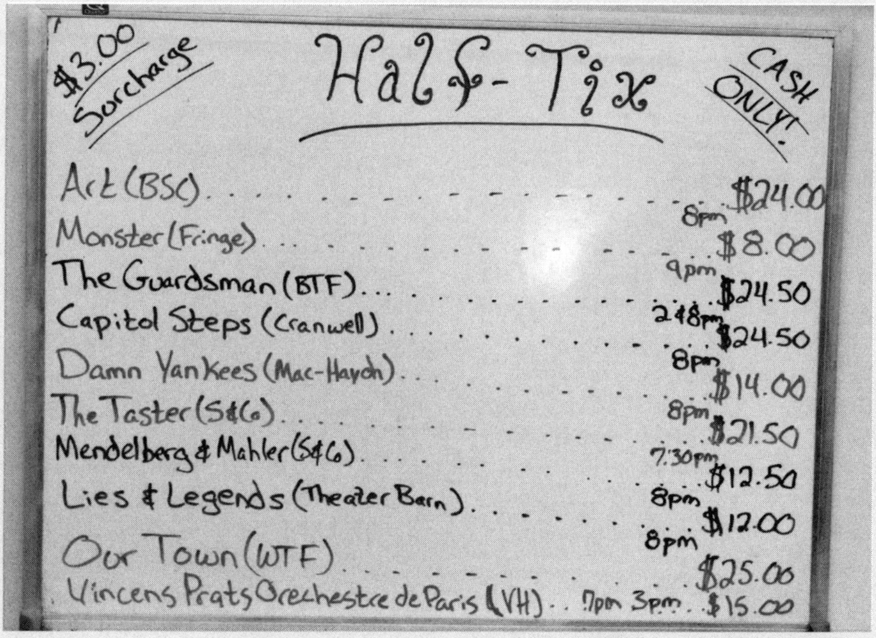

Christina Tree

Northeast. **Shakespeare & Company** (shakespeare.org) in Lenox, performing May through October, is in a class of its own, and the **Berkshire Theatre Festival** (berkshire theatre.org) in Stockbridge is still thriving after 75 years of summer productions. In Pittsfield the **Barrington Stage Company** (barringtonstage-co.org) annually orchestrates original hits that go on to Broadway, and the magnificently restored **Colonial Theatre** (thecolonialtheatre.org) stages a variety of live entertainment, as does the **Mahaiwe Performing Arts Center** (mahaiwe.org) in Great Barrington. In Chester the **Chester Theatre Company** (chestertheatre .org) offers frequently provocative small productions, and in Ashfield the **Double Edge Theatre** (double edgetheatre.org) is a highly professional company performing both indoors and out on its own 100-acre farm. **CityStage** (symphonyhall.com) in Springfield stages professional theater September through May, as does **Shea Theater** (theshea.org) in Turners Falls.

TRACKING With or without snowshoes, tracking is proving to be a new way into the woods year-round for many people. The idea is to track animals for purposes other than hunting. Naturalist Alan Emond (413-624-95444) in Colrain, the local guru, offers half- and full-day tours. Massachusetts Audubon Sanctuaries (see *Birding*) also offer tracking programs.

TRUSTEES OF RESERVATIONS (413-298-3239; thetrustees.org) The nation's oldest private statewide conservation and preservation organization, the Trustees, as this nonprofit is simply known, was founded in 1891 by Charles Eliot, who proposed to preserve parcels of land "which possess uncommon beauty and more than usual refreshing power . . . just as the Public Library holds books and the Art Museum pictures—for the use and enjoyment of the public." So it happens that the Trustees now own and manage hilltops, waterfalls, islands, barrier beaches, bogs, historic houses, and designed landscapes, among other things, more than 20 in Western Massachusetts alone. Within this book we describe properties as they appear within chapters. Note that holdings include the outstanding Guest House at Field Farm in Williamstown. Also note the beautifully maintained historic houses in Stockbridge, Sheffield, and Cummington.

WATERFALLS We long thought that someone should make a poster of Massachusetts waterfalls, not only because there are so many, but also because most are so little known. Happily, such a poster—which depicts 20 Berkshire County waterfalls in full color—is now available from Berkshire Photos (berkshirephotos.com). Check out the falls in Ashfield, Becket, Blandford, Cheshire, Chesterfield, Dalton, Middlefield, Mount Washington, New Marlboro, North Adams, Sheffield, Shelburne Falls, Williamsburg, and Worthington, all of which we have visited and describe. Also check Joe Bushee's book, *Waterfalls of Massachusetts: An Explorer's Guide to 55 Natural Scenic Wonders.*

WHEELCHAIR ACCESS The wheelchair symbol ♿ indicates lodging and dining places that are handicapped accessible. Also note the pamphlet detailing the universal access program in state forests and parks (see above).

WHITE-WATER RAFTING Since 1989, when New England Electric began releasing water on a regular basis from its Fife Brook Dam, white-water rafting has become a well-established pastime on the Deerfield River. **Zoar Outdoor** (zoaroutdoor.com) in Charlemont pioneered the sport in this area and offers lodging and a variety of programs. Maine-based **Crab Apple Whitewater** (crabapplewhitewater.com) provides stiff competition with its own attractive base on the river down the road, as does **Moxie Outdoor Adventures** (moxierafting.com), also headquartered in Maine.

WINERIES **West County Winery** (westcountycider.com) in Shelburne has been producing widely marketed and respected apple wines since 1984 and has won numerous awards for its annually changing selection. Its annual CiderDays (ciderday.org) open house attracts cider makers from throughout the continent. **Furnace Brook Winery** at Hilltop Orchards (hilltoporchards.com) in Richmond specializes in oak-aged cider, but also offers free tastings of its varietal grape and specialty wines. In New Marlborough check out **Les Trois Emme Winery and Vineyard** (413-528-1015; ltewinery.com), which is open for tours and tastings of its wines (including pumpkin wine) made from homegrown and California grapes. **Pioneer Valley Farm & Vineyard** (pioneervalleyvineyard.com) in Hatfield is a sixth-generation farm crafting grape and fruit wines; check the website for hours.

Zoar Outdoor

ZIP LINES This new high-wire sport can be sampled seasonally in Berkshire County at **Catamount Adventure Park** (catamounttrees.com) in South Egremont, at **Jiminy Peak Mountain Aerial Adventure Park** (jiminypeak.com) in Hancock and in the West County town of Charlemont at both **Zoar Outdoor** (deerfieldzipline.com) and at **Berkshire East** (berkshireeast.com).

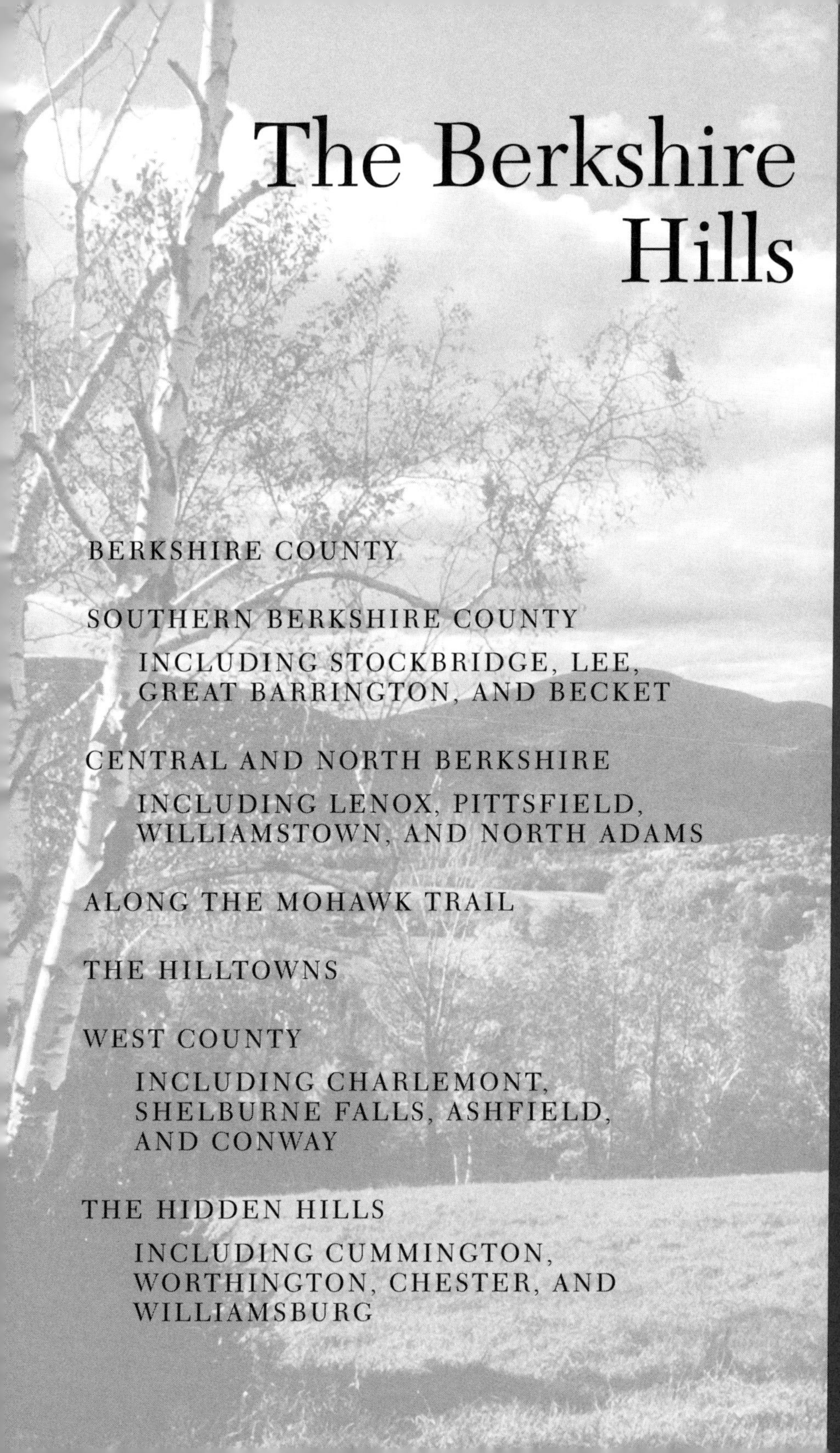

The Berkshire Hills

1

BERKSHIRE COUNTY

SOUTHERN BERKSHIRE COUNTY

INCLUDING STOCKBRIDGE, LEE, GREAT BARRINGTON, AND BECKET

CENTRAL AND NORTH BERKSHIRE

INCLUDING LENOX, PITTSFIELD, WILLIAMSTOWN, AND NORTH ADAMS

ALONG THE MOHAWK TRAIL

THE HILLTOWNS

WEST COUNTY

INCLUDING CHARLEMONT, SHELBURNE FALLS, ASHFIELD, AND CONWAY

THE HIDDEN HILLS

INCLUDING CUMMINGTON, WORTHINGTON, CHESTER, AND WILLIAMSBURG

BERKSHIRE COUNTY

Berkshire has the best name recognition of any Massachusetts county. Ask residents where they come from and the answer is invariably "the Berkshires," not "Massachusetts."

The Berkshires is a fairly recent name created to promote Berkshire County. Never mind that the Berkshire Hills themselves roll east through the Hilltowns and south into Connecticut.

This westernmost strip of Massachusetts has always been a place apart. Its first settlers were easygoing Dutchmen rather than the dour Puritans, and while parts of Berkshire County are equidistant from both Boston and New York City, visitors and ideas tend to flow from the south rather than the east.

This distinctive roll of hill and valley extends the full 56-mile length of the state, from the Vermont to Connecticut borders. Its highest mountains, including Mount Greylock (3,491 feet) in North Berkshire and Mount Everett (2,264 feet) in South Berkshire, are actually strays from New York's Taconic Range; the county is walled from New York state on the west by the Taconics and from the rest of "the Bay State" by hills high enough for 18th-century settlers to have called them the Berkshire Barrier.

History, topography, and politics aside, what sets the Berkshires apart from anywhere else in the U.S. is the quantity and quality of the music, art, dance, and theater found there. In July and August this serene landscape is the backdrop for the liveliest music, theater, and dance presentations in the Northeast, arguably in the entire country. It's a phenomenon that's been more than a century in the making.

Writers Nathaniel Hawthorne, Herman Melville, and Oliver Wendell Holmes Sr. were among the first Berkshire summer residents. Their lyrical descriptions of the area's inspirational scenery helped attract wealthy rusticators who terraced cornfields into formal gardens and built some 75 summer mansions (coyly called "cottages") between 1880 and 1920, most in and around Lenox and Stockbridge.

The stock market crash of 1929, the Depression, and the federal income tax thinned the ranks of the Berkshires' wealthy elite. The mansions remained, however, and were frequently taken over by private schools, religious orders, or cultural institutions.

In 1937 the Boston Symphony Orchestra (BSO) made Tanglewood, a Lenox

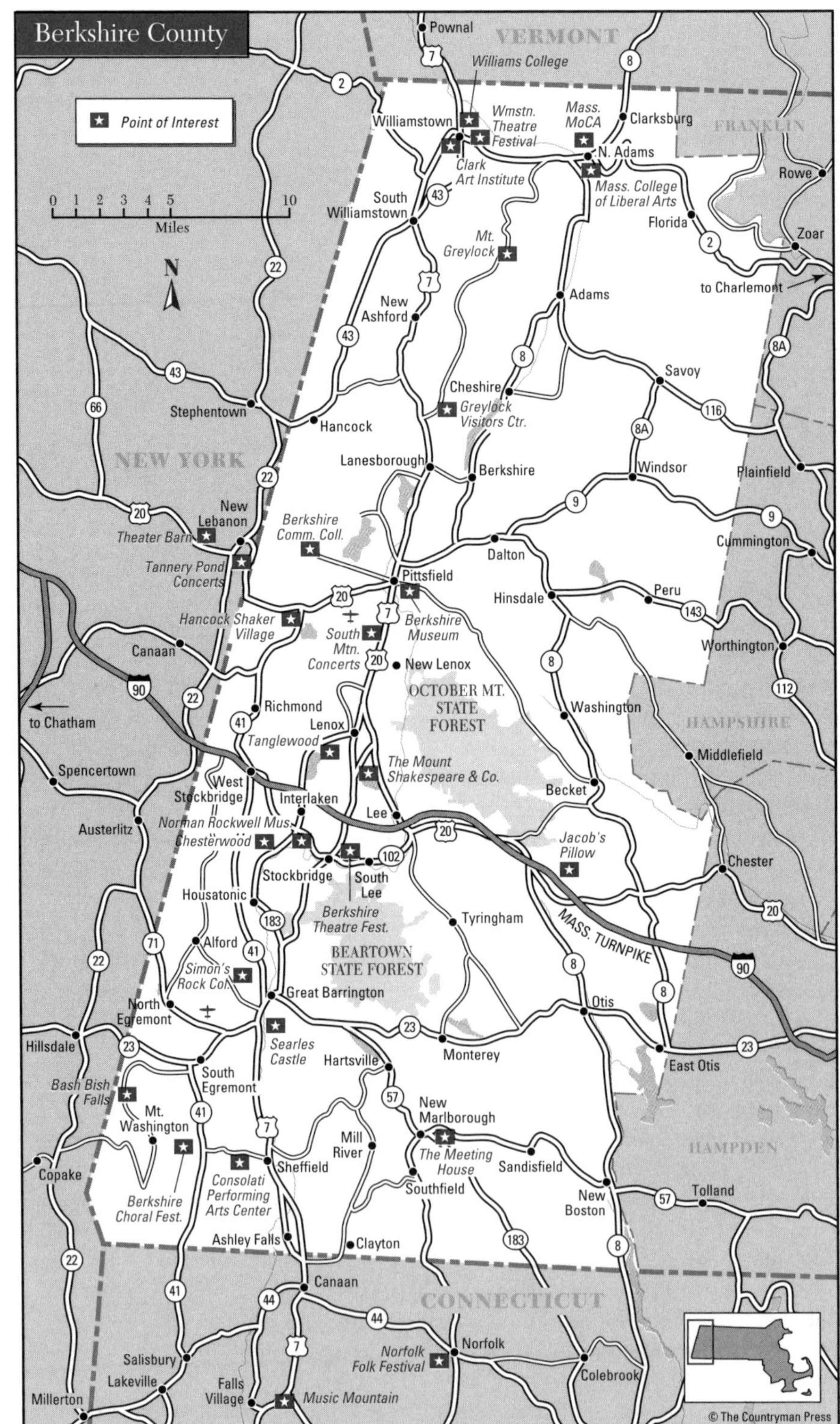
Berkshire County
Point of Interest
0 1 2 3 4 5 10
Miles
N
VERMONT
NEW YORK
FRANKLIN
HAMPSHIRE
HAMPDEN
CONNECTICUT
Pownal
Williams College
Williamstown
Wmstn. Theatre Festival
Mass. MoCA
Clarksburg
N. Adams
Clark Art Institute
Mass. College of Liberal Arts
Rowe
South Williamstown
Florida
Zoar
Mt. Greylock
to Charlemont
Adams
New Ashford
Savoy
Cheshire
Greylock Visitors Ctr.
Stephentown
Hancock
Lanesborough
Berkshire
Windsor
Plainfield
New Lebanon
Theater Barn
Berkshire Comm. Coll.
Dalton
Cummington
Tanney Pond Concerts
Pittsfield
Hinsdale
Peru
Hancock Shaker Village
South Mtn. Concerts
Berkshire Museum
Worthington
Canaan
New Lenox
OCTOBER MT. STATE FOREST
to Chatham
Richmond
Washington
Lenox
Tanglewood
Middlefield
The Mount Shakespeare & Co.
Spencertown
West Stockbridge
Interlaken
Becket
Austerlitz
Norman Rockwell Mus.
Lee
Chesterwood
Jacob's Pillow
Stockbridge
South Lee
Chester
Housatonic
Berkshire Theatre Fest.
Tyringham
MASS. TURNPIKE
Alford
BEARTOWN STATE FOREST
Simon's Rock Col.
Great Barrington
Otis
North Egremont
Hillsdale
Searles Castle
Monterey
East Otis
South Egremont
Hartsville
Bash Bish Falls
Mt. Washington
New Marlborough
Mill River
The Meeting House
Sandisfield
Copake
Sheffield
Consolati Performing Arts Center
Southfield
New Boston
Tolland
Berkshire Choral Fest.
Ashley Falls
Clayton
Canaan
Norfolk
Norfolk Folk Festival
Salisbury
Colebrook
Lakeville
Falls Village
Music Mountain
Millerton
© The Countryman Press

estate donated by an orchestra patron, its summer home. Dancers, musicians, actors, and writers began flocking to the area, also lured by the presence of the Berkshire Playhouse (now the Berkshire Theatre Festival) in Stockbridge and Jacob's Pillow Dance Festival in Becket. This burgeoning summer scene was interrupted by World War II, however, and for years after this remained the sleepy small-town America which illustrator Norman Rockwell depicted, based on what he saw within bicycling distance of his Stockbridge studio.

Unexpectedly, the Cold War boosted Berkshire County as a cultural destination. Fearing a nuclear attack on Manhattan, Singer Sewing Machine heirs Sterling and Francine Clark chose to display their legendary art collection in the ivied college town of Williamstown, building a marble museum to house it. The 1955 opening of the Clark Art Institute drew art lovers from around the world—and the steady stream continues.

Even more unexpectedly, the Vietnam War brought the Berkshires a different artistic fame. Folksinger Arlo Guthrie wrote "Alice's Restaurant," an 18-minute-long saga recounting Guthrie's arrest for illegally dumping litter and how it kept him out of the draft. The song became the anti-battle cry of a generation, and the 1969 movie version brought it all visually home: the same small-town scenes and people Rockwell had depicted once more evoked the feel—this time a different feel—of small towns across the country.

In the 21st century Berkshire County is once more enjoying a Gilded Era, this time shared by a far larger group than that of 100 years ago. Once more there's no question that Stockbridge and Lenox are not just any small towns. Visitors from everywhere rock on the porch of the Red Lion Inn, and Lenox offers dozens of princely mansions in which to sleep and half a dozen in which you can dine at princely prices.

Few Berkshire County lodging places or restaurants now close for the winter. Lodging rates, on the other hand, vary wildly with the season and even with the day of the week. On weekends during "Tanglewood season" (July and August), you can pay Manhattan prices for a modest room and frequently must stay a minimum of three days. Weekdays, even in August, generally cost less. Rates remain high through October as foliage colors linger. Winter offers skiing at some of the country's oldest family-geared ski areas and reduced prices for all those elegant rooms with fireplaces; it's also a good time to take advantage of lower rates at both the day and full-service spas.

We have divided Berkshire County in two: "Southern Berkshire County," also known as "South County," includes Lee and Stockbridge as well as Great Barrington and the surrounding rural villages. We also include attractions just south of the border in Connecticut and west in New York's Columbia County. The Central Berkshire communities of Lenox, Pittsfield, and Hancock are combined with Williamstown and North Adams in "Central and Northern Berkshire County."

Southern and North Berkshire County are distinctive entities linked by the Pittsfield area, but it's debatable where Lenox—with its Tanglewood Music Festival, which dictates high season in The Berkshires—fits in. In previous editions we have included it in South Berkshire. However, with the ever-growing attraction of North Adams's MASS MoCA, one of the world's largest contemporary art

Christina Tree

BALDWIN HILL IN SOUTH EGREMONT.

centers, and the recent clustering of theater and art galleries in Pittsfield, we have placed Tanglewood within the context of these cultural draws.

Year-round the countryside remains far more than a backdrop. Since the 1840s, both picnicking and hiking along bench-spotted paths and up gentle mountains have been considered the thing to do in summer, and now snowmobiles, snowshoes, and cross-country skis access many trails in the county's more than 125,000 acres of public preserves.

GUIDANCE

Countywide information services

Berkshire Visitors Bureau (413-743-4500 or 1-800-237-5747; berkshires.org; info@berkshires.org) offers a countywide online reservation service. Request *The Berkshires Visitors Guide,* an annual booklet listing attractions, lodgings, and dining. The office at 3 Hoosac St. in Adams is open weekdays 8:30–5.

Also see *Guidance* for **Southern Berkshire** and **Central and North Berkshire.**

Rural Intelligence (ruralintelligence.com) is the best website we have found covering dining, shopping, and the cultural scene in Columbia County, N.Y., and Litchfield County, Conn., as well as Berkshire County. We find its reviews consistently on target.

WHEN TO COME High season here is synonymous with the Tanglewood Music Festival (bso.org) in July and August in Lenox (see the "Central and North Berkshire" chapter). Many concert-goers book their rooms a year ahead or as soon as the season's concert schedule is published. May, June, September, and October are less lively and pricey, but still delightful. Christmas through February weekends bring skiers, but prices are low midweek.

SOUTHERN BERKSHIRE COUNTY

INCLUDING STOCKBRIDGE, LEE, GREAT BARRINGTON, AND BECKET

The southwest corner of Massachusetts has its own distinctive beauty and pace. The Housatonic River is slower, and the roads are more heavily wooded, winding through classic old villages, by swimming holes, and past hiking paths that lead to waterfalls.

The towns that have changed most visibly in South County in recent years are the formerly workaday Lee and Great Barrington. Paper is still made in Lee and both the vintage 1855 Morgan House and 1955 Joe's Diner are still Main Street staples, while Victorian-era buildings house a number of restaurants. Capitalizing on its status as the county's prime gateway from the Massachusetts Turnpike, a large designer outlet mall, Premium Outlets, is just off the Pike exit. Gracious B&Bs are scattered along the town's wooded upland roads.

Great Barrington is said to be equidistant from New York and Boston—2 hours, 15 minutes (traffic permitting) from both. The largest town in south Berkshire County, it has always been a place to buy a wrench, catch a bus, or see a movie. Currently it's also a place to shop for linen clothing and country furnishings, to purchase artist materials and vintage posters, and to choose from an ever-widening variety of menus. The friendly visitors center also houses Half Tix, selling same-day, half-price tickets for dance at Jacob's Pillow, theater and music throughout the Berkshires.

South from Great Barrington, the Housatonic spirals lazily through a broad valley hemmed in by rolling hills to the west and walled by the abrupt Taconic Range that includes Mount Everett on the west. Sheffield is the Berkshires' oldest town and now aptly synonymous with antique dealers. Its village of Ashley Falls, almost on the Connecticut line, is the site of the Colonel Ashley House in which the Sheffield Declaration, a 1773 statement of grievances against British rule, was drafted. This exceptional home is owned by the Trustees of Reservations, the venerable Massachusetts organization that also maintains several of the area's outstanding historic houses and preserves, notably the vintage 1793 Mission House and Naumkeag, a 26-room, 1894 "Berkshire cottage," both in Stockbridge, 6 miles north of Great Barrington.

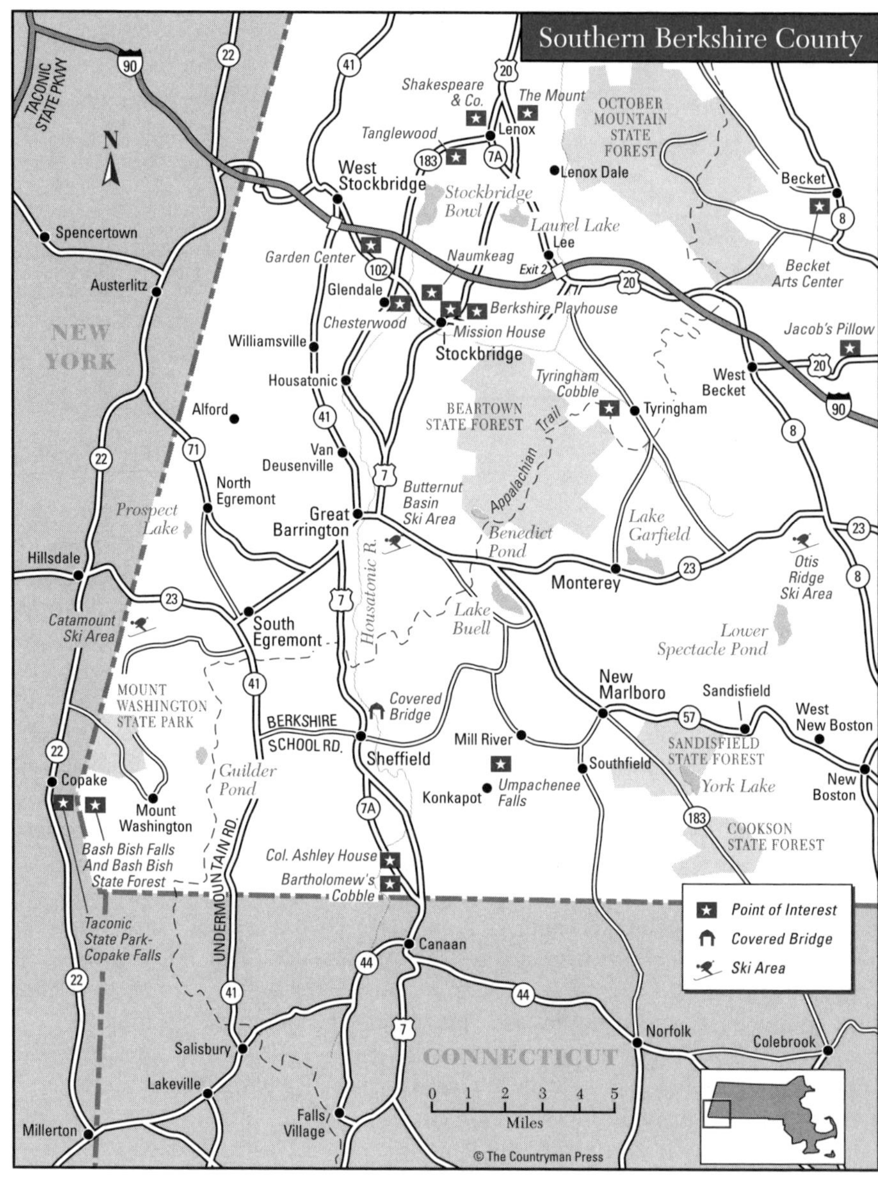

Main Street Stockbridge looks much the way Norman Rockwell, who lived there from 1953 until his death in 1978, painted it in the 1950s (see page 60). The museum showcasing his work is well worth a visit. Continue on to West Stockbridge, a former mill village with exceptional shopping and dining.

More than other parts of the Berkshires, the often breathtaking beauty of South County is found along back roads. From West Stockbridge head south along MA 41 or the Alford Road to North Egremont. Continue over Baldwin Hill to South Egremont (blink and you're through) with its clutch of restaurants and antique shops. More adventurous travelers, certainly hikers, should turn on Mount Washington Road, just west of town, as it winds into the town of Mount Washington, following signs for Bash Bish Falls.

Southern Berkshire harbors thousands of acres of state park and forest acquired when land was cheap, after 75 percent of its trees were chopped down to feed either the area's lime kilns or its paper mills. In the 1890s vast estates were also acquired by private owners, and segments of these are also now preserved by the state and by the Trustees. Public lands offer camping, swimming, and fishing as well as hiking and cross-country skiing. The Appalachian Trail cuts across the Housatonic Valley, offering numerous access points, from the heights of Mount Everett in the southwest corner to Benedict Pond in Beartown State Forest. Cross-country trails web these preserves and alpine trails draw loyal followers to Butternut, just east of Great Barrington, and to Catamount, west of South Egremont. Both are family-friendly areas with 1,000-foot verticals.

East of the Housatonic Valley, gentle hills are webbed with back roads, many still dirt, climbing through old farms and some estates dating from land speculation before railway routes were determined. (A railway never materialized.) The east–west Massachusetts Turnpike follows US 20 through Becket to Lee, backroading Otis, Tyringham, and Monterey and even further back-roading the 18th-century towns of Sandisfield and New Marlborough.

AREA CODE 413 applies to all of Western Massachusetts.

GUIDANCE **Southern Berkshire Chamber of Commerce** (413-528-1510; southernberkshirechamber.com; visitor@southernberkshirechamber.com), 362 Main St. at the southern edge of Great Barrington (MA 23–US 7), across from Searles Castle. Open year-round, Tues.–Sun. 10–4:30. Limited hours off-season, weekends. Lodging hotline: 1-800-269-4825.

The **Lee Chamber of Commerce** (413-243-0852; leechamber.org), 3 Park Place, is well marked and conveniently sited just after you make the turn (northbound) onto US 20 (Main Street) in a small park with plenty of adjoining parking. Open Mon.–Sat. 10–4, Sun. 1–4.

Columbia County Tourism (1-800-724-1846; bestcountryroads.com) publishes a handy booklet guide to the roads and towns in New York west of Southern Berkshire.

GETTING THERE *By air:* See **Albany Airport** and **Bradley International Airport** in Windsor Locks, Connecticut, under *Airports* in "What's Where."

By bus: From Boston, **Peter Pan Bus Lines** (1-800-343-9999; peterpanbus.com) serves Lee via Springfield, and from Manhattan its buses run up US 7, stopping on the green in Sheffield, at the chamber booth in Great Barrington, on Main Street in Stockbridge, and at the Morgan House Inn in Lee.

By train: From New York City, **Metro-North** (212-532-4900 or 1-800-METRO-INFO; mta.info). On weekends from July through Labor Day, Friday evening trains travel from Grand Central to Wassaic Station in Amenia, New York. Return service is offered Sunday afternoon. The price is surprisingly reasonable.

Christina Tree

MA 57 IS A PICTURESQUE WAY TO GET FROM SOUTHWICK TO MARLBOROUGH.

Connecting service: **Taxi Co.** (413-528-0911) or **All Points Courier** (413-429-7397).

By car: From Boston, the obvious route is the Massachusetts Turnpike to Exit 2 at Lee (2 hours on the button). For a more scenic approach, take Mass Pike Exit 6 (I-291) to I-91 South to MA 57 West (see *Scenic Drives*).

From New York City, the obvious approach is the Major Deegan Expressway or the Henry Hudson Parkway to the Saw Mill River Parkway, then to the Taconic Parkway; take the South Berkshire exit, Hillsdale/Claverack, N.Y., then MA 23 East. About 2½ hours.

GETTING AROUND A car is the way to go, but you can hire a taxi or rent a car (check chamber listings in Lee and Great Barrington). Local car rental agencies deliver cars to the bus stops or local inns. Given the many scenic but confusing roads that web this area in particular, we recommend securing a Berkshire County map, free from the sources listed under *Guidance.*

The **Berkshire Regional Transit Authority** (1-800-292-2782; berkshirerta.com) links Great Barrington, Lee, Lenox, and Stockbridge with Pittsfield; hours are geared to commuters rather than visitors.

PARKING It's free in Lenox, Stockbridge, and Great Barrington, but there's a two-hour limit that is strictly enforced. In Great Barrington, downtown lots are accessed from Railroad and Elm Streets as well as Main and Bridge Streets; there's also a small lot at the end of Castle Street.

MEDICAL EMERGENCY Dial **911.**

✷ Towns and Villages

Becket (population: 1,802). Technically within Berkshire County, the village center is marked by the **Becket Arts Center of the Hilltowns** (becketarts center.org) and it borders Blandford and Chester (see "Hidden Hills" chapter) to the east. It's best known as home to **The Jacob's Pillow Dance Festival** (jacobspillow.org), a major Berkshires summer destination (see *Must See*), just 8 miles east of Lee on US 20. There several distinct parts to Becket. The 1840s arrival of the Western Railroad shifted population to Becket Village, 5.5 miles north up MA 8 from the Old Center. From there many visitors continue on County Road to **Dream Away Lodge** (*Entertainment*), **Yokum Pond,** or on into **October State Forest.** A vestige of the town's defunct granite quarrying in South Becket is now a great place to walk (becketlandtrust.org). Heavily wooded and pond-pocked, Becket harbors several summer camps and many second homes.

Egremont (population: 1,150). There is no village of Egremont; instead, there's North Egremont and South Egremont, divided by Baldwin Hill. **South Egremont** is the livelier village, one known for antique shops. Note the fan window in the **Congregational Church** and the town hall in the southern village. Don't miss **Baldwin Hill,** with its surviving farms and sense of serenity. **North Egremont** offers a general store, inn, and lakeside campground.

Great Barrington (population: 7,288). The shopping hub of southern Berkshire County, Great Barrington is known for the quality and quantity of its restaurants, and also of its downtown shopping. Railroad Street is restaurant row; neighboring film, music, and live performance venues complement the dining and shopping. There were once three large and fashionable inns in town, including the Berkshire Inn (1868–1963), which more than filled the site that's now occupied by the Southern Berkshire Chamber of Commerce, CVS Pharmacy, and Days

MAIN STREET, GREAT BARRINGTON.

Christina Tree

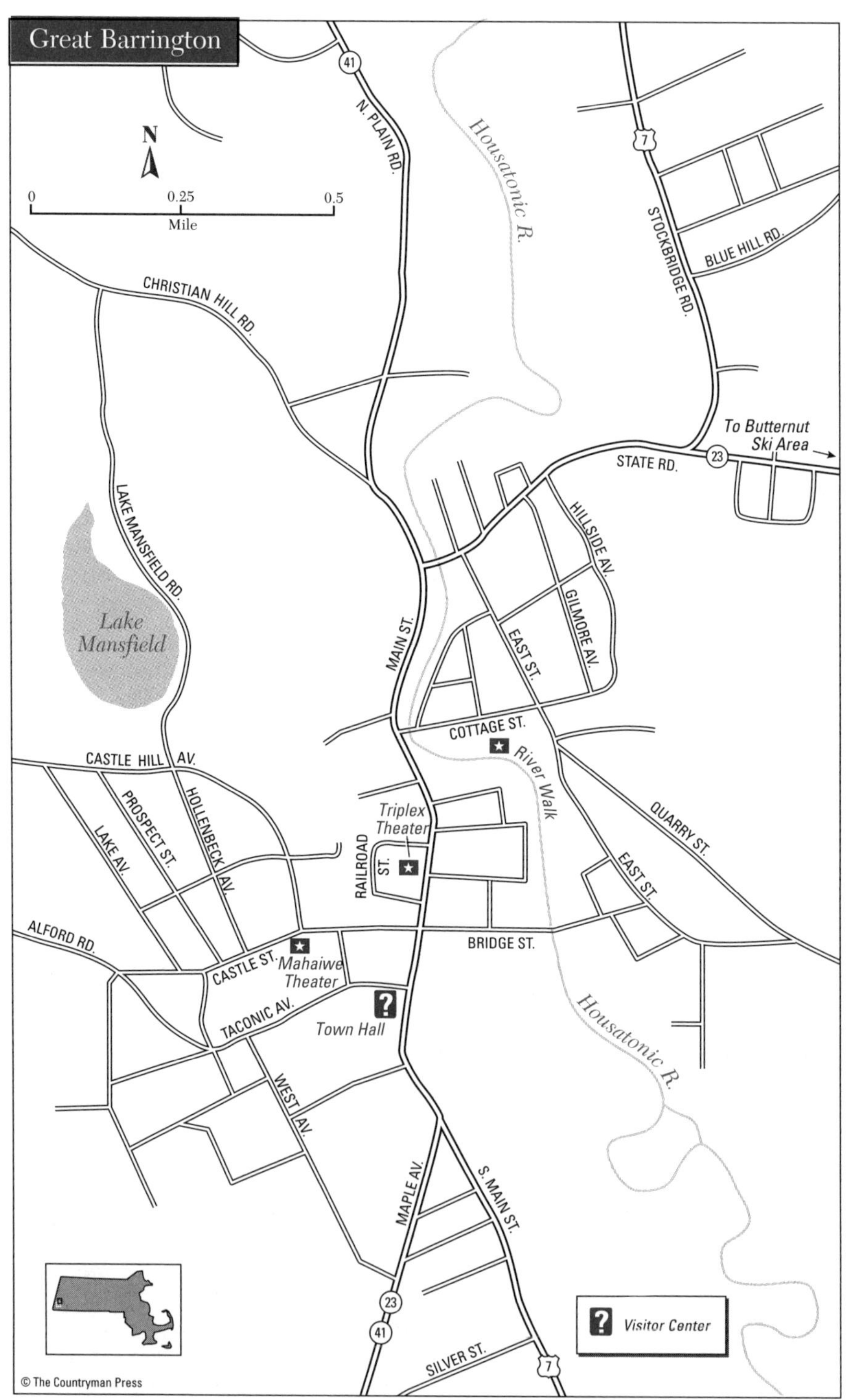
Great Barrington
N
0
0.25
0.5
Mile
41
N. PLAIN RD.
Housatonic R.
7
STOCKBRIDGE RD.
BLUE HILL RD.
CHRISTIAN HILL RD.
To Butternut Ski Area
23
STATE RD.
HILLSIDE AV.
LAKE MANSFIELD RD.
Lake Mansfield
GILMORE AV.
MAIN ST.
EAST ST.
COTTAGE ST.
River Walk
CASTLE HILL AV.
PROSPECT ST.
HOLLENBECK AV.
LAKE AV.
Triplex Theater
RAILROAD ST.
QUARRY ST.
EAST ST.
ALFORD RD.
CASTLE ST.
Mahaiwe Theater
BRIDGE ST.
TACONIC AV.
Town Hall
Housatonic R.
WEST AV.
MAPLE AV.
S. MAIN ST.
23
41
Visitor Center
SILVER ST.
7
© The Countryman Press

Inn. Searles Castle, across the street, was designed by Stanford White and built of local blue dolomite stone from 1882–86 for the widow Mary Hopkins, founder of the Central Pacific Railroad. Main Street's three stone churches also evoke this opulent era.

Worth noting: The ancient-looking (and barely readable) stone marker in front of the town hall with the inscription: near this spot stood the first court house of berkshire county. here, august 16, 1774, occurred the first normal resistance to British Rule in North America. *Also worth finding:* **River Walk,** still evolving but offering benches and views of the Housatonic in several segments as it flows behind Main Street. At the entrance beside the Rite Aid Pharmacy, a brief history credits **W. E. B. Du Bois** with inspiring the project, pleading with townspeople to "Rescue the Housatonic . . . restore its ancient beauty." A sociologist and civil rights activist, Du Bois (1868–1966) was born in Great Barrington by what he called this "golden river," explaining that it was "golden because of the woolen and paper waste that soiled it." The woolen and paper mills were, however, several miles upstream in **Housatonic,** a village that still has a working paper mill as well as a number of artists working in former mill buildings.

Lee (population 5,985). The county's only access from the Massachusetts Turnpike, Lee boasts that it is "The Gateway to the Berkshires." It is also home to Premium Outlets, a large shopping complex just off the turnpike exit with more than 60 designer and brand-name outlet stores. Another visitor magnet is 16,500-acre October State Forest, the largest park of its kind in the state, attracting hikers, bikers, campers, and boaters in summer and cross-country skiers and snowmobilers in winter. First settled in 1760, Lee has long been the commercial hub of an area that includes the villages of South and East Lee and surrounding towns such as Tyringham, Becket, Otis, and Sandisfield. It was once a paper-making center with 25 mills operating in the mid-19th century. Today only one small company making specialty paper remains. The town was also once famous for its marble, which can be viewed in a wing of the Capitol in Washington and St. Patrick's Cathedral in New York City. A legacy of Lee's 19th-century prosperity is the many handsome buildings along Main Street, a number of which house restaurants serving everything from fast food and pizza to haute cuisine.

MAIN STREET, LEE.

Christina Tree

Stockbridge (population: 2,300). Stockbridge was founded in 1734 to contain and educate the local Mahicans. Just four white families were permitted to settle, theoretically to "afford civilizing examples to the Indians." But predictably, the whites multiplied and the Native Americans dwindled. After distinguishing themselves as the only tribe to serve in the Revolution and the first to be given U.S. citizenship, the Stockbridge tribe was banished to the west, eventually to Wisconsin, where a few hundred descendants still live. Stockbridge boasts that the Laurel Hill Association was the country's first village-improvement society. Residents will tell you that the same number of notables have been summering in town for the past century; only the faces change periodically. The rambling, wooden **Red Lion Inn,** a short walk from the restored **Mission House,** forms the heart of the village. **Naumkeag,** the quintessential Gilded Age mansion, is just a short way up the hill, and the **Berkshire Theatre Festival** is on the northern fringe of town.

The village green is west of the MA 102–US 7 junction, and many visitors miss it entirely. Here stand the imposing brick **Congregational Church** (1824), the pillared **Old Town Hall** (1839), and the **Field Chime Tower,** which marks the site of the original Native American mission. The **Indian Burial Ground** is nearby—the large mound topped by a stone obelisk and overlooking the golf course. The **Village Cemetery,** across from the green, contains the remains of John Sergeant, Native American chief John Konkapot, 19th-century tycoons such as Joseph Choate, and town aristocrats like the Fields and Sedgwicks, the latter buried in a large circular family plot known as "the Sedgwick Pie."

West Stockbridge (population: 1,416). West Stockbridge (weststockbridgetown.com) is an old town, dating back to a 1724 purchase from Sachem Konkapot. In the 19th century its marble was quarried and used in the Boston State House and New York City Hall. The heart of town today is a former mill village on the Williams River, a great spot for shopping and dining.

ELM STREET, STOCKBRIDGE.

Christina Tree

Monterey (population: 918). Much of this town has been absorbed into **Beartown State Forest,** and it is largely a second-home community. Lake Garfield is ringed with summer homes, and its beach is private. Head north from the village center and turn onto Art School Road to find the **Bidwell House,** an exceptionally well-furnished 18th-century home with walking trails through its extensive grounds. This was once a dairy center producing more cheese than any other location in the county, and **Monterey Chèvre** from Rawson Brook Farm is still the county's best.

Mount Washington (population: 135). This town is the southwesternmost, the highest, and one of the smallest in Massachusetts. Best known as the home of **Bash Bish Falls,** the state's most photographed cascade, it is also the site of one of the highest peaks (2,600-foot **Mount Everett**) and the highest lake (**Guilder Pond**) in Massachusetts. The community, settled by the Dutch in the 1690s, is also arguably the oldest in Berkshire County. The town is webbed with hiking trails—including one of the more dramatic, open ridgeline sections of the **Appalachian Trail.** Given that you can park at several trailheads that access high-elevation trails—and paths to several waterfalls (the cascades of Race Brook and Bear Rock as well as Bash Bish)—you would assume this was one of the better-known, more popular spots to hike. Not so. Mount Washington seems to be a well-kept hikers' secret. The center of the village is marked by the small **Union Church** (ecumenical, open summers only) and tiny town hall. Note the old cemetery on West Street and **Blueberry Hill Farm.**

New Marlborough (population: 1,494). Lying within a beautiful roll of hills pocked by shallow valleys carved by the Konkapot River and its offshoots, New Marlborough (new-marlborough.info) is webbed with roads connecting its villages: Mill River, Southfield, Hartsville, New Marlborough Center, and Clayton. At the center stand the **Old Inn on the Green** and a domed, white-clapboard **New Marlborough Meeting House,** the venue for year-round music, films, etc., sponsored by **Music and More**, as well as a seasonal gallery.

Sheffield (population: 2,967). This town was the first in the Berkshires to be chartered (1733). Its wide main street (US 7) is lined with stately old homes, and the town boasts the greatest number of antique dealers of any town in the Berkshires. North of the green, the 1770s brick **Dan Raymond House,** maintained by the **Sheffield Historical Society** (413-229-2694; sheffieldhistory.org), reflects the lifestyle of this prosperous merchant, his wife, and their nine children. It's part of a seven-building complex that includes a regional research center, a vintage-1820 law office, a carriage house with a tool exhibit, and an oddly shaped building once used to grow vegetables for nearby hotels, now an education center. There's also an 1830s smokehouse and the Old Stone Store, which houses changing exhibitions and a museum store. The 1760 **Old Parish Church** is a beauty, one of the oldest churches in Berkshire County and the site of a seasonal Friday afternoon farmers' market as well as the annual three-day **Sheffield Antiques Fair,** always the third weekend in August. Several miles south on US 7 is Ashley Falls. It's well worth allotting several hours in which to tour the **Colonel Ashley House** (1735), the oldest in the Berkshires, and to walk along the glassy Housatonic in **Bartholomew's Cobble.** Note the covered bridge, originally built in 1827, just off US 7 at the northern end of the village.

Sandisfield (population: 809). With the largest area of any Berkshire County town, this was once a thriving industrial center with six taverns and churches and a population said to surpass Pittsfield's. It's difficult to believe. Land sales boomed when a railroad was proposed to run through town, but it never happened. The most visible village in Sandisfield is New Boston, at the junction of MA 8 and MA 57. The **New Boston Inn**—said to date to 1737—has a well-documented resident ghost and still offers food and lodging. Much of the town now lies within the **Sandisfield State Forest.**

Tyringham (population: 375). Hemmed in on three sides by mountains, this village was the site of a major Shaker community from the 1790s until the 1870s (a group of privately owned Shaker buildings still stands on Jerusalem Road near Shaker Pond). The village then began attracting prominent summer residents, including Samuel Clemens. In fact, a number of 19th-century writers eulogized Tyringham. Two miles of hiking trails, including a section of the AT, pass over the twin knobs of **Tyringham Cobble,** 206 acres maintained by the Trustees of Reservations.

Over the hills and south of the border: While a range of the Taconics forms a natural boundary between Southern Berkshire and New York state, this is also part of a genuine tri-state area that includes the New York towns of Chatham, Hillsdale, Copake, and Millerton as well as Salisbury, Canaan, and Lime Rock, Connecticut. We include their attractions; also see *Scenic Drives.*

✷ Must See

Jacob's Pillow Dance Festival (413-243-0745; jacobspillow.org), 358 George Carter Rd., Becket (off US 20, 8 miles east of Lee). America's oldest dance festival and still its most prestigious, Jacob's Pillow presents a 10-week summer program of classic and experimental dance. Located on a one-time hilltop farm, the Pillow was founded in the 1930s by famed dancer Ted Shawn as both a school for dancers and a performance center. In addition to scheduled productions, informal impromptu performances are ongoing during the festival. There are talks, class observations, and tours. Picnicking is allowed on the Great Lawn, and the pleasant Pillow Café opens for dinner and drinks before evening performances. Tickets for performances in the Ted Shawn Theater, the first in the country built exclusively for dance, are $30–68. Inquire about performances in the Doris Duke Studio Theater, as well as children's programs and some 200 free performances.

Norman Rockwell Museum (413-298-4100; nrm.org), MA 183 south of its junction with MA 102, 3 miles west of Stockbridge. Open daily 10–5 in summer (until 7 Thurs. in July and Aug.); Nov.–Apr., weekdays 10–4, weekends 10–5. Rockwell's studio, located on the museum grounds, is open May–Oct. Closed Thanksgiving, Christmas, and New Year's Day. Adults $15, seniors $13.50, college students with ID $10, under 18 free if accompanied by an adult. Norman Rockwell (1894–1978), America's most beloved illustrator, spent his last 50 years

Jacob's Pillow Dance Festival
JACOB'S PILLOW DANCE FESTIVAL, HELD IN BECKET, IS AN ANNUAL SUMMER ATTRACTION.

in Stockbridge and often used it as a backdrop and local residents as models. The museum displays some 200 of his works, including the famous World War II poster series *The Four Freedoms,* along with many original paintings done for covers of *The Saturday Evening Post,* at the time a national institution. Even if you didn't grow up with the *Post,* Rockwell's iconic yesteryear images of small-town American life retain their charm and are a delight to look at. Also on view are powerful paintings, quite different from the folksy *Post* covers, that he did for *Look* magazine to illustrate articles on 1960s civil rights incidents. Although Rockwell is the focus, the museum always features special exhibits on other illustrators and aspects of contemporary illustration, too. The handsome museum building, which includes a large gift shop and a café, is on a 36-acre former estate with tranquil views from benches (and picnic facilities) overlooking the Housatonic River.

✷ Also See

HISTORIC HOMES **Chesterwood** (413-298-3579; chesterwood.org), MA 183, south of its junction with MA 102 in the Glendale section of Stockbridge. Open late May–mid-Oct., daily 10–5. Adults $15, seniors and students $9, ages 6–18 $5, family rate $25. This 160-acre estate served for 33 years as the summer home of Daniel Chester French (1850–1931), whose *Minute Man* statue in Concord established his eminence as a sculptor at age 25. By 1895, when he discovered Stockbridge, he was internationally respected and able to maintain this

HOME FOR CHRISTMAS AT THE NORMAN ROCKWELL MUSEUM.
Printed by permission of the Norman Rockwell Agency © The Norman Rockwell Family Entities

elaborate summer home and studio, which commands, as he put it, the "best dry view" he'd ever seen. The National Trust offers guided tours of the residence, a newly renovated barn gallery with special exhibits, and the studio, now exhibit space for plaster casts of many of the sculptor's works, including the statue that now sits in Washington's Lincoln Memorial. Visitors are welcome to stroll the grounds, which include a wooded path—the Hemlock Glade—overlooking Monument Mountain. Frequent events are staged throughout the summer, notably an outdoor sculpture show July into October, a summer gala and auction in August, and a pumpkin festival in October.

Mission House (413-298-3239; thetrustees.org), Main St., Stockbridge. Open Memorial Day weekend–Columbus Day, daily 10–5. Adults $6, ages 18 and under free. John Sergeant, idealistic young missionary to the Stockbridge tribe of the Mahican nation, constructed this house for his bride in 1739. He built it not on MA 102, where it now stands (known as the Plain at the time, this site held Native American wigwams), but up on the hill where the town's few white families lived, among them the Williamses. Sergeant's wife was Abigail Williams, a lady of pretensions, and the house is elaborate for its time and place. Salvaged and moved to this site in 1929, it's maintained by the Trustees of Reservations. An outbuilding houses an exhibit on the Stockbridge Indians. The beautiful "Colonial Revival" garden, a mix of flowers and herbs, is the work of the noted landscape architect Fletcher Steele, who also designed the famous formal gardens at Naumkeag.

Naumkeag (413-298-3239; thetrustees.org), Prospect Hill Rd., Stockbridge. Open late May–Columbus Day, daily 10–5. Adults $15 for house and garden, members and children 12 and younger free. The Trustees of Reservations maintain this fantasy gabled and shingled 26-room "cottage." It was designed by McKim, Mead & White in 1885 for one of the leading lawyers of the day, Joseph Hodges Choate, who endeared himself to his wealthy colleagues by securing the reversal of an income tax law that Congress had passed in 1894. It's the most evocative of the region's Gilded Age mansions because it retains many of its original furnishings and because its tours are so good. The view from the terrace is one of the finest in the Berkshires. The gardens, designed by leading landscaper Fletcher Steele, are as exceptional as the house and filled with imaginative touches and surprising elements, such as the famous curving blue steps set for contrast in a grove of white birches.

Ashley House (413-298-3239; thetrustees.org), 117 Cooper Hill Rd. in Ashley Falls, Sheffield. Well marked from US 7, south of Sheffield Village. The grounds are open without charge daily from sunrise to sunset year-round. The house is open for guided tours Memorial Day weekend through Columbus Day, Sat.–Sun. 10–4. Adults $5, members and children age 12 and younger free. The oldest house in Berkshire County (1735), this was the site of the 1773 drafting of the Sheffield Declaration denouncing the British Parliament. The Ashley family had a black servant, Mum Bett, who in 1780 sued for and won her freedom on the grounds that slavery was unconstitutional in Massachusetts, the first such court case in the country. The home is beautifully paneled, restored, and furnished. Along with nearby Bartholomew's Cobble, also maintained by the

Trustees of Reservations

THE NAUMKEAG MANSION IS A LANDMARK IN STOCKBRIDGE.

Trustees of Reservations, this is one of the most interesting corners of south Berkshire County.

The Bidwell House (413-528-6888; bidwellhousemuseum.org), 100 Art School Rd., Monterey. Open Memorial Day–mid-Oct., Thurs.–Mon. 11–4. Admission fee. A genuine center-chimney Colonial house, built circa 1750 as a parsonage by the Rev. Adonijah Bidwell. But what's special about this place is the way it's furnished. In the 1960s it was purchased by Jack Hargis and David Brush, New York interior designers who not only painstakingly restored the home, but also expertly furnished it with their collections of earthenware and china, including redware, slipware, and delft, some fine early samplers, antique quilts, pewter, domestic hand tools, and lighting devices. It's a must for anyone interested in 18th-century decorative arts. The house is set in period gardens, and footpaths lead through 196 acres of fields and woods. Inquire about lectures, workshops, and other special events.

SCENIC DRIVES **Southwick to New Marlborough**. Take Exit 6 (I-291) off the Massachusetts Turnpike to I-91; continue south to MA 57 in Agawam. This leads to Southwick, where we recommend the fresh peach at **MooLicious Ice Cream,** and on to **Granville,** a classic old village with a general store that's worth a stop to pick up the **Granville Cellar Cheddar** that's been aged and sold on this spot since the 1850s (open most days until 6:30). It only gets prettier after that, passing though **West Granville** with its early-18th-century meetinghouse and **Tolland** with its state forest (with lakeside campsites on Otis

Reservoir). Note the **New Boston Inn** that's been standing at the junction of MA 57 and MA 8 since 1737 and still boasts good food and lodging. Just over the New Marlborough line, note the turnoff for **York Lake** (swimming and fishing). Farther along in **New Marlborough,** the **Old Inn on the Green,** vintage 1760, offers fine dining as well as hospitality. From here roads radiate to most corners of South County.

Great Barrington to Lee is one of our favorite routes. Follow MA 23 East to MA 57, wandering through the historic village of **New Marlborough,** and turn north at the Old Inn on the Green onto the (dirt) New Marlborough–Monterey Road. It climbs up into high meadows, then dips down through woods. Bear left at the fork and you'll soon see a sign for **Rawson Brook Farm;** stop to visit the goats and pick up some exceptional goat cheese. At MA 23 turn left into the center of Monterey and head north on the Tyringham Road (also called Main Road). A left turn will take you to the **Bidwell House;** otherwise, continue into the breathtaking Tyringham Valley. Stop at **Tyringham Cobble,** park by the cow pasture just above the village, and walk to the top of the cobble (a limestone hill); the trail also winds through forest and meadow. The road brings you into Lee, near MA 102 and Exit 2 on the Mass Pike.

Egremont–Sheffield Road. For both history and beauty, it's difficult to beat the road from South Egremont to Sheffield. This country road runs south from the village. Woods soon give way to fields with views of the hills to the west. This is the "Sheffield Plain." At the corner of Kiln Road look for the suitably ancient-looking marble monument commemorating the last battle of **Shays Rebellion** in 1787. Follow the road to US 7 and look on your left for the **covered bridge,** originally built in 1837 and reconstructed in 1998.

Ring Around the Mountains. From Millerton, N.Y., MA 22 runs north along the Harlem Valley at the western base of a Taconic Range that rises to more than 2,000 feet. It shadows the bed of the defunct Harlem Railroad, now the **Harlem Valley Rail Trail** (hvrt.org). At Copake Falls it accesses **Taconic State Park** (nysparks.com), which offers extensive camping and other lodging facilities, and here you can cut over on NY 344 to **Bash Bish Falls** in Mount Washington. **Millerton** (enjoymillerton.com) is a lively destination, best known as home to Harney & Sons Teas (harney.com). It's 17 miles from Millerton up MA 22 to **Hillsdale,** N.Y., then east on MA 23, 10 miles to **South Egremont,** 12 miles south on MA 41 along the eastern base of the range to **Salisbury,** Conn., and 6 more miles on US 44 to Millerton.

✷ To Do

BICYCLING *Berkshire Bike Touring,* a version of the *Rubel Western Massachusetts Bicycle and Road Map,* is currently available from local information booths and centers. Bicycles can be rented from **Berkshire Bike & Board** (413-528-5555), 29 State Rd. (US 7), Great Barrington. Check southernberkshirechamber.com for suggested routes. Catamount Ski Area in South Egremont (catamountski.com) offers mountain biking. Also see **Harlem Valley Rail Trail** in the above entry.

BOATING The placid **Housatonic** is ideal for lazy rides down the river, especially between Great Barrington and Bartholomew's Cobble. Trips are detailed in *Discover the Berkshires of Massachusetts: AMC Guide to the Best Hiking, Biking & Paddling.*

Rental kayaks, kayaking information, and tours are available at **Expeditions Outdoor Store** at Ski Butternut (413-528-2000), 380 State Rd. (MA 23), Great Barrington, the **Berkshire chapter of the Appalachian Mountain Club** (outdoors.org), and **Berkshire South Regional Community Center** (413-528-2810; berkshiresouth.org). By far the largest lake in the area is **Otis Reservoir** in the **Tolland State Forest** (413-269-6002); rowboats can be rented at **Camp Overflow** (413-269-3036).

CAMPING The obvious way to beat the high cost of lodging during the Tanglewood season is to take advantage of one of the four state park campgrounds in this area. The best bet for finding a site is in **Tolland State Forest** (93 campsites, 26 lakeside). The other options are **October Mountain State Forest** (50 sites) and **Beartown State Forest** (12 year-round sites). For reservations, call 1-877-422-6762. The Department of Conservation and Recreation (DCR) maintains an excellent website, mass.gov/dcr. Each of the state forests is described in more detail under *Green Space.*

For commercial campgrounds, check out the free guides published by the **Massachusetts Association of Campground Owners** (campmass.com).

CAR RACING **Lime Rock Park** (1-800-722-3577; limerock.com), 60 White Hollow Rd., Lakeville, Conn. Open Memorial Day weekend.–Oct., Sat. and holidays. Known as "the Road Racing Center of the East," Lime Rock hosts car shows, vintage races, and world-class sports car events. Admission free for children under 12.

FISHING Fishing licenses are required. Log onto mass.gov/dfwele for a list of trout-stocked waters. South Berkshire's many options include Center Pond and Yokum Pond in Becket, Prospect Lake in Egremont, Goose Pond and Laurel Lake in Lee, Benedict Pond in Monterey, Thousand Acre Swamp in New Marlborough, Benton Pond and East Otis Reservoir in Otis, and Stockbridge Bowl in Stockbridge. **The Berkshire Fishing Club** (413-243-5761; berkshirefishing.com) offers access to a private, secluded, 125-acre lake stocked with largemouth bass. The **Berkshire National Fish Hatchery** (413-528-9761), 240 Hatchery Rd. off MA 57/MA 183 in New Marlborough, raises Atlantic salmon, rainbows, and brown trout and maintains a visitors center.

FOR FAMILIES ✐ **Rainbow's End Miniature Golf** (413-528-1220), 18 holes at the **Cove Lanes,** 109 Stockbridge Rd. (US 7), Great Barrington. If the kids are along, this indoor mini golf is great for evenings or rainy days.

Catamount Adventure Park (413-528-1262; catamounttrees.com), MA 23 on the South Egremont/Hillsdale, N.Y., line. An "Aerial Forest" with zip lines designed by Swiss Alpine mountaineers. For ages 8 and up.

✐ **Berkshire Theatre Festival** (413-298-5576; berkshiretheatre.org) offers children's theater written by local children.

✐ The **Norman Rockwell Museum** (413-298-4100; nrm.org) is free to children under age 18.

✐ **Pleasant Valley Wildlife Sanctuary** (413-637-0320; massaudubon.org) in Lenox; **Berkshire Botanical Garden** (413-298-3926; berkshirebotanical.org) in Stockbridge; and **Bartholomew's Cobble** (413-229-8600) offer special programs for children.

✐ Both the **Stockbridge Library** (413-298-5501) and **Lenox Library** (413-637-0197) have extensive children's collections; inquire about story hours.

Also see Farms.

GOLF **Egremont Country Club** (413-528-4222; egremontcountryclub.com), MA 23, South Egremont. Eighteen scenic holes, driving range, pro shop, private lessons, moderate greens fees.

Greenock Country Club (413-243-3323), West Park St., Lee, has nine holes; moderate greens fees.

HIKING This is major hiking country, with the **Appalachian Trail** (AT) traversing the county. See *Green Space* in this chapter for details about suggested hikes in **Beartown State Forest** and at the Trustees of Reservations sites: **Monument Mountain, Bartholomew's Cobble,** and **Tyringham Cobble.**

LLAMAS STAND READY TO TRANSPORT GUESTS AT HAWKMEADOW FARM LLAMA HIKES.

William A. Davis

HORSEBACK RIDING **Sunny Banks Ranch** (413-623-5606; sunnybanksranch.com), 2299 Main St. (MA 8), Becket. Western-style trail rides on a 200-acre horse and cattle ranch. Lessons in riding, also team roping and cattle sorting.

Also see listings for Lenox in the "Central and North Berkshire" chapter.

LLAMA HIKES **Hawkmeadow Farm Llama Hikes** (413-243-2224; hawkmeadowinlee.com), 322 Landers Rd., Lee. Guided one- to three-hour hikes with llamas. Rates for an hour-long hike range from a minimum of $60 for a group of up to three people to $90 for 10 or more. Accommodations available.

RAILWAY EXCURSION ✐ **Berkshire Scenic Railway Museum** (413-637-2210; berkshirescenicrailroad.org), 10 Willow Creek Rd., Lenox. On weekends and federal holidays from Memorial Day weekend through October with some special events through December. Adults $15, seniors $14, children under 14 $8 for the Stockbridge trip; $9, $8, and $5, respectively, for Lee. There are two daily 90-minute excursions between Lenox and Stockbridge, as well as a 45-minute journey between Lenox and Lee. Vintage coaches and a veteran diesel locomotive are used, and a uniformed conductor narrates the scenic trip along the banks of the Housatonic River. Excursions begin from the old Lenox depot, which houses a gift shop and a museum that includes model train displays and an exhibit on the role of railroads in the Berkshires' Gilded Age.

SWIMMING For a fee, you can swim at **Prospect Lake Park** (413-528-4158), a private campground in North Egremont with a sandy swim beach, and at **Card Lake** in West Stockbridge. Inquire locally about swimming in the **Stockbridge Bowl** and **Laurel Lake.** Another favorite local spot is the swimming hole in the **Green River** on MA 23 about a mile west of Great Barrington between MA 71 and Alford Road, and on MA 23 south of Great Barrington (look for the lineup of cars along a cornfield).

Under *Green Space,* check 40-acre **York Lake,** off MA 57 in Sandisfield State Forest; **Otis Reservoir** in Tolland State Forest; **Benedict Pond** in Beartown State Forest; and **Umpachenee Falls** in New Marlborough.

✷ Winter Sports

ALPINE SKIING ✐ **Butternut** (413-528-2000; skibutternut.com), Great Barrington; east on MA 23. Still owned by the same family that founded it in 1963, Butternut is known for its grooming and for the beauty of its design by founder Channing Murdock—both on and off the slopes.

Vertical drop: 1,000 feet.

Terrain: 22 trails, 110 skiable acres; longest run: 1.5 miles.

Lifts: Three quads, one triple, double chair, four surface lifts.

Snowmaking: 100 percent of area.

Programs: Children's ski and boarding programs, ski school, tubing.

Special Features: Seven-lane tubing center, telemark rentals and lessons.

Rates: Adults $60 holiday periods, $55 weekends, $25 Mon.–Fri. nonholiday; kids $15–25; junior/senior $20–50; students $20–35.

✐ **Catamount** (413-528-1262; snow conditions, 1-800-342-1840; catamountski.com), MA 23, South Egremont. Straddling the New York–Massachusetts line and overlooking the rolling farm country of the Hudson Valley, Catamount has been in business as a family area for 65 years. The base lodge is pleasant.

Vertical drop: 1,000 feet.

Terrain: 33 trails including 2.5-mile-long Upper/Lower Promenade, 119 skiable acres.

Butternut, Great Barrington

BUTTERNUT'S RAINBOW RAIL.

Lifts: Six, including a quad, a triple chair, and two double chairs.

Snowboarding: Megaplex with 400-foot half-pipe.

Snowmaking: 99 percent of area.

Special Features: Night skiing on 15 trails including the half pipe.

Programs: Mountain Cats for ages 4–12; also Tiny Tot lessons for ages 4–6.

Rates: Adults $59 weekends ($100/two days), $27 weekdays; juniors and seniors $48 weekends; seniors $20 weekdays; children $25 weekends, $10 weekdays.

Otis Ridge (413-269-4444; otisridge.com), MA 23 in Otis. A long-established family ski area whose ski camp (ages 8–15) is the oldest in the country and has its own dedicated tow.

Vertical drop: 400 feet.

Terrain: 11 trails.

Lifts: One double chair, four tows.

Snowmaking: 90 percent of area.

Facilities: Lodging and food at the slope-side Grouse House (413-269-4446).

Rates: Adults and juniors $30 weekends, $15 weekdays; $12 nights Wed.–Sun.; seniors $15, $10, $5; seniors 70 or older ski free.

Also see **Jiminy Peak** in "Central and North Berkshire."

CROSS-COUNTRY SKIING **Canterbury Farm** (413-623-0100; canterbury-farms.com), 1896 Fred Snow Rd., Becket. Generally open Dec.–Mar., closed

Christmas and nonholiday Tuesdays. More than 13 miles of tracked, wide trails to a lake and around a beaver pond, with an average elevation of 1,700 feet, rental equipment (including snowshoes), skate skiing and regular lessons, a fireplace room with drinks, hot soup, chili, and snacks; also see *Lodging*.

Some of the best cross-country skiing is to be found in public preserves described in the *Green Space* section of this chapter. Because of its elevation, the **Mount Washington State Forest** is a standout. **Bartholomew's Cobble** in Ashley Falls and **Beartown State Forest** in Monterey also invite skiers and snowshoers.

SNOWMOBILING Several state forests and parks in this region permit snowmobiling; see *Green Space* below.

✷ Green Space

Note: More than 100,000 acres of Berkshire County (75 percent) is wooded, and 86 miles of the **Appalachian Trail** traverse the county. The number and variety of walking and hiking trails, many dating to the 19th century, are amazing. They are described in several books, notably *Hikes & Walks in the Berkshire Hills* by Lauren R. Stevens, *A Guide to Natural Places in the Berkshire Hills* by René Laubach, and *Wildflowers of the Berkshire & Taconic Hills* by Joseph G. Strauch Jr., all published by Berkshire House, based in South Lee. The *Appalachian Mountain Club Guide to Massachusetts* is also extremely helpful, published by AMC Books. Also see the trails described in this chapter's *Green Space*.

STATE PARKS AND FORESTS The Massachusetts Department of Conservation and Recreation (mass.gov/dcr) publishes a handy map/guide and maintains a regional office at 740 South St. (US 7) in Pittsfield (413-442-8928), open Mon.–Fri. 8–5. Contact the respective park for a trail map. Please note: Specified day-use recreation areas charge a nominal parking fee per vehicle from May through Labor Day or Columbus Day. Parking is free for vehicles with handicapped or disabled veteran plates/placards, annual ParksPass holders, or seniors 62 and older with the Massachusetts Senior Citizen ParksPass, available at most parks, or call 617-626-4969 for details. Camping reservations may be made through ReserveAmerica.com or by calling 1-877-422-6762.

Beartown State Forest (413-528-0904), Blue Hill Rd. (off MA 23), Monterey; about 12,000 acres. This is high tableland stretching northwest from Monterey, the upper end dropping down to the Housatonic River in South Lee. Accessible from MA 102 in South Lee and from both Blue Hill Road off MA 23 or Tyringham Road in Monterey. In summer the big attraction is 35-acre **Benedict Pond,** an artificially formed pond good for **swimming** (there are sanitary but no changing facilities), picnicking, boating (nonmotorized), and fishing. A parking fee is charged from May–Labor Day. A section of the **Appalachian Trail** (AT) joins the pond, and the 1.5-mile **Benedict Pond Loop Trail** circles it. There are also a dozen **campsites** (open year-round; reservations are needed in summer, but Oct.–Apr. it's first come, first served) plus backpacker lean-tos along the

AT. There's a satisfying hour-long hike along the AT to the summit of **Mount Wilcox** (2,155 feet).

Four DCR properties cluster in the extreme southwestern corner of the state. The best known of these is **Bash Bish Falls State Park.** The centerpiece here is a dramatic waterfall that rushes down a 1,000-foot-deep gorge, finally plunging some 60 feet around two sides of a mammoth boulder and dropping into a perfect pool that's signed NO SWIMMING. Needless to say this sign is frequently ignored (park rangers patrol the area during the summer) and, sad to say, divers occasionally die here. Don't swim, but do explore this special place. Access is via MA 23, MA 41, and Mount Washington Road from South Egremont; take Mount Washington Road to East Street, then Cross Road back up West Street to Falls Road to the parking lot. Signage is sparse; keep an eye out for blue trail blazes. The rugged 0.25-mile trail meanders steeply down through pines to the falls. Don't lose heart at the point the blue blazes disappear (after you cross the stream); they pick up below.

Locals who want to bring folding chairs and picnics usually drive down the road instead (it becomes NY 344 in New York state) to the "lower parking lot" in New York's **Taconic State Park** in Copake, which offers extensive camping facilities. It's a longer but level walk to the bottom of the falls, which are referred to as Copake Falls in New York. Not to confuse things, but the best source of information in Massachusetts is from **Mount Washington State Forest** (413-528-0330), with headquarters on East Street in Mount Washington. Inquire about primitive, walk-in (0.5-mile) camping sites with pit toilets, spring water, and fireplaces, and about access to the AT. The AT is also accessible from Jug End Road in the **Jug End State Reservation & Wildlife Management Area,** adjacent to the **Mount Everett State Reservation** that's accessible from both MA 41 and Mount Washington Road in South Egremont. The **Mount Everett State Reservation** is accessible from East Street (north of Cross Street) in Mount Washington. The dirt road up Mount Everett is open seasonally, ending in a parking lot less than a mile below the 2,602-foot-high peak, the second highest in Massachusetts. It commands an overview of Berkshire County to the north and is worth the hike up. Dogwood blooms in

BASH BISH FALLS.

Christina Tree

spring, mountain laurel in June and early July, and there are wild blueberries in late July and early August.

Guilder Pond, a little more than half a mile up the road, is filled with pink water lilies during late July and much of August; the **AT** leads north and south of the pond along the ridgeline. Within the reservation a popular trail climbs up to the AT via **Race Brook Falls** from MA 41 in Sheffield. South of Mount Race, the AT skirts beautiful Plantain Pond.

October Mountain State Forest (413-243-1178), 256 Woodland Rd., Lee. With a total of 16,500 acres, this is the largest state forest in Massachusetts. **Camping** (mid-May–mid-October) is the big draw here; options include three yurts and some wheelchair-accessible sites, but there are just 47 campsites (flush toilets, showers, picnic tables, and a dumping station but no electrical hookups); reservations are recommended. **Schermerhorn Gorge** is a popular hike and has many miles of trails also used for winter skiing and snowmobiling. Much of this area was once impounded as a game preserve (it included buffalo, moose, and Angora goats as well as smaller animals) by wealthy landowner and President Grover Cleveland's secretary of the Navy, William C. Whitney. **Halfway Pond** is a good fishing spot.

Otis State Forest (413-269-6002), off MA 23 on Nash Rd. in West Otis. This is undeveloped forest. Boating (no motors) is permitted on **Upper Spectacle Pond,** and cross-country skiing and snowmobiling on the unplowed roads, which include the original road that Henry Knox labored over, hauling cannons from Fort Ticonderoga to Boston in the winter of 1775–76.

Tolland State Forest (413-269-6002), off MA 23 in Otis, offers 92 campsites, Memorial Day–Columbus Day (most for tents; flush toilets, showers, picnic tables, fireplaces). Campsites are on a peninsula jutting out into **Otis Reservoir** (reservations recommended). There is a picnic area with a sandy swim beach and a boat launch; also fishing and boating in the reservoir. A day-use parking fee is charged in-season. This is a spot to hike and cross-country ski.

Sandisfield State Forest (in winter, 413-528-0904; in summer, 413-229-8212). The state forest holdings are scattered around Sandisfield; the most popular section is just over the New Marlborough line (MA 57) at **York Lake,** a 40-acre dammed area near the headwaters of Sandy Brook. Here you can swim, boat (no motors), and picnic (there are tables, grills, and fireplaces). The forest harbors five more lakes, all stocked with trout and accessible to nonmotorized boats. Winter trails for skiing and snowmobiling. Hunting is permitted in-season.

TRUSTEES OF RESERVATIONS Contact 413-298-3239 or thetrustees.org.

Bartholomew's Cobble (413-229-8600), 106 Weatogur Rd., Sheffield. (Marked from MA 7A in Ashley Falls, south of Sheffield Village.) Open year-round sunrise to sunset. Natural History Museum and Visitor Center (restrooms) open 9–4:30 but closed Sun. and Mon., Dec.–Mar. Adults $5, children 6–12 $1. This 329-acre tract takes its name from the high limestone knolls or cobbles of marble and quartzite that border the glass-smooth Housatonic River. We recommend the pine-carpeted Ledges Trail, a (theoretically) 45-minute loop with

Trustees of Reservations

CLIMBERS LOVE MONUMENT MOUNTAIN.

many seductive side trails down to the river or up into the rocky heights. The Cobble is noted for the diversity of its fern species and woodland wildflowers, at their best in April and May. A booklet guide is available from the naturalist. Leashed dogs welcome. Inquire about special kayaking and nature programs. Note that the Colonel Ashley House (see *Historic Homes*) is just up the road.

Monument Mountain, US 7 north of Great Barrington. Open year-round sunrise to sunset. Free. This peak is one of the most distinctive in the state: a long ridge of pinkish quartzite, scarcely 15 feet wide in some places, 1,700 feet high. The climb is lovely any day, whether by the Hickey or the Monument Trail. The hillside is covered with red pine and, in June, with flowering mountain laurel. A Bryant poem tells of a Native American maiden, disappointed in love, who hurled herself from Squaw Peak. Nathaniel Hawthorne, Herman Melville, and O. W. Holmes all picnicked here in 1850.

Tyringham Cobble, 20 Jerusalem Rd. (0.5 mile from Tyringham Center), Tyringham. Open daily, sunrise to sunset, year-round. The AT crosses a portion of this 206-acre property: steep upland pasture and woodland, including a part of Hop Brook, with views of the valley and village below.

Ashintully Gardens, Sodem Rd. (marked from Main Rd. between Tyringham Center and Monterey), Tyringham. Open mid-June–mid-Sept., Wed. and Sat. 1–5. Free to individual visitors; group tours by appointment. These elaborate gardens are sited on a 120-acre property below the ruins of the "Marble Palace," a pillared white mansion completed in 1912 as the centerpiece of the 1,000-acre Ashintully Estate. The design of the garden is described as "episodic"—an artistic creation incorporating paths, fountains, bridges, stairs, gates, and lawns.

McLennan Reservation, Fenn Rd., off Main Rd. south of Tyringham Center. Open daily, year-round. Free. This 491-acre property adjoins Ashintully Gardens (see above) and was once part of the same 1,000-acre estate. Round Mountain and Long Mountain are the backdrop for paths through the woods, along brooks, and by a beaver pond.

Questing, New Marlborough. Open daily, year-round. Free. From New Marlborough Center, take New Marlborough Hill Road for 0.6 mile. A 2-mile loop trail threads hardwood forest, upland field, pockets of wetlands, and the Leffigwell settlement, where the first non–Native American children were born in Berkshire County.

OTHER **Bowker Woods,** MA 183 between Stockbridge and Chesterwood; drive in at the sign. There's a pine grove by a small pond, good for picnics.

Laurel Hill, Stockbridge. The best access is from the end of Park Street off US 7 just south of the village. A trail along the Housatonic River leads to a seat designed by Daniel Chester French, and marked trails continue across the Housatonic to Ice Glen (a ravine) and to Laura's Tower (a steel tower); another trail leads along the crest of the spur of Beartown Mountain.

✐ **Berkshire Botanical Garden** (413-298-3926; berkshirebotanical.org), junction of MA 102 and MA 183, Stockbridge. Gardens and gift shop open May–Columbus Day, daily 9–5. Greenhouses open year-round. Adults $12, seniors and students $10, children under 12 free. The 15 acres include a pond, woodland trail, and children's garden. There are shrubs, trees, perennial borders, greenhouses, herbs, and periodic lectures and workshops. Picnickers welcome.

LAUREL HILL TRAILS BEGIN IN DOWNTOWN STOCKBRIDGE.

Christina Tree

Du Bois Homesite (413-528-3391; duboishomesite.org), MA 23 in Great Barrington, 0.25 mile west of the junction with MA 71. Interpretive panels along wooded trails on the roadside property, a national historic landmark, describe the life of W. E. B. Du Bois (1868–1963), who became a leading scholar, the first African American to earn a doctorate at Harvard, a founder of the NAACP, and an activist in the civil rights movement in the U.S. and around the world. This is one of 50 sites in town associated with

Christina Tree

THE DU BOIS HOMESITE IS A PLEASANT WALK IN GREAT BARRINGTON.

Du Bois; check the website for details about the Du Bois Center at Great Barrington.

WATERFALLS **Bash Bish Falls.** The area's most famous and dramatic waterfall—a 60-foot cascade plunging through a sheer gorge (also see *State Parks and Forests*).

Becket Falls, 0.2 mile up Brooker Hill from the Becket Arts Center (MA 8 and Pittsfield Rd.); there is a shallow turnout in which to park. It's a steep scramble down to view the 25-foot-high cascade.

Campbell Falls State Park, accessible from MA 57 in New Marlborough, then a forest road to this site. The Whiting River pours over a split ledge and cascades 80 feet down a precipitous declivity. There are picnic tables, toilets, and foot trails.

Race Brook Falls in Sheffield: a series of five cascades and a picnic area. From the turnout on MA 41 north of the Stagecoach Inn, follow red blazes for 1.5 miles.

Sages Ravine. A strikingly cut chasm with a series of falls, best accessed from Salisbury Road in Mount Washington and from MA 41 between Sheffield and Salisbury, Conn.

Umpachenee Falls. At the New Marlborough Church in the village center, turn south; follow signs to Mill River. Just before the metal bridge there is a dirt road forking right; from here follow signs. While this is the least dramatic of the falls, it's the best swimming hole.

✷ Lodging

Note: Tax varies from town to town, so inquire when making a reservation. Most places also have a two- or three-day requirement for weekends July through October, and many inns offer midweek discounts, even in July and August. B&Bs with fewer than four rooms are not required to charge tax. Check with local chambers of commerce for seasonal B&Bs and apartments.

INNS

In Stockbridge

Williamsville Inn (413-274-6118; williamsvilleinn.com), MA 41, West Stockbridge 01266. Kandy and Erhard Wendt have renovated this old (1797) inn, adding among other improvements a new kitchen wing to house their culinary school. The dining room, open to the public for dinner (see *Dining Out*), is a showcase for gourmet cuisine. There are nine rooms in the main house, four in the restored 18th-century barn, and two cottages, all with private baths. The 10-acre grounds include flower and herb gardens, a tennis court, swimming pool, and seasonal sculpture garden. $165–260 includes a full breakfast and afternoon tea.

In New Marlborough

(ᵍ) ♂ ✿ **Mepal Manor & Spa** (413-229-8236 or 1-800-286-3139; mepalmanor.com), 100 Stone Manor Dr., New Marlborough 01230. The latest and most ambitious undertaking by Brad Wagstaff and Leslie Miller, who also restored New Marlborough's Old Inn on the Green and transformed Gedney Farm into a fantasy wedding venue, this 1906 stone mansion was a boys prep school when the couple bought it. In just a few years it's been lavishly reborn, the former gym transformed into an elegant spa. The setting for the inn is key. The manor sits high above sweeping lawns with a view of hills rolling away south into Connecticut. Paths through meadows lead to a beaver pond and into the neighboring nature preserve. There are just 12 guest rooms (each with private bath), some in the octagonal towers and some with wood-burning hearth and arches, all with many small-paned windows. Even the smallest rooms have been imaginatively and comfortably decorated using William Morris wallpapers, rich colors, and fabrics. Common space includes several smaller rooms as well as the formal parlor and a breakfast room. All rooms may be reserved on

MEPAL MANOR & SPA USED TO BE A BOYS PREP SCHOOL.

Christina Tree

INN THE HEART OF STOCKBRIDGE

The Red Lion Inn (413-298-5545; redlioninn.com), 30 Main St., Stockbridge 01250. Probably the most famous inn in Massachusetts, the Red Lion is a rambling white-clapboard beauty first opened in 1773, gradually expanded, and virtually rebuilt after a major fire in 1897. Staying here is like stepping into a Norman Rockwell painting. Even the least expensive, shared-bath rooms are furnished with real and reproduction antiques and interesting art, and there are some splendid rooms and baths.

In summer the inn's long porch, festooned with flowers and lined with rockers, is the town's true center. This is also true of the lobby hearth in winter. There is a large, formal dining room, the informal Widow Bingham's Tavern, nightly entertainment in the Lion's Den (never a cover charge), and, in summer, a popular garden café (see *Where to Eat* for all). In all there are 108 guest rooms (90 with private baths, two handicapped accessible) divided between the main inn and six guest houses, one of them the old Stockbridge firehouse that Rockwell pictured in paintings. Upper floors are accessed by an antique birdcage elevator and a more modern version.

In the main inn no two rooms are alike and all have been sensitively updated, preserving charm while adding comfort. The wide halls on each floor are worth a wander, filled with art, furnishings, and two centuries' worth of collectibles (some rescued from the 1897 fire). In 1968, when it seemed doomed to make way for a gas station, it was rescued and reopened by John and Jane Fitzpatrick; it is currently owned and ably operated by their daughter Nancy.

Red Lion regulars opt for rooms overlooking Main Street, the pool, or in one of the guest houses, rather than an outside room facing US 7 (trucks

weekends for weddings, but just as frequently they aren't, and spa packages are the specialty. A number of rooms have twin beds, the better for two women to share. The spa includes a salon and outdoor whirlpool and offers a variety of massages, a full menu of spa treatments, and a schedule of yoga and Pilates classes. There is also a complement of fitness machines and a gym. $195–285 includes breakfast and afternoon tea; less midweek and off-season. Spa packages: two nights with massage and treatments cost $240 per person per night. Bridal packages a specialty. Also see *Dining Out*.

The Old Inn on the Green (413-229-7924; oldinn.com), 134 Hartsville-New Marlborough Road, New Marlborough 01230. This classic, double-porched, 1760 stagecoach inn is a gem in the classic setting of a small village green. It's a widely celebrated dining destination under current ownership by Peter Platt and have to downshift here before making the turn onto Main Street). Otherwise the location is terrific, handy to village shops and restaurants and to walking trails along the Housatonic and up Laurel Hill (see *Green Space*). From $89–95 for a shared-bathroom with breakfast on a weekday off-season. Rooms with private bath are $235–325 in-season (late June to Labor Day and foliage weeks); two-room suites with connecting bath are $335–410 (cheaper midweek than weekends). Children are free, but there's a charge per cot. Well-behaved pets are welcome but cost another $40.

Inquire about **Meadowlark at Chesterwood,** a studio hideaway built by sculptor Daniel Chester French in 1905, across the road and down a wooded road from the current public part of his estate. The living and dining area features a big skylight and a view of Monument Mountain from its deck, and the cottage includes two bedrooms, a bath, and a small kitchen. It's a graceful, comfortable, and historic space.

THE PORCH AT THE RED LION INN. Christina Tree

Meredith Kennard. Platt was executive chef for a dozen years at Wheatleigh in Lenox, and the atmospheric old tavern rooms are reputedly the setting for some of the best food to be had in the state (see *Dining Out*). The 11 guest rooms (all with private bath) are divided between the inn with its appropriate antiques and neighboring Thayer House, a 19th-century home with six elegant rooms, several with fireplaces and Jacuzzis and more privacy. Room rates are $225–410 depending on the season, but drop to $99 per person midweek, dinner included.

Gedney Farm (413-229-3131 or 1-800-286-3139; gedneyfarm.com), 34 Hartsville-New Marlborough Rd., New Marlborough 01230. In the 1970s Bradford Wagstaff and Leslie Miller restored the Old Inn (see above), then moved on to transform the nearby Norman-style barn at Gedney Farm into 16 fantasy guest rooms (our favorite is Room 138) and

THE OLD INN ON THE GREEN.

suites, many with a fireplace and tiled whirlpool. The neighboring barn is a reception and banquet center, and both the farm and barn are booked most weekends for weddings. Midweek, however, this remains a great getaway spot. $195–250 includes a continental breakfast; frequently cheaper midweek; lunch and dinner available. Also see **Mepal Manor.** $50 fee for pets. Children welcome.

New Boston Inn (413-258-4477; newbostoninn.com), 101 N. Main St. (junction of MA 8 and MA 57), Sandisfield 01255. This authentic 1737 inn sits at the junction of two country roads. It's pleasant and informal. Current innkeeper Barbara Colorio is a chef, so tables fill more of the common space than in the past (see *Eating Out*). The seven upstairs guest rooms have wide floorboards, private baths, and furnishings that are a bit funky but comfortable. The former second-floor ballroom with its matching fireplaces (one is now gas) at either end of the room was set up for a banquet when we stopped by, but still contained a corner with armchairs. The resident ghost—a 19th-century bride shot at the top of the stairs by her thwarted lover—is sighted regularly, usually around 3:30 AM. $149–169 double, $99 off-season; $35 per extra person; $35 per pet.

BED & BREAKFASTS

In Great Barrington

Windflower (413-528-2720 or 1-800-992-1993; windflowerinn.com), 684 South Egremont Rd. (MA 23), Great Barrington 01230. We keep returning to this gracious, turn-of-the-20th-century country mansion set on expansive grounds. The common rooms are just the right combination of elegance and comfort. All 13 guest rooms have a private bath and queen-sized bed (most are canopy or four-poster), and five have a working fireplace. Check out the deep claw-foot tub in Room 5 and the vintage, many-needled shower in Room 7—which is actually our favorite with its window seat, fireplace, and maple cottage furniture. Our second favorite is ground-floor Room 12 with its huge stone fireplace and easy access to the big screened porch and its wicker furniture. Several of the rooms have both queen and twin beds. But what really makes this place is the welcoming family that runs it: veteran innkeeper and sensational chef Claudia Liebert with her green-thumbed and handy husband, John Ryan. Whether you are traveling solo, as a family, or as a couple looking for a romantic getaway, this is one place that works for all—plus tunes you in to local dining and happenings. The grounds include a landscaped pool; golf and tennis are across the road at the Egremont Country Club. $125–265 in-season, from $100 off-season, with a full country breakfast—maybe cottage cheese pancakes with yellow raspberries from the garden—and afternoon tea featuring homemade cookies. The charge for an extra person in the room is $25, less for infants. Checks or American Express, please.

Baldwin Hill Farm (413-528-4092; baldwinhillfarmbandb.com), 121 Baldwin Hill Road N/S, Great Barrington 01230. Open year-round. On a hilltop overlooking hundreds of acres of fields, woodland, and rolling hills, Priscilla and Richard Birdsall have been warmly welcoming guests since 1990. The Victorian farmhouse has been in Richard's family for more than three generations. In summer guests relax in wicker chairs on the screened porch or by the landscaped pool in the orchard. In winter a large hearth warms one of the two living rooms; there's also a piano and a multitude of books. Most of the antiques and paintings have been passed down through the family. Upstairs all the guest rooms offer charm, comfort, and views; the Bay Window Room is our favorite. $110–175 includes a full breakfast.

WINDFLOWER INN, GREAT BARRINGTON.

Wainwright Inn (413-528-2062; wainwrightinn.com), 518 S. Main St. (US 7 south of town), Great Barrington 01230. Said to date to 1766, this large, Victorian-looking house was expanded to its current shape by Franklin Pope, an electrical genius recognized for a number of inventions (a couple in partnership with Thomas Edison), who died while tinkering with a transformer in his basement here. A place to stay for many decades, it's been thoroughly renovated and brightened by current innkeeper Marja Tepper. There's an attractive living room with an upright piano and fireplace, and a crisp, sunny breakfast room. The nine guest rooms vary from fireplaced to family-geared, so we suggest asking for details when booking. You might want one in the quieter, rear wing of the building. $189–225 in-season, from $100 off-season includes a three-course breakfast. Inquire about a two-bedroom unit with kitchenette.

The Acorn's Hope (413-528-2573; theacornshope.com), 85 Alford Rd., Great Barrington 01230. This expanded 1930s shingle Cape sits surrounded by large oak trees across from the Simon's Rock campus. There are expansive lawns and a rear guest room with private entrance that is good for families. Another attractive ground-level room with private entrance is handicapped accessible. The remaining two upstairs rooms are also inviting, each with a private bath and AC. Both the living and dining room have working fireplaces. A full breakfast is served. A resident gray parrot contributes to conversation. $115–179.

In Lee

Devonfield (413-243-3298 or 1-800-664-0880; devonfield.com), 85 Stockbridge Rd., Lee 01238. This

THE LIVING ROOM AT DEVONFIELD IN LEE.

Christina Tree

comfortably elegant mansion is set on 32 acres with a tennis court, an inviting pool, and a view of hills set off across meadows. The house has an 18th-century core, but was modernized at the turn of the 20th century by George Westinghouse Jr. While Queen Wilhelmina of Holland was a houseguest in 1942, President Franklin Roosevelt paid a visit. This was already an inn though not for sale when current innkeepers Ronnie and Bruce Singer fell in love with the property, and their enthusiasm for the inn and its guests persists. The nine rooms and suites are all furnished in antiques; several have a working fireplace and Jacuzzi. A one-bedroom cottage beyond the pool has kitchen facilities and a fireplace in the living room. Common areas include a living room with grand piano, a library with fireplace, a TV room, screened porch off the pool, and a fully stocked guest pantry. Rates include a bountiful breakfast. Children older than 10 welcome. Rooms are $275–325 during Tanglewood season, $200–285 during summer/foliage, and otherwise $185–260; the cottage is $300–375.

The Inn at Laurel Lake (413-243-9749; theinnatlaurellake.com), US 20 West, Lee 01238. This inn has served Berkshire travelers since 1900. One of its nicest features is the small, private beach just 150 feet downhill from the house. Tom Fusco bought the inn in 1996 and has improved and brightened it considerably. Of the 19 rooms and suites, 17 have a private bath. Facilities include a music room with more than 1,000 classical recordings, tennis court and sauna, picnic tables on a bluff overlooking the lake, and a paddleboat, canoes, and kayaks. A well-behaved dog can be accommodated in the room with a separate entrance. The Cork 'n Hearth restaurant (see *Dining Out*) is next door. Supervised children are welcome. Rates include continental breakfast. Picnics and dinner can be ordered. $95–285 in-season, $95–245 in foliage season, otherwise $50–165.

Historic Merrell Tavern Inn (413-243-1794 or 1-800-243-1794; merrell-inn.com), 1565 Pleasant St. (MA 102), South Lee 01260. This is a standout: a double-porched inn built in 1794 with a third-floor ballroom added in 1837. It was one of the first places in Berkshire County to be placed on the National Register of Historic Places. A stagecoach stop for much of the 19th century, it stood vacant for 75 years before previous owners painstakingly restored and furnished it appropriately. Current owners George and Joanne Crockett appreciate what they have and maintain the place lovingly. All guest rooms have a private bath and TV and have been carefully decorated with an eye to comfort as well as style. The Riverview Suite in a separate wing at the back has a king-sized bed, a wood-burning fireplace, and a private balcony overlooking the grounds and the Housatonic River. Real wood fires glow in the old keeping room where guests breakfast (choosing from a full menu) and in the taproom with its original birdcage bar in the corner, now a cozy sitting room. Grounds slope gently in back to a gazebo beside the Housatonic. $115–225 in high season ($225–325 for the suite), $100–175 off-season ($175–215 for the suite) with full breakfast. $25 per extra guest.

Hawkmeadow Farm (413-243-2224; hawkmeadowinlee.com), 322

Christina Tree

THE HISTORIC MERRELL TAVERN INN.

Lander Road, Lee 02138. Located on the highest ridge in Lee, Hawkmeadow Farm has a spectacular view to the west, particularly at sunset. Other attractions include the opportunity to explore nearby October Mountain State Forest, a resident llama herd (see **Hawkmeadow Llamas**), and optional instruction in yoga breathing, exercise, and meditation techniques by owner Richard Cleaver, who also leads llama hikes. His yoga expertise comes from 12 years spent at the Kripalu Center in Lenox when it was still operating as an ashram. There are three bedrooms, all with great views. One room has a private bath, another a half bath, and the third access to a full bath. The en suite room is $135 a night, the others $110. A full breakfast is served. Hawkmeadow Farm is open as a B&B May through November.

Applegate Bed and Breakfast (413-243-4451 or 1-800-691-9012; applegateinn.com), 279 W. Park St., Lee 01238. This place is a winner: a 1920s mansion with a pillared portico that's spacious and comfortable. Gloria and Len Friedman, longtime Staten Island residents, bring people skills acquired in their previous careers to innkeeping. The living room is huge, bright, and comfortably furnished, with built-in bookcases and window seats, a fireplace, and space for reading or playing backgammon. Welcoming touches include flowers and chocolates in the rooms. The five rooms in the main house vary in size from huge (Room 1, with its king-sized four-poster, fireplace, and steam shower with two showerheads) to snug but cozy. There are also three suites in the house. Two more suites, along with a two-bedroom "cottage" apartment, are in the adjacent carriage house, all with patio and whirlpool tub. Amenities include a pool, a guest pantry/fridge, borrowable bicycles, and plenty of lawn. $195–395 in-season, from $150 off-season. Inquire about winter and spring packages.

Federal House Inn (1-800-243-1824; federalhouseinn.com), 1560 Main St. (MA 102), South Lee 01260. This is a graceful Federal-era house, built of mellow brick with white columns in 1824. The guest rooms—two downstairs and six upstairs—all have private bath, WiFi, TV, and AC; three have a gas fireplace, and most have a four-poster bed. Guests have the use of a downstairs parlor. Owners Brian and Kolleen Weinrich are former educators who offer a warm welcome to guests. A full breakfast is served, always with a hot entrée. $175–275 high season, $150–200 off-season.

Jonathan Foote 1778 House (413-243-4545 or 1-888-947-4001; 1778 house.com), 1 East St., Lee 01238. One of the oldest houses in Lee, the Jonathan Foote House was lived in by the Foote family for 200 years. Current owners JoAnne and Bruce Zarnoch have preserved the historic character while transforming it into an elegantly comfortable B&B. Eighteenth-century features that have been retained include wide plank floors, four fireplaces (one a 7-foot-wide hearth) and a beehive oven. There are five units: three rooms and two suites. All have private baths, air conditioning, queen- or king-sized four-poster beds, and are furnished with art and antiques. $150–235 with full breakfast.

♿ **Chambery Inn** (413-243-2221 or 1-800-537-4321; berkshireinns.com), 199 Main St., Lee 01238. This unlikely lodging place, a parochial school built in 1885, was rescued from the wrecking ball and moved to its current site by Joe Toole, whose grandfather was in the first class to attend the school. As you might suspect, the rooms are huge, with 13-foot-high tin ceilings, 8-foot-tall windows—and blackboards (chalk is supplied). Separate stairs are marked for girls and boys, but guests don't get their knuckles rapped with a ruler if they take the wrong one. A continental breakfast is delivered to your room. $85–289, depending on the season and day.

In Sheffield 01257

Broken Hill Manor (1-877-535-6159; brokenhillmanor.com), 771 West Rd. Many try but few are equal to the challenge of converting ponderous vintage 1900 Edwardian mansions into truly inviting places to stay.

LEE'S CHAMBERY INN DATES TO 1885.
William A. Davis

Mike Farmer and Gaetan Lachance, however, have both the savvy and the furniture it takes. The colors and many details are authentically Edwardian, and while the furniture is comfortable, much of it is exotic, appropriate to the pervading sound and theme of opera music. The eight guest rooms are each named for an opera's heroine. Tosca, as you might suspect, is the most elegant, featuring an Egyptian brass canopy bed, but our favorite is Violetta with its golden walls and coverlet and slightly less ornate (also Egyptian) bed. We could spend hours in the Great Room with its mix of comfortable and exotic furnishings (most rugs are also Egyptian) around the stone hearth. The dining room is formal, but there are also tables on the back terrace, beyond the totally revamped kitchen, surrounded by landscaped gardens. Farmer and Lachance spent four years rewiring, plumbing (they installed five bathrooms), and landscaping. The 12 hilltop acres are just minutes from either US 7 or MA 23, but seem totally removed. $150–235 includes a full breakfast.

1802 House (413-229-2612; berkshire1802.com), 48 S. Main St. This much-expanded early-19th-century house rambles back from US 7 in the village of Sheffield. Dan Rossi and Ron Smith have created an unusually relaxing and welcoming B&B with a choice of seven rooms with queen or double bed, five with a private bath (two small rooms share). There's a stocked guest pantry, an inviting screened porch, and nicely landscaped gardens in the rear. Breakfast is flexible in its timing and full, maybe a frittata or buttermilk pancakes. $110–190; packages and midweek discounts.

Staveleigh House (413-229-2129 or 1-800-980-2129; staveleigh.com), 59 Main St. Ali Winston maintains the 1817 parsonage just off the Sheffield village as a gracious B&B. She has a sure touch with colors, and the seven guest rooms (each with private bath) are furnished with a mix of well-chosen antiques and an eye for comfort. There's a hearth in the parlor and a breakfast room filled with flowers and sunlight. We dropped by at teatime and the aroma of fresh-baked chocolate chip cookies was heady. Ali is an enthusiastic cook whose breakfasts are special, perhaps a home-grown melon and light little pancakes drizzled with baked apples, served with locally raised and cured bacon. $149–195. One-time $25 pet fee.

The B&B at Howden Farm (413-229-8481; howdenfarm.com), 303 Ronnapo Rd. When we first met artist Bruce Howden, he was operating the (then) only bed & breakfast in Burlington, Vermont. He has since inherited the family homestead, a Victorianized Greek Revival farmhouse and a 250-acre pumpkin farm, famous for having developed its own varieties and for its pick-your-own policy. It's all beautifully sited in Ashley Falls near Bartholomew's Cobble and the Colonel Ashley House. Guests can launch a canoe on the river and hike in the fields and woods. There are three rooms with private bath. All are nicely furnished, but the beauty is Room 104, which offers a sitting room with bow windows overlooking fields. $109–179 in high season, otherwise $99–149, which includes a very full breakfast, perhaps featuring eggs from resident chickens.

Race Brook Lodge (413-229-2916; rblodge.com), 864 S.

Undermountain Rd. (MA 41). Architect David Rothstein has transformed a 1790s barn into one of Berkshire County's more distinctive places to stay. "This is a chintz-free zone," Rothstein quips about the lack of antiques and frills in his 32 guest rooms (14 in the barn, many with private entry; six in the brick Federal-era Coach House; and the rest divided among cottages). The open beams and angles of the rustic old barn remain, but walls are white and stenciled; rooms are furnished with Native American rugs and quilts or spreads. As you would expect in a barn, the common room is large and multileveled, with some good artwork; a wine bar is in one corner. The lodge caters to hikers and walkers (as individuals and couples as well as groups), encouraging guests to climb the Race Brook Trail, which measures 1.5 miles in distance and rises almost 2,000 feet in elevation—past a series of five cascades—to Mount Race. There's a landscaped pool and a Meeting Barn (also used for wedding receptions). Children are welcome, as are well-behaved dogs (in certain rooms). There are also rooms in the neighboring brick Federal Coach House and four cottages; two units have kitchenettes. Dinner is served in the Stagecoach Tavern (see *Dining Out*). $85–210.

In Stockbridge

The Taggart House (413-298-4303; taggarthouse.com), 18 Main St., Stockbridge 01262. "For a big house, it's warm and there's plenty of light," remarks August Murko, who since acquiring this grand village manor has installed a new heating system, roof, and storm windows, redone the chimneys, and generally injected it with informality and comfort. The rambling mid-19th-century "cottage" has some grand common rooms. The four upstairs guest rooms are lush, with decor to match their names: the French, Russian, Willow Bough (with William Morris paper and matching curtains and linens), and Clara Bow Rooms, the last graced by the silent film star's own ornate bed. Guest amenities include deep soaking tubs, a butler's pantry stocked with complimentary beverages, canoes and kayaks, and a small beach on the Housatonic River, which winds along below the grounds. Breakfast is served in the formal dining room. $250–350 in-season, $175–250 Nov.–May.

The Stockbridge Country Inn (413-298-4015; stockbridgecountry inn.com), MA 183, Box 525, Stockbridge 01262. Handy to Chesterwood and the Norman Rockwell Museum in the Glendale section of Stockbridge, this 1856 farmhouse offers an unusual amount of common space, including an elegant living room with fireplace, a less formal sitting room, and a sunporch overlooking the garden. The eight guest rooms all have private baths and are tastefully furnished with four-poster queen-sized bed, antiques, Laura Ashley fabrics and prints, bright chintzes, and hooked rugs. The walls are hung with original Audubon prints—which are for sale, as is much of the furniture, because innkeepers Diane and Vernon Reuss are antique dealers. There is a large, heated outdoor pool. The full breakfast is cooked to order and in summer served on a screened porch looking out on the garden. $160–399 in summer and fall, less off-season.

♿ **The Inn at Stockbridge** (413-298-3337; stockbridgeinn.com), US 7, Box 2033, Stockbridge 01262. This white-pillared mansion was built in 1906 and set on 12 acres with ample woods and meadows. Alice and Len Schiller preside over afternoon wine and cheese served by the hearth in the pleasant living room. Common space also includes a library and a more private computer/writing room; there's WiFi throughout. The wicker- and flower-filled back porch overlooks a garden and pool. Full breakfast is served by candlelight at the formal dining room table. In addition to the guest rooms in the main house—each different, most with a king-sized bed, and all with a private bath—there are eight large, luxurious rooms in two new annexes, the Cottage House beside the pool and the Barn Suites set farther back amid greenery. These all are themed and fitted with gas fireplaces; six have baths featuring deep, two-person whirlpool tubs. All rooms have air-conditioning and telephone. There's also a well-equipped fitness center and a massage room. $195–375 in-season, $160–280 off-season.

Conroy's Bed & Breakfast (413-298-5188 or 1-888-298-4990; conroysinn.com), US 7, P.O. Box 191, Stockbridge 01262. Set up and off US 7 on 3 acres of lawn and woods, this 1830 brick farmhouse has a homey feel. There is a bright dining room and a small sitting area; the eight rooms—five in the main house (two with private bath) and three (all with private bathroom) in the old post-and-beam barn—are all country comfortable. Two of the barn rooms have decks, and the third offers a patio. The real treasure here, however, is the seasonal apartment in the barn with a deck, a sleeping loft, and a great downstairs space with fully equipped kitchen, great for families (four people).

A PEACEFUL PORCH AT THE INN AT STOCKBRIDGE.

Christina Tree

Amenities include a pool in landscaped grounds that contain the foundations of the former dairy barn. $140–185 for rooms in summer, $325 for the apartment; in winter, rooms from $120, apartment $225. Breakfast is served in the dining room.

North Egremont

The Silo B&B (413-528-5195), 6 Boice Rd., P.O. Box 544, North Egremont 01230. What a great spot! An artfully designed home attached to an authentic silo, it is set atop a knoll and surrounded by fields. The airy living room maximizes the view, beyond flowers and ever-popular bird feeders. Innkeeper Marion Jansen is an artist, and walls are hung with her locally inspired work. Two guest rooms share an upstairs sitting area, and a third is on the ground floor. $115 midweek, $125 weekends year-round; includes a full breakfast either in the breakfast room or on the screened porch. Maybe a tart with tomatoes or zucchini from the garden. The Green River is handy for wading and Prospect Lake is down the road, good for a swim. No credit cards.

LAKESIDE TERRACE BED & BREAKFAST ALONGSIDE LAKE GARFIELD.

Christina Tree

The Inn at Sweet Water Farm (413-528-2882; innsweetwater.com), 1 Prospect Lake Rd. (at MA 71), North Egremont 01230. This early-19th-century post-and-beam farmhouse is sited at a country crossroads, part of a cluster that also includes the village general store. Innkeeper Lynda Fisher is an artist—reflected in the color and art on the walls—and a cook, with a breakfast menu that draws nonguests. The herb omelet from the house chickens and Monterey Chèvre is a winner. We like the open-timbered living room with its hearth and upright piano and the feel of the six guest rooms, each so different we suggest you check out the website. *Sweet water* refers to the taste of the inn's own water, served fresh to guests each day in delectable blue bottles. Rooms are $150–225, including breakfast.

Elsewhere

Lakeside Terrace (413-528-3371; off-season, 516-527-5371; lakesideterracebb.com), 24 Lakeside Terrace, P.O. Box 33, Monterey 01245. Open Memorial Day weekend through Columbus Day. This is a 150-year-old summer cottage on Lake Garfield with rockers on the expansive screened porch and a fireplace in the living room, all set on 9 acres sloping to the lake on two sides. It's been in Merry Oislander's family since 1962 and catered to paying guests long before that, though it was a closely guarded secret. "Now most of the guests who came every year are gone, and we need to let people know we're here," Merry says about why this hidden gem has finally surfaced. There are seven bedrooms, five with

Christina Tree

COBBLE VIEW BED & BREAKFAST, TYRINGHAM.

private bath (the smallest rooms share or are rented together). $140–150 per room includes breakfast, served on the porch when possible, otherwise in the dining room. There's a swim dock with a rowboat, and guests are welcome to bring kayaks. Children only over age 5, please. No weddings, but this is a great place for groups.

Cobble View Bed and Breakfast (413-243-2463 or 1-800-467-4136; cobbleviewbandb.com), 123 Main Rd., Tyringham 01264. Located across the road from Tyringham Cobble (hence the name), this handsome early-19th-century house is just 4 miles from the Mass Pike exit, but has a way-off-the-beaten-path feel. Lifelong Berkshire residents Lynn Bertelli and Alan Wilcox offer four large guest rooms with air-conditioning and private bath, also a studio with its own kitchen and a separate entrance, good for families. A large loft in the barn can accommodate four people. Decor throughout is a pleasantly appropriate mix of antiques and reproductions. Guests have the use of two downstairs parlors and the grounds, which include flower gardens and a croquet course. Rooms are $110–190, studio $210–245, loft $225–295. The enhanced continental breakfast, which might include Lynn's special puffed apple pancakes or dishes made with eggs from the resident flock of hens, is served by candlelight.

The Inn at Freeman Elms Farm (413-229-3700; www.vgernet.net/freeman), 566 Mill River Great Barrington Rd., New Marlborough 01230. This is a find: a handsome farmhouse still in the same family that's owned it for nine generations. Obviously it was built very grandly in 1797. Later additions are limited to a spacious, screened front porch furnished with plenty of rocking chairs, and a rear ell with a classic Mission-style dining room. The six guest rooms (private baths) are furnished in family antiques and quilts, the kind most innkeepers covet. We especially like the "cottage" room with its mint-condition Cottage furniture. The property totals 600 acres with fields, woods, gardens, an orchard, and cattle. Children must be 12 or older. $150–225 includes continental breakfast.

Canterbury Farm B&B (413-623-0100; canterburyfarms.com), 1986 Fred Snow Rd., Becket 01223. Best known as a cross-country skiing center, this vintage farmhouse also offers three attractive guest rooms with private baths, a dining area with guest pantry, and leather couches by the fire. $60–90 includes breakfast. Handy to Jacob's Pillow, October Mountain State Forest, and summer camps, with gardens and hiking trails in summer.

Linden-Valley (518-325-7100), P.O. Box 157, Hillsdale, NY 12529. Sited on the New York–Massachusetts border at Catamount ski area, but really in a landscaped world of its own. Linda Breen has created an exceptional hideaway: seven large, nicely designed and decorated rooms, the upper units with cathedral ceilings and those on the garden level with small terraces. Each has a TV, coffeemaker, and wet bar with icemaker. A full breakfast is served in the dining room, an inviting space with a fireplace, or, weather permitting, on the garden terrace. The magnificently landscaped grounds include a spring-fed pond with a sandy beach, a swimming pool, and two tennis courts. The previous owner of the nearby Swiss Hutte (see *Dining Out*), Linda is Bavarian, clearly a scrupulous housekeeper, and an enthusiastic cook. $145–155 midweek, $165–175 on weekends, includes a full breakfast.

Hallig Hilltop House (413-644-0076; hallighilltophouse.com), 68 West St., Mount Washington 01258. In the very southwestern corner of Massachusetts, this is about as away-from-it-all as you can get. The turn-of-the-20th-century Dutch Colonial–style house is surrounded by thousands of acres in the Mount Washington State Forest, handy to some of the region's best hiking trails and to Bash Bish Falls. Chef Oskar Hallig is happy to prepare lunch and dinner, as well as picnic versions of both—which is a good thing, because once you get here you won't want to leave, and you certainly won't want to have to find the place again after dark (it's 12 miles to South Egremont). There are three guest rooms, all with private bath; other amenities include a stone fireplace in the living room, a porch lined with rockers, a swimming pool, and a wood-burning cedar sauna. In winter there can be great cross-country skiing—you're at 1,300 feet, and there are plenty of trails through the woods. $125–250 per room in summer and fall (from $75 in winter/spring) includes a full breakfast; $15 for a picnic lunch; $40 for a five-course dinner. Inquire about renting the whole house.

✷ Where to Eat

DINING OUT

Note: Reservations are a must for pre-performance dining throughout the summer season. Seating is less of a problem after 8 PM.

In Great Barrington

Castle Street Café (413-528-5244; castlestreetcafe.com), 10 Castle St. Open for dinner except Tues., also Sun. brunch. Reservations advised.

Next door to the Mahaiwe Performing Arts Center, Michael Ballon's casually elegant restaurant was the first high-end place to dine in Great Barrington, and it remains one of the best. Linen-draped tables and changing art set the tone for a frequently changing menu that features local farm products. Entrée choices ($21–29), served with green salad, might include Ioaka Valley Farm grass-fed beef with red wine sauce and straw potatoes, or chicken breast stuffed with Berkshire Blue and fresh fig wrapped in prosciutto; burgers and organic soba noodles with mixed vegetables and ginger sauce are always available along with the bar menu, which includes small plates and sandwiches as well as the likes of meatloaf and pizza. A choice of menus is available at seasonable outdoor café tables. Saturday nights serve up live jazz in the **Celestial Bar** (no cover charge).

Allium Restaurant + Bar (413-528-4001; alliumberkshires.com), 42–44 Railroad St. Open for dinner nightly and Sun. brunch. The brightest spot of Railroad Street, this is an imaginatively designed and decorated restaurant filling two old deep storefronts with an open kitchen and (weather permitting) street front. Like its sister-restaurant, Mezze, in Williamstown, the menu is locally sourced. It may, however, need some translating for nonfoodies; i.e., "wood-oven whole roasted branzino, sautéed greens, lemon, evoo" ("branzino" is sea bass and "evoo" is extra-virgin olive oil). Reviews suggest that you stick to a "small" or "medium" rather than the "large plates" ($19–28).

Café Adam (413-528-786; cafeadam.org), 325 Stockbridge Rd. (US 7), #4. Open Wed.–Sat. 11–9, Sun. 10–9, Mon. 11–3. Cheapskates that we are (an occupational hazard that goes with weeks on the road), we ignored our innkeeper's hints that guests repeatedly told her this was the best restaurant in town. We compromised by trying it for lunch of mussels in fennel and pastis and cold smoked

MICHAEL BALLON AT HIS CASUALLY ELEGANT CASTLE STREET CAFÉ.

Christina Tree

Christina Tree

CAFÉ ADAM IN GREAT BARRINGTON HAS A BISTRO FEEL.

salmon with grilled local asparagus. Superb. Berkshire-grown chef-owner Adam Zieminski is a graduate of Johnson & Wales and a prestigious list of restaurants. Tables are well-spaced and decor is contemporary bistro, with long blackboard menus *and* a frieze of wine bottles high along the walls. The menu changes seasonally, but ranges from grilled organic pizza to New Zealand lamb and various grades of steak, $15–32.

♿ **Bizen** (413-528-4343), 17 Railroad St. Open daily for lunch and dinner. Michael Marcus opened this restaurant and sushi bar in 1997 to serve the food for which his pottery is intended. Marcus studied the distinctive pottery of Bizen in Japan for four years and has been creating it in his Joyous Spring Pottery in Monterey since 1982. The restaurant has expanded several times and now includes a sake bar and an area of traditional tatami rooms specializing in "Kaiseki" cuisine with a prix fixe menu. The main menu features three dozen varieties of sushi, sashimi, and maki, all made from the freshest fish, seafood, and organic vegetables. Dinner entrées ($8.95–18.95) include seafood, chicken, vegetables, tempura, and noodles.

🖍 ♿ **Aegean Breeze** (413-528-4001; aegean-breeze.com), 327 Stockbridge Rd. (US 7). Reservations advised. Open daily 11–10. The winning combination here is light, bright, and airy decor plus good service, unusual Greek appetizers, and a wide variety of pastas and very fresh fish entrées. You might begin with a Metzedes platter or char-grilled octopus and dine on spanikopita (baked stuffed filo with spinach, feta cheese, dill, and scallions), a calamari santorini (individual casserole), char-grilled swordfish kabobs, or a grilled platter. Children's menu. Dinner entrées $16.95–32.

Shiro (413-528-1898), 105 Stockbridge Rd. (at the junction of MA 23 and US 7). Open daily for lunch and dinner. Closed Tues. off-season. This is a local favorite, a Japanese restaurant with two hibachi tables (reserve if you want one) and an attention to presentation. More than 20 varieties of sushi are featured, along with hibachi-grilled steak and seafood, tempura dishes, and noodle dishes. Full bar. Most dinner entrées are around $20.

In Lee

Chez Nous (413-243-6397; cheznousbistro.com), 150 Main St. Open for dinner daily in summer, fewer days off-season; closed in March. French chef Franck Tessier and pastry chef Rachel Portnoy have created one of the hottest dining venues around. You may have to reserve a night or two in advance. The setting: three romantically lit dining rooms in a rambling village house. The à la carte menu usually includes escargot and frog legs with champagne garlic-herb butter and locally grown mushrooms, as well as a homemade pâté selection. Main courses ($18.95–29.95) might include braised veal sweetbreads with wild mushrooms, grilled sirloin of beef with green peppercorn and Jack Daniels sauce, or various cuts of certified Black Angus beef. This is not a place to pass up dessert—perhaps a dark chocolate peanut butter hazelnut crunch torte or ginger maple crème brûlée. The wine list is extensive and moderately priced.

Perigee (413-394-4047; perigee-restaurant.com), 1575 Pleasant St. (MA 102), South Lee. Open daily except Tues., 5–9. Perigee claims to be "the birthplace of Berkshire cuisine," defined as an innovative cuisine based on local ingredients prepared with imagination and international flair. Menu standards include traditional New England dishes such as clamcakes, international ones like a tempura sampler with ponzu dipping sauce, and pub favorites such as fish-and-chips. Entrées are $15–35. Wine pairings are suggested for each entrée. There are special menus throughout the week. Fridays, for instance, has a different "outside the box" lobster dish each week.

Cork 'N Hearth (413-243-0535; corknhearth.com), US 20. Open for dinner except Mon.; call ahead in the off-season. Dine overlooking Laurel Lake if you can get a table near the large glass windows in the Lake Room; there's also a stone fireplace in the barnboard-sided Brass Room, hung with brass antiques. Chef-owner Chris Ryan offers a varied à la carte menu. Try the pan-roasted seafood medley with ginger teriyaki sauce, the veal Oscar, or the boneless roast prime rib. Children's menu. Entrées are $18.50–28.

Sullivan Station (413-243-2082; sullivanstationrestaurant.com), 189 Railroad St. Open daily for lunch and dinner. Housed in the old Lee railroad depot (still a stop on the Lenox-based Berkshire Scenic Railway), this has been a local institution for more than 25 years. The wood-lined dining room with its ornate former waiting room stove has a cozy, old-fashioned feel. The menu features stick-to-the-ribs fare such as prime rib, baked stuffed shrimp, and grilled pork chops with applesauce. Dinner entrées (from 4:30) $16.95–22.95. Burgers and sandwiches are also available at dinner.

In Stockbridge

The Red Lion Inn (413-298-5545; redlioninn.com), 30 Main St. Breakfast, lunch, and dinner served daily. Reservations recommended. The main dining room is an elegantly formal space but, with the exception of tank tops, there is no dress code. Chef Brian Alberg honors the inn's traditional dishes, but with pleasantly unexpected, locally sourced twists. The Culinary Institute of America grad, who raises his own pigs, smokes his own bacon, and makes his own chips, relies heavily on local farms for meat, cheese, and produce. A winter menu might include (local) lamb ragout over soft polenta. In summer, lunch on salmon cakes or a grilled chicken salad, and dine on vanilla-cured pork loin or lemon-thyme roasted pheasant breast. For dessert you can't go wrong with Red Lion Indian pudding, but there are other options. *Boston Globe* food editor Sheryl Julian recently raved about Alberg's individually cupped panna cotta, a cold, creamy Italian custard he makes with apple cider, buttermilk, and vanilla bean. It's topped with apple salad and a hot buttered rum sauce. The wine list is extensive. Dinner entrées $23–34. Also see **Widow Bingham's Tavern** under *Eating Out*.

Once Upon a Table (413-298-3870; onceuponatablebistro.com), 346 Main St. Tucked away in the Mews, around the corner from the Red Lion Inn, this popular and cozy (just 11 tables) place is open for lunch and dinner daily in July and August (variable days at other times). The menu changes with the seasons. Dinner entrées $22-27.

West Stockbridge

Rouge Restaurant and Bistro (413-232-4111; rougerestaurant.com), 3 Center St., West Stockbridge. Open for dinner only, Wed.–Sun. 5–10. Up a side street in a small wooden building on the banks of the Williams River, Rouge draws diners by the droves with its Americanized international cuisine and elegantly casual atmosphere. It can get crowded and reservations are recommended. Chef de cuisine William Merelle's moderately priced but imaginative menu includes dishes such as pan-seared salmon with Shiitake mushrooms; braised free-range duck and shredded potato cake; persillage of frog legs pan-sautéed with sauce à la Rouge and polenta; and seared tuna encrusted with peppercorns and ginger with ratatouille. Tasting menus are available. The cozy bar serves memorable martinis, among other drinks, as well as tapas, a "croque madame," and mini burgers. Entrées $21–24.

Williamsville Inn (413-274-6118; williamsvilleinn.com), MA 41, West Stockbridge. Dinner by reservation Thurs.–Sun. Kandy and Erhard Wendt (he is a certified master chef and culinary instructor) also offer cooking classes. While the à la carte menu includes a choice of dishes, the specialties are German—perhaps Rhenish beef sauerbraten with raisin sauce, red cabbage, and potato dumplings, or Wiener schnitzel with sauce tartar. Desserts include Bavarian-style warm apple strudel. Appetizers $9–14, entrées $20–30.

Truc Orient Express (413-232-4204; trucorientexpress.com), 3 Harris St., West Stockbridge. In summer open daily for lunch (11–3) and dinner (5–9). Off-season open for dinner only, every day except Tues. Nguyen and Drai Duong still offer the personalized service they have been known for since opening this Vietnamese restaurant and local institution in 1979. On a recent visit we arrived a few minutes before our friends and soon became absorbed in the coffee-table books about Vietnam piled beside comfortable seating. The large dining room is pleasant, decorated with woven straw, Vietnamese art, and white tablecloths. Dishes can be as spicy as you specify. Specialties include Truc's special triangular shrimp rolls (with crab, pork, and vegetables surrounding a large shrimp wrapped in crisp, golden rice paper) and many vegetarian selections. Our hot-and-sour soup was outstanding. We also recommend the Banh Xeo ("happy pancake"), a crispy rice flour crêpe stuffed with shrimp, pork, mushroom, onions, and bean sprouts. Dinner entrées range from $11.95 for Truc's special fried rice (combined with peas, carrots, onions, shrimp, pork, chicken, and sausage) to $22.75 for "Bo Luc Lac" ("shaking beef"). Another specialty is lemongrass duck: crispy boneless duck topped with chopped lemongrass and chili sauce and served with fine rice noodles ($25). Out of Vietnam, a gift shop selling Vietnamese crafts, is attached to the restaurant.

Olio Mediterranean Kitchen (413-232-4005), 32 Main St., West Stockbridge. Open for dinner Tues.–Sun. As the name indicates, the emphasis here is on food, particularly local specialties, from around the Mediterranean. This means tapas, mezze, and antipasto for appetizers, and main dishes such as a fish soup with clams, mussels, shrimp in garlic, wine and fresh tomatoes; and chicken breast sautéed with mushrooms and Madeira sauce. Entrees $16–26.

In Egremont

The Old Mill (413-528-1421; oldmillberkshires.com), 53 Main St. (MA 23), South Egremont. Dining nightly from 5, Sunday brunch 11–2; closed Mon. off-season. Reservations for more than five, otherwise it's first come, first served. This is on the top of many restaurant lists. Chef-owner Terry Moore has been creating some of the most reliably superb fare in the county since 1978, and the reviews are still over-the-top. The vintage-1797 gristmill dining room by Hubbard Brook, with wide-board floors, low beams, and an open fire, makes a rustic but elegant setting. A celebratory feast might begin with Terry's country-style pâté with red onion jam and peasant toast, then move on to grilled rib lamb chops with fig, olive, and balsamic relish and potato gratin (entrées: $22–34) or grilled Angus New York steak with tarragon butter sea salt fries. More reasonably priced staples include vegetarian lasagna and pan-seared calf's liver. The cozy tavern area has its own reasonably priced menu. Special care is taken to make single diners feel at ease in either venue.

John Andrews (413-528-3469; jarestaurant.com), MA 23, South Egremont near the New York line. Open for dinner nightly; closed Wed. in winter. We love the warm, earth-toned walls and soft lighting, not to mention the menu that includes so many of our favorite foods: starters like lobster ravioli with lemon, pine nuts, and fried parsley followed by sautéed duck breast with duck leg confit, mashed potatoes, and maple-balsamic glaze. Pastas such as fettuccine with mushrooms, parsley, and pine nuts begin at $22, and other entrées are $25–30. From $14 in the bar for a grilled hamburger, fries, and chèvre. Leave room for dessert.

Swiss Hutte Inn & Restaurant (413-528-6200; swisshutte.com), MA 23 at Catamount ski area in South Egremont. Open in the winter and summer seasons for lunch on weekends and dinner Wed.–Sun. We should explain that "at Catamount" simply means within the grounds, which are delightfully green and landscaped in summer. The current chef-owner is Swiss, and choices include Wiener schnitzel and "bundnerteller"—but it's a varied menu. Entrées may range from seafood curry to herb-crusted rack of lamb with a red wine glaze. The ambience is polished wood and linen. There's also an outdoor patio, weather permitting. Dinner entrées $28–34.

In New Marlborough

The Old Inn on the Green (413-229-7924; oldinn.com), 134 Hartsville-New Marlborough Road (MA 57), village green, New Marlborough. Open for dinner except Tues. Also closed Mon., Nov.–June. Reservations a must. This is a beautifully restored 18th-century inn set in the middle of a gem of a village. The four small, candlelit (the only other light is from the hearth) dining rooms are furnished with worn Windsor chairs and mahogany tavern tables. In July and August there's additional seating on a tented terrace. Chef-owner Peter Platt, former executive chef at Wheatleigh, gets some of the best reviews of any restaurateur in New England. He offers a different four-course prix fixe menu on Saturday for $75. An eight-course $90 tasting menu is also offered. Three-course weeknight special menus are $30, and the frequently changing à la carte menu offering a choice of appetizers ($9.50–15) and entrées ($26.50–32) is wide. A $30 Thursday menu in July included chanterelle soup, slow-braised barbecued Angus boneless short ribs, and apricot linzer tart with pistachio gelato. See *Lodging* for reasonably priced midweek packages.

Mepal Manor (413-229-7501; mepalspa.com/dining.php), 100 Stone Manor Dr., New Marlborough. Open Wed. and Thurs. Reservations suggested. Known primarily as an inn, spa, and wedding venue, the Terrace dining here is a local secret and can be magical on a summer night, with the sun setting and moon rising over the hills beyond landscaped grounds. Honestly, we were there. The menu changes frequently, but you might begin with chilled beet brûlée with tossed fresh herbs and gazpacho sauce, and dine on the dayboat fish (maybe a crispy bass) with coriander spinach, capered cucumbers, and soba noodles ($24). The wine list is extensive and reasonably priced. Other options might include a spiced vegetable tangine and charred sirloin.

Elsewhere

The Stagecoach (413-229-8585; stagecoachtavern.net), 845 S. Undermountain Rd. (MA 41), Sheffield. Open for dinner Thurs.–Sat. This handsome brick Federal-style house became a tavern in 1829 and has been many things since—but never anything better than its current look and use. Now owned by neighboring Race Brook Lodge, the timbered, candlelit tavern is both informal and romantic, the setting for dining on a menu that ranges from rigatoni with vodka cream sauce to rib eye with crushed potatoes and blue cheese. Entrées $13–28.

EATING OUT

In Great Barrington

20 Railroad Street (413-528-9345), 20 Railroad St. Open daily for lunch and dinner, also for Sunday brunch. Railroad Street was still dingy in 1977, when this friendly pub opened. Since then the side street has filled with boutiques and restaurants, but this one still stands out and, while ownership has changed, the atmosphere remains relaxed and welcoming. The menu features Angus burgers, sandwiches, and pub food along with 20 craft beers. The ornate, 28-foot-long bar was moved from the Commodore Hotel in Manhattan to Great Barrington in 1919 and served as the centerpiece of a speakeasy until 1933—when it became one of the first legal bars in town.

MEPAL MANOR.

Martin's (413-528-5455), 49 Railroad St. Open daily 6–3 for breakfast and lunch. Breakfast is an all-day affair, the omelets are a feast, and the burgers are outstanding, too. Beer and herbal teas are served, and crayons are at every table so inspired customers of all ages can design their own place mats. Martin Lewis worked in several of New York's most famous restaurants, but his wife is from Sandisfield. Fifteen years ago he opened this spotless, family-run diner-with-a difference, good for a veggie sandwich or Berkshire Breeze (avocado, cucumber, tomato, sprouts, and Swiss or cheddar on farmer's bread) as well as a BLT or burger.

Baba Louie's Sourdough Pizza Restaurant (413-528-8100), 286 Main St. Open Tues.–Sun. for lunch and dinner. Unusual wood-fired pizzas ("Pizza Festival" is topped with broccoli rabe, fresh tomatoes, roasted peppers, yellow squash, zucchini, mozzarella, and oregano) are the specialty, but there are also a surprising variety of salads and a hearty antipasto.

Siam Square (413-644-9119), 290 Main St. Open daily for lunch and dinner. This is a deep, deep storefront with a pleasant decor. In addition to a choice of reasonably priced and quickly prepared curry and noodle dishes, you'll find an intriguing array of house specialties and Thai hot-and-sour salads. Try the Chicken Volcano: marinated Cornish hen with herbs, spices, and a sweet hot chili sauce. Wine and beer is served.

Barrington Brewery & Restaurant (413-528-8282), 420 Stockbridge Rd. (US 7) in Jennifer House Commons. Open daily for lunch and dinner. Both the brew and the food are good, and the scruffy barn atmosphere works. Barn Brewed is the original micro-brew here; there are usually half a dozen on tap. The menu includes a plowman's lunch and hearty classics like shepherd's pie.

Route 7 Grill (413-528-3235; route7grill.com), 999 S. Main St. (US 7) near the Sheffield line. Open daily for dinner, also lunch on weekends (but maybe more often in-season; check). Take-out, too. Decor is attractive and a back deck overlooks a tree farm. Meat and produce is local and BBQ is house-smoked, with the sauce made from scratch. House specialties include pot roast braised in Guinness as well as meaty baby back ribs, but the menu is broad. The calamari is outstanding. Kids' menu.

The Neighborhood Diner (413-528-8226), 282 Main St. Open daily for breakfast through dinner. Breakfast all day, but you can also get an 8-ounce steak or a panini. Reasonable prices, relaxing atmosphere.

Four Brothers (413-528-9684), US 7. This restaurant is part of an upstate New York chain, but it doesn't seem that way. The decor is classic Greek, complete with plants and fake grape arbor. Generally regarded as having the best pizzas, Greek salads, and lasagna around; there's also fried fish and eggplant casserole. Dinners range from a small pizza to honey-dipped fried chicken.

Xicohtencati (413-429-4743; xicohmexican.com), 50 Stockbridge Rd. (US 7). Open daily 11:30–9, until 10 Fri.–Sat.; from 4 PM weekdays off-season. Pronounced "Ski Ko Ten," cheerful ambiance with moderately spicy food is the rule here. Moderately priced margaritas ($8–13) are best in warm weather, when you can sit on the patio or porch.

The Great Barrington Bagel Company (413-528-9055), 777 S. Main St. (US 7 South), across from Guido's Market. Open 7–4 daily; Fri.–Sat. until 5. Our New York friends tell us these are the best you can get north of Manhattan. We counted 19 varieties, from sesame to jalapeño to chocolate chip. This is a small, attractive deli with soups made daily, eight kinds of smoked fish, and more than a dozen spreads. Good to eat in or take out. Breakfast served until 11 AM.

East Mountain Café at the Berkshire Co-op Market (413-528-9697; berkshirecoop.org), 42 Bridge St. Open Mon.–Sat. 8–8, Sun. 10–6. The parking is easy, the food is good, and so, amazingly, is the view. For visitors this is also a place to pick up a range of local produce and products.

The East (413-528-8850), 305 Stockbridge Rd. (US 7). Open daily for lunch and dinner. The menu includes sushi and sashimi; the specialties are Chinese, fresh and flavorful vegetarian, and seafood dishes.

SoCo (413-528-9420), 5 Railroad S., Great Barrington. SoCo of-course stands for South County. The factory on US 7 in GB styles itself as a "microbatch creamery" and turns out more than 100 flavors. Check it out!

In Lee

Salmon Run Fish House (413-243-3900), 78 Main St. The decor is minimal, but the price is right and the seafood menu extensive. We enjoyed the fish-and-chips, but the specialty really is salmon, and it's served 10 different ways. There's also a choice of chicken and steak and a good kids' menu.

Cakewalk Bakery and Café (413-243-2806), 56 Main St. Open daily except Tues., 7–5. This is a great spot for lunch, with a wide choice of sandwiches on freshly made breads. Also soups, salads, and good quiche. There's more seating than apparent from out front. The cakes—mocha cream, carrot, lemon raspberry, and many more—are the thing here, but so are breakfast scones, muffins, croissants, and breads. Everything is made from scratch.

Pho Sai Gon (413-243-6288), 5 Railroad St. This Vietnamese restaurant is sparking clean, cheerful, and so good that we wish we lived within take-out range. We feasted on a lunch special ($7.95) of pan-fried salmon with black bean sauce that was exquisite, the salmon marinated in chunks and delicately spiced. A cup of piping hot jasmine tea arrived in a very large, bright cup. The extensive menu features a number of noodle soups and noodle stir-fries as well as seafood, meat, and vegetarian dishes. Another diner raved about the crispy spring rolls, each served in a wrapping of lettuce.

Alpamayo Restaurant (413-243-6000), 60 Main St. Open Tues.–Sun. 11–9. The first Peruvian restaurant in Lee, and probably the Berkshires, Alpamayo showcases a savory national cuisine. Distinctive dishes include parihuela, a Peruvian version of bouillabaisse that includes fish, calamari, shrimp, mussels, clams, and crab. Entrées are $12–15.

Timothy's Restaurant & Pizzeria (413-243-8220; timothysrestaurantinlee.com), 54 Main St. Open for lunch, Mon.–Sat. 11:45–3; for dinner, Mon.–Thurs. 4–9 and Fri.–Sat. 4–10. Although particularly known for its pizza and oven-baked grinders, Timothy's has a full lunch and dinner menu that includes dishes such as veal marsala, baked seafood casserole, and chicken piccata. Most entrées $13.99–16.99.

Paradise of India Restaurant (413-243-0500), 5 Railroad St. Just off the main drag, a pleasant place for curries and tandoori dishes—and a real bargain at lunch and dinner, too. BYOB.

Claire's Café (413-243-1775; berkshiresgreengrocer.com), 42 Park St. Open Mon.–Fri. 8–6, Sat. 9–6, Sun. 11–4. The emphasis here is on food is that is organic and wherever possible also local. With sandwiches, for instance, there is a choice of flax seed or sourdough bread, and the daily soup specials always include a vegan and gluten-free option.

Joe's Diner (413-243-9756), 85 Center St., South Lee. Open Mon.–Fri. 5:30–9, Sat. 5:30–6:30, Sun. 7–2. The scene of a famous Norman Rockwell *Saturday Evening Post* cover (the one where a burly but kindly state trooper counsels a young runaway sitting at the counter), this is still a local hangout. So choose from a counter stool or a booth and watch the town saunter in and out. The food is good, and when particular specials are on the menu, such as corned beef or slow-roasted prime rib, there can be a line of diners waiting to get in.

Morgan House (413-243-3661; morganhouseinn.com), 33 Main St., Lee. A reliable dining spot since stagecoach days, Morgan House is open for dinner nightly and lunch Thurs.–Mon. Both the tavern and main dining room are wood-paneled and welcoming. The menu features filling fare such as pot roast dinner, filet mignon, chicken parmigiana, and fish-and-chips. Entrées $13.95–23.95.

In Stockbridge

Widow Bingham's Tavern at the Red Lion Inn (413-298-5545), Main St. Open daily for all three meals. More casual and intimate than the formal dining room and good for lighter fare. The Red Lion burgers are legendary, and dinner stews are a good bet. You might also want to try the "plowman's plate" of local Camembert, dried sausage, and Berkshire Mountain bread. In summer the garden itself is a pleasant café. The Lion's Den, opening at 4 on weekdays and noon on weekends, features live entertainment (no cover) and reasonable prices.

Elm Street Market (413-298-3634), 4 Elm St. A good little grocery store with hand-cut meats and a deli menu with a choice of sandwiches; a few tables. Good for breakfast, too. When Stockbridge is flooded by a bus group, this is a find.

Stockbridge Coffee (413-298-3169), 6 Elm St. Fresh roasted organic coffees, bread and pastries, soup and quiche.

Main Street Café (413-298-3060), 40 Main St. The obvious place for a quick lunch. Fresh homemade food, including vegetarian.

Also see **Once Upon a Table** under *Dining Out.*

In Sheffield

♿ 🖉 **The Bridge** (413-229-9000), 650 N. Main St. Open daily except Mon. for dinner from 4:30. A friendly, family-owned and -geared restaurant with a varied menu, reasonable prices, and consistent quality, filling the need and space that was formerly Limey's. It's by the old covered bridge.

((ψ)) **The Marketplace Café** (413-248-5040, ext. 1; marketplacekitchen.com), 18 Elm Court, just off Main St. Open Mon.–Sat. 7–7, Sun. 9–4. Great sandwiches with names like Bartholomew's Gobble (roast turkey with house-made stuffing) and Shay's Rebellion (roast beef, horseradish mayo, peppers, cheese, and more). Also panini, salads, and Harney tea.

Also see **Route 7 Grill** under "Great Barrington," but almost in Sheffield.

Elsewhere

Mom's Restaurant (413-528-2414), 67 Main St., South Egremont. Open daily 6–3. A welcome way stop that's open for breakfast and lunch, with a shady deck in back overlooking a stream. A good choice of burgers, sandwiches, soups, and salads for lunch. Beer and wine are served.

New Boston Inn (413-258-4477; newbostoninn.com), MA 8 and MA 57, New Boston. Open Thurs.–Sun. for lunch and dinner. This is a genuine 18th-century inn and the current owner, Barbara Colorio, is a former corporate chef. Now the old taproom and three large, light-filled rooms are filled with tables. You can opt to dine in the pub or in the formal dining rooms with a full menu ranging from meatloaf to New York strip steak. Most dinner entrées remain priced under $20 and include crabmeat-stuffed haddock and crispy roasted duck. We lunched on a delicious minestrone soup and a half-sandwich of Italian cold cuts on a flaky roll.

The Southfield Store Café (413-229-5050; southfieldstore.com), Southfield Village. Café hours: Mon.–Sat. 7–5, Sun. 8–5; dinner Thurs.–Sun. 5:30–9 (check off-season). Owned by Chef Peter Platt and Meredith Kennard of the Old Inn on the Green, this landmark store is now primarily a place to eat, good for freshly prepared foods to go as well as great sandwiches, salads, and pastries. Also, a full Sunday brunch with a choice of omelets, maybe challah French toast with a mixed berry compote. The dinner menu changes nightly (entrées $20–25). Follow the Southfield signs from MA 57 in New Marlborough.

Perks Café at Hotchkiss Gallery (413-232-0200), 8 Center St., West Stockbridge. Open May–Oct., Wed.–Sun. 8–4. A pleasant breakfast and lunch spot with espresso and fresh-made desserts, including gluten-free brownies.

Otis Poultry Farm (413-269-4438; otispoultryfarm.com), 1570 N. Main Rd., North Otis. Home of "the custom laid egg." Still in the same family that established this as a working poultry farm in 1904, but there no longer seems to be resident chickens. The old chicken house is now a vast store selling Yankee Candles, wine and beer, souvenirs, and homemade pies, breads, and eggs. A café is open seasonally for breakfast and lunch.

✱ Entertainment

MUSIC **Aston Magna Festival** (413-528-3595 or 1-800-875-7156; astonmagna.org), Daniel Arts Center, Simon's Rock College, Great Barrington. The country's oldest annual summer festival devoted to baroque, classical, and early romantic music, very professionally played on period instruments.

THE SOUTHFIELD STORE CAFÉ, NEW MARLBOROUGH.

Christina Tree

Berkshire Choral Festival (413-229-8526; www.choralfest.org), 245 Undermountain Rd. (MA 41), Sheffield. Held in the concert shed of Berkshire School, this is a summer series of concerts combining hundreds of voices with music by the Springfield Symphony. Come early for a picnic and a preconcert talk.

Close Encounters with Music (1-800-843-778; cewm.org) or through the Mahaiwe Box Office (413-528-0100). A respected chamber music series Sept.–Memorial Day weekend at the Mahaiwe in Great Barrington.

Music & More in the Meetinghouse (newmarlborough.org), 154 Hartsville-New Marlborough Road, New Marlborough. A series of chamber music and other programs staged in this 300-year-old church.

Guthrie Center (413-528-1955; guthriecenter.org), 4 Van Deusenville Rd., Great Barrington. This is the actual church immortalized as "Alice's Restaurant," and it now belongs to folksinger and writer Arlo Guthrie, who periodically performs here himself. Other well-known and not-so-well-known talent also performs.

Celestial Bar at the Castle Street Café (413-528-5244; castlestreet cafe.com), 10 Castle St. Live music nightly (except Tues.): piano, guitar, jazz groups. Check to see who's on. No cover. An attractive bar with its own menu; also see *Dining Out*.

❀ **The Dream Away Lodge** (413-623-8725; thedreamawaylodge.com), 1342 County Rd., Becket. Open Wed.–Sun. (for brunch) from Mother's Day to Halloween, weekends only from New Year's to Valentine's Day. A Berkshire legend for more than 90 years, this old farmhouse was a speakeasy and brothel during the Depression. Under the ownership of Daniel Osman, a former Shakespeare & Company of Lenox actor, it has become a very hip music, bar, and dining venue with a diverse and devoted clientele. The decor is eclectic, as is the music and the cuisine, which Osman describes as "a daily happening." Burgers and pizza, also baked marinated tofu and grilled rack of lamb are on the printed menu ($8–26). Name performers are booked on weekends, but the very popular Wednesday "open acoustic" night in the intimate music room attracts area musicians who can include, among others, local resident Arlo Guthrie. Check out The Loo Gallery. Reservations are encouraged and often essential. Credit cards not accepted.

The Gypsy Joint (413-644-8811), 393 Stockbridge Rd. (US 7 North), Great Barrington. Closed Mon., otherwise open 11AM–9 PM, midnight on weekends. Popular all day for pizza, salads, sandwiches, and wraps, but music is the nightly draw.

FILM **Mahaiwe Performing Arts Center** (413-528-0100; mahaiwe.org), 14 Castle St., Great Barrington. In addition to frequent live performances, this restored vaudeville house screens "Live in HD" performances by London's National Theater and The Metropolitan Opera. Classic films, too.

Triplex Cinema (413-528-8885; the triplex.com), 70 Railroad St., Great Barrington. First-run and some art films; four screens with surround sound. Check for the "Upstairs Live" series.

✷ Selective Shopping

ANTIQUES SHOPS South Berkshire is one of the antiques centers of New England. Visit bcaada.com or pick up the locally available pamphlet listing more than 40 antique dealers here and in neighboring Litchfield and Columbia Counties. **Sheffield** alone has a dozen dealers and **Bradford Auctions**, Great Barrington has more than a dozen varied dealers.

ART AND ARTISANS

In Great Barrington
Berkshire Art Gallery (413-528-2690; berkshireartgallery.com), 80 Railroad St. Open weekends noon–5 and by appointment. The gallery specializes in 19th- and early-20th-century American artists as well as Berkshire paintings.

MAHAIWE PERFORMING ARTS CENTER, SITE OF GREAT PERFORMANCES IN GREAT BARRINGTON.

Christina Tree

Vault Gallery (413-644-0221; vaultgallery.net), 322 Main St. Housed in the former Mahaiwe Bank Building, the gallery features well-established contemporary paintings, photography, film, and sculpture by Clemens Kalischer, Leonard Baskin, and Barry Mosher, among many others.

Great Barrington Pottery (413-274-6259), MA 41, Housatonic. The handsome, nicely glazed pieces are fired in a Japanese wood-burning kiln. Visitors are invited to view demonstrations of *ikebana* or the tea ceremony between 1 and 4 in the Kyoto-style teahouse.

In West Stockbridge
🏵 **Hotchkiss Mobiles Gallery** (413-232-0200; artmobiles.com), 8 Center St. Joel Hotchkiss likes to watch jaws drop as unsuspecting tourists step into his gallery and register the dozens of moving, one-of-a-kind sculptures suspended from the ceiling and gloriously colored artifacts spaced through the rooms. A vast studio stretches beyond. Hotchkiss makes more mobiles than anyone in the country, supplying museum shops with a variety of models (from $85 to $2,000). He also creates original mobiles on commission. A stunning array of glass and glass-beaded jewelry selected by Sandra Hotchkiss is also sold.

🏵 **Hoffman Pottery** (413-232-4646; ehoffmanpottery.com), south of the village at 103 MA 41. This is a must-stop. Open daily during summer, weekends during the school year. Elaine Hoffman's brightly colored house/studio/shop stands in a flower

Christina Tree

JOEL HOTCHKISS IS SURROUNDED BY HIS WORK AT HOTCHKISS MOBILES GALLERY IN WEST STOCKBRIDGE.

garden peppered with pottery masks that represent the good spirits guarding the house. Check her website for a sense of the variety of patterns and colors in which she has created plates, mugs, bowls, vases, and other functional pottery over the years.

Elsewhere

Schantz Galleries (413-298-3044; schantzgalleries.com), 3 Elm St., Stockbridge. A gem well worth finding (it's hidden behind a bank), this is a showcase of museum-quality contemporary glass sculpture, some of the finest around.

Sheffield Pottery (413-229-7700; sheffield-pottery.com), US 7 north of the village, Sheffield. This family-owned business began in 1946 by supplying Sheffield clay to make "redware" pottery. It now imports clays from across the country, blending them for use by potters throughout the East. The showroom displays and sells work by a wide range of the craftspeople it supplies.

Joyous Spring Pottery (413-528-4115), Art School Rd., Monterey. Striking unglazed vases and other decorative pieces.

Becket Arts Center of the Hilltowns (413-623-6635; becketarts center.org), 12 Brooker Hill Rd, off MA 8, Becket. A major summer gallery with biweekly receptions for changing exhibits as well as a variety of seasonal workshops, summer music, and theater camps.

BOOKSTORES **The Bookloft** (413-528-1521; thebookloft.com), Barrington Plaza, US 7, Great Barrington. A large, long-established, independent bookstore with a knowledgeable staff. Out-of-print and hard-to-find books, also self-publishing. Berkshire authors a specialty.

Main Street Books (413-243-0243), 69 Main St., Lee. An independent bookstore in the heart of town. The

CONTEMPORARY ART AT SCHANTZ GALLERIES IN STOCKBRIDGE.

store's two sunny rooms have comfortable reading chairs and are decorated with art, mainly by local artists.

ANTIQUARIAN BOOKS North Star Rare Books (413-644-9595), 684 S. Main St. (US 7), Great Barrington. Specializing in 18th- through 20th-century historical and literary manuscripts and rare volumes. Sited unexpectedly in a mini shopping mall, Randy Weinstein's shop seems as much gallery as bookshop, a serene space displaying valuable vintage manuscripts and illustrations, all said to come from local collections.

Yellow House Books (413-528-8227), 252 Main St., Great Barrington. Bonnie and Bob Benson's store fills several rooms in a house. They specialize in rare books, photographs, children's illustrated books, and folklore. Browsing encouraged. We always come away with something we never meant to buy but are grateful we did.

CHARLES H. BALDWIN & SONS, AN EMPORIUM ON CENTER STREET IN WEST STOCKBRIDGE.

Christina Tree

SPECIAL SHOPS Country Curtains (413-298-5565; countrycurtains.com) at the Red Lion Inn, Stockbridge (see *Lodging*). A phenomenon rather than just a store, Country Curtains is nationally known through its catalog. It is a source of a wide variety of matching curtains, bedding, and pillows, beautifully displayed in the rear of the inn.

Charles H. Baldwin & Sons (413-232-7785; baldwinextracts.com), 1 Center St., West Stockbridge. This aromatic emporium has been in the same family since 1888 and on the same spot since 1912, making and selling its own "table syrup" (a blend of maple and cane sugar syrup), pure vanilla extract, and other cooking extracts and flavorings. Also, house-made scents like rose water. The shop is chock-full of gifts and souvenirs, but most customers are looking for extracts, particularly the hard-to-find pure vanilla. Check out the family's fabulous hardware store across the street.

Kenver, Ltd. (413-538-2330; kenverltd.com), 39 Main St. (MA 23), South Egremont. Housed in an 18th-century tavern, family-owned since 1959, Kenver is a source of snow sport and skating equipment and clothing for kids as well as adults. Sportswear in summer.

Guido's Fresh Marketplace (413-528-9255; guidosfreshmarketplace.com), 760 S. Main St. (US 7), Great Barrington. The standout place to shop for a full line of vegetables, health food, and deli items as well as seafood and meat. Great baked goods and deli, too.

The Snap Shop (413-528-4725; thesnapshop.biz), 14 Railroad St. Open Tues.–Fri. 9–5:30, Sat. 8:30–4.

Steve Carlotta and his nephew, Tony Carlotto, have been running this friendly camera shop since 1972. We tried to buy an expensive new card for our digital camera and instead were given a lesson in how to work with what we had.

Byzantium (413-528-9496), 32 Railroad St., Great Barrington. Our favorite for women's clothing and accessories.

Robin's Candy Shop (413-528-8477), 288 Main St., Great Barrington. Open Mon.–Fri. 11–9:45; weekends from 11 with varying closing hours. This is more like a quirky boutique for sweets lovers than the old mom and pop corner candy store. The 10,000 candy items for sale range from bubble gum, jelly beans, and M&Ms to garlic-flavored "vampire repellent" mints, bacon-specked candy bars, vegan Italian gelato, chocolate-covered farm-raised ants, and cheese-coated larvae. (The last reportedly tastes like popcorn.) It is also home to the World's Largest Gummy Bear, weighing in at 5 pounds ($39.98) and an 11-pound bar of premium Belgian chocolate that goes for $130. Then there's the licorice. Owner Robin Helfand carries 85 varieties of licorice imported from a dozen countries. There are frequent licorice tastings and seminars, too. Candy purchases are nicely wrapped and come with a free toothbrush so customers can keep that sweet tooth healthy.

Barrington Coffee Roasting Co. (1-800-528-0998), 165 Quarry Hill Rd., Lee. Open Mon.–Fri. 9–5. Source of the outstanding local brew. Tours are not offered, but visitors are welcome to stop buy to pick up a freshly roasted bag of beans and a sample cup.

Rubiner's Cheesemongers & Grocers (413-528-0488), 264 Main St., Great Barrington. A mecca for cheese lovers, with more than 100 to choose from. Pricey but worth it for those who care. The same holds for deli meats, breads, and more.

OUTLET MALLS **Premium Outlets at Lee** (413-243-8186 or 1-800-866-5900; primeoutlets.com) at Mass Pike Exit 2 in Lee. A nicely grouped array of more than five dozen outlets offering upscale and everyday wares, from Liz Claiborne and Polo Ralph Lauren to Reebok and OshKosh B'Gosh. There is a central food court and plenty of parking. In summer a shuttle bus runs to and from downtown Lee.

* Farms

Note: **Berkshire Grown** (berkshire grown.org) is the community group promoting locally grown food, flowers, and plants. Its website lists farmers' markets for each town.

In Great Barrington

Farmers' market at the old train station, Castle St. and Taconic Ave. (behind town hall). Early May–Oct., Sat. 9–1. Organic vegetables, fruit, dairy products, prepared foods, special events.

Windy Hill Farm (413-298-3217), 686 Stockbridge Rd. (US 7), Great Barrington. Open Apr.–Christmas, daily 9–5. Pick-your-own apples (more than 25 varieties), pies, and fresh-pressed cider in fall, extensive container-grown nursery stock, and hardy perennials; staff members are very knowledgeable.

Taft Farms (413-528-1515 or 1-800-528-1015; taftfarms.com), Division St.

and MA 183. More than 400 produce items, baked goods, and free-range chickens. Call to find out what's in-season in the way of PYO fruits and vegetables.

In Monterey

Gould Farm's Harvest Barn (413-644-9718; gouldfarm.org), marked from MA 23. Memorial Day–late Oct., weekdays 9–4. Produce, maple syrup, Monterey Mint Tea (made from organically grown apple mint leaf, dried and packaged in tea bags), herbs, salsa and sauces, and an artisan cheddar cheese that's a big draw.

Lowland Farm (413-528-0728), 128 New Marlborough Rd. Open daily year-round with mulch hay, maple syrup, and PYO raspberries in-season.

Rawson Brook Farm (413-528-2138), off New Marlborough Rd., 2 miles from MA 23 in Monterey. Getting there is half the fun, since the back roads to the farm are beautiful. Susan Sellew has chosen to supply local restaurants and customers rather than go big time—an option that is very real given the quality of her Monterey Chèvre goat cheese. The cheese is available in various sizes from the fridge at the dairy at prices well below what you pay in local stores. Children will love seeing the baby goats, but adult supervision is a must.

In Sheffield

Howden Farm (413-229-8481; howdenfarm.com), 303 Rannopo Rd. From US 7 in Ashley Falls, follow signs for Bartholomew's Cobble and the Ashley House. Rannopo Road runs north between these two sites. Also off MA 7A south of Sheffield. Home of the Howden pumpkins, two varieties developed by John A. Howden. Family run since 1937; PYO pumpkins on weekends and holidays starting in late September. PYO blueberries and raspberries in July and August. Good for sweet corn and eggs, too. Also see *Lodging*.

Equinox Farm (413-229-2266), 489 Bow Wow Rd. Open daylight hours, Memorial Day–Labor Day. From US 7 south, turn right onto Cook Road, then right onto Bow Wow. A variety of greens, mesclun, salad greens, herbs, and heirloom tomatoes.

Moon in the Pond Organic Farm (413-229-3092), 819 Barnum St. A wide variety of organic meats, eggs, greens, and herbs as well as heirloom vegetables.

Elsewhere

Les Trois Emme Winery & Vineyard (413-528-1015; ltewinery.com), 8 Knight Rd., New Marlborough. Open for tours and tastings ($5) Apr.–Dec., Thurs.–Sun. 1–5. Tastings include five wines and nibbles. The specialty is Berkshire Red.

High Lawn Farm (413-243-0672), 535 Summer St., Lee. Source of the creamiest milk around. Visitors are welcome.

✷ Special Events

March: **Southern Berkshire Chamber of Commerce Winterfest Auction** (southernberkshires.com).

May: **Chesterwood Antique Auto Show,** Stockbridge. **Memorial Day Parade,** Great Barrington.

Mid-August: **Berkshire Crafts Fair** (berkshirecraftsfair.org) at Monument Mountain Regional High School, Great Barrington. **Annual Flower Show** at Berkshire Botanical Garden. **Zucchini Festival,** West Stockbridge. **Antique Car Show,** Great Barrington.

October: **Housatonic Heritage Walks** (heritage-hikes.org) feature guided walks in and around town on Columbus Day weekend. **Berkshire Botanical Garden Harvest Festival,** Columbus Day weekend in Stockbridge. **Halloween Walk through Ice Glen** is a Stockbridge tradition, usually followed by a bonfire. **Spirits of Sheffield Rise Again** is a dramatized tour of the town's 14 cemeteries on Halloween weekend.

December: **Stockbridge Main Street at Christmas** finds Main Street decorated to re-create the way it looked in Norman Rockwell's famous painting (first weekend). **Naumkeag** is also decorated for Christmas. Great Barrington hosts a **Christmas Stroll**.

CENTRAL AND NORTH BERKSHIRE

INCLUDING LENOX, PITTSFIELD, WILLIAMSTOWN, AND NORTH ADAMS

Northern Berkshire and Southern Berkshire are distinct areas, physically different and tucked respectively in the northwest and southwest corners of Massachusetts, one bordered by Connecticut and the other by Vermont. Central Berkshire County is more difficult to define.

Lenox is a hinge, linked closely to Lee and Stockbridge on the south and blurring seamlessly along US 7's motels, restaurants, and mini malls into Pittsfield on the north. Home of the Tanglewood Music Festival, Shakespeare & Co., Edith Wharton's "The Mount," the state's most famous resorts and spas, as well as a clutch of dining destinations and boutiques, Lenox looms larger than it is. As a tourist destination it overshadowed Pittsfield for much of the 20th century. No longer.

The original heart and hub of Berkshire County, Pittsfield is in the midst of a vibrant renaissance. It's the place to see a hot new play by the Barrington Stage Company, a performance at the lovingly restored (1903) Colonial Theatre, or a film at the cutting edge Beacon Theater. Terrific art galleries and restaurants, cafés and shops are filling mile-long North Street while upper floors are now condos and studios. Just south of Park Square, the Berkshire Museum represents the city's long-standing cultural core.

Hancock Shaker Village, 5 miles west of Pittsfield, displays the largest collection of Shaker artifacts on any original Shaker site and evokes a sense of the rare and beautiful places (not just things) that Shakers created. It's also worth finding your way to Arrowhead on the southern fringe of the city. Novelist Herman Melville spent 13 of his happiest years in this still-rural farmhouse. He penned *Moby-Dick* in a study overlooking Mount Greylock, which is said to have inspired his grandly conceived epic about a great white whale.

Mount Greylock isn't an isolated peak, but part of a range that includes four of the highest mountains in Massachusetts, rising abruptly from the countryside, dividing the north–south flow of traffic in this region the way a big boulder divides the flow of a narrow stream. US 7, running from Williamstown down to

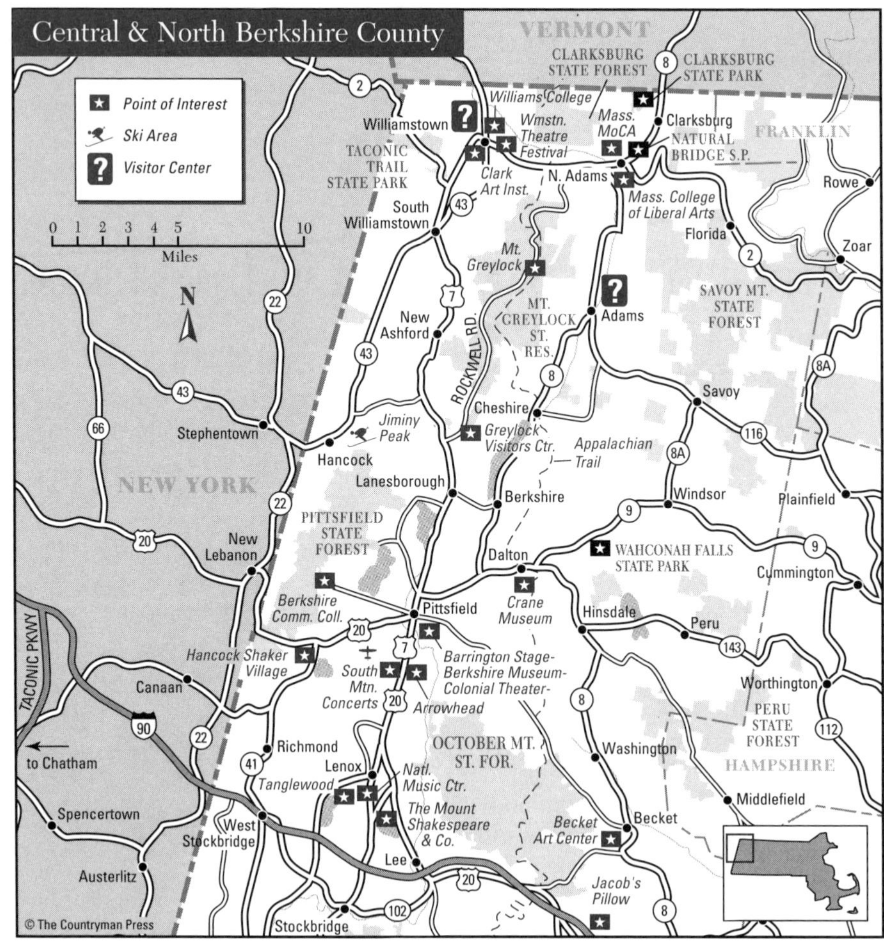

Pittsfield on the western side of the range, is the main road, while MA 8, from North Adams south through Adams and Cheshire, is the road less taken.

The access road from US 7 north of Pittsfield to the Mount Greylock State Reservation Visitor Center (1.7 miles) is open year-round. Mid-May through Oct. 31, you can drive another 7 miles up to the summit of the state's highest mountain (3,491 feet). Along with a second access road from North Adams on the north, this newly resurfaced, 16.3-mile network of mountain roads constitutes the state's most dramatic Scenic Byway. The view from the summit is truly spectacular and can be enjoyed at both dawn and sunset if you stay on the summit at Bascomb Lodge, built in the 1930s by the Civilian Conservation Corps and also recently upgraded, now offering comfortable lodging, reputable dining, and a series of workshops, lectures, and live entertainment.

Williamstown is the area's "village beautiful," home to prestigious Williams College and to the Sterling and Francine Clark Art Institute, internationally known for its collection of paintings by French impressionists and 19th-century American masters. The Williams College Museum of Art also displays several icons of American art, and in summer the Williamstown Theater Festival—staged in a stunning, recently expanded facility—draws theater buffs from throughout the Northeast.

For decades this cultured northwestern corner of the state was perceived as isolated, but that's changed. The Massachusetts Museum of Contemporary Art (MASS MoCA), one of the world's largest contemporary art and performance centers, is housed in former mill buildings in neighboring North Adams and has sparked a genuine renaissance in that proudly gritty little city, which now also offers upscale dining and lodging. North Adams is also the beginning or end, depending on how you look at it, of the Mohawk Trail.

Turning South on MA 8 through Adams, the Ashuwillticook Rail Trail runs south along Cheshire Reservoir (from which the Hoosic River flows north). Below Cheshire and Lanesborough, the landscape opens expansively into a broad valley with Pittsfield at its center. The two branches of the Housatonic River and all roads meet in Pittsfield.

AREA CODE 413 applies to all of Western Massachusetts.

GUIDANCE Berkshires Visitors Bureau (413-743-4500 or 1-800-237-5747; berkshires.org), 3 Hoosac St., Adams. Open daily; hours vary seasonally. Online lodging reservation service; ½ TIX ticket booth, June–Labor Day. The State's Regional Tourism Council office for Berkshire County maintains a walk-in visitors center, a useful website, and an annual free guide.

Lenox Chamber of Commerce (413-637-3646 or 1-866-515-3649; lenox.org). A walk-in visitors center in Lenox Town Hall, 6 Walker St., provides free lodging referral, which during Tanglewood season includes many private homes, along with guidance about shopping, dining, and attractions. There is also a half-price ticket booth. The town hall has public restrooms. Open Tues.–Sun. 11:30–4:30.

Pittsfield Visitors Center (discoverpittsfield.com), is located at the Colonial Theatre, 111 South St. The website has a full events calendar plus dining and shopping. At this writing the visitor center has no phone, but **Creative Pittsfield** (413-499-9348; pittsfield-ma.org), maintained by the city's Office of Cultural Development, does the job. It's based at **The Lichtenstein Center for the Arts**, 28 Renne Ave., Pittsfield. Open Wed.–Sat. noon–5.

North Adams. Phone inquiries: **North Adams Office of Tourism** (413-664-6180; tourist@northadams-ma.gov). Walk-in information: **Western Gateway Heritage State Park** (413-663-6312), marked and accessible from State St. (MA 8 South). Open year-round, daily 10–5. A seasonal information booth at **Windsor Mill** is on your right as you enter the city on MA 2 (Union St.) from the east.

Williamstown Chamber of Commerce (413-458-9077 or 1-800-214-3799; williamstownchamber.com) maintains an unstaffed information booth with restrooms at 100 Spring St., across from the village parking lot, and another at the junction of MA 2 and US 7.

GETTING THERE *By air:* See Albany Airport and Bradley International Airport under *Airports* in "What's Where."

By bus: An **Intermodal Transportation Center** (413-499-2782 or 1-800-292-2782), corner of Columbus Ave. and North St. in downtown Pittsfield, serves local and long-distance buses as well as AMTRAK under one roof. From New York City, **Peter Pan/Trailways** (1-800-343-9999; peterpanbus.com) serves Pittsfield via Lenox and Lee; from Boston service is via Springfield. From Albany, **Greyhound** offers service to Pittsfield.

By train: **AMTRAK** (1-800-USA-RAIL) stops at convenient times in Pittsfield en route from Boston to Chicago.

By car: From Boston to Lenox and Pittsfield: take the Mass Pike to Lee. For Williamstown and North Adams, MA 2 (see "Along the Mohawk Trail") is a half-hour shorter and far more scenic.

From the New York area the Taconic State Parkway exit is your way north, but where you get off varies. For Lenox or Southern Berkshire it's at MA 23 east through Hillsdale, New York, to Great Barrington and then US 7 north. For Pittsfield, exit at NY 295 East for 12 miles, then left onto MA 41 North and right on US 20 East.

For Williamstown, follow NY 295 to MA 22 North to MA 43 East to US 7 North into town.

GETTING AROUND Williamstown, North Adams, Adams, Cheshire, and Lanesborough are all served by the buses of **BRTA,** the **Berkshire Regional Transit Authority** (413-499-2782 or 1-800-292-BRTA).

PARKING It's free in Pittsfield, but there's a two-hour limit, strictly enforced.

MEDICAL EMERGENCY 911 reaches police, fire departments, and ambulances throughout this area.

Berkshire Medical Center (413-447-2834), 725 North St., Pittsfield.

North Adams Regional Hospital (413-664-5256), Hospital Ave.

✷ Towns and Cities

Lenox (population: about 5,000). Lenox evolved in stages. Its 1787 status as county seat gave it graceful Federal buildings like the courthouse; the recently renovated library with its luxurious reading rooms, gallery, and outdoor reading park; Lenox Academy; and the Church on the Hill. In the 1860s county government shifted to Pittsfield and summer visitors began buying up large holdings. By the turn of the century more than 90 elaborate summer "cottages" were scattered along every ridge in the area. Lenox's glory years as the inland Newport were brief, ended by the Great Depression and the federal income tax. The resort might have vanished entirely had it not been for the Boston Symphony Orchestra's Berkshire Music Festival. Concert halls were not yet air-conditioned, and symphony music typically ceased during summer. The orchestra selected

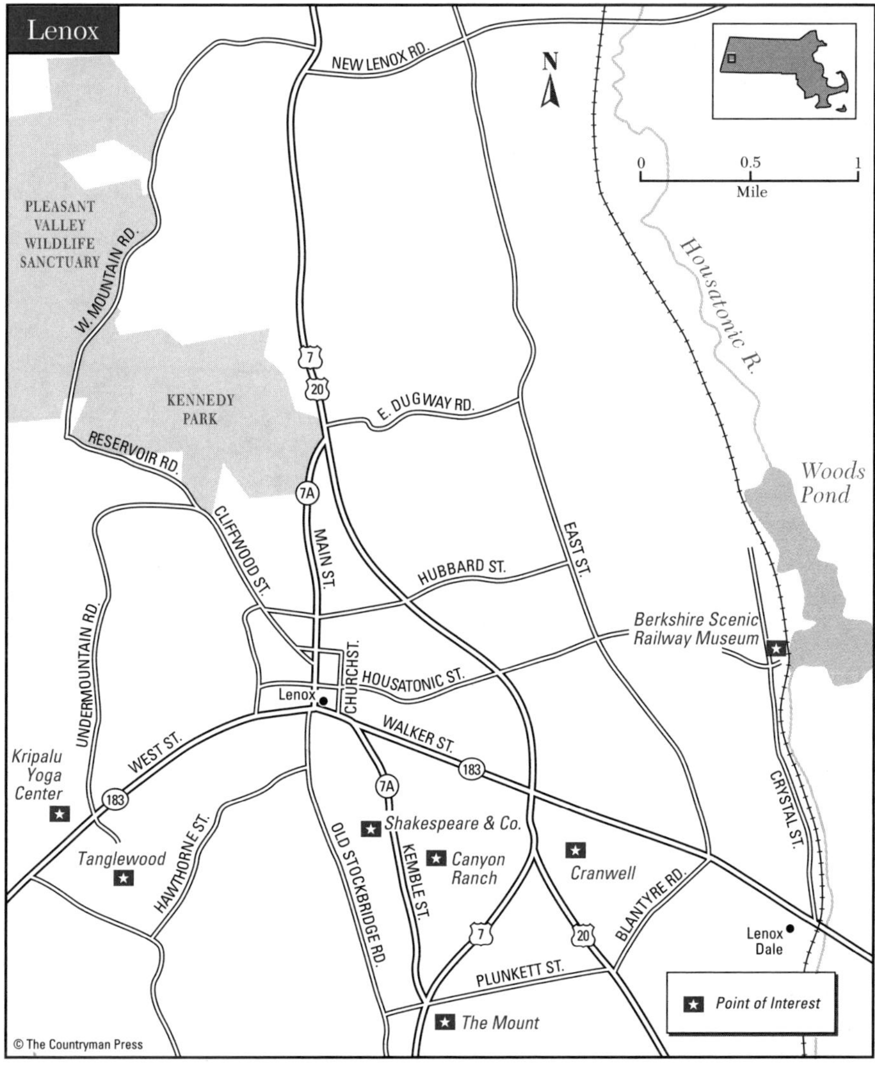

Lenox as its summer home because **Tanglewood** (a forested estate named by Nathaniel Hawthorne, who wrote *Tanglewood Tales* there) was given to it by a patron.

More than 50 grand "Berkshire Cottages" still cluster in and around Lenox. **The Mount,** former residence of novelist Edith Wharton (whose best-known work, *Ethan Frome,* is set in the Berkshires), has been restored and is open to the public. Bellefontaine, another baronial cottage, is now a spa (**Canyon Ranch**), several are inns, and the site of one of the grandest—Andrew Carnegie's mansion, which unfortunately burned, though its million-dollar view remains—is now occupied by the **Kripalu Center for Yoga and Health.**

Christina Tree

A QUAINT SIDEWALK IN LENOX.

Pittsfield (population: 45,793). "Pittsfield was, and will be, the downtown of the Berkshires," maintains the city's mayor, James M. Ruberto, explaining that while the old downtown was about retail, what's evolving is a mix of restaurants and shops, with offices, lodging, and creative enterprises on upper floors and side streets. It's happening thanks in good part to a zoning change creating a downtown arts district that encompasses the city's commercial core.

PITTSFIELD MURAL

Christina Tree

Until recently Pittsfield was a company town that had lost its company. In the 1950s some 15,000 General Electric employees worked in Pittsfield; today it's one-tenth that number. There is, however, a silver lining to GE's legacy of toxic waste and deflated property values: a $250 million settlement that includes $1 million a year for 10 years. A healthy percentage of this discretionary fund is seeding cultural projects—such as the splendid **Colonial Theatre,** closed in 1949, now beautifully restored and reopened. The **Barrington Stage**

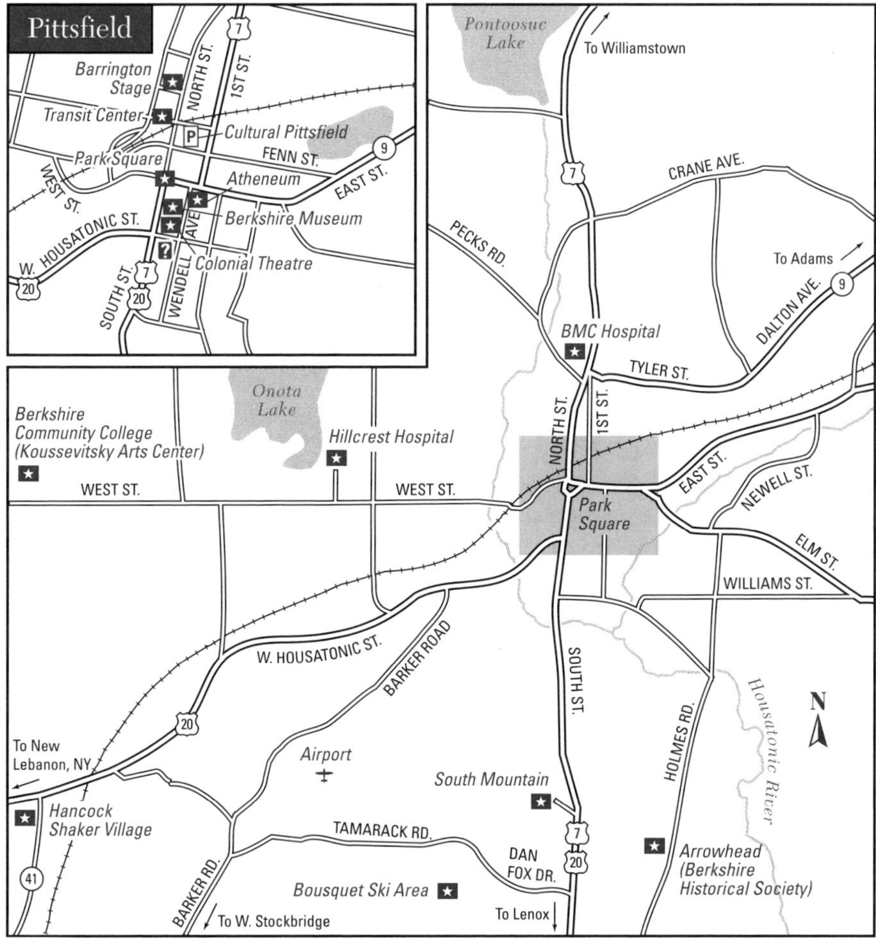

Company took advantage of the city's financial incentives, moving up from South County, restoring another major theater, and mounting smaller productions in other venues around this town that is now studded with public art. Around Park Square and along North Street long-vacant storefronts have filled with cafés, restaurants, and galleries beside long-established utilitarian stores. The **Berkshire Museum** continues to attract families with fine art and family-friendly exhibits.

This isn't the first time Pittsfield has reinvented itself. First settled in 1752, the town grew in the late 18th century around the common that still survives as Park Square, a centerpiece from which radiate streets aptly named North, South, East, and West. It was in Park Square in 1807 that Elkanah Watson introduced the first merino sheep to New England, inaugurating an era in which this particular breed transformed the region's landscape from woods to open pasture dotted with mills to process their wool. Watson founded the Berkshire Agricultural

Society and in 1811 held one of the country's first agricultural fairs on the square.

In the second half of the 19th century the arrival of the railroad changed Pittsfield from agricultural center to industrial metropolis, transporting its burgeoning products, principally textiles and paper, and bringing visitors to stay in its hotels and build summer homes. This boom was also fueled by local inventors like William Stanley, who developed the electric transformer and employed 5,000 people before General Electric bought him out in 1903. For a sense of the city's Gilded Era, walk up quiet, gracious Wendell Avenue (visitors are welcome in the Women's Club of Pittsfield at No. 42) and around the common, noting the Victorian Gothic athenaeum (now the registry of deeds), the courthouse built of Sheffield marble, and St. Stephen's Church with its stained-glass windows by Louis Comfort Tiffany. Most of these buildings date to 1870–1903, years during which the city's population grew from 11,000 to 40,000.

Pittsfield remains headquarters for GE's Plastics Division, which has, in turn, spawned a number of local plastics companies. It's also recently become corporate headquarters for several other companies of various sizes, and the feel is that of a small city rather than a tourist destination, one with a variety of reasonably priced standout restaurants, galleries, theaters, and frequent cultural happenings.

POPCORN IN PITTSFIELD.

Christina Tree

Williamstown (population: about 4,600). From its earliest years Williamstown has been an orderly, elegantly planned, and education-minded community. It was founded in 1753 as West Hoosac, and at their first meeting the seven original proprietors passed what would now be called zoning laws. Meadows and uplands were divided, and settlers were required to clear a minimum of 5 acres of land and build a house at least 15 by 18 feet—a substantial dwelling by frontier standards. An exact replica of one of these "regulation" houses, built as a town bicentennial project using mid-18th-century tools and methods, stands in **Field Park,** a remnant of the original town green. Two years after the settlement was founded, Colonel Ephraim Williams Jr.—who had commanded the local fort and first surveyed the area—wrote a will endowing "a free school forever," pro-

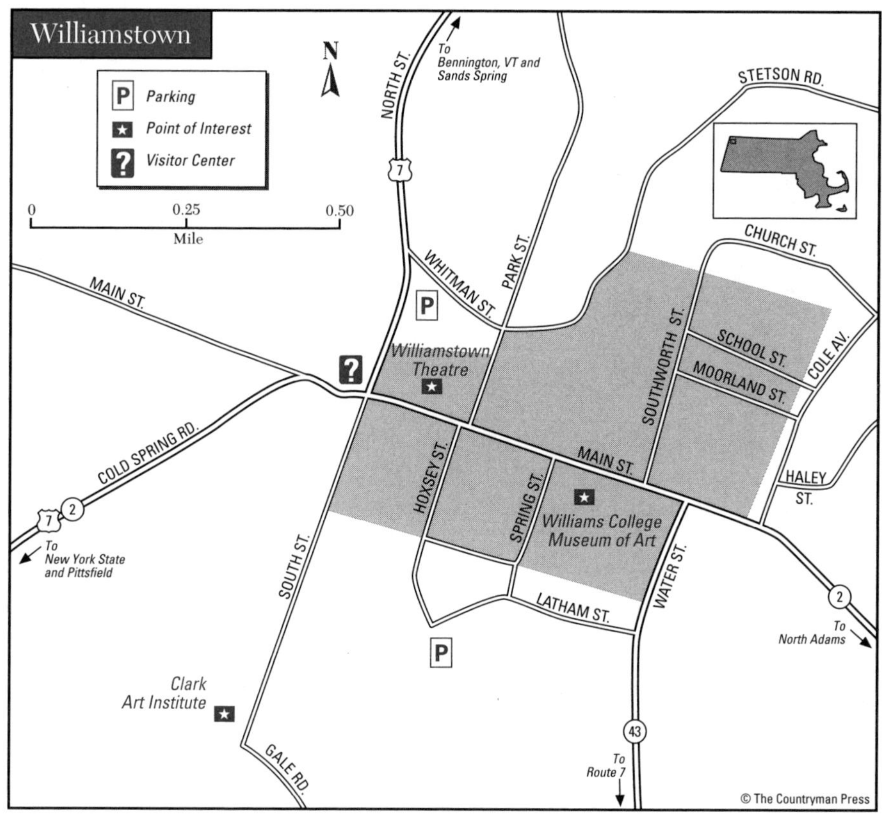

vided that the township fell within Massachusetts (New York claimed it) and was renamed Williamstown. Shortly after making his will, Williams was killed in upstate New York fighting the French, but the conditions of his will weren't met for many years.

Because the border between Massachusetts and New York was long disputed, the school, now **Williams College,** couldn't be founded until 1791. It quickly became central to town life, however. In 1815, when finances were shaky and the trustees considered moving the school to a less isolated location, local people pledged enough money to keep it in town. **Williams College** (413-597-3131; williams.edu) currently enrolls some 2,000 students, almost equally divided between men and women and drawn from throughout the U.S. and more than 40 countries. Tours of the 450-acre campus are available at the admissions office (next to the Adams Memorial Theater). Few other colleges are as entwined with their communities. Be sure to pick up the *Guide to the Campus,* which includes a map that covers half of town. Buildings of interest to the general public (in addition to the art museum) include **Chapin Library** (413-597-2462) of rare books in Stetson Hall, which sits behind Thompson Memorial Chapel, across

Christina Tree

SCULPTURE ON THE CAMPUS OF WILLIAMS COLLEGE.

Main Street from the Museum of Art. It's worth visiting to see the college's priceless collection of documents from the American Revolution. Original copies of the Declaration of Independence, the Articles of Confederation, two early versions of the Bill of Rights, and a draft of the Constitution are exhibited. Closed Sat.–Sun. **Hopkins Observatory** (413-597-2188), dedicated in 1838, is one of the first observatories in the country. Free shows are offered here in the Milham Planetarium most Fridays; since space is limited, make reservations.

The town has been a tourist destination since the mid-19th century. As early as the 1830s, local mineral springs began attracting visitors, and by the Civil War, Williamstown was an established resort with some large hotels and palatial summer homes. The old resort hotels are long gone, but there are many appealing places to stay. Bucolic South Williamstown still has a number of gentlemen's farms, some quite grand. **Sterling and Francine Clark Art Institute** alone is worth a trip to Williamstown, and its world-class collection is complemented by that of the first-rate **Williams College Museum of Art.**

The **Williamstown Theatre Festival** is one of the best of its kind in the country. Also check out the **Williamstown House of Local History** in the Elizabeth S. Botsford Memorial Library (413-458-2160), 1095 Main St. (open Mon.–Fri. 10–noon and 1–3, or by appointment: nancywb947@aol.com). Built in 1815 as a residence for the college treasurer, this homey library building retains many original features, including a curved staircase and graceful fireplace mantels. The House of Local History wing contains an extensive and eclectic collection that includes spinning wheels, Civil War uniforms, old ice skates, photos, and much more. All in all, Williamstown, a jewel of a village set within a circle of mountains, deserves more than a quick stop.

North Adams (population: 13,816). Few communities in Massachusetts have had a more dramatic death and rebirth than its smallest city. A 1939 guide, *The Berkshire Hills* (American Guide Series), described a Main Street lined with "mid-Victorian blocks, small drygoods stores, taverns, colorful fruit stands and markets, and ten-cent stores. . . . There is a constant hum of noise and a confusion of tongues: French-Canadian, Italian, nasal Yankee. . . . North Adams is nervous with the energy of twentieth century America." The engines of that energy—the railway, the vast Arnold and Windsor Print Works and other textile mills, along with other small manufacturing—are long gone. Arnold Print Works was supplanted by Sprague Electric Company, which flourished during World War II, producing circuitry that, among other things, was used to detonate atomic bombs and later helped launch systems for Gemini and moon missions. Sprague closed in 1985, but it had atrophied long before and the downtown was decimated by "urban renewal." One entire side of Main Street was razed.

The idea of utilizing Sprague's vast, vacant mill buildings to display contemporary art was first suggested in 1986, but a dozen years of ups and downs for the project intervened before MASS MoCA opened, quickly becoming a major draw and anchor for galleries in storefronts and mills throughout the small city. Much of the old railyard is now the **Western Gateway Heritage State Park,** with sophisticated displays dramatizing construction of the Hoosac Tunnel—the phenomenon that created this brick city in the first place. Because the Hoosac Range, just east of North Adams, is so steep, early locomotives were unable to climb it, which meant a railroad couldn't run directly westward from Boston. Massachusetts's industries were handicapped, and Boston's future as a major port was in doubt until 1875, when—after 25 years of nonstop work, at a cost of nearly 200 lives—a 4.75-mile-long railroad tunnel was finally blasted through the Hoosac Tunnel.

Beyond the narrow downtown, North Adams's streets climb steeply up the hills. At the foot of Main Street, turn at the Blackinton Mansion (now the public library) onto Church Street, lined with turn-of-the-20th-century mansions. Follow it up by the **Massachusetts College of Liberal Arts** and turn onto Kemp Avenue to find **Windsor Lake.**

Adams (population: 9,213). In McKinley Square at the center of Adams stands a bronze statue of President William McKinley, arms outstretched pleadingly as they were when he asked Congress to pass a tariff protecting American textile manufacturers from foreign competition. The protective tariff was responsible for Adams's period of greatest prosperity and directly benefited a local industrialist and longtime friend of McKinley, William Plunkett, owner of the Berkshire Cotton Manufacturing Company. A grateful and grieving Plunkett erected the statue after McKinley's assassination in 1901.

Adams was founded by Quakers, and their 1782 meetinghouse still stands on Friend Street. The town's most famous daughter is Susan B. Anthony (1820–1906), the daughter of Quakers who became a leading suffragist, instrumental in passing legislation that gave married women legal right over their children, property, and wages. A plaque at the southern end of Main Street commemorates her as the only woman to have ever graced the face of an American (silver) dollar. Approaching Adams from the north on MA 8, you pass an unsightly operation mining calcium carbonate from Mount Greylock—but persevere. At the McKinley statue, turn onto Hoosac Street to find the town's prime outlet and the **Berkshires Visitor Center.** Or head up Maple Street through orchards to **Greylock Glen** with its trails and views. Bicyclists note the new **Ashuwillticook Rail Trail** running south through Cheshire.

MUSIC

Tanglewood Music Festival (413-637-5165; off-season, 617-266-1492; box office, 617-266-1200 or 1-888-266-1200; bso .org), Tanglewood, entrance on West St. (MA 183) west of Lenox village. The Boston Symphony Orchestra's summer concert series, which opens July 4 and runs through August, has been held since the 1930s in a fan-shaped, open-sided hall understatedly referred to as "the Shed." The Koussevitzky Music Shed actually seats 5,000 people and has splendid acoustics. More than 14,000 patrons regularly converge on Tanglewood on weekends, but a concert is rarely sold out, and then it's usually for an appearance by a pop music superstar such as James Taylor. There is always room on the 500-acre grounds, though parking lots can fill up and postconcert traffic jams are legendary (which is why inns and B&Bs within walking distance of the main gate can charge premium rates). Many concertgoers actually prefer sitting on the lawn and come several hours early, dressed in high resort style (or any old way at all), bearing elaborate picnic baskets that have been known to include white linen tablecloths and candelabra. (*Note:* It does rain and bugs do bite on the lawn, so come prepared.) The lawn at Tanglewood is one of New England's great people-watching places, too. Many concerts are also staged in the 1,200-seat Seiji Ozawa Hall, which has an adjoining lawn that can accommodate several hundred.

Hilary Scott

JOHN WILLIAMS CONDUCTS THE BOSTON SYMPHONY ORCHESTRA AND YO-YO MA AT TANGLEWOOD ON PARADE.

Symphonic concerts (Fri. and Sat. evenings and Sun. afternoons) aside, the Tanglewood calendar is filled, beginning in mid-June, with classical music and other special concerts; there's also an annual Festival of Contemporary Music and a Labor Day weekend Jazz Festival, plus almost daily concerts by young musicians of the Tanglewood Music Center (TMC) Orchestra. The Boston Pops perform each summer, and there are Friday Prelude Concerts and Saturday morning open rehearsals. For information, call 1-888-266-1200 or visit tanglewood.org. Prices for seats in the Shed are $21–115 depending on seating and event, while lawn seats run $11–20; Ozawa Hall, $33–97. Open rehearsals in the Shed are $17, and opera performances in the theater are $65 and $110. TMC tickets are $11–51. Request a detailed schedule and order form. Children under 18 are free on the lawn.

THEATER

Shakespeare & Company (box office, 413-637-3353; off-season, 413-637-4274; shakespeare.org), 70 Kemble St., Lenox. Productions late May–Oct.; tickets run $10–65 depending on seating, theater, and performance. On opening and Saturday nights, $85 premium tickets that include early seating in choice seats, a glass of wine, and "a decadent dessert" also are available. There are a variety of discounts as well as some free performances. In existence for more than 30 years, this exciting theater company with a core of some 150 artists has a 30-acre property with two stages. The grounds are open to the public for strolling and picnicking. Although Shakespeare is the main dramatic fare, the company also does other classic plays as well as work by contemporary authors and short "salon" pieces based on stories by Edith Wharton and others. Major productions are staged at Founders Theatre, which can seat nearly 500 people. One of the company's long-term projects is a re-creation of The Rose—a three-tiered, thatch-roofed Elizabethan-era London theater. Until the money is raised to begin construction, the group makes do with "The Rose Footprint." This is a simple outdoor theater on the site of and with the same dimensions as the planned Elizabethan replica. It is covered with a tent in midsummer and is often used for productions featuring student actors.

SHAKESPEARE & COMPANY'S 2006 PRODUCTION OF THE *MERRY WIVES OF WINDSOR*.
Kevin Sprague

Barrington Stage Company (413-236-8888; barringtonstageco.org), 30 Union St., Pittsfield. Mainstage tickets $15–58; senior and student discounts; children free. Productions late May–late Oct. and Dec. Artistic director Julianne Boyd has orchestrated a number of major musical hits, most notably *The 25th Annual Putnam County Spelling Bee,* which became a long-running hit on Broadway. The company has restored a 500-seat vaudeville theater just off North Street for its main stage. Its Stage 2 is two blocks north in the Pittsfield VFW at 36 Linden St. BSC also mounts youth theater productions and sponsors a summer musical theater camp at St. Joseph's High School, 22 Maplewood Ave. Also check for special one-night performances and free events.

SANDY DUNCAN IN THE BARRINGTON STAGE COMPANY'S 2006 PRODUCTION OF *MAME.* Kevin Sprague

Williamstown Theatre Festival (413-597-3400; wtfestival.org), Williamstown. Since 1955 this festival has offered some of the best theater in the Northeast, staging some 200 performances of classic and new plays from the last week of June through August. It was the country's first summer theater to receive a Tony Award for sustained excellence, and it is housed in the sleek "62 Center for Theatre and Dance" at Williams College. Full-scale productions aside, you'll also find Nikos Stage performances, late-night musical cabarets, staged readings, and free theater. Parking is free, both across the street and in the neighboring garage.

THE NEW '62 CENTER FOR THEATRE AND DANCE AT WILLIAMS COLLEGE. Williams College

MUSEUMS

♿ **Sterling and Francine Clark Art Institute** (413-458-2303; clarkart.edu), 225 South St., Williamstown. Open July–Labor Day, daily 10–5; otherwise closed Mon. Free Nov.–May, adults $15 June–Oct.; also free for children under age 18 and students with ID. Inquire about the combination ticket with MASS MoCA and other cultural venues in the region. The permanent collection rivals those of many city museums. There are medieval works like a 15th-century panel painting by Piero della Francesca and works by such masters as Fragonard, Turner, and Goya. The museum is best known for its French impressionist paintings (Monet, Degas, Pissarro, and more than 30 Renoirs) and for its American period pieces by Winslow Homer, John Singer Sargent, and Frederic Remington. R. S. Clark (1877–1956), grandson to a founding partner in the Singer Sewing Machine Company, settled in Paris and began collecting art in 1912. When he met Francine (1876–1960), she was an actress with the Comedie Française. The couple collected avidly for their own pleasure, but considered donating everything to the Metropolitan Museum of Art before deciding in 1950 to build a museum to house it in this serene, safe town, far from the threat of nuclear war then felt in New York City. The white-marble building at the center of the current museum was opened in 1955. It has since been substantially expanded. The seasonal **Stone Hill Center** houses galleries for changing exhibits and a café with views of the Green Mountains and Taconics. The Clark is set on 140 acres of lawns, meadows, and walking trails spotted with picnic tables and benches.

THE IMPRESSIONIST GALLERY AT THE STERLING AND FRANCINE CLARK ART INSTITUTE.

Sterling and Francine Clark Art Institute

Inquire about concerts and other special programs, including a series of films and lectures.

♿ **Williams College Museum of Art** (413-597-2429; wcma.org), MA 2. Open Tues.–Sat. 10–5, Sun. 1–5. Free. This is one of the finest college art museums in the country, too often overlooked by visitors. It's easily accessible from Spring Street (Williamstown's shopping drag) as well as from Main Street (MA 2). The striking building combines an 1846, two-story octagon with a major three-story addition designed by Charles Moore and filled with unconventional spaces. The museum has an outstanding permanent collection of American 19th- and 20th-century works by Eakins, Hassam, Feininger, Rivers, and Hopper, and represents the world's largest collection of works by Charles and Maurice Prendergast. Exhibits change frequently.

♿ **Massachusetts Museum of Contemporary Art** (MASS MoCA; 413-662-2111; massmoca.org), 87 Marshall St., North Adams. Open daily 11–5, closed Tues. except in July and Aug., when it's open every day 10–6. Adults $15, ages 6–16 $5, students $10. Inquire about Kidspace, an interactive area with special exhibits for kids, open daily in summer months noon–4 and weekends off-season (but call to check). Also inquire about the seasonal combination ticket with the Clark Art Institute. Check the schedule of upcoming programs, which might include weekend films, Saturday night dance parties, and varied special exhibits and events. MASS MoCA exhibits change so constantly that it's pointless to describe what we last saw here, but one thing we notice consistently is that as we wander from gallery to gallery, our perceptions alter. In contrast to a traditional museum in which you focus on one painting or sculpture after another, here the size of the viewing space itself changes constantly: One moment you are in a small blackened room mesmerized by a computer-composed choreography, and the next you are faced with a gallery as big as a football field, its walls stamped and streamed with myriad shapes and colors. Finally stepping outside, you may see actors filming while in another mill yard workers may be installing a stage for the night's performance. The mill's old bell tower tolls the quarter-hour in muted tones (the volume of this "sound art" varies with the intensity of the sun), while in front of it upside-down trees, presented by the Clark Art Institute as a welcoming present, appear to thrive. If conventional museums are boxes, MASS MoCA is more of an open platform. The lines between the exterior and interior of the building, between art and urban reality, blur. The 15 galleries fill four large buildings in this 25-building complex connected by the courtyards, viaducts, and elevated walkways that evolved to house Arnold Print Works (1860–1942), one of the world's leading textile producers. Sprague Electric Company occupied the complex from

1942–85, at its height employing 4,137 workers. In 1986, when Williams College Museum of Art director Thomas Krens was searching for a space to display large modern art pieces, North Adams mayor John Barrett III showed him the vacant Sprague mill buildings. The ups and downs of the project, shepherded by MASS MoCA's current director, Joseph Thompson, over the next dozen years, easily fill a book. **Lickety Split,** the museum's café, is open for breakfast (you can come in before the museum opens) and lunch as well as during after arts events; **Gramercy Bistro** (see *Dining Out*) is next door. Inquire about guided tours and audio guides. Local historian Paul W. Marino (413-663-3809; historyman@fiam.net) offers free, seasonal tours of downtown.

✐ **Hancock Shaker Village** (413-443-0188; hancockshakervillage.org), 5 miles west of Pittsfield on US 20 at its junction with MA 41; use the Mass Pike West Stockbridge exit (take MA 41 north to US 20 west). Open Apr.–Oct., daily 10–5. Adults $17, ages 13–17 $8, children 12 and younger free. Inquire about frequent special events. Founded in 1783, this "City of Peace" was the third of what would eventually number 19 Shaker communities stretching from Maine to Kentucky (see *Shakers* in "What's Where"). In the mid-19th century it numbered some 250 brethren divided among six "families" farming 3,000 acres. It survived until 1959.

THE MASSACHUSETTS MUSEUM OF CONTEMPORARY ART, BETTER KNOWN AS MASS MOCA.

Christina Tree

In 1960 the village's buildings were about to be sold to a neighboring racetrack when a group of Pittsfield residents rallied and bought the entire community—including more than 1,000 acres—from its last Shaker sisters. Since then it has evolved into a 20-building museum housing the premier collection of Shaker artifacts on any original Shaker site. The buildings have been restored, including the much-copied and -photographed Round Stone Barn, and the five-story Brick Dwelling House, built in 1830 to house 100 Shaker brethren and sisters.

A scattering of tidy buildings surrounded by its own orchards and meadows, the village looks like some primitive painter's vision of the heavenly kingdom. The guides, craftsmen, and furnishings all tell about the dancing sisters and brethren who turned farming, craftsmanship, and invention into visible prayers. Note the frequent special events staged throughout the year. During fall and on holiday weekends, Shaker Suppers are served in the Brick Dwelling House (call or visit the website for reservations). The visitors center includes a Center for Shaker Studies and a gallery displaying the village's "spirit drawing" collection, an orientation theater, a changing exhibit gallery, and a gift shop selling yarn, herbs, books, tapes, and crafts made on the premises. It also includes a café with a children's menu. Families should take care not to miss the hands-on Discovery Room in the 1910 barn: Visitors can weave and spin, try on Shaker-style clothes, milk MaryJane (a life-sized replica cow), sample 19th-century toys and games, and check out the beehive and newly hatched chickens. Inquire about the **Shaker Trail** leading to the adjacent **Pittsfield State Forest,** traveling past the sites of old Shaker dwellings and religious ceremonies. During summer months inquire about the day's schedule of thematic tours and crafts demonstrations.

HANCOCK SHAKER VILLAGE.

Christina Tree

MORE MUSEUMS 🏵 ✐ **Berkshire Museum** (413-443-7171; berkshiremuseum.org), 39 S. Main St. (US 7, just south of Park Square), Pittsfield. Open Mon.–Sat. 10–5, Sun. noon–5. Adults $13, seniors and students $6.50, ages 3–18 $6. An example of what a regional museum should be. Founded in 1903 by Dalton philanthropist Zenas Crane, its no less than eight galleries display both permanent and changing exhibits. Check the website for current special exhibits, as these are invariably worth a visit. The permanent collection includes American and European paintings, 15th- to 18th-century European works, and contemporary art, along with ancient artifacts that include a 2,000-year-old mummy. There are also interactive exhibits based on toys by Alexander Calder, and children love the "Dino Dig" in the Gallery of Dinosaurs; the natural history collection of shells, gemstones, and fossils; and the aquarium featuring fish from throughout the world, as well as reptiles, spiders, local animals, and birds. Note the annual Festival of Trees in Nov.–Dec. There are frequent films, performances, lectures, and concerts in the **Little Cinema,** a 300-seat theater.

Crane Museum of Papermaking (413-684-6481; crane.com/about-us), off E. Housatonic St. (MA 8/I-90), 30 South St., Dalton. Open early June–mid-Oct., weekdays 1–5. Free and worth a stop. Housed in the rag room of the **Old Stone Mill** (1844) beside the Housatonic, the displays and a video tell the story of papermaking from rags and include a fascinating variety of paper money. Crane Paper is the sole supplier of "money paper" to the U.S. Mint; the company has been in the family for five generations.

Frelinghuysen Morris House & Studio (413-637-0166; frelinghuysen.org), 92 Hawthorne St., Lenox. Open June 23–Labor Day, Thurs.–Sun. 10–3; Labor

OUTSIDE THE BERKSHIRE MUSEUM.

Christina Tree

BERKSHIRE AUTHORS

Christina Tree

THE MOUNT, EDITH WHARTON'S HOME IN LENOX.

The Mount (413-551-5111; edithwharton.org), 2 Plunkett St. (junction of US 7 and MA 7A), Lenox. Open early May–Oct., daily 10–5. Adults $16, students $13, children younger than 18 free. The Georgian-style home of novelist **Edith Wharton** (1862–1937), built in 1902, incorporates many of the ideas articulated in her influential book *The Decoration of Houses,* which denounced the excesses of Victorian interior design and urged a return to the simplicity of earlier eras. Wharton had a hand in designing the formal gardens as well as the building, and also chose its furnishings. The resulting mansion is special indeed and once more looks as it did in Wharton's day: Nearly $9 million was spent to restore the 42-room house and magnificent formal gardens. Also meticulously restored was Wharton's sumptuous bedroom suite—it has French marble fireplaces, oil-painted floral wall panels, gilded mirrors—and the gardens where she did much of her writing. Her original 2,700-volume library is on display as well. Included in the admission price is a 45-minute tour (given by volunteers from Edith Wharton Restoration, Inc.) that conveys a sense of her life and work. A café on the long terrace off the dining room, open daily 11–4, has a superb view over the gardens to the hills beyond. Special events include changing exhibits on aspects of Wharton's life, free dramatic readings of her works, and talks, readings, and book signings by well-known writers. Although best known for novels that examined the social mores of her day, Wharton was also a master of the ghost story. On Friday nights from June through October, The Mount presents "Friday Night Fright," a 90-minute tour of parts of the estate reputed to be haunted. Adults $20, children under 18 $10. The tour is not recommended for children under 8. Reservations required.

Herman Melville (1819–91) spent 13 of his happiest, most productive years at Arrowhead, a farm on the southern edge of Pittsfield that's now headquarters for the Berkshire County Historical Society. Forced to work after his father's bankruptcy and death, Melville held a number of jobs, joined the Merchant Marines, and—at age 22—set sail on the whaler *Acushnet.* He jumped ship in the Marquesas Islands and spent time in Hawaii before returning to Boston, where he wrote *Typee,* followed by several more South Seas–based novels. Established as a writer, he married and in 1850 brought his wife, Lizzie, and baby son, Malcolm, to spend the summer at his uncle's fine house (now the Pittsfield Country Club) on US 7.

It was on a famous rainy picnic atop Monument Mountain that he met Nathaniel Hawthorne (then living at Tanglewood in Lenox). The two young writers bonded instantly, and Melville was influenced by Hawthorne to become a year-round Berkshire resident. He bought a farm just up the road from his uncle, one commanding the same splendid view of Mount Greylock—which is said to have inspired his grandly conceived story of the great white whale and the mad sea captain. Melville penned *Moby-Dick* in a study overlooking the mountain. In all he wrote four novels, a collection of short stories, 10 magazine pieces, and the beginning of a book of poetry in this wonderfully rambling 18th-century house with its central hearth (described in the short story *I and My Chimney*). Unlike his far more famous neighbor, Oliver Wendell Holmes, Melville seems to have been somewhat aloof, preferring to farm and write rather than to party.

Arrowhead, which is furnished with many original pieces, evokes Melville the author and father who had difficulty supporting his wife and four children despite his prodigious literary output. Melville eventually sold the farm to his brother and moved to New York, where he worked in the Customs House for more than 20 years, earning $4 per hour and finding time to write only poetry and, eventually, *Billy Budd,* published in 1924, 33 years after his death.

Arrowhead (413-442-1793; mobydick.org), 780 Holmes Rd. (off US 7/20), Pittsfield, is open Memorial Day–Columbus Day, daily 9:30–5; tours on the hour or by appointment. Adults $12, students with ID $8. There is a gift shop selling books by and about Melville, and the 44-acre grounds include a walking trail. Inquire about special exhibits.

Note: Melville buffs should also find the **Herman Melville Memorial Room** in the **Berkshire Athenaeum** (413-499-9480, ext. 204), Pittsfield's public library at 1 Wendell Ave. on Park Square. It contains every book about, as well as by, the author and such artifacts as the desk on which he wrote *Billy Budd.* **Canoe Meadows,** the former property of Oliver Wendell Holmes (see *Birding*), is just up Holmes Road.

AN 1861 PHOTO OF HERMAN MELVILLE.

Rodney Dewey, courtesy of Berkshire Athenaeum

Day–Columbus Day, Thurs.–Sat. 10–3. Adults $12, seniors $10.50, students with ID $6. An architecturally interesting 1940s house (a starkly white Bauhaus-style building with art deco decor) on 46 acres bordering Tanglewood. The furnishings are original (cutting-edge modern for the era) and the walls hung with paintings by the owners and their contemporaries, including Picasso, Braque, Léger, and Gris.

Ventfort Hall (413-637-3206; gildedage.org), 104 Walker St., Lenox. Open daily, except holidays, weekends 10–3, weekdays 10–5. An imposing Elizabethan-style mansion in the center of Lenox built in 1894 for Sarah Morgan, sister of financier J. P. Morgan, Ventfort Hall is now "the Museum of the Gilded Age." A popular venue for weddings and private functions, the building is also used for lectures, theatrical performances, and "Victorian teas," and also has permanent and changing exhibits. Some rooms have been restored and furnished in period style. An ongoing exhibit, "Les Petites Dames de Modes," features 59 doll-sized "models" illustrating changing fashions from 1855–1914. Admission with guided tour: adults $16, ages 5–17 $5.

Western Gateway Heritage State Park (413-663-6312), Furnace St., North Adams. Open year-round, daily 10–5. Housed in a former railroad freight shed, its sophisticated displays tell the epic story of the construction of the 4.75-mile-long Hoosac Tunnel, one of 19th-century America's greatest engineering feats. The tunnel took 25 years to build, from 1850–75, claimed nearly 200 lives, pioneered use of the explosive nitroglycerine, and cost $20 million—a vast sum for the time. An audiovisual presentation takes visitors back in time with the sounds of dripping water, pickaxes striking stone, nitroglycerine explosions, and a political debate about the merits of the massive project. Displays also depict other aspects of North Adams's history and include a miniature railroad with a precise diorama of the city in its heyday. There are changing arts and crafts exhibits, too. Other buildings in the "Park" contain the Freight Yard Pub, shops, and the volunteer-operated.

VENTFORT HALL, "THE MUSEUM OF THE GILDED AGE."

Christina Tree

North Adams Museum of History and Science (413-664-4700; northadamshistory.org). Open Apr.–Dec., Thurs.–Sat. 10–4, Sun. 1–4; off-season, Sat. 10–4, Sun. 1–4. Free. This fascinating museum fills three

DEM/John Crispin

WESTERN GATEWAY HERITAGE STATE PARK.

floors of a former coal storage shed with exhibits on North Adams history and industry. Hands-on history and science discovery rooms are geared to children, and working model trains will delight rail buffs. Donations requested.

SCENIC DRIVES **Mount Greylock Scenic Byway.** The 16.3-mile road system accessing the 3,491-foot-high summit of Mount Greylock has been recently resurfaced and is the most dramatic and scenic drive in the Berkshires (see the "Mount Greylock" sidebar for details).

Mohawk Trail Scenic Byway. Even if you don't drive to the northern Berkshires via MA 2, better known as the Mohawk Trail, be sure to drive from North Adams up along MA 2 to the western summit and park at the Wigwam Cabins for "the three-state view" before plunging back down the well-named Hairpin Turn as it zigs and zags its way into North Adams. See the "Along the Mohawk Trail" chapter.

Williamstown to Pittsfield. Along US 7 south through South Williamstown, the views are of high meadows and mountains. Turn onto MA 43 and follow it through the steep, mostly wooded Jericho Valley to the village of Hancock; continue on into New York state and turn south onto MA 22. At the high school in New Lebanon, make a sharp left east onto US 20 and continue over Lebanon Mountain. Stop by **Hancock Shaker Village,** then continue east to Pittsfield.

Greylock Glen, Adams. MA 8 is the main north–south drag through Adams, but find your way up to parallel West Road and then take Gould Road. This quiet old road climbs up past an apple orchard to the glorious high meadow that's been the object of a series of development schemes, including a ski area, a gambling casino, and a high-altitude cross-country resort. Today it is a Department of

Conservation and Recreation state park. There is a small parking lot at the trailheads for the Bellows Pipe and Gould Trails. It is a scenic but steep climb to the summit from here. While the area is webbed with hiking and biking trails, few are marked. A pavilion and field by a small pond offer a scenic location to picnic. Dogs must be kept leashed because there are beavers in the pond. It's a magical spot.

✷ To Do

BIKING Ashuwillticook Rail Trail (berkshirebikepath.com) is an 11-mile, paved, multiuse trail from the visitors center in Adams south to Berkshire Mall Road in Lanesborough. It parallels MA 8, but also follows the shores of Berkshire Pond and Cheshire Reservoir for several miles, replacing tracks first laid in 1845 that remained in use until 1990.

Rental bikes are available at **Berkshire Outfitters** (413-743-5900; berkshire outfitters.com) on MA 8 south of Adams.

The Mountain Goat (413-458-8445; themountaingoat.com), 130 Water St. in Williamstown, is an excellent source of biking information in the Williamstown area. Recommended: MA 43 along the Green River. **Plaine's Bike & Ski** (413-499-0294; plaines.com), 55 W. Housatonic St. (US 20) in Pittsfield, also rents bikes and is a source of local cycling info.

Jiminy Peak (413-738-5500; www.jiminypeak.com) rents mountain bikes in summer, along with use of lifts and 14 trails, some singletrack and some downhill cruises. Helmets are required. An all-day trail and lift access pass is $24 (bikes and helmets not included).

THE ASHUWILLTICOOK RAIL TRAIL IS A GREAT PLACE TO WALK OR BIKE.
A. Blake Gardnew/Berkshire Visitors Bureau

Jiminy Peak
MOUNTAIN BIKING AT JIMINY PEAK.

Berkshire Cycling Association (www.berkshirecycling.org), based in Pittsfield, schedules frequent rides. And *Rubel Western Massachusetts Bicycle and Road Map* (Rubel Bike Maps) is highly recommended for its in-depth coverage of the area. At this writing, an excellent, free *Berkshire Bike Touring* map/guide, based on Rubel, is available from the regional information sources listed under *Guidance*.

BOATING In Lenox, the **Arcadian Shop** (413-637-3010; arcadian.com) rents both kayaks and canoes. **Berkshire Canoe Tours** (413-442-2789; berkshirecanoetours.org) offers guided tours on the Housatonic from Decker's Landing, and guided tours are available through the **Pleasant Valley Wildlife Sanctuary** (413-637-0320; massaudubon.org).

The Hoosic River flows north from **Cheshire Lake,** offering some good kayaking and canoeing along the way. Check in with **Berkshire Outfitters** (413-743-5900; berkshireoutfitters.com), MA 8 south of Adams, for canoe and kayak rentals as well as sales and guidance (closed Mon.).

Canoes and boats also can be rented at **Windsor Lake** (413-662-3198) in North Adams.

Cheshire Reservoir (also known as Hoosac Lake) on MA 8 in Cheshire offers a good launch area, as does **Richmond Pond** on Swamp Road in Richmond. **Berry Pond** in Pittsfield State Forest (see *Green Space*), one of the highest ponds in the state, is also accessible for kayaks and canoes. On **Pontoosuc Lake** in Pittsfield, **U-Drive-A-Boat** (413-442-7020 or 413-281-4916; 1651 North St.) offers a variety of boat rentals. On neighboring **Onota Lake, Onota Boat Livery** (413-442-1724; onotaboat.com) rents motorboats, pontoon boats, sailboats, kayaks, and canoes.

PONTOOSUC LAKE IN PITTSFIELD OFFERS EXCELLENT BOATING AND FISHING.
Christina Tree

Berkshire Rowing and Sculling Society (413-442-7769; berkshirerowing.com), Pittsfield. Lew Cuyler rents and offers instruction in an unusually lightweight and stable scull for use on Onota Lake.

CAMPING The Massachusetts Department of Conservation and Recreation publishes a handy map/guide and maintains a visitor-friendly regional office on US 7 south of Pittsfield (413-442-8928; mass.gov/dcr). For reservations, call 1-877-422-6762. Primitive campsites can be found in the **Mount Greylock State Reservation** (see sidebar under *Green Space*) and in **Pittsfield State Forest** (13 rustic campsites on Berry Pond at the top of Berry Mountain, 18 at the Parker Brook campground at the mountain's base; flush and nonflush toilets, no showers or hook-ups).

♿ **Historic Valley Park Campground at Windsor Lake** (413-662-3198), 200 Windsor Lake Rd., North Adams. Open May–mid-Oct. This city-operated facility on a quiet lake minutes from downtown, North Adams, and MA 2 offers 100 campsites ranging from water and electric hook-up sites to tent-only sites; some walk-in tent sites and some lakeside. Under new management in 2011, the campground now has handicapped-accessible bathrooms with hot showers. Even in August there are usually vacancies midweek.

For other private campgrounds, contact the **Massachusetts Association of Campground Owners** (781-544-3475; campmass.com).

State Forests and Parks

The Massachusetts Department of Conservation and Recreation publishes a handy map/guide and maintains a visitor-friendly regional office on US 7 south of Pittsfield (413-442-8928; mass.gov/dcr). For reservations, call 1-877-422-6762. Campsites are located in **Clarksburg State Park** (50 campsites near Mauserts Pond; flush toilets and showers but no hook-ups); **Mount Greylock State Reservation** (primitive campsites and backpacker shelters; no flush toilets, showers, or hook-ups); and **Pittsfield State Forest** (13 rustic campsites on Berry Pond at the top of Berry Mountain, 18 at the Parker Brook campground at the mountain's base; flush and nonflush toilets, no showers or hook-ups). See *Green Space* for details about these preserves; also see **Savoy Mountain State Forest** in "Along the Mohawk Trail."

FOR FAMILIES Jiminy Peak Mountain Adventure Park (413-738-5500; jiminypeak.com), Corey Rd. between US 7 and MA 43, Hancock. Open mid-June–Labor Day, daily 10–8; Memorial Day–mid-June and early Sept.–mid-Oct., weekends 10–6. A dozen attractions include the Mountain Coaster, which provides a ride through the woods down several thousand feet of twisting track, an Alpine slide, a giant swing, a rock climbing wall, and an Aerial Adventure Park.

Play Bousquet (413-442-8316; www.bousquets.com), Dan Fox Dr., Pittsfield. Open Memorial Day– Columbus Day. This small ski area is a summer family fun park with waterslides and an activity pool, miniature golf and a driving range, a go-cart track, a climbing wall, and chairlift rides.

Also see Museums, Farms, and Special Events.

Jiminy Peak

A THRILLING TRIP AT JIMINY PEAK'S AERIAL ADVENTURE PARK.

FISHING Licenses (required for age 15 and older) are available at local sporting goods stores and by contacting the **Division of Fisheries and Wildlife** (413-447-9789; masswildlife.org), 400 Hubbard Ave., Pittsfield. The Green River is a famous trout stream. Anglers should also check out Cheshire Reservoir in Cheshire, Mauserts Pond in Clarksburg, Windsor Lake in North Adams (where you can rent a boat), Onota and Pontoosuc Lakes in Pittsfield, and Richmond Pond in Richmond. Also see **Savoy Mountain State Forest** in "Along the Mohawk Trail"; it's accessible from MA 2 just east of North Adams.

GOLF **Cranwell Golf Course** (413-637-1364; cranwell.com), Lee Rd. (US 20), Lenox, is an 18-hole championship par-70 course. There's a *Golf Digest* School as well as a driving range, pro shop, and full-service spa. Sloane's Tavern serves lunch. Also see *Lodging*.

Bas Ridge Golf Course (413-655-2605; basridge.tripod.com), 151 Plunkett Ave. (off MA 8), Hinsdale. Eighteen challenging but user-friendly holes.

Donnybrook Country Club (413-499-7888), 755 Williamstown Rd. (US 7), a recent addition with sweeping views.

Pontoosuc Lake Country Club (413-445-4217), Kirkwood Dr., Pittsfield. Eighteen holes, reasonable rates, snacks, beverages.

Skyline Country Club (413-445-5584), 405 S. Main St. (US 7), Lanesborough. Eighteen holes; dining area with pub menu.

Wahconah Country Club (413-684-1333), Orchard Rd. in Dalton. Eighteen holes, highly rated, full facilities.

Taconic Golf Club (413-458-3997), Meachem St., Williamstown. Open daily mid-Apr.–mid-Nov., but only Tues.–Fri. to the public.

Waubeeka Golf Links (413-458-8355; waubeeka.com), 137 New Ashford Rd. (US 7), South Williamstown. Open daily, Apr.–mid-Nov. Eighteen holes, driving range, full practice facility, great views.

North Adams Country Club (413-663-7887), River Rd., Clarksburg. Nine holes.

HIKING More than 100,000 acres of Berkshire County (75 percent) is wooded, and 86 miles of the **Appalachian Trail** traverse the county. The number and

Sterling and Francine Clark Art Institute

IN WILLIAMSTOWN, THE CLARK ART'S 140 ACRES INCLUDE HIKING PATHS THAT ARE OPEN TO THE PUBLIC YEAR-ROUND.

variety of walking and hiking trails, many dating to the 19th century, are amazing. They are described in several books, notably *Hikes & Walks in the Berkshire Hills* by Lauren R. Stevens, *A Guide to Natural Places in the Berkshire Hills* by René Laubach, and *Wildflowers of the Berkshire & Taconic Hills* by Joseph G. Strauch Jr., all published by Berkshire House. The *Appalachian Mountain Club Guide to Massachusetts*, published by AMC Books, is also extremely helpful. Also see the trails described in this chapter's *Green Space.*

A GREAT SPOT TO PICNIC ON MOUNT GREYLOCK RESERVATION

Christina Tree

Mount Greylock. More than 70 miles of trails in the Mount Greylock Reservation include more than 11 miles of the Appalachian Trail. The (literally) top hike in North Berkshire is from the summit of Mount Greylock. See the "Mount Greylock" sidebar under *Green Space.*

Hopkins Memorial Forest (413-597-2346), Northwest Hill Rd., Williamstown. A 2,050-acre preserve owned by Williams College with a network of hiking (and, in winter, cross-country skiing) and nature trails. The **Hopkins Farm Museum** and a botanical garden are also here.

Field Farm (413-458-3135; thetrustees.org), Sloan Rd., South Williamstown. Four miles of foot trails wander through meadows, cropland, marsh, and forest with spectacular views of Mount Greylock to the east. Waterfowl frequent the pond and the lime-rich soil nurtures an abundance of wildflowers. There are two buildings on the property, an outstanding 1950s home (see **The Guest House at Field Farm** under *Lodging*) and "The Folly," a small house designed by noted architect Ulrich Franzen and open to the public by appointment ($5 per adult for nonmembers). From the intersection of MA 43 and US 7, take MA 43 west and then make an immediate right onto Sloan Road; the reservation is 1 mile down the road. This is also a favorite local cross-country skiing venue.

Sheep Hill (413-458-2492; www.wrlf.org), 671 Cold Spring Rd., Williamstown. This 50-acre spread of woods and meadows offers trails, access to more trails, and the Mary and Craig Lewis Center for Nature (open Mon.–Fri. 9–5)—a farmhouse by Josiah's Pond that's home to the Williamstown Rural Lands Foundation and offers educational nature programs for all ages.

Taconic Crest Trail. The 35-mile ridgeline trail along the western rim of Berkshire County is accessible from Hopkins Memorial Forest, Field Farm, and several other trailheads in North Berkshire, but it should not be attempted without a trail map.

Hoosac Range Trail. Begun in the summer of 2010, this 3-mile hiking/snowshoeing path is due to open this summer (2011) with access from the top of the Hairpin Turn in North Adams. It begins just east of the former Wigwam Shop and continues along the ridge with spectacular views, ending at Spruce Hill in Savoy Mountain State Forest.

Serious hikers should pick up a copy of the *North Berkshire Outdoor Guide* published by the Williams Outing Club and available at The Mountain Goat (see *Bicycling*). *Nature Walks in the Berkshire Hills* by Charles W. G. Smith (AMC) and *Hikes & Walks in the Berkshire Hills* by Lauren Stevens (Berkshire House) are both very useful.

Also see *Green Space.*

HORSEBACK RIDING **Undermountain Farm** (413-637-3365; undermountainfarm.com), 400 Undermountain Rd., Lenox. Year-round lessons, trail rides.

Berkshire Horseback Adventures (413-637-9090; berkshirehorseback.net), 293 Main St., Lenox. Located in the Aspinwall Adult Equestrian Center. Scenic trail rides and overnight camping trips.

✐ **Harmony Trails Horseback Riding** (413-442-6101), 659 Kirchner Rd., Dalton. Family-friendly horseback and pony rides, beautiful views.

DeMayo's Bonnie Lea Farm (413-458-3149; bonnielea.com), US 7, Williamstown. Guided cross-country trail rides for riders older than 13; by appointment only.

Also see **Sunny Banks Ranch** in the "Southern Berkshire County" chapter for Western-style riding.

RAILWAY EXCURSION ✐ **Berkshire Scenic Railway Museum** (413-637-2210; berkshirescenicrailroad.org), 10 Willow Creek Rd., Lenox. Weekends and federal holidays from Memorial Day weekend through October, with some special events through December. There are two daily 90-minute excursions between Lenox and Stockbridge, as well as a 45-minute journey between Lenox and Lee. Vintage coaches and a veteran diesel locomotive are used, and a uniformed conductor narrates the scenic trip along the banks of the Housatonic River. Excursions begin from the old Lenox depot, which houses a gift shop and a museum that includes model train displays and an exhibit on the role of railroads in the Berkshires' Gilded Age. Adults $15, seniors $14, children under 14 $8 for the Stockbridge trip; $9, $8, and $5, respectively, for Lee.

SPAS AND FITNESS CENTERS The region's destination spas—**Cranwell, Canyon Ranch,** and **Kripalu**—are listed under *Lodging.* The **Lenox Fitness Center and Spa** (413-637-9893; lenoxfitnesscenter.com) also offers a fitness center and daily programs plus spa treatments. Thanks to the destination spas, there are also probably more massage therapists per capita in this area than anywhere in the country. Several more day spas are around, and many inns have massage therapists on call.

YOGA ON THE LAWN AT KRIPALU.
Kripalu Center for Yoga and Health

TENNIS Berkshire West Athletic Club (413-499-4600), Dan Fox Dr., Pittsfield, has four outdoor and five indoor courts. **Ponterril/YMCA** (413-499-0687), US 7, Pontoosuc Lake, Pittsfield, has six clay courts; fee for nonmembers.

SWIMMING ✐ **Sands Spring Pool and Spa** (413-458-5202), Sands Spring Rd. (off US 7 north of Williamstown; turn at the Cozy Corner Motel and Restaurant). Open May–Sept., daily 11–7. This attractive 50-by-75-foot pool is fed year-round by mineral springs that were well known to the Native Americans for centuries. It's surrounded by lawn on which patrons spread their towels; there are picnic tables and some lawn sports. Billed as the oldest spa in the U.S., it was formally established in 1813 and in 1842 became the centerpiece for a resort hotel. The century-old pavilion survives and includes a snack bar, changing rooms, and whirlpool. The pool is sparkling clean,

Christina Tree

SANDS SPRING POOL AND SPA IN WILLIAMSTOWN.

74 degrees, and genuinely exhilarating. There's a separate wading pool for preswimmers and a sauna. Inquire about fitness classes and swim lessons.

Windsor Lake (413-662-3198), off Kemp Ave., North Adams. This pleasant city-run beach is set in a 180-acre preserve and seems miles from the mills that are just blocks away. There's a pavilion, lifeguards, and, just off the lake, 100 campsites (see *Camping*). Nonresidents pay a nominal fee per car.

Margaret Lindley Park (MA 2 and US 7), Williamstown, is a well-kept town pool with changing rooms and picnic tables; daily charge for nonresidents. Open summer and school vacation, daily 11–7.

See also **Clarksburg State Park and Pittsfield State Forest** under *Green Space,* and **North Pond** in Savoy Mountain State Forest under "Along the Mohawk Trail."

✷ Winter Sports

DOWNHILL SKIING ✐ **Jiminy Peak** (413-738-5500; snow phone: 1-888-4-JIMINY; jiminypeak.com), 37 Corey Rd., Hancock, open mid-Nov.–mid-Apr., full time from Dec. on, weather permitting, 8:30 AM–10 PM. Set high in the Jericho Valley, a narrow corridor that runs east–west between MA 43 and US 7. Jiminy Peak is a self-contained four-season resort—the largest ski and snowboarding resort in southern New England—with two- to four-bedroom rental condos. You'll also find a 105-suite inn (see *Lodging*). Family geared, it offers a full range of children's programs. On-site dining includes **John Harvard's Restaurant & Brewery** and **Christiansen's Tavern**.

Vertical drop: 1,150 feet.

Terrain: 45 slopes and trails.

Lifts: One six-passenger, two quads, three triples, one double chair, two surface lifts.

Snowmaking: 96 percent of area.

Facilities: The Children's Center accommodates up to 350 SKIwee and Explorer program participants and has its own rental shop and cafeteria; it also offers a playroom for children not skiing. Restaurants include John Harvard's Restaurant & Brewery and Hendrick's Summit Lodge. Winter Mountain Coaster.

Rates: Adults $59, teens $51, juniors and seniors $44; less for four hours, more on holidays. Lodging-skiing packages.

✐ **Bousquet** (413-442-8316; bousquets.com), Dan Fox Drive, Pittsfield. Marked from US 7/US 20 south of town. The Berkshires' oldest ski area, opened in 1932, and the one that pioneered both the ski train and night skiing. Noted for friendly slopes ideal for beginning and intermediate skiers. Open daily 9–9 (closes Sun. at 4) in winter for skiing, snowboarding, and tubing; also nightly except Sunday for skiing and boarding. Inquire about condo lodging on the adjacent property.

Vertical drop: 750 feet.

Terrain: 23 trails.

Lifts: Three double chairs, two surface lifts.

Facilities: Restaurant, ski school, rentals.

Rates: $37 weekends and holidays, Sun. $25; Mon.–Thurs. $20; night skiing $20; snow tubing $15; Thurs. night skiing $10.

JIMINY PEAK'S SIX-PASSENGER CHAIRLIFT.

Jiminy Peak

CROSS-COUNTRY SKIING **Hilltop Orchards** (1-800-833-6274; hilltop orchards.com), 508 Canaan Rd. (I-295) off MA 41, Richmond. Open Thurs.–Sun., possibly more depending on snow. This 200-acre hilltop orchard straddles the New York/Massachusetts line, offering fairly dependable conditions and sweeping views. Trails are designed by Winter Olympic athlete John Morton. Trails are tracked for skating and traditional stride, and there are snowshoe trails as well (rentals available). Trail fee. The lodge with its big hearth doubles as a site for free tastings of Furnace Brook Wine, made here. The Farm Winery Store also offers hot chocolate, cider, baked goods, and cheeses. No cross-country rentals. Inquire about guided tours.

Cranwell Resort (413-637-1364 or 1-800-272-6935; cranwell.com), Lee Rd., Lenox, offers more than 6 miles of groomed golf course trails, equipment rentals, and instruction. Full-service spa and dining.

Notchview Reservation (413-684-0148; notchview.org), 83 Old MA 9, Windsor. The highest cross-country trails in Massachusetts are found on this 3,000-acre Trustees of Reservations property. Admittedly, it takes a new snowfall to work your way up to the summit of 2,297-foot-high Judges Hill, but 17 miles of the 25-mile system are groomed, winding through 3,100 acres of forest and meadow. The panoramic view from this open area includes the notch in the hills cut by the Westfield River. Trail fee.

Kennedy Park in Lenox also offers easy access to an extensive trail system; rental equipment is available next door at the Arcadian Shop.

Also see **Canterbury Farm** in Becket in the "Southern Berkshire County" chapter and **Stump Sprouts** in "The Hilltowns" and "West County." Rentals are available in Lenox at the **Arcadian Shop** (413-637-3010; arcadianshop.com) and in Adams at **Berkshire Outfitters** (413-743-5900; berkshireoutfitters.com), MA 8. Cross-country skiers are welcome on the **Taconic Golf Course** and on the **Stone Hill** trails. Also see *Green Space.*

SNOWMOBILING Snowmobiling is permitted in six local state parks and forests, including the Mount Greylock Reservation (413-499-4262) on summit access roads, conditions permitting. Check with the Pittsfield office of the Department of Conservation and Recreation (413-442-8928).

✷ Green Space

STATE PARKS AND FORESTS *Note:* The Massachusetts Department of Conservation and Recreation publishes a handy map/guide and maintains a visitor-friendly regional office on US 7 south of Pittsfield (413-442-8928; mass.gov/dcr).

✐ **Natural Bridge State Park** (413-663-6392), MA 8, North Adams. Open Memorial Day–Columbus Day. $2 parking fee. The centerpiece of this 47-acre park is an unusual geologic formation, a white-marble bridge spanning a steep chasm that has attracted tourists since the 1830s, when Nathaniel Hawthorne compared the stream churning through its depths to "a heart that has been rent asunder by a torrent." A series of dramatic (but child-safe) paths and stairways offers views of the waterfall and rock formations. There are picnic tables, nature

MAGNIFICENT MOUNT GREYLOCK

Mount Greylock State Reservation (413-499-4262; mass.gov/dcr/parks /mtGreylock). The highest point in Massachusetts is an extraordinary place, easily accessible by recently resurfaced roads (open mid May–Nov. 1, weather permitting).

The 60- to 90-mile, five-state vistas from the 3,491-foot-high summit was described in 1799 by Timothy Dwight, president of Yale University, as "immense and of amazing grandeur." Dwight's widely read guidebook may have inspired many subsequent visitors, including Nathaniel Hawthorne, who compared the "high mountain swells" of the Taconics on the west to "immense, subsiding waves," and Henry David Thoreau, who bushwhacked up and spent the night on top, waking to "an ocean of mist . . . and undulating country of clouds."

Currently at the summit you can climb spiraling steps in the 92-foot high 1930s futuristic **Veterans War Memorial Tower.** Picnic on the grass above ledges that drop away to the east or enjoy the view south to Pittsfield from a table in the many-windowed dining rooms at **Bascom Lodge** (413-743-1591; bascomlodge.net). This handsome stone lodging was built in the 1930s by the Civilian Conservation Corps and has been upgraded under current management, offering meals and lodging late May–Oct 31. It's currently a destination for sunset dining, workshops, and lectures (check the website and see *Dining Out*). Rooms for families and couples as well as groups are also offered (see *Other Lodging*). It's truly magical to watch the sky color at sunset and then the stars appear while the villages and city of Pittsfield light up far below, and it's especially enjoyable when you don't have to drive down that night.

Note the "interpretive stones" scattered along trails around the summit recalling the experiences here of notables who have come

THE MASSACHUSETTS VETERANS WAR MEMORIAL TOWER, A DISTINCTIVE FEATURE OF THE MOUNT GREYLOCK STATE RESERVATION. Christi

Christina Tree

A SUMMER DAY ON MOUNT GREYLOCK'S SUMMIT.

this way in the past. Our favorite remains the description by Thoreau, who spent a July night up here in 1844 when only a "rude observatory," built by Williams College students, stood on the top. In *A Week on the Concord and Merrimack Rivers,* Thoreau describes the way he built a fire and "encased" himself in boards to keep warm. At dawn he found himself above the clouds, which he described as "floating on this fragment of the wreck of the world, on my carved plank, in a cloud land." Imagine the novelty of sitting above the clouds before the era of airplane windows.

As noted in the chapter introduction, Mount Greylock is the highest peak in a range that includes five other of southern New England's highest peaks. These are Saddle Ball Mountain (3,247 feet), Mount Fitch (3,110 feet), Mount Prospect (2,690 feet), Mount Williams (2,951 feet), and Ragged Mountain (2,451 feet). Known as Greylock since the 1830s, the range spreads across six towns: Adams, Cheshire, Lanesborough, New Ashford, North Adams, and Williamstown.

GETTING THERE

The primary route is from the southeast in Lanesborough, not far north Pittsfield. It's 1.7 miles from US 7 to the **Mount Greylock Visitor Center** (413-499-4262; open year-round, daily 9–5); worth a detour even if you don't have an extra hour to devote to the summit trip. The visitor center is already high enough to offer expansive views south, and there's a diorama of the mountain and access to trails. Inquire about summertime guided hikes. There is no fee to enter the park, but parking at the summit is $2. Dogs are welcome but must be leashed. In winter the visitor center is accessible open, weather permitting.

From the visitor center the **Rockwell Road** winds its way 7 miles up the southern flank of the mountain, joining the **Notch Road,** an even windier access from MA 2 in North Adams. Both roads access the final half mile to the summit. From North Adams we recommend beginning the ascent at the **Western Gateway Heritage State Park** (see *Museums*) in North Adams and following **Reservoir Road** to its junction with Notch Road. In spring and fall the drive can be especially dramatic as foliage changes with the altitude.

Even in summer it's obvious that the range is an inland island, with vegetation zones changing as you climb. On the lower slopes expect northern hardwoods: red oak, beech, birches, black cherry, ash, and maple. At 2,600 feet there's a transition to boreal or spruce-fir forest set off by mountain ash and yellow birch. Above this come subalpine balsam fir trees and wildflowers.

HIKING TRAILS

In 1898, 400 acres on Mount Greylock was the first property acquired by the commonwealth, becoming the foundation for the Massachusetts State Park system. Managed by the Department of Conservation and Recreation, the reservation now consists of more than 12,500 acres with 70 miles of trails. Roughly one-third of the reservation's visitors hike. Stop by the visitor center for advice and a map of the most popular trails.

The Appalachian Trail crosses the summit and offers great views along the segment accessed from the marked trailhead just below, at 3,000 feet. Hike south along Saddle Ball Ridge and return, 1–2 miles, 60–90 minutes.

Bradley Farm Trail: A 1.8-mile loop from the visitor center, beginning in a former orchard, skirts a ravine and many stone walls while traversing varied woodland. It's suitable for cross-country skiing, conditions permitting.

Stony Ledge offers a dramatic view of the Hopper, a steep, semicircular valley. It's an easy 4-mile walk out and back along Sperry Road to a great picnic spot.

CAMPING

Primitive backpacking sites are accessible only by hiking in: There are 15 tent sites, seven group sites; reservations are required (through Reserve America.com) from Memorial Day to Columbus Day. Potable water is available. For the more intrepid, five backcountry lean-to shelter areas are available; registration is suggested. For more information, call the visitor center or check the website.

trails, and a visitors center with restrooms; in summer a park interpreter is on hand to explain the geological forces that created the bridge. It's also a popular local fishing spot.

Clarksburg State Park and **Clarksburg State Forest** (413-664-8345), 1199 Middle Rd., Clarksburg. Off MA 8 north from MA 2. The park covers 368 wooded acres that are particularly beautiful in foliage season. **Mauserts Pond** has a day-use area with swimming, picnic facilities, a bathhouse, and pavilion. There is a 3-mile scenic nature trail around the pond and 50 wooded campsites nearby (reservations suggested). (In "Along the Mohawk Trail," also see **Savoy Mountain State Forest,** with its beautiful **Tannery Falls,** swimming in North Pond, and camping at South Pond, all not far from Adams.)

♿ **Pittsfield State Forest** (413-442-8992) totals more than 10,000 acres along the Taconic Mountain Range. From the corner of US 20 and US 7 in Pittsfield, drive west on West Street, north on Churchill Street, and west on Cascade to the entrance. A 5-mile circular paved road follows Lulu Brook to high, scenic **Berry Pond,** the highest natural body of water in the state that's also good for boating (no motors); swimming, however, is permitted only in smaller **Lulu Brook Pond.** A rustic Civilian Conservation Corps–built ski lodge that serves as a warming hut in winter can also be rented by groups in summer. **Tranquility Trail,** a paved, 0.75-mile loop through spruce and pine woods, has been designed for wheelchair access. There are also taped descriptions of flora and fauna. In June the forest harbors 40 acres of azaleas atop Berry Mountain. Nearby **Balance Rock**—a 165-ton limestone boulder poised on another rock—is accessible via Balance Rock Road from US 7 in Lanesborough.

Peru State Forest (413-442-8992), off MA 143 in Peru; south on Curtin Rd., 1 mile from Peru Center. Garnet Hill (2,178 feet) yields a good view of the surrounding country, and there is fishing in **Garnet Lake.**

NATURAL BRIDGE STATE PARK IN NORTH ADAMS.

Christina Tree

OTHER **Kennedy Park** on US 7 in Lenox. The grounds of the former Aspinwall Hotel offer trails for hiking, biking, and cross-country skiing.

WATERFALLS **Becket Falls,** 0.2 mile up Brooker Hill from the Becket Arts Center (MA 8 and Pittsfield Rd.), has a shallow turnout in which to park. It's a steep scramble down to view the 25-foot-high cascade.

The Cascades, a property of the Berkshire Natural Resources Council not far from downtown North Adams, is a 45 foot-high waterfall formed by Notch Brook as it tumbles into a pool below. Park on Marion Avenue (off MA 2) and pick up the path at the end of the street. Cross the footbridge and follow the trail.

Stone Hill, a 55-acre town park, is accessible from Stone Hill Rd. off South St., Williamstown. Wooded trails and a stone seat with a view.

Wahconah Falls State Park (c/o Pittsfield State Forest; 413-442-8992), off MA 9 in Dalton, is located 3 miles east of the town center. A 2-minute walk brings you from the parking area down to picnic tables scattered among the smooth rocks above the falls. Swimming is not permitted due to dangerous conditions.

✷ Lodging

Note: Tax varies from town to town, so inquire when making a reservation. Most places also have a two- or three-day requirement for weekends July through October, and many inns offer midweek discounts, even in July and August. B&Bs with fewer than four rooms are not required to charge tax. Check with local chambers of commerce for seasonal B&Bs and apartments.

RESORTS

In Lenox 01240

♿ **Blantyre** (413-637-3556; blantyre.com), 16 Blantyre Rd. Built in 1902 to replicate an ancestral home in Scotland, this magnificent, Tudor-style mansion—open year-round—was lovingly restored to its original glory by Jack and Jane Fitzpatrick, owners of the Red Lion Inn in Stockbridge. There is a baronial entry hall and a truly graceful music room with crystal chandeliers, sofas covered in petit point, a piano, and a harp. Guests enjoy their meals in the paneled dining room around the long formal table, or in the adjoining, smaller, octagonal room (see *Dining Out*). The 25 guest rooms are impeccably furnished with antiques, and most have a fireplace. There are 117 well-kept acres with four tennis courts, a swimming pool (with Jacuzzi hot tub and sauna), a spa, and competition croquet courts. Including continental breakfast, rates begin at $550 for a room and run to $1,800 per night for the two-bedroom Ice House Cottage. Dinner in the elegant and formal (jackets and ties for men in the evening) dining room is expensive but a true culinary experience (see *Dining Out*).

Cranwell Resort, Spa & Golf Club (413-637-1364 or 1-800-272-6935; cranwell.com), 55 Lee Rd. (US 20). A 380-acre resort with 107 units—rooms, suites, and town houses—scattered in five varied buildings. An imposing, Tudor-style 1890s summer mansion is the centerpiece, and both its common and guest rooms are large and luxurious, furnished with period antiques. Less formal options in other buildings include family-friendly suites with large bedrooms, a living room with a sleeper sofa, and a galley kitchen. Buildings reflect the property's varied history, including its use for much of the 20th century as a famous Jesuit prep school. There are three restaurants, a lounge, meeting rooms, four claylike Har-Tru tennis courts, heated indoor and outdoor pools, and cross-country skiing in winter. The big attractions, however, are the 18-hole, PGA championship golf course and a luxurious spa complex, built at a cost of $9 million and one of the largest resort spas in the Northeast. The spa offers some 50 different treatments and has a 60-foot-long indoor heated pool along with a fitness room, sauna, whirlpool, juice bar, fireplace lounges, and café. Glass-enclosed heated passageways connect it with several resort buildings so that guests in about half the rooms can access the spa without going outdoors—a welcome convenience in winter. Room rates are $275–575 a night in high season, $175–475 low season. Rates include full use of the spa, exclusive of spa and fitness services. The resort offers a number of packages, including golf and spa. Weddings and meetings are a specialty; before booking you might want to ask what else is booked for your stay.

Wheatleigh (413-637-0610; wheatleigh.com), Hawthorne Rd. This yellow-brick palazzo was built in 1893, set on 22 acres that now include a heated outdoor swimming pool and a tennis court. Tanglewood is around the corner. There are 19 large and elegantly decorated rooms, all with private bath, about half with a fireplace. The restaurant is expensive (see *Dining Out*) and award winning. Rates are $715–2,100 without breakfast.

SPAS AND YOGA CENTERS

Lenox is the spa center of the Northeast and said to have one masseuse

THE POOL AT CRANWELL RESORT, SPA & GOLF CLUB.

Cranwell Resort, Spa & Golf Club

for every 60 residents. Augmenting the residential centers described below are several day spas, a resource for all visitors, especially in the off-season when inn prices are so reasonable. Nowhere else in New England is it so possible to combine the comforts of an inn or B&B with so many services that improve the health of both body and spirit.

Canyon Ranch in Lenox (413-637-4100 or 1-800-742-9000; canyon ranch.com), 165 Kimble St., Lenox. Sister to the famous spa in Arizona, this spectacularly deluxe, 120-acre fitness resort is blessed with a superb setting. The focal point is a grand 1890s manor house that is a replica of the Petit Trianon of Louis XVI. Guests sleep in the adjoining 126-room inn, a clapboard building in traditional New England style. Just about every health and fitness program imaginable is offered, and instruction and equipment are state of the art. The setting is luxurious, but the emphasis on wellness is serious. The staff-to-guest ratio is about three-to-one. Meals are dietary but also gourmet and delicious. Guests (who have included many celebrities) almost invariably depart glowing and enthusiastic. Three-night packages start at $3,000 in high season, $1,930 off-season. Packages include meals and a wide variety of spa and sports services. Inquire about special deals such as discounts for returning guests who bring a first-timer friend or relative with them, mothers and daughters sharing a room, and off-season one-day "Spa Renewal" programs.

Kripalu Center for Yoga and Health (1-800-741-7353; kripalu.org), MA 183, Lenox. This yoga-based holistic health center offers a structured daily regimen and a variety of weekend, weeklong, and longer programs. A mecca for spiritual and physical renewal, nonprofit Kripalu is housed in a former Jesuit seminary (once the estate of steel magnate Andrew Carnegie) on 150 acres and just a stone's throw from Tanglewood. Founded as a guru-centered yoga ashram (*kripalu* means "compassion" in Sanskrit), it is now staffed primarily by paid professionals, and the atmosphere and programming are mainstream New Age. The country's largest holistic health center, Kripalu accommodates nearly 500 guests and has a national reputation for training instructors in its own style of yoga. It also attracts nationally known lecturers and teachers. Facilities include whirlpools, saunas, hiking and cross-country trails, a beach, boats, and tennis; also a children's program during summer months. A recent addition is a striking, architecturally innovative, and environmentally friendly 80-room annex, linked to the main building by a grass-covered passageway. All rooms in the annex have private baths and floor-to-ceiling windows with views of the grounds overlooking Stockbridge Bowl. More than 750 variously priced programs are offered; they include healthy meals, workshops, and yoga classes. The per-day cost of a two-night "Retreat and Renewal" package, a popular introduction to Kripalu, ranges from $166 for a bed in a dormitory with communal bathroom midweek to $394–453 for a private room with bath weekends and holidays. Kripalu also has a day-guest program priced at $100, which includes breakfast, lunch, dinner, and all "Retreat and Renewal" program activities.

Cranwell Resort, Spa & Golf Club (see *Resorts*) has an elaborate spa facility that boasts a 60-foot-long heated indoor pool and offers some 50 different spa treatments. Both day and overnight spa packages are available.

INNS

In Lenox 01240

Village Inn (413-637-0020 or 1-800-253-0917; villageinn-lenox.com), 16 Church St. Dating from 1771 and one of the oldest houses in Lenox, this is an authentic old New England inn but after many enlargements and renovations has all the modern conveniences. All of the 32 rooms have private bath (some with Jacuzzi tub) and are comfortably furnished with antiques or reproductions, period prints, and country quilts. Many rooms have four-poster beds, and some also have a working fireplace. The restaurant, Rumplestiltzkin's (see *Dining Out*), is open for breakfast and dinner but not lunch. The tavern, Rumpy's, is a popular hangout. $202–304 in high season and $122–189 off-season, with breakfast (continental only, weekdays in winter and spring).

Apple Tree Inn (413-637-1477; appletree-inn.com), 10 Richmond Mountain Rd. This century-old house sits high on a hill overlooking the waters of the Stockbridge Bowl, near the main entrance to Tanglewood. The main house, an 1880s mansion, offers 12 rooms and two suites, four with a working fireplace. The 21 rooms in the modern lodge are motel-style but pleasant and handy to the pool, which has the best view from any pool around. (The one from the terrace off the lobby is terrific, too.) Landscaping includes a wide variety of roses that bloom from spring into fall, as well as apple trees. Well-behaved children are welcome. The inn is a very popular wedding venue. Depending on season and day of the week, nightly rates are $90–400 in the main house and $60–290 in the lodge.

Gateways Inn (413-637-2532 or 1-888-492-9466; gateways.inn.com), 51 Walker St. Built by Harley Procter of Procter & Gamble in 1912, the inn has been said to resemble a cake of Ivory soap, but it is more elegant than that, with black shutters and a central skylit mahogany staircase designed by the firm of McKim, Mead & White. Owners Fabrizio and Rosemary Chiariello have made many improvements and are welcoming hosts. The 12 guest rooms all have a private bath, telephone, television, and individually controlled central air-conditioning. Three, the only ones where children are accepted, are on the first floor, along with a restaurant, terrace café, and popular bar (see *Dining Out*). Second-floor rooms include a suite with two fireplaces (Arthur Fiedler's favorite place to stay when he conducted at Tanglewood) and another nice touch: a flat-screen TV that looks like an antique mirror until you switch the TV on. Another suite, named for *Romeo and Juliet,* features a king-sized sleigh bed under a small skylight. High-season rates are $150–515, low season $100–250, with full breakfast.

In Williamstown 01267

The Williams Inn (413-458-9371 or 1-800-828-0133; williamsinn.com), 1090 Main St. (junction of MA 2 and US 7). The slight, grandmotherly lady pouring your morning coffee may well be Marilyn Faulkner.

Son David is now GM of this 125-room, full-service inn, but Marilyn and husband Carl have been hands-on owner/hosts at the hospitable heart of Williamstown since 1991. Rooms are comfortable, motel-style, crisply and attractively furnished in reproduction antiques, with full bath, TV, phone, computer hook-up, and air-conditioning; the 24 "premier rooms" in the new wing are better than comfortable. Request a corner room. Amenities include an indoor swimming pool, sauna, and hot tub. The dining room is open for breakfast, lunch, and dinner, and lighter fare is served in the tavern lounge, known for its burgers. This is, incidentally, the ideal place to stay without a car—it's a short walk from the museums and steps from the Adams Memorial Theater (venue for the Williamstown Theatre Festival), and its outer lobby (open 24 hours) doubles as the Peter Pan bus stop. Rooms $140–190; more for suites. No charge for children 14 and younger in the same room.

♿ **The Orchards** (413-458-9611; orchardshotel.com), 222 Adams Rd. (MA 2). Walled away from a commercial strip on the eastern edge of town, The Orchards faces inward on a landscaped courtyard. The feel is of a small, elegant, slightly tired but friendly country hotel. Common spaces are fitted with Oriental rugs, crystal chandeliers, inviting seating, and a hearth. There are 45 rooms and two suites, many unusually spacious with gas fireplace and window seats. Soundproofing can be an issue if you are a light sleeper. The **Gala Restaurant** is formal but gets mixed reviews. Amenities include a pool and an exercise center with a sauna. $111–556; check packages.

BED & BREAKFASTS

In Lenox 01240

⚤ **Stonover Farm** (413-637-9100; stonoverfarm.com), 169 Undermountain Rd. Stonover Farm is a luxurious gem of a place with a setting to match: a quiet woods- and meadow-lined rural road just 0.6 mile from the entrance to Tanglewood. After spending more than 20 years in Los Angeles (where Tom was a successful record producer), Tom and Suky Werman moved to the Berkshires for a complete change of scene and lifestyle. They bought what had been the farmhouse of a former grand estate, a stone-and-shingle building built in the 1890s, and spent a year restoring and remodeling the house and its outbuildings. They also cleared and landscaped the 10-acre grounds, which include a spring-fed duck pond. The result is an elegant, small B&B that has lots of character and tasteful touches and all the high-tech comforts. Walls are decorated with original paintings and prints—there is also an art gallery on the grounds—and guests have the use of a library, a greenhouse solarium, and a computer with high-speed Internet access. Units are air-conditioned and have cable TV and phones with voice mail. There are three large suites in the main house. The adjacent Rock Cottage has a large, sunny living room (one wall is lined with windows), a kitchen, a master bedroom, and a smaller twin-bedded room in a turret, accessed by circular staircase, that makes an ideal children's room. The new School House suite adjacent to the pond is a renovated 1850s schoolhouse with heated floors for winter use, gas fireplace, and a luxurious bathroom that includes a Jacuzzi for two. The rate for house suites is $275–425; Rock Cottage $435–575; the School House $395–485. There is a three-night minimum over weekends at peak times, a two-night weekend minimum the rest of the year. Rates include afternoon wine and cheese and a full, cooked-to-order breakfast.

The Summer White House (413-637-4489 or 1-800-832-9401; thesummerwhitehouse.com), 17 Main St. Originally called "The Lanai" (Hawaiian for "veranda") because of its many inviting porches, this is an authentic Berkshire cottage built in 1885 for a wealthy New Yorker. President Chester K. Arthur stayed here once, hence the name. The decor is distinctly Gilded Age, with lots of period furniture, paintings, and antiques. There are two guest parlors and a formal dining room where a full breakfast is served. The seven large bedrooms, all air-conditioned and with private baths, are named for the wives of U.S. presidents and contain books and framed documents relating to their time in the White House. One room has twin beds, all the others have four-posters that are either antiques or were custom-made of Honduran mahogany. Innkeeper Frank Newton is a knowledgeable guide to Lenox and also sometimes entertains guests on the back parlor piano. $195–225 high season, $160 off-season.

♿ **Rookwood Inn** (413-637-9750 or 1-800-223-9750; rookwoodinn.com), 11 Old Stockbridge Rd. A turreted, 20-room Victorian inn within walking distance of Tanglewood. All rooms have a private bath, some have a small private balcony, and 12 have a fireplace. We liked Victorian Dream on the second floor, with its fainting couch, fireplace, and bath with both claw-footed tub and extra-large shower. But our favorite was Revels' Retreat, a third-floor room with queen bed, gas fireplace, and an octagonal space with daybed four steps up in a turret with oval windows and incredible views. Suites have phone and TV. Well-behaved, supervised children are welcome, and two first-floor rooms are handicapped accessible. Dogs are allowed in two ground-floor suites. A three-room suite is available for rentals of a week or more. Rates, which include afternoon refreshments as well as a full, "heart-healthy" breakfast, are $199–400 in summer, $175–325 the rest of the year, except holidays.

♿ **Hampton Terrace** (413-637-1773 or 1-800-203-0656; hamptonterrace.com), 91 Walker St. Stan and Susan Rosen have completely renovated this handsome white frame turn-of-the-20th-century house, filling it with antiques and many family heirlooms. A 1929 Steinway grand piano graces the living room, for instance, and a hand-painted cabinet holds the family doll collection. The 14 rooms all have private baths. Some units have a whirlpool tub; every room has a TV, VCR, and CD player. WiFi access is free. Guests can relax in the parlor of the main house; there is a separate lounge area in the carriage house. Breakfast is served in the dining room and sunporch. $260–345 high season, $175–249 the rest of the year.

The Cornell Inn (413-637-4800; cornellbb.com), 203 Main St. This inn on the edge of the village has 28 rooms in three very different structures: a Gilded Age mansion built in 1888; the adjacent MacDonald

House, dating to 1777; and a restored former carriage house. Most rooms have a fireplace; all have a private bath and some have a Jacuzzi tub. The decor in the mansion is Victorian, but the decorative theme is Colonial in MacDonald House and "country primitive" in the carriage house. Amenities include a pub-style guest lounge with access to a deck looking out on the Japanese rock garden and koi pond. $150–375 in high season, $100–275 low season with full breakfast.

The Garden Gables Inn (413-637-0193 or 1-888-243-0193; gardengables inn.com), 135 Main St. (MA 7A). This triple-gabled, white-clapboard house dating in part to 1780 is set well back from the road, but is within walking distance of the village shops and restaurants. Nice touches include fresh flowers in rooms and afternoon sherry in the parlor. The 18 rooms are bright and comfortable, all with private bath, telephone, and air-conditioning, several with whirlpool, many with fireplace or private porch. Our favorites are in the back of the main house, particularly east and west facing sunrise and sunset, which have elaborately carved four-poster beds and large fireplaces. Four suites in the orchard cottages have cathedral ceilings and sitting areas. The ample grounds convey a sense of being out in the country, and the outdoor, guests-only heated pool is one of the biggest in Berkshire County. Breakfast, at a common table in the gracious dining room or at individual tables out on the porch, includes fresh fruit, yogurt, and cheeses as well as a hot dish. $197–515 in-season, $157–377 off-season.

♿ **Birchwood Inn** (413-637-2600 or 1-800-524-1646; birchwood-inn.com), 7 Hubbard St. Ellen Gutman Chenaux has brought out the best of this grand old house, which dates in part to 1767. There are nine rooms in the main house, all with private bath and telephone, and two in the carriage house. The library parlor—the real thing with four walls lined with books, many recent purchases of Ellen's—is a gracious, welcoming room with window seats, a fireplace, and tea and a plate of brownies in the afternoon for guests. The front porch, with its homey wicker furniture, is a popular gathering place in summer. Kennedy Park (good for walking and cross-country skiing) is across the street. Amenities include a sociable dog called Quinn. All rooms are nicely furnished, some with four-poster beds; six have a fireplace. Rates are $175–335, including a full breakfast. (Fondue Florentine is a particular specialty.)

♿ **Brook Farm Inn** (413-637-3013; brookfarm.com), 15 Hawthorne St. A handsome yellow Victorian house on a quiet byway south of the village, Brook Farm has been tastefully furnished to fit its period (1882) by owners Phil and Linda Halpern. There are 15 guest rooms, all with private bath, nine with a fireplace. The carriage house annex has two rooms and a suite, all with whirlpool tub. Two annex units are handicapped accessible. Breakfast, featuring homemade baked goods, is buffet-style in the elegant green dining room overlooking the garden, and afternoon tea with scones is also served. There is a heated outdoor pool, a comfortable lounging parlor with fireplace, and a large library of poetry books and tapes. Linda, a storyteller, sometimes entertains at teatime. $175–425 in-season, $145–325 the rest of the year.

Whistler's Inn (413-637-0975; whistlersinnberkshires.com), 5 Greenwood St. (at corner of MA 7A). A mostly Tudor-style mansion with large common rooms, including a ballroom, library, music room, and baronial dining room. The decor is high Victorian. It's across from the Church on the Hill and an easy walk from both village shops and Kennedy Park. The grounds include 7 acres of garden and woodland. The 14 guest rooms all have private baths. In the carriage house, a very large room on the second floor has wide pine floors, two sitting areas, a TV, a small refrigerator, and lots of light, as well as African artifacts and books; the rustic suite on the first floor has a woodstove, a sitting/sleeping/TV room, and a private deck. Continental breakfast is served. The library is well stocked, the walls hung with interesting art, and the atmosphere distinctly cultural. It's also rumored to have a ghost, like so many of the English country houses it resembles. $110–300 in summer and fall, $90–225 off-season.

Cliffwood Inn (413-637-3330 or 1-800-789-3331), 25 Cliffwood St. On a quiet street just a block off Main, Cliffwood is the home of Joy and Scottie Farrelly and a Yorkshire terrier named Charlie. Built in 1889 as the summer home of a former American diplomat, the inn is airy and elegant with three guest rooms. Only coffee is served in the morning, but there are several good breakfast places nearby. Children 11 years of age and older are welcome, but credit cards are not. $192–264 in-season, $132–264 the rest of the year.

Walker House (413-637-1271 or 1-800-235-3098; walkerhouse.com), 64 Walker St. This expanded Federal-era (1804) house in the heart of town is decorated with eclectic art, has a lot of common space, and features amenities such as a large library of videos and DVDs that guests can watch on a 12-foot-high screen. Peggy and Richard Houdek have been innkeepers for more than 30 years, and Walker House has a definite lived-in feeling: There are always a number of cats in residence, and there are currently two grand pianos in the parlor. A long flower-garnished and wicker-furnished veranda overlooks the expansive back garden. Five of the eight guest rooms, each named for a composer, have a fireplace, and all have charm. A continental breakfast with fruit and afternoon tea are included in the rates: $90–220 June–Oct., $90–160 the rest of the year.

In Pittsfield 01201

Thaddeus Clapp House (413-499-6840 or 1-888-499-6840; clapphouse.com), 74 Wendell Ave. Just a block off South St. (US 7) and a leafy stroll from Park Square, this 1871 mansion evokes a sense of what Pittsfield once was as well as what it is becoming. Innkeeper Becky Smith is herself at the heart of the city's current renaissance and enjoys plugging guests into the best of all the city has to offer. A dilapidated apartment house when Smith began renovations, this is now an elegant B&B with eight suites. Each has a fireplace, cable TV, fridge, AC, and dataport; all are spacious and airy, furnished in handsome antiques. Several have a whirlpool bath as well as shower. Woodwork is extraordinary throughout, set off by Oriental rugs. An enthusiastic historian, Smith likes to tell guests about Thaddeus Clapp, the president of the

Pontoosuc Woolen Mill who had a passion for acting. These spacious public rooms were designed as venues for musical performances, poetry, and theatrical readings as well as elaborate dinner parties (inquire about occasional theatrical presentations in the parlor). In warm weather the wicker-filled front porch is a favored gathering spot. Breakfast and tea are served in the dining room. $125–295 rates vary with the season and day and include a full breakfast. Note minimum stay policy in high season.

White Horse Inn (413-442-2512 or 1-877-442-2512; whitehorsebb.com), 378 South St. (US 7). Two generations of Pittsfield's McGovern family have worked together to totally renovate this handsome century-old home, adding a spacious deck and landscaping the ample back garden. Host Gary McGovern, former assistant manager at a San Francisco hotel, puts his all into breakfast, which is served on the deck or in a sunny breakfast room heated by a wood-pellet stove. A similar stove also glows in the comfortable, uncluttered living room. The eight guest rooms (one on the ground floor) all have the same unfussy feel. The emphasis is on comforts such as a good mattress (from full to king), new (private) bathroom, and small TV in each room. $140–220 in high season, $110–125 in low.

In Williamstown 01267

Williamstown Bed and Breakfast (413-458-9202; williamstownbandb.com), 30 Cold Spring Rd. Since 1989 Lucinda Edmonds and Kim Rozell have been welcoming guests to this spacious 1880s house nicely but unfussily furnished in period style. It's steps from Field Park (the town green) and within walking distance of downtown restaurants and shops. There's a sitting room opening onto the oak-furnished dining room, the setting for a full breakfast that always includes a hot entrée and home-baked breads. Guests tend to talk to one another over breakfast or while relaxing on the porch or lawn. The three good-sized guest rooms, each with private bath, are furnished with a mix of well-chosen antiques and a sure eye to comfort. We especially like the upstairs front room with its small-patterned paper, marble-topped dresser, and coral couch set in a window bay. Children over 12, please. $150–200 double, $130–180 off-season. Tax is included.

The Birches at Steep Acres Farm (413-458-8134; birchesbb.com), 522 White Oaks Rd. High on a hill with an out-there feel but just 2 miles from Williams College. This is a comfortable home built by host Daniel Gangemi along traditional lines, but with inviting open spaces, a large hearth, and outdoor deck with grill. It's part of a larger property that has been in his family since the 1970s and includes a swimming pond. The three guest rooms include one with a king-sized bed, fireplace, and whirlpool; two smaller rooms share a bath. $100–175 includes a full breakfast and afternoon refreshments.

Upland Meadow House (413-458-3990; uplandmeadowhouse.com), 1249 Northwest Hill Rd. This contemporary house is set on 160 acres, high on a hill adjacent to Hopkins Forest but less than 3 miles from the middle of town. It's very much Pan Whitman's home, but the two rooms (sharing one bath) are private, with their own sitting room and a splendid view east to the Green Mountains. It's a great spot for birders, cross-country skiers, and hikers as well as anyone who savors mountain meadows and views. Pan is known for her blueberry and raspberry jams. $100 per room includes breakfast served, when possible, on the big deck. Two-night minimum only on major weekends.

The House on Main Street (413-458-3031; houseonmainstreet.com), 1120 Main St. This lovely, centuries-old house has been taking in "guests" since the 1930s. Thoroughly remodeled and modernized by the Riley family, it now offers five large, sunny, and cheerfully decorated guest rooms, two with private bath and the others sharing a bath and a half. A full breakfast is served in the country-style kitchen. Guests have the use of a parlor and a large screened porch. $95–147 includes a full breakfast.

Clover Hill Farm (413-458-3376; cloverhillfarm.net), 249 Adams Rd. This quixotic but comfortable hilltop farm caters to horse and dog lovers and welcomes children. Your first impression is of an imposing mansion, spreading across the crest of a hill. Carolyn and Robert Henderson built the post and beam house a decade ago. The 19th-century dairy barn is now filled with horses, the centerpiece of a full equine center. Carolyn also raised beagles. The informal, imaginative house has three guest rooms ($150–220). Inquire about the 1,200-square-foot, condo-style guest house. Farm animals include chickens and cats, and there is a pool. All this just minutes from downtown Williamstown.

In North Adams 01247

Also see "The Porches Inn" sidebar.

Blackinton Manor (413-663-5795; blackinton-manor.com), 1391 Massachusetts Ave. Obviously a mill owner spared no expense in 1832, when he built himself this exquisite Italianate mansion in the middle of the small, leafy mill village that bears his name. It was restored as a B&B under previous owners, but Laura and Paul Micionus have substantially raised the comfort level. Common space includes elegant living/dining rooms with floor-to-ceiling windows and a grand piano. The grounds include an inviting pool. There are two ground-floor guest rooms and three more up the graceful staircase; all have private baths and one (the Parlor) has a Jacuzzi. From $150 weekdays off-season for the Blue Room to $220 on a summer weekend for the Parlor. Rates include a full breakfast.

Elsewhere

The Inn at Richmond (413-698-2566 or 1-888-968-4748; innatrichmond.com), 802 State Rd. (MA 41), Richmond 01254. Handy to Hancock Shaker Village, this is an attractive inn with three guest rooms, three suites, and three cottages on a gentleman's horse farm. Formerly separate from the farm, it's now under the same ownership; guests can take lessons and ride (see **Berkshire Equestrian Center** under *Horseback Riding*). All rooms have air-conditioning and phone as well as private bath and queen- or king-sized bed. Landscaped grounds include perennial gardens and woodland trails; inside there's an attractive parlor and library. Cottages have fully equipped kitchens, and some suites and cottages have fireplaces and whirlpools. High-season rates are $280–340 on weekends, $160–240 off-season. All rates except

HISTORIC WILLIAMSTOWN B&BS

Riverbend Farm (413-458-3121), 643 Simonds Rd. (US 7), Williamstown 01267. Open late Apr.–Oct. Many B&Bs try to cultivate a colonial ambience, but Riverbend Farm doesn't have to try: It's an authentic 1770 former tavern listed on the National Register of Historic Places. The current parlor is the original tavern taproom in which the Battle of Bennington was planned. Owners David and Judy Loomis have lovingly restored the place, uncovering and preserving the wood paneling, wide floorboards, and massive central chimney serving five working fireplaces. Whenever it's cool enough, a fire glows afternoons and evenings in the parlor and is lit in the old "keeping room" or kitchen in time for breakfast. The two common rooms are as comfortable as they are historic, and there is a fridge for guest use. Each of the five guest rooms reflects careful, scholarly restoration: period lighting fixtures, latch doors, and exposed original wallpaper lend authenticity. One of the two shared baths has a claw-foot tub; the other, downstairs, has a slate-lined shower and shelves filled with antique glass bottles, pottery, and jugs. A substantial continental breakfast featuring homemade breads and granola is served in front of the hearth. This is a great place to rent as a whole for reunions. $120 per room, $20 for a third person in a room.

Christina Tree

RIVERBEND FARM HAS FIVE CAREFULLY RESTORED GUEST ROOMS.

((ψ)) **The Guest House at Field Farm** (413-458-3135; guesthouseatfieldfarm.org), 554 Sloan Rd. (off MA 43, near the intersection with US 7), Williamstown 01267. Owned and maintained by the Trustees of Reservations on 316 upland acres with a spectacular view of Mount Greylock. Lawrence Bloedel had a house built in 1948 that represents, both inside and out, the best of 1950s design. He filled it with furniture to match and with a priceless collection of modern art. A 1923 graduate of Williams College and heir to a fortune earned in the Pacific Northwest and Canada, Bloedel himself designed and made furniture, some of which survives in the house. He died in 1976; on the later death of his wife,

Eleanor, the most valuable paintings found their way into museums. Most went to the Whitney in Manhattan, but one of the most moving—*Morning in the City* by Edward Hopper—hangs in the Williams College Museum of Art. The property was donated to the Trustees, but without funds to maintain the house, the initial idea was to tear the house down. Preservationists David and Judy Loomis, who had meticulously restored Williamstown's 18th-century tavern as a bed & breakfast, suggested they might do the same with this exceptional home. Luckily they prevailed, serving as its initial hosts.

Guests will appreciate the enormity of the loss this house would have been. Field Farm's meadows and woods are beautiful, webbed with 4 miles of trails, good for cross-country skiing as well as walking (see *Green Space*), but to stay in this house is a gift. We sat mesmerized at the dining room table, facing the picture window through which clouds quickly shaped and reshaped above Mount Greylock, drifting toward us above the pond and landscaped lawns below the house. Beside the living room picture window, which commands the same view, there's a telescope and Eames chair. The room is sparely, comfortably furnished with clean-lined, bright, and comfortable pieces, sculpture, and paintings. The hearth here, as in other rooms, features unusual hand-painted tiles. The cork floors are warmed by copper pipes, corners are rounded, and lighting is recessed. In all there are five guest rooms, and at this writing all except the ground-floor room (a former study with its own balcony) retain their original furnishings. The large master bedroom with its balcony and glass-faced hearth is the indisputable gem. A swimming pool, sequestered in a corner of the garden, is available June–Sept. $150–295 includes a full breakfast and use of the guest pantry to store a picnic and drinks. While weekends are booked far in advance, midweek nights are frequently wide open.

THE LIVING ROOM AT THE GUEST HOUSE AT FIELD FARM IN WILLIAMSTOWN. Christina Tree

ALL IN A ROW

The Porches Inn (413-664-0400; porches.com), 231 River St., North Adams 01247. These six wooden row houses, each containing four apartments, were built facing the vast brick Arnold Print Works around 1900. With slate roofs, some shingle detailing under their sharply peaked gables, and distinctive, continuous porches, they were a cut above the city's typical, no-frills workers' housing. The mill across the river (then Sprague Electric) closed in 1985, and the by-then-dilapidated row houses continued to deteriorate. Fortunately, however, they remained clearly visible from a major gallery in the mill, which reopened in 1999 as MASS MoCA (see *Museums*). Thanks to foresight and funding by the current owner, the wooden row houses were thoroughly but sensitively renovated to form one of New England's most unusual lodging places. Each building is now painted a different, tasteful color (red, yellow, sage, gray, and blue); together they house 47 guest rooms, including 25 suites.

The decor is a combination of sleek contemporary and 1950s funky. Specially designed steel cupboards hiding flat-screen TVs, Blu-ray players, and mini bars resemble mill lockers; windows are bare except for natural linen ingeniously hung. In the luxurious bathrooms large mirrors, set into the original, battered window frames, hang above marble sinks. Furnishings are simple and comfortable, walls are hung with paint-by-the-number oils that cleverly conceal mini safes, and bedside tables are topped with 1950s futuristic lamps. Top-floor rooms as well as suites feature skylights; suites have a Jacuzzi tub and separate living room; two-bedroom suites feature two baths with Jacuzzis plus a sitting room.

Guests check in at a central reception desk in a row house that also

weekly cottage rentals include a full breakfast.

Harbour House Inn (413-743-8959; harbourhouseinn.com), 725 N. State Rd. (MA 8), Cheshire 01225. Eva and Sam Amuso are the warm and welcoming hosts of this mansion-sized country house in the shadow of Mount Greylock. As a stop on the Albany–Springfield stage, it first welcomed guests in 1793, but it was substantially expanded in the 1880s as the manor of a 500-acre gentleman's farm. The name *harbour* refers to safety—this was also a known stop for fleeing slaves on the Underground Railroad. With its immense, long sitting room and six guest rooms, it works well as a B&B. The master suite with its fireplace, many windows, and paneling (it was the former library) is beloved by brides, and there is a two-room suite with fireplace and balcony on the third floor. We thoroughly enjoyed a night in Country Sunshine, a comfortable offers two comfortable sitting rooms, one with a fireplace and plenty of local reading material, and a large, sunny breakfast room. A cozy and intimate cocktail bar is set up in the evenings. There's a sauna in the small 1850s River Street house out back beside the landscaped pool that's usable year-round. River Street itself has not been rehabbed, but it's a short, safe walk to downtown restaurants, shorter still to MASS MoCA with its many evening performances. From $180–$252 mid-May–mid-Oct; $130–195 off-season.

In "Along the Mohawk Trail," also see the rustic **Wigwam Cabins,** a vintage 1930s collection of rustic cabins due to reopen in 2011 after extensive restoration by Nancy Fitzpatrick; guests share access to The Porches' amenities.

THE PORCHES INN, A UNIQUE PROPERTY IN NORTH ADAMS.

Nicholas Whitman

room cleverly decorated in lemon yellow and Wedgwood blue. A full breakfast is served at the long dining room table. The Ashuwillticook Rail Trail, just down the road, runs along Cheshire Reservoir, and the main access road up Mount Greylock and hiking trails in Greylock Glen are both handy. Come to think of it, while it's quite far from anywhere else to stay, Harbour House is handy (because of the way the roads run) to most of Berkshire County and to much of the Hampshire Hilltown area as well. $145–185, more in-season.

MOTOR INNS AND MOTELS

The 1896 House (413-458-1896 or 1-888-999-1896; 1896house.com), 910 Condspring Rd. (US 7), Williamstown 01267. Brookside Motel, a neighboring red barn that housed a restaurant for many decades but has been expanded to include luxury suites, and the Pondside Motel across MA 2 are now all under the same ownership.

The six "Barnside" suites are elaborately decorated, each evoking a different era or theme. All have a sitting area, gas fireplace, spacious bath with dual whirlpool tubs, TV, DVD/CD player, dataport, and more. They are, however, all rather dark, with windows only at the entrance ($219–289 in-season; from $179 off-season). Rooms in the Brookside Motel are crisp and cheerful. Across the road, Pondside units have been decorated to look more like B&B than motel rooms; the Sweetheart Room has a canopy bed and whirlpool, and a three-room suite has a full kitchen and whirlpool bath ($64–169 for motel rooms; $189–219 for the suite).

Crowne Plaza Hotel (413-499-2000; berkshirecrowne.com), Berkshire Common at West St., Pittsfield 01201. This is the Berkshires' only high rise and very much a part of the county seat. There are 179 rooms, an attractive indoor pool, and restaurant. Rooms: $129–349 in summer and fall, otherwise $99–159. Pets are $50 per stay.

North Adams Holiday Inn (413-663-6500; holidayinnberkshires.com), 40 Main St., North Adams 01247. This seven-floor, 87-room hotel, the only place to stay during North Adams's darkest era, has risen to the city's change in status. It's been thoroughly, tastefully renovated, but continues to offer one of the best values around. On a downtown site that has been occupied by a hotel since the city's inception, it continues to serve as the heart of town. Rooms vary in configuration, with king beds or two queens. There's a restaurant/lounge, an indoor pool, sauna, game room, and weight room in the basement. No minimum two-day stay on weekends except during college graduations. $99–169.

Jericho Valley Inn (413-458-9511; jerichovalleyinn.com), 2541 Hancock Rd., Williamstown 01267. This family-owned and -geared motel is 5 miles south of Williamstown on MA 43, 3 miles from Jiminy Peak. There's a fireplace in the breakfast room off the reception area. The 24 units range from one to three bedrooms, some with efficiencies. There are also several cottages with full kitchens and fireplaces. From $89 for rooms, $128–248 for suites with kitchen facilities and hearths. Inquire about cottages.

OTHER LODGING **New England Country Inn at Jiminy Peak** (413-738-5500; outside Massachusetts, 1-800-882-8859; jiminypeak.com), Jiminy Peak, Corey Rd., Hancock 01237. At the base of the ski mountain, this facility offers one-bedroom efficiency suites as well as a restaurant and lounge, an outdoor pool, indoor and outdoor whirlpools, and an exercise and game room. Each suite has a master bedroom with a king-sized bed, a living room with a queen-sized sleep sofa, two cable TVs, a bathroom, a powder room, and a fully equipped kitchen. Two- and three-bedroom condominiums are also available. Units are nicely laid out and furnished. $129–539; larger units run $179–999. Rates are based on double occupancy. Children 13 and younger stay free. See *Skiing, Biking,* and *For Families.*

Bascom Lodge (413-743-1591; bascomlodge.net), Mount Greylock Reservation, accessible by road from both North Adams and Lanesborough. This handsome vintage

1930s stone lodge on the summit of Mount Greylock is open late May–Oct 31. It accommodates 34 overnight guests in private rooms for two or in "family rooms" with a queen and bunk beds, sleeping up to four; there is also one single and two coed bunk rooms, each sleeping 10. Baths are shared. Comfortably rustic with working hearths and a wraparound, many-windowed dining porch, the facility has been recently renovated. The entire place can be rented and lends itself to small weddings or family reunions. Three daily meals are served, and the dinner under current management is itself a reason to come. $125–150 for private rooms, $35 per person in the bunk rooms.

WEDDINGS AND GROUP VENUES ⚤ **Eastover** (413-637-0625; www.eastover.com), 430 East St., Lenox 01240. For more than 60 years, this 1,000-acre Gilded Age estate was a resort known for its varied programs, themed weekends, and quirky amenities such as a buffalo herd and Civil War museum. New owners have upgraded the infrastructure; they now describe the property as "a boutique hotel" and no longer offer organized activities. The 60 rooms now in use are all motel-style units in buildings outside the original grand "Berkshire cottage," built in 1910. Room rates are $229–399, double or single occupancy, with continental breakfast. Guests have access to a swimming pool, volleyball court, and a network of walking trails.

⚤ ✐ 🐾 ♿ **Seven Hills Inn** (413-637-0060 or 1-800-869-6518; www.sevenhillsinn.com), 40 Plunkett St., Lenox 01240. Open May–Oct. A popular venue for weddings and functions, this 1911 Tudor Revival mansion, with its wonderfully ornate carved woodwork, is set on 27 terraced and landscaped acres next to Edith Wharton's former home, The Mount. The manor itself has 11 various-sized "guest chambers," all with elegant period decor and some with working fireplace and jet tub. A restored carriage house has five suites, all with fireplace, jet tub, and kitchenette; 29 more units (motel-style doubles) are in the adjoining Terrace Country Motel (several are handicapped-accessible and pets are allowed in some). Facilities include a landscaped pool and tennis courts; a path leads down to Laurel Lake. Pets and children are welcome. Rates with breakfast (continental only on weekdays) are $155–295 in-season in the manor house and carriage house, $125–175 in the motel, which is closed off-season.

✷ Where to Eat

DINING OUT

In Lenox

Church Street Café (413-637-2745; churchstreetcafe.biz), 65 Church St. Open daily for lunch and dinner May–Feb. Billing itself "An American Bistro," this lively, popular restaurant has an eclectic and always interesting menu which changes with the seasons. There is a pleasant dining patio and several connecting dining rooms, the walls of which are hung with paintings by local artists. Lunch on a spiced grilled swordfish or St. Louis–style ribs with homemade BBQ sauce; for dinner try seared duck breast with roast duck and potato hash or a roasted vegetable enchilada plate. Dinner entrées $22.50–28.50.

Bistro Zinc (413-637-8800; bistro zinc.com), 56 Church St. Open daily for lunch and dinner. Very popular, with a contemporary decor and cuisine but a cozy bistro atmosphere. Dinner choices might include pan-seared Maine scallops, sautéed calves liver, or roasted free-range chicken. Entrées $18–28. The bar is known for its martinis and other cocktails, and serves a wide variety of domestic and imported wines by the glass. Usually crowded and lively in the evening, it's separate from the main dining room but very visible—an impressive array of bottles behind the bar is dramatically illuminated—through a floor-to-ceiling glass wall.

Nudel (413-551-7183; nudelres taurant.com) 37 Church St. Open Tues.–Sat. 11:30–3 for lunch; Tues.–Sun. 5:30–9:30 for dinner. Nudel is about "seasonally inspired food" using local, organic, and natural ingredients whenever possible. "Nudels" (i.e., pasta dishes) include mustard spaetzle with olives, zucchini, and saffron broth, and semolina gnocchi with shiitakes, chèvre, and braised greens. Entrées include pan-seared beef with shiso butter, smoked soy, and balsamic-braised portobello and crimini mushrooms; and brown butter poached rainbow trout with almonds, fried garlic green and flat beans, mashed potatoes, and shallot and caper vinaigrette. Nudels are $18, main plates $25.

Café Lucia (413-637-2460; cafelucia lenox.com), 80 Church St. Open for dinner Tues.–Sat.; Sundays on holiday weekends and summer months. A remodeled art gallery is the setting for appreciating fine Northern Italian regional dishes such as *osso buco con risotto* or veal cutlet alla Lucia. The Caesar salad is rich and garlicky. Try the tiramisu for dessert. Good wine list. Deservedly popular, and reservations are recommended. Entrées $25–39.

Village Inn (413-637-0020; village inn-lenox.com), 16 Church St. The restaurant, Rumplestiltzkin's, is open to the public for dinner year-round and lunch in summer and fall. Entrées, $17.95–27.95, include dishes such as Shaker-style cranberry pot roast and pistachio-encrusted rack of lamb. **Rumpy's**, the basement tavern, serves pub food and has entertainment on weekends.

Gateways Inn (413-637-2532; gate waysinn.com), 751 Walker St. Open daily for lunch and dinner. The inn's restaurant, La Terrazza, is in an elegant formal dining room with an adjoining casual bar and lounge. (The bar stocks 200 different kinds of malt whisky.) The Italian-flavored menu includes dishes such as chicken piccata, roasted branzino, and spinach and ricotta ravioli with marinara sauce. Entrees $20–30.

Blantyre (413-637-3556; blantyre .com), 16 Blantyre Rd. Blantyre is a baronial mansion that epitomizes the Berkshires' Gilded Age glory. Dining in its grand restaurant is a memorable and rather formal experience. (Men are required to wear jackets and ties.) The cuisine is French, of course, prepared with care and served with flair. The wine list is vast and varied. The prix fixe three-course menu is $125 per person, the four-course menu $145. The tasting menu is $165; $240 with wine tasting. A 20 percent gratuity is added. Dinner is by reservation only. The restaurant is closed to the public on Mon. In July and Aug. lunch is also served on the terrace overlooking the splendid formal garden. A three-course prix fixe menu is $55.

Wheatleigh (413-637-0610; wheat leigh.com), Hawthorne Rd. Open for lunch and dinner; check off-season. By reservation only. The formal dining room in this Florentine palazzo, within walking distance of Tanglewood, features contemporary French and American interpretations of classic dishes such as Scottish salmon with parsnips, bok choy and mustard glaze, and ravioli with mushrooms, asparagus, and piquillo sauce. The four-course prix fixe dinner menu is $125, and the chef's tasting menu is $165. The wine list is long and includes some superb vintages.

Cranwell (413-637-1364; cranwell .com), US 20. Breakfast, lunch, and dinner. "Wyndhurst," the main dining room of the baronial manor (Wyndhurst was its original name), is grandly appointed and its cuisine appropriately first rate. The $38 prix fixe menu has steak, chicken, salmon, and vegetarian entrée choices, The **Music Room** offers a grill menu with dishes such as coriander-encrusted tuna, roasted lobster tails, and a mixed grille with lamb loin chop, petit filet mignon, and scallops; entrées $28.75–36.75. It also has live entertainment on weekends. **Sloane's Tavern**, a seasonal English-style pub, is on the golf course. The spa also has a café serving light fare.

Prime Italian Steakhouse & Bar (413-637-2998; primelenox.com), 15 Franklin St. Still in the same family, this is the successor to Antonio's, an unpretentious Italian restaurant that had a strong local following. Proprietor Gennaro "Jerry" Gallo, who started working in the restaurant when he was 8 years old, has given the old place a sleek contemporary decor with black tile, red leather, polished wood, glass-enclosed booths, and colorful artwork. Emphasis obviously is on beef—the signature steak is the 8-ounce center-cut filet mignon, "The Queen of Beef"—but traditional Italian dishes such as veal parmigiana and pasta Bolognese are also on the menu. The wine list is extensive. Most entrées are $22–34.

Fin Sushi & Sake Bar (413-637-9171; finsushi.com), 27 Housatonic St. Open daily 5:30–9:45. Varied as its restaurant scene has been, Lenox lacked a good sushi bar for a long time. That void has been more than filled by Fin Sushi & Sake, which has a genuine Japanese menu that includes tuna, salmon, and yellowtail sushi and sashimi along with items such as squid salad, barbecued eel, sea urchin roe, and miso soup. The decor is uncluttered but pleasant in the Japanese style. Beer and wine as well as sake are served. Entrées $17–22; sushi $6–9; sashimi, $8–14.

Firefly (413-637-2700; fireflylenox .com), 71 Church St. Open daily for dinner and for lunch on Sat. and Sun.; closed Tues. and Wed. off-season. Live entertainment Wed. nights. This cheery, popular place has an uncluttered, contemporary decor and an eclectic menu. Summer diners have the option of eating inside or outside on the porch. Tapas are served in the popular but often noisy bar, which also mixes high-octane drinks such as "Green Mambo" (apple vodka, sour apple schnapps, apple juice, and cinnamon sugar) and "The Lava Lamp" (prosecco, Johnny mash, calvados, and dried cranberries). Entrées $14–28.

Alta Restaurant and Wine Bar (413-637-0003; altawinebar.com), 34 Church St. A nice, casual atmosphere and a menu that blends American and Mediterranean cuisine. You can have a Berkshire pork chop or a New York strip steak, but also Spanish paella or Moroccan tangine. The menu recommends a wine by the glass for each entrée. There is dining on a porch facing the street. Entrées $19–29.

Frankie's Ristorante Italiano (413-637-4455; frankiesitaliano.com), 80 Main St. Open for dinner Sun.–Thurs. 5–9; Fri.-Sat. 5–9:30. The kind of restaurant that used to be found in every Italian neighborhood, Frankie's serves the sort of food your mother used to make, presuming she came from southern Italy. House specialties include steak fiorentina served with goat cheese, stuffed tomatoes, and potato gratin; lasagna made with spinach dough, Parmesan, Bolognese, and bechamel sauce; and fresh shrimp and lobster ravioli. Entrées $19–29.

Trattoria il Vesuvio (413-637-4904; trattoria-vesuvio.com), 242 Pittsfield Rd. Housed in a remodeled barn on the outskirts of Lenox, this family-owned restaurant has long had a devoted local following. We've enjoyed meals here in the past, but on our most recent visit found both the food and the service seriously wanting. The menu features Italian dishes such as roast breast of veal stuffed with prosciutto and spinach, chicken piccata, and osso buco. Entrées $14–34.

In Pittsfield

Note: In recent years the number of quality restaurants has increased and many now cluster companionably at the southern end of North Street and adjoining McKay Street, handy to parking garages, the new Beacon Cinema Center, The Colonial Theatre, and Barrington Stage.

Trattoria Rustica (413-499-1192; trattoria-rustica.com), 27 McKay St. Open for dinner daily except Tues. Reservations suggested. Davide Manzo hails from Pompeii and is a purist when it comes to things Italian (even the floor tiles); likewise, the authenticity of everything, including bread, emerging from his brick oven. The menu might include just half a dozen choices of antipasti, pasta, and "secondi." You might begin with caprese (homemade mozzarella, fresh basil, tomato, and olive oil), then dine on homemade ricotta-stuffed ravioli in tomato basil sauce, or oven-roasted veal loin chop (locally, organically raised). Entrées range from $14 for penne in spicy tomato sauce, to $32 for oven-roasted rack of lamb. Nightly exotic specials such as buffalo steak or wild boar.

Brix Wine Bar (413-236-9463; brixwinebar.com), 40 West St. (between North and McKay). Open for dinner Tues.–Sat. and Sun. brunch. As authentic as a French wine bar can be in the Berkshires: The zinc bar was carved by hand in Paris by one of the last craftsmen to produce them, and red as well as white wines are kept at their proper temperatures in a "cave" behind the bar. Some 120 wines, many by the glass; each bottle is air-sealed after opening to prevent degeneration. Beer and a full bar is also available. Needless to say, no one is rushed here, and friends meet for "wine flights" (samplings of four wines), hors d'oeuvres, and entrées ranging from croque monsieur and tarte du jour to grilled, marinated lamb chops and a locally raised pork served with wild mushrooms and house-made spatzle. In summer we dined on a delicious salad Niçoise (entrées: $11–26).

Elizabeth's Restaurant (413-448-8244), 1264 East St. (across from the GE plant). Open Wed.–Sun. for dinner. Reservations are a must. This long-established gem is not in restaurant row, but is not difficult to find. Request a table in the kitchen. The dining room, with its dozen or so tables, is also funky and friendly. This place is all about the food: Soups are great; real Italian polenta is a specialty. There are marvelous salads. Daily specials.

Brulées Restaurant & Catering (413-443-0500; brulees.com), 41 North St. Ken Peckham, a former executive chef who catered functions at Tanglewood, orchestrates the kitchen, and his wife Cara, the dining room. The menu blends French, Italian, and American dishes. Live entertainment on weekends. Entrées range from eggplant roulade ($16) to grilled filet mignon with a wild mushroom ragout ($23.50) with plenty of choices in between.

Flavours Restaurant (413-443-3188; flavoursintheberkshires.com), 75 North St., entrance on McKay St. Open for lunch and dinner Tues.–Fri., dinner only Sat.–Sun. Recently moved from a less inviting location on US 7, this Malaysian American cuisine is getting rave reviews for freshness, authenticity, variety, and service. Ambiance is minimal but pleasant. No MSG, gluten-free and vegan options, full bar, pub menu. Entrées $9–21.

Mazzeo's (413-448-2095; mazzeos ristorante.com), 1015 South St. (US 7). Open for dinner from 4; closed Mon. Reservations suggested. A long-time local favorite, recently relocated from downtown to US 7 south of town, is substantially expanded but still usually crowded. The large menu remains traditional Italian with many antipasti, a wide choice of homemade pastas such as cavatelli baked with sweet Italian sausage fettucini Bolognese ($16–24); other entrées range from eggplant parmigiana ($17) and veal saltimbocca ($24) to a variety of bisteca ($30).

Jae's Spice (413-443-1234; eatatjaes .com) 297 North St. Open from 11AM daily. Jae Chung is a North Adams native who established a reputation for pan-Asian, primarily Korean cuisine in Boston's South End. His restaurant in North Adams has since closed. This is an ambitious space and we wish Jae the best of luck with it, but reviews have been mixed. There is a complete sushi meal menu. Appetizers include meat dumplings, tempura, and flatbreads; entrées range from chicken and mango stir fry ($13.95) to carmelized scallops ($19.95). Rice and noodle dishes begin at $13.95.

Shiro (413-528-1898; berkshiro.com), 48B North St. Harry Yu opened this Japanese sushi restaurant just off Park Square after more than a decade of success with his place in Great Barrington. We haven't eaten there, but the word seems to be that, while the food is middling good, service is rushed and unfriendly. Hope this changes.

Mission Bar & Tapas (missionbar andtapas.com), 438 North St. Open daily for lunch and dinner, noon–midnight, Sun. brunch. Jim Benson's place is so hip that contact info is a gmail account, no phone. The contemporary lounge features hot and cold tapas, beer, and live entertainment. Check the website for current happenings.

Dakota Steak House (413-499-7900; dakotarestaurant.com), 1035 South St. (US 7). Open daily 4–10 for dinner, Sun. brunch 10–2. A big, cheery place, it specializes in beef and seafood and does both well, often together. Signature dishes include Crabby Filet (a petite filet mignon topped with sweet blue crabmeat), teriyaki sirloin, steak kebab (chunks of sirloin skewered with bell peppers, mushrooms, and tomatoes, then grilled), shrimp scampi, and Steak & Cake (grilled sirloin with a Maryland-style crabcake). Entrées $16.99–26.99.

In Williamstown

Mezze Bistro + Bar (413-458-0123; mezzeinc.com), 777 Cold Spring Road (US 7). Open nightly for dinner with the bar open most nights until 1 in summer months, later Sat. evenings. Reserve and be aware that during theater season it's quieter after curtain time (8 PM). The best fine dining in the northwest corner of the state. This third incarnation of Nancy Thompson's restaurant is housed in the nicely redesigned first floor of the much-loved former inn/restaurant Le Jardin. Opened in 2010, this new location offers more widely spaced tables than Mezze's former Water Street Site, and the large, attractive bar is itself a dining venue. Thompson was one of the area's first farm-to-table advocates, and Chef Joji Sumi spends part of every day talking to local farmers and purveyors, with a resulting à la carte menu that reflects what's seasonally available. On a winter night you might begin with a plate of house-cured olives and dine on Northeast Family Farm rib eye ($27) or sirloin burger ($12); house-made local sausages; a cassoulet of duck confit, smoked mutton sausage, and braised bacon; or house-made cavetelli with roasted balano broth, smoked chicken, and chorizo ($18).

THE LARGE BAR AT MEZZE BISTRO + BAR IS ITSELF A DINING VENUE.

Gala Restaurant (1-866-928-1108; galarestaurant.com), 222 Adams Rd. Open for breakfast, lunch, dinner, and Sun. brunch. Overlooking inner courtyard at The Orchards (see *Lodging*). This is the kind of upscale, lodging-based restaurant that tends to get AAA four-star ratings. Honestly, we haven't dined here, just read the online reviews, which are wildly mixed. Gala offers an informal sports bar with couches and a hearth, and the formal dining room with a locally sourced, à la carte menu. Entrées from $20 for a roasted half chicken to $29 for soy-braised Cavendish Farm pheasant with grilled fries and braised leeks in a cognac butter sauce.

The Williams Inn (413-458-9371; williamsinn.com), Main St. The formal inn's dining room offers a traditional American menu with such entrées as roast pork tenderloin Shaker-style ($17.25), New England scrod baked with tomatoes and smothered leeks topped with choron sauce ($17.50), and roast rack of lamb ($24.95). Sunday brunch is a huge buffet.

In North Adams

Gramercy Bistro (413-663-5300; gramercybistro.com), 87 Marshall St. Open nightly from 5; lunch Wed.–Sat. noon–2; Sun. brunch 11–2. Alexander Smith's popular restaurant has moved from its former storefront to a larger contemporary space adjacent to the MASS MoCA entrance. The cuisine is styled "contemporary classics." A recent dinner menu included seafood paella, filet mignon with blue cheese, sweet breads au beurre noire, and lamb osso buco with roasted vegetables. Entrées $18–26.

Taylor's Restaurant (413-664-4500; taylorsfinedining.net), 34 Holden St. Longtime owners of The Freight Yard Pub now also operate this white-cloth restaurant with a dining-out atmosphere. The menu ranges from comfort food and sandwiches through pasta to steaks and Alaskan king crab ($10–24).

Elsewhere

Mill on the Floss (413-458-9123; millonthefloss.com), US 7, New Ashford. Dinner nightly except Mon. A long-established favorite among Berkshire regulars, this 18th-century farmhouse with an open kitchen specializes in French country cuisine. Entrées might include crabcakes in Dijon sauce, tournedos béarnaise, and rack of lamb; $27.50–34.

Bascom Lodge (413-743-1591; bascomlodge.net), Mount Greylock Summit (see the "Mount Greylock" sidebar). Mid-May through Oct., three daily meals are served in this rustic summit lodge, but what got our attention is the Wednesday night dinner and entertainment series, a showcase for Chef Peter's skills with local, seasonal produce. Reservations are a must for these three-course meals ($25 including tax and gratuity). On an August evening we began with a white bean soup with squash followed by grilled beef with lemon, summer beans, and fingerling potatoes (the vegetarian option was Gorgonzola and walnut gnocchi with fresh tomato sauce with summer vegetables). Beer and wine are served. Tables are assigned, and next time we would request the sunporch, which offers the best sunset views south across the broad valley and the lake of lights in Pittsfield. Dinner is preceded by a free talk or live entertainment, open to the public and listed on the website.

In Lenox

The Olde Heritage Tavern (413-637-0884; theheritagetavern.com), 12 Housatonic St. Open for lunch and dinner. A no-nonsense pub housed in an 1881 building. There are tables out front in summer, while the dining room and bar areas are cozy and unpretentious. The burgers are the best we found in Lenox; wraps, steak, and fish-and-chips are reputed to be very good, too. The bar stocks 42 different beers. Dinner entrées $10–15.

Haven Café & Bakery (413-637-8948; havencafebakery.com), 8 Franklin St. Open Mon.–Sat for breakfast and lunch; 8–2 for Sun. brunch. Haven offers a varied and moderately priced menu for all three. Eggs Benedict and huevos rancheros are staples of the brunch menu. Lunch choices include pizza, brisket burger, pan-seared salmon, and grilled polenta. Price range is $6–14.50.

Shots Café (413-841-4150) 27 Housatonic St. A popular gathering place open from 7:30 AM for breakfast and lunch. Fresh pastries, organic coffee. Paninis a specialty. Homemade soups and desserts.

Chocolate Springs Café (413-637-9820; chocolatesprings.com), 55 Pittsfield Rd. (US 7). The café is open Sun.–Thurs. 10–8, Fri.–Sat. until 9. Serious hot chocolate, freshly made cakes, biscotti, espresso, huge tea list, homemade sorbet and gelato—everything is made here, especially fabulous chocolates.

In Pittsfield

Café Reva (413-442-6161), 238 Tyler St. Open Wed.–Mon. 6–2. Chef-owner Aura Whitman established her reputation at Seven Hills in Lenox, but decided to call her own hours when she became a mother. The cheerful storefront eatery is frequently packed, but worth a try. Breakfast all day on a "frittata of the moment," or a huge choice of omelets, pancakes, and waffles. Daily specials, too.

Dottie's Coffee Lounge (413-443-1792; dottiescoffeelounge.com), 444 North St. Open weekdays 7–5, Sat. 8–3, Sun. 9–3. Outdoor dining in summer. An inviting café specializing in artisan coffee, espressos, teas, local ingredients. Vegan/gluten-free options. A popular gathering spot for North Street's arts community.

Baba Louie's (413-499-2400), 34 Depot St. Open for lunch and dinner. Below North Street and handy to parking and the Beacon Cinema, this newest in a local chain is warmly welcomed. The specialty is wood-fired pizza, but there are delectable soups and salads, antipasto, and pastas.

The Lantern (413-448-2171), 455 North St. Open for all three meals except Sun. A landmark local eatery, great hot corned beef and New York pastrami sandwiches, soups, and salads. Claims the best burger in the Berkshires.

On a Roll Café (413-236-5671), 75 North St. Open weekdays 7–3. Hidden away in the middle of the "Central Block" (a shortcut from the parking garage to North Street), this is a cheery space with a great choice of salads, quesadillas, and individual pizzas as well as a frittata of the day. Handy to Beacon Cinema.

Hot Dog Ranch (413-499-0055), 20 Linden St., Pittsfield. Open from 11 for lunch and dinner daily, serving until 11 PM Sat. and Sun. A must for

Christina Tree

DOTTIE'S COFFEE LOUNGE, PITTSFIELD.

hot dog connoisseurs. These are baby hot dogs, served in the flakiest of buns, slathered with onions, mustard, and the mystery sauce that has made this a local favorite for generations. We lunched on two hot dogs and a Coke for a grand total of $3.

♿ **Marketplace Café** (413-358-4777), 55 North St. in the Beacon Cinema. Open daily 6:30 AM–9:30, Sun. from 9. This is part of a popular local chain, good for coffees, teas, hot chocolate, and butter beer. Sandwiches are above par.

House of India (413-443-3262), 261 North St. Open daily for lunch and dinner. The best thing here is the lunch buffet, a varied and flavorful value.

Court Square (413-442-9896), 95 East St., Pittsfield. Open daily for breakfast, lunch, and Sunday brunch. Full breakfast menu and many salads and sandwiches; also known for pies.

Patrick's Pub (413-499-1994), 26 Bank Row. Open for lunch and dinner; closed Sun. Dark, pubby atmosphere. Sandwiches and wraps at lunch, reasonably priced staples such as baked stuffed sole and honey-Dijon chicken at dinner. Mixed reviews.

The Highland (413-442-2457), 100 Fenn St. An oasis for the frugal diner since 1936. Open for lunch and dinner; closed Mon. Reasonably priced

THE LANTERN, PITTSFIELD

Christina Tree

road food. No credit cards, no reservations, no pretensions.

In Williamstown

Spice Root (413-458-5200; spiceroot.com), 23 Spring St. Open daily for dinner, Tues.–Sun. for lunch. Lunch on the bargain-priced buffet or on mulligatawny soup and honey sesame nan or poori. Rave reviews for authenticity, service, atmosphere, and value. The large menu features a wide choice of lamb and vegetarian dishes, including vegan.

Coyote Flaco (413-458-4240; mycoyoteflaco.com), 505 Cold Spring Rd (US 7). Open for dinner except Mon. Authentic, upstanding Mexican fare and reasonable prices. Tequilas a specialty.

The '6 House Pub (413-458-1896; 6housepub.com), 866 Cold Spring Rd. (MA 2) west of town. Part of the 1896 lodging complex but a good bet for both lunch and dinner. A comfortable pub atmosphere with microbrews and a full, reasonably priced menu. Outside tables in season.

Papa Charlie's Deli and Sandwich Shop (413-458-5969), 28 Spring St. Open daily from breakfast through dinner. Overstuffed sandwiches and bagels, many named for actors at the Williamstown Theatre Festival and other notables, are what this place is about. In off-hours it's a great place to play student, even if you aren't one, sipping slowly and reading a book in a deep wooden booth. The overflow basement area is less inviting.

Thai Garden (413-458-0004), 27 Spring St. Open for lunch and dinner daily. An attractive atmosphere and reasonably priced, fresh, and tasty food are an irresistible combination. The menu features both Thai and Japanese dishes. Dine on tamarind tofu or duck, steamed ginger salmon, or a variety of sushi and sashimi.

Chef's Hat (413-458-5120), 905 Simonds Rd. (US 7, north of town). Open for breakfast from 6:30 (7 on Sun.) and lunch until 3; closed Mon. The Pudvar family will tell you that if you know where to look, the original diner car is still here, but they have expanded, adding knotty pine and booths. Locals crowd in on weekends to breakfast on hash and eggs (steak and eggs is also on the menu) and a wide choice of omelets and pancakes, diner classics like a hot turkey sandwich or liver and onions; also salads, stir-fries, and a surprising variety of fish and seafood. The children's menu features a foot-long hot dog with fries.

Cozy Corner Restaurant (413-458-3854), 850 Simonds Rd. (US 7). Breakfast, lunch, and dinner daily. An unpretentious roadhouse with low prices and a loyal following. Fish-and-chips and pizza; also Greek specialties, including a great eggplant. A selection of beers. Our Mediterranean-style cod was delicious.

Hobson's Choice (413-458-9101; hobsonsrestaurant.com), 159 Water St. Open from 5 for dinner. The ground floor of an 1830s house is the setting for the most popular, moderately priced place to dine in town: a friendly, unpretentious, roadhouse-style restaurant with old-fashioned wooden booths. The menu is vast, ranging from vegetarian pasta to prime rib, with plenty of seafood and chicken options. All dinners include the big salad bar as well as starch and vegetable. Beers and specialty drinks. Entrées are $14–24.

Water Street Grill (413-458-2175; waterstgrill.com), 123 Water St. Open for lunch and dinner until 11, bar until midnight. A more formal grill and an informal tavern, but nothing's very formal. Burgers and steaks are certified Angus, and there's a nice choice of entrée salads

Michael's Restaurant (413-458-2114; michaelsofwilliamstown.com), 460 Main St. (MA 2). Open Tues.–Sun. for dinner from 4. Charles (the original Papa Charlie) opened this place as an A&W root beer stand more than 40 years ago. Now his children, Cindy and Michael, continue to run the area's favorite Greek restaurant. Friendly atmosphere, booths, good beers on tap, and all the classics: spanakopita, salads, seafood with kalamata olives and garlic, terrific soups. Honestly, however, we were disappointed in the eggplant.

Misty Moonlight Diner (413-499-2483; themistymoonlightdiner.com), 565 Dalton Ave. A family restaurant with a contrived but pleasant 1950s atmosphere with a jukebox. Open Mon.–Sat. 6:30 AM–9 PM, Sun. 6:30 AM–2 PM, serving breakfast all day as well as a large choice of burgers, sandwiches, vegetarian dishes, BBQ ribs and chicken, pastas, and fried seafood. Daily specials, too. Fancy rum as well as nonalcoholic smoothies and margaritas are house specialties, and there's a choice of beer on tap.

Lickety Split (413-458-1818), 69 Spring St. This lunch place offers good soups, sandwiches, and salads.

Tunnel City Coffee (413-458-5010), 100 Spring St. Open 6:30 AM–6 PM. With coffees, teas, light snacks, and WiFi, this big, pleasant café at the far end of Spring Street is understandably a big student hangout.

In North Adams

The Hub (413-662-2500), 55 Main St. Open Tues.–Fri.11–9:30, Sat. 8 AM–11 PM, Sun. 8–1 (breakfast only). This spacious, comfortable space made a great lunch stop and gets raves for dinner, like porch chops and apple sauce or jambalaya. Great blackboard sandwich specials usually include a portobello pesto burger and "grown-up grilled cheese" on artisan bread with creamy Muenster cheese, shaved ham, and tomato.

Petrino's Café (413-346-4558; petrinoscafe.net), 67 Main St. Open for breakfast, lunch, and Sunday "jazzy" brunch. Mark Petrino is committed to things fresh and local. The place is known for made-to-order salads and options like grilled eggplant and portobello mushroom cap topped with tomato, mozzarella, fresh spinach, and avocado on a bun. Baking is all done here.

Boston Seafood (413-663-8740), 160 American Legion Dr. Open for lunch and dinner except Mon. Just off Main Street, this is a classic family-style seafood restaurant, which doesn't mean you can't get a burger, Reuben, or chicken teriyaki. Specialties include baked salmon with lobster stuffing and a seafood casserole. Beers on tap and full liquor.

Jack's Hot Dogs (413-664-9006), 12 Eagle St. (off Main St.). Lunch, dinner, and noshing in between. A local institution that's been in the same family for more than seven decades. If you like hot dogs with all the trimmings (including sauerkraut), Jack's is the place.

Isabella's (413-662-2239; isabellasrest.com), 896 State Rd. (MA 2 next to Stop & Shop). Open for dinner except Mon. A reasonably priced dinner option, Isabella's has a cheerful atmosphere with dining on the outdoor deck, weather permitting. Pastas, regional Italian cuisine. No surprises but no complaints.

COFFEE HOUSES ✐ ♿ ((·)) **Elf Parlor** (413-664-7303; elfparlor.com), 303 Ashland St. Open from 8 AM weekdays (6 PM Sat., closed Sun.). A family-run and -geared coffee shop in a vintage house near the Massachusetts College of Arts with an emphasis on teas (loose leaf, organic), coffees (Barrington Coffee Roasters), and healthy pastries. Cocoa, soy drinks and "hot creams" for kids are also served. Also open Thurs.–Sat. nights for jam sessions. Patrons are encouraged to use the house electric piano and acoustic guitar. Beer and wine are served.

Brew Haha (413-664-2020; cafebrewhaha.com), 20 Marshall St., North Adams. Daily except Wed., 7–5. An attractive café handy to MASS MoCA. Breakfast all day with espresso and teas.

Elsewhere

✐ **Miss Adams Diner** (413-776-7372), 53 Park St. (MA 8), Adams. Open Mon.–Thurs. 7–2, Fri. 7–7, Sat.–Sun. 7–noon. An expanded 1940s classic (Worcester lunch car No. 821) diner with an expanded traditional diner menu.

✷ Entertainment

THEATER Colonial Theatre (413-997-4444; thecolonialtheatre.org), 111 South St., Pittsfield. Built in 1903, the playhouse in its heyday hosted a dazzling array of performers, from the Barrymores and Sarah Bernhardt to Will Rogers. Eventually refitted for movies, it closed in 1949 and for half a century was preserved as a warehouse by the Miller family, who sold art and paint supplies from a storefront they added on. In 1998 Hillary Clinton declared the Colonial "a national treasure," which triggered initial efforts to reclaim the theater's glory. It was finally and completely restored in 2006, opening with a performance of *Rent*. At this writing performances include children's productions, jazz (T. S. Monk), Arlo Guthrie, *The Nutcracker* by the Albany Berkshire Ballet, and the Irish Rovers.

MUSIC South Mountain Concerts (413-442-2106; southmountainconcerts.com), US 7/US 20, 2 miles south of Park Square, Pittsfield. A Berkshire tradition since 1918. This is a series of five Sunday afternoon chamber concerts by world class ensembles, September through the fist weekend in October. They are performed in an acoustically fine, vintage music hall that seats 440.

Concerts at Tannery Pond (1-888-820-9441; tannerypondconcerts.org), New Lebanon, N.Y. The setting for outdoor chamber music concerts, staged on selective Saturday evenings late May through mid-October, is beautiful: the pond on the grounds of the former Mount Lebanon Shaker Village, now the Darrow School, a coed boarding school with a campus that occupies and sensitively enhances the former Shaker Village, just over the New York line from Hancock and off US 20.

OTHER Albany Berkshire Ballet (413-445-5382; berkshireballet.org), 116 Fenn St., Pittsfield. Performances

Christina Tree

SUMMER CHAMBER MUSIC CONCERTS AT TANNERY POND DRAW PATRONS TO THIS FORMER SHAKER VILLAGE IN NEW LEBANON, N.Y.

of classic and contemporary ballet are staged periodically year-round at a variety of venues, reviewed respectfully in New York and Boston.

Massachusetts Museum of Contemporary Art (413-662-2111; massmoca.org), 87 Marshall St., North Adams. See *Museums.* MASS MoCA sponsors a year-round series of live concerts and other performances.

Main Street Stage (413-663-3240; mainstreetstage.org), 57 Main St., North Adams. Year-round performances are given in a storefront theater.

FILM **The Beacon Cinema** (413-358-4780; thebeaconcinema.com), 57 North St., Pittsfield. The Kinnel-Kresge building is classic 1918, but inside a new, six-screen, all-digital theater features The Metropolitan Opera "Live in HD" as well as art films, sports, and first runs in surround sound. Hot hits can appear on all screens at once—in 3D. A vintage escalator accesses the wine bar and **New Stage** performances upstairs.

Little Cinema (413-443-7171), 39 South St., Pittsfield. This 300-seat theater in the Berkshire Museum features art and classic films.

Williams College's **Williams Theatre** performs during winter months.

Sterling and Francine Clark Art Institute (413-458-2303; clarkart.edu), 225 South St. Presents a variety of films, lectures, and plays throughout the year.

Images Cinema (413-458-5612; imagescinema.org), 50 Spring St., Williamstown. A classic college-town movie house showing foreign films and interesting domestic ones.

✷ Selective Shopping

ANTIQUE SHOPS **The Library Antiques** (413-458-3436; libraryantiques.com), 70 Spring St., Williamstown. Open daily. An ever-expanding series of spaces filled with fine antiques of all sorts, as well as many unusual gifts. Browsers welcome.

Collector's Warehouse (413-458-9686; collectorswarehouse-williamstown.com), 723 Cold Spring Rd. (US 7), Williamstown. Open daily except Tues. June–Dec.; otherwise Thurs.–Sun. Miscellaneous antiques and collectibles, including glassware, jewelry, frames, dolls, linen, and furniture.

ART AND ARTISANS

In Lenox

DeVries Fine Art (413-637-3462; andrewdevries.com) 62 Church St. This gallery mainly displays sculptures, reliefs, sketches, and watercolors by internationally known artist Andrew DeVries. Many of the smaller sculptures on view are models for larger commissioned works. In summer open Wed.–Mon. 11–5, Fri –Sat. 5–9; spring and fall hours, Fri.–Sun. 11–3:30; winter by appointment.

Hoadley Gallery (413-637-2814; hoadleygallery.com), 21 Church St. An established gallery featuring paintings, jewelry, ceramics. Glass, and home furnishings. Nearly 150 artists are represented. Everything on view has been carefully selected and the quality is outstanding. Open daily 10–6, extended hours in summer.

In Pittsfield

Note: Third Thursdays of every month are open gallery nights (5–8) with receptions up and down North Street and live entertainment at local theaters, special dining and café happenings throughout downtown; for details see culturalpittsfield.com.

DEVRIES FINE ART IN LENOX FEATURES THE WORK OF ANDREW DEVRIES.

Christina Tree

Leslie Ferrin Ceramic Art & Sculpture Gallery (413-442-1622; ferringallery.com), 437 North St., Pittsfield. Open daily 11–5 in summer, Wed.–Sun. off-season. Leslie Ferrin established an enviable reputation with her gallery, primarily devoted to pottery and ceramics, moving from Northampton to Lenox and on to Pittsfield when artistic energy shifted to North Street as a showcase for both established and cutting-edge art. Check the website for "Dish and Dine" events, gallery dinners showcasing both pottery and local chefs.

Lichtenstein Center for the Arts (413-499-9348; culturalpittsfield.com), 28 Renne Ave., Pittsfield. Open Wed.–Sat. noon–5. Just behind the vest-pocket park on Main Street, a handsome gallery hosting exhibitions by nationally known professionals; also the setting for performances and concerts.

Museum Facsimiles Gallery (413-499-1818; museumfacsimiles.com), 431 North St. Exhibiting established contemporary Berkshire artists; also locally handcrafted cards, framing.

Storefront Artist Project (413-442-7201; storefrontartist.org), 31 South St. Founder Maggie Mailer has been a force in revitalizing downtown Pittsfield through a strategy: using vacant storefronts to exhibit local artists. An artist herself, Mailer has a sense of what makes good art and continues to mount exceptional exhibits in ever-changing venues. Check the website for current happenings.

Zeitgeist Gallery (413-446-3772), 648 North St. Open Fri. 4–7, Sat. 1–7. A community art space exhibiting a broad range of media and genre.

Berkshire Fine Handcrafts (413-441-6926), 431 North St. A surprising variety of items, most of them locally crafted. Well worth a stop.

Fern Leslie Studio (413-446-0723; fernleslie.com), 249 North St. Fabric art: one-of-a-kind scarves, T-shirts, bags, and cards.

In Williamstown

The Harrison Gallery (413-458-1700; theharrisongallery.com), 39 Spring St. Changing exhibits of work by a stable of established artists.

In North Adams

Note: Late June through Columbus Day weekend, more than 30 art venues in town welcome visitors at least Mon.–Wed. Pick up a **DownStreet Art Map,** which locates and describes each of the galleries and lists special

CROWDS FLOCK TO NORTH STREET IN PITTSFIELD FOR THE MONTHLY THIRD THURSDAY EVENT.

Karl Volkman

A "DISH & DINE" EVENING AT THE FERRIN GALLERY, GREENFIELD

events; these include citywide gallery openings on the **4th Thursday**, June–Sept. Also see DownStreet Art.org.

Galleries open year-round include:

North Adams Artists' Co-Op Gallery (413-664-4003; naacogallery .org), 33 Main St. Open Mon. and Thurs.–Sat. 11–6, Sun. noon–4. An impressive gallery showcasing works in a wide variety of media; exhibits change frequently.

Kolok Gallery (413-346-1046; kolok gallery.com), 121 Union St. (MA 2), Suite 1E. Open Thurs.–Sun. afternoons. This classy contemporary gallery in the Windsor Mill mounts changing exhibitions of contemporary work.

MCLA's Gallery 51 (413-662-5362; mcla.edu/gallery51), 51 Main St., North Adams. Open daily in summer, Wed.–Sun. off-season. Changing exhibits feature established contemporary artists as well as faculty and students at the Massachusetts College of Liberal Arts; inquire about Studio21South in the Beaver Mill, displaying work by locally based artists.

KOLOK GALLERY, NORTH ADAMS.

Christina Tree

Eclipse Mill (413-664-9101; eclipse mill.com), 243 Union St., #102. This complex of artist lofts and galleries holds gallery hours on weekends, noon–5.

BOOKSTORES **The Bookstore** (413-637-3390; bookstoreinlenox .com), 11 Housatonic St., Lenox. An inviting independent bookshop of the kind that's getting harder to find, with a large, well-chosen, and varied selection of new and used books. Regional interest and authors with local connections are featured, but there's something for just about every kind of reader. There's a wine bar, too.

Chapters Bookstore, Inc. (413-443-2665; chapterspittsfield.com), 78 North St., Pittsfield. Kelley Wright's large, cheerful bookstore fills three storefronts and invites browsing; there's a reading room for kids.

Papyri Books (413-662-2099; papyri books.com), 45 Eagle St., North Adams. Open May–Dec., Mon.–Sat. noon–6; also closed Mon. off-season. Lois and Michael Daunis now maintain this oasis for book lovers: mostly used books, but some new titles. Inviting seating and a full schedule of readings, signings, and music.

Water Street Books (413-458-8071), 26 Water St., Williamstown. The town's independent, full-service bookstore.

Barnes & Noble (413-496-9051), Berkshire Crossing Mall, MA 9, Pittsfield. A superstore and a Starbucks.

SPECIAL STORES

In Lenox

Weaver's Fancy (413-637-2013) 65 Church St. Specializes in handcrafted clothing and accessories by leading fabric artists, including owner Katharine Pincus. Open year-round, always on weekends, but check for weekday hours off-season.

In Williamstown

Where'd You Get That? (413-458-2206; wygt.com), 100 Spring St., Williamstown. Open daily. Ken and Michele Gietz are enthusiastic purveyors of some wild toys geared to children of all ages: strategy games, gizmos, gadgets.

The Mountain Goat (413-458-8445; themountaingoat.com), 130 Water St. The founding store in what's become an upcountry chain specializing in outdoor clothing, equipment, and bicycles (rentals, too); also local books and plenty of advice about where to do whatever you do outdoors.

✱ Farms, Flowers and Farmer's Markets

Farmer's markets are detailed on two excellent websites: berkshiregrown .com and farmfresh.org. They are held seasonally each week in Adams, Lanesborough, Lenox, North Adams, Pittsfield, and Williamstown. The sites also describe local farms, among them:

In Cheshire

♿ **Lightwing Farms** (413-743-4425), MA 8, site of Saturday farmers' market, 10–4. Also open July–early Oct. for vegetables, flowers, and honey. No pesticides or herbicides.

✐ **Whitney's Farm Stand** (413-442-4749), MA 8, 2.5 miles north of Berkshire Mall. Open Easter–Christmas. Homegrown fruits and vegetables, including melons, sweet corn, and apples; also, bedding plants, perennials, a deli, bakery, dairy bar, and petting zoo. PYO blueberries and pumpkins in-season.

In Hancock

Ioka Valley Farm (413-738-5915; iokavalleyfarm.com), 3475 MA 43, near Jiminy Peak. Call ahead for seasonal hours. Uncle Don's Barnyard and seasonal events, especially at Halloween, when there's a corn maze outside and a very dark hay bale maze inside the barn. Major fun. Also seasonal maple syrup and a pancake café. PYO strawberries mid-June–mid-July, pumpkins in fall, cider and apples, farm-theme playground, picnic area.

In Lanesborough

Lakeview Orchard (413-448-6009; lakevieworchard.com), 94 Old Cheshire Rd. Open early July–Thanksgiving. From MA 8, take Old State Rd. to Summer St. to Old Cheshire Rd.; from US 7, take Summer St. to Old Cheshire. Sixteen varieties of apples along with sweet cherries, peaches, plums, blueberries, shallots, onions, homemade doughnuts, pies and turnovers, jams, and apple butter. Sweet cider pressed in-season. A beautiful location.

Mountain View Farm (413-445-7642), 90 Old Cheshire Rd. (see directions above). Open mid-June through Oct. Sweet corn, PYO tomatoes, and strawberries in-season. Another beautiful location.

In Richmond

Furnace Brook Winery at Hilltop Orchards (413-698-3301; furnacebrookwinery.com), 508 Canaan Rd. off MA 41 (look for the sign). Open Thurs.–Sun. 11–5. Free wine tasting in a lodge that doubles as a cross-country ski center in winter. Visitors are welcome to walk the paths and enjoy the long views. John Vittori makes varietal grape and specialty wines, also Johnny Mash Hard Cider and French Cidre, aged in oak barrels. PYO apples, pears, plums in summer and fall; picnics encouraged, special events.

Bartlett's Orchard (413-698-2559; bartlettsorchard.com), 575 Swamp Rd. Four miles south on Barker Rd. from US 20. Open year-round, daily 8–5:30. Generations of Bartletts have grown, sold, and shipped apples from these 52 hillside acres. There are 18 varieties of apples plus a full bakery (try the cider doughnuts) and specialty foods; also milk, bread, ice cream, and more.

In Williamstown

Green River Farms (413-458-2470; greenriverfarms.com), on MA 43 at its junction with US 7. PYO strawberries, blueberries, tomatoes, and peppers. Full greenhouse and nursery. Corn, summer squash, tomatoes, winter squash, Indian corn, pumpkins, and cider press in-season. Petting farm and hayrides.

Cricket Creek Farm (413-458-5888; cricketcreekfarm.com), 1255 Oblong Rd. at the end of Sloan Rd. (at the junction of MA 43 and US 7), just up the road from Field Farm. A special farm: 500 acres with grass-fed Brown Swiss and Jersey cows. The farm store is open year-round: farmstead cheeses, raw milk, homemade breads, grass-fed beef and whey-fed pork, fruits and veggies, maple syrup and honey.

✱ Special Events

May: **Memorial Day Parade** in North Adams.

June–December: **Third Thursday** (413-664-6180) with music and food, late-night shopping in Pittsfield.

June–September: **Fourth Thursdays** (413-663-5253) in North Adams.

July 4: Pittsfield boasts one of the biggest **Fourth of July parades** in the country. **Fireworks** and Independence Day music at Tanglewood.

July–August: **Tanglewood Music Festival,** Lenox. For more seasonal concerts, see *Entertainment/Music.*

Late July–early August: **Susan B. Anthony Days** in Adams commemorate the suffragette, who was born in Adams. Main Street is closed off and filled with booths, games, and food stalls.

Late September: The **Tub Parade** in Lenox is a re-creation of the Gilded Age end-of-summer procession in which carriages and carts were decked with flowers. **Country Fair and Crafts Festival at Hancock Shaker Village,** featuring New England Heritage Breeds Conservancy Exhibition of Heritage Livestock, crafts, lawn games, daily parade of animals.

October: **Fall Foliage Festival** (413-664-6180) in Pittsfield includes a parade and week of festivities. Columbus Day weekend **Northern Berkshire Fall Foliage Festival** in North Adams includes races, games, suppers, and sales, and culminates with a big parade on the Sunday before Columbus Day weekend, which is observed by holding citywide open studios. In Adams it's the **Mount Greylock Ramble,** a traditional mass climb of "their" mountain by Adams residents. **Williamstown Film Festival** (williamstownfilmfest .com) honors major figures in American cinema (*mid- to late month*).

ALONG THE MOHAWK TRAIL

Beyond North Adams the Berkshire Hills rise steeply on the east, traversed by one of the country's first roads designed specifically for auto touring.

The Mohawk Trail Scenic Byway, as this stretch of MA 2 is known, loosely (very loosely) shadows an ancient Indian trail that ran from the Hoosac Valley up over the Hoosac Range and along a wooded ridge, then dropped down into the wide Deerfield River Valley and followed the Deerfield to the Connecticut River Valley. In the late 18th century both a toll road and a "shunpike" traversed this high country, an era evoked by the fine old houses along the Deerfield in Charlemont and by the Charlemont Inn, built in 1787 to accommodate stagecoach traffic.

"Peaks of one or two thousand feet rush up either bank of the river in ranges, thrusting out their shoulders side by side. . . . I have never driven through such romantic scenery, where there was such a variety and boldness of mountain shapes as this," Nathaniel Hawthorne wrote in 1850.

For all practical purposes, however, north Berkshire County continued to be isolated from eastern Massachusetts until the opening of the 4.75-mile-long Hoosac Tunnel in 1875. In the first decades of the 20th century, the speediest, safest way from Boston to North Adams was still by train through the tunnel. By then, however, rail travel was old hat.

Everyone wanted to escape the narrow dictates of the rails and to get off on their own four wheels. Cars could drive from Greenfield to Charlemont and then along the Deerfield River, but there they met the same mountain that had stumped railroad builders for so long. Already motor traffic (almost all recreational at the time) was flowing along "Jacob's Ladder" (present US 20) and into South Berkshire instead. The city fathers of North Adams rose to the challenge, and on October 22, 1914, 15 miles of carefully graded (no more than 7 percent), unpaved but well-oiled road over Hoosac Mountain was formally dedicated and hailed by the *North Adams Transcript* as a "symphony of sylvan delight." In 1921 the eastern end of this "Mohawk Trail" was rerouted from less dramatic Shelburne Road to climb over a high shoulder of Greenfield Mountain. Given the absence of official route numbers (the U.S. Highway System was adopted in 1926), white-and-red-striped markings for the Mohawk Trail extended east much

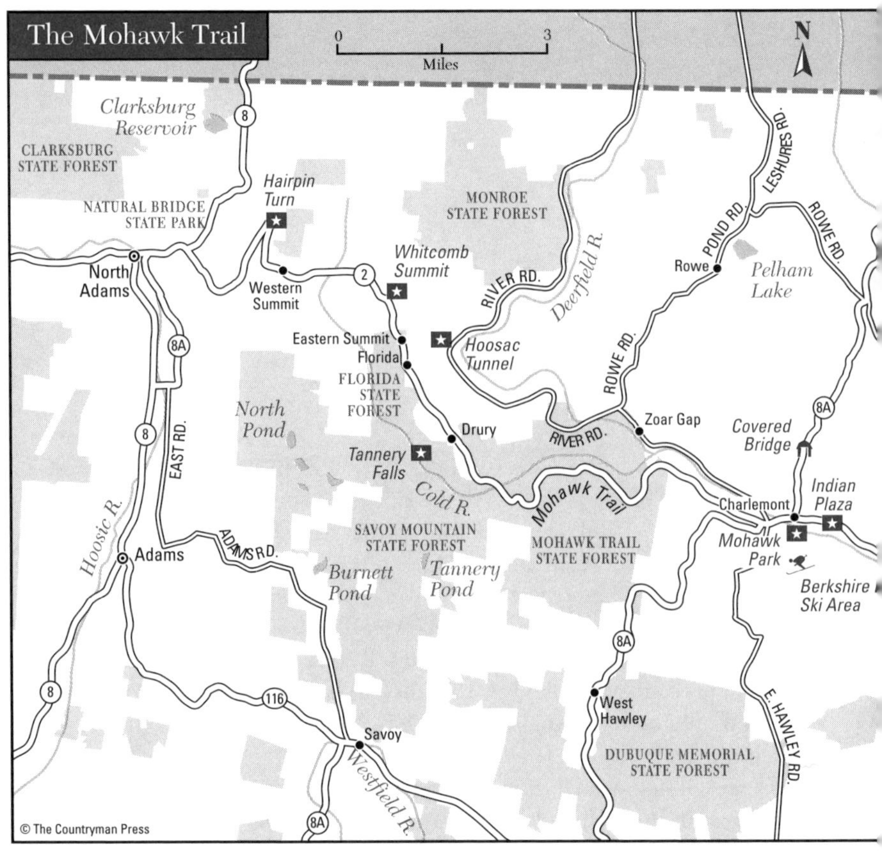

of the way to Boston. The current Mohawk Trail officially extends from Williamstown to Millers Falls.

It's the 38 miles between North Adams and Greenfield that we focus on here. This was the stretch of the trail recognized as a destination in its own right from the 1920s through the 1950s, a period during which it sprouted tea shops and gift shops, motor courts, motels, and campgrounds (both private and state), and seasonally accommodated more than 1,000 tourists.

Take its very name and theme. Ignoring the century in which this route evolved as an 18th- and 19th-century way west, *Mohawk Trail* conjures up the narrow path blazed by Indians, not even local Indians (the Mahicans on the western side and Pocumtucks on the eastern side of the Hoosac Range), but the more famous marauders from (current) upstate New York who used it as a warpath.

In 1914 America's first affordable cars were just beginning to transform the way ordinary folks vacationed. Between 1908 and 1927, 15 million Model T's were produced. In the 1920s motor touring along the Mohawk Trail increased

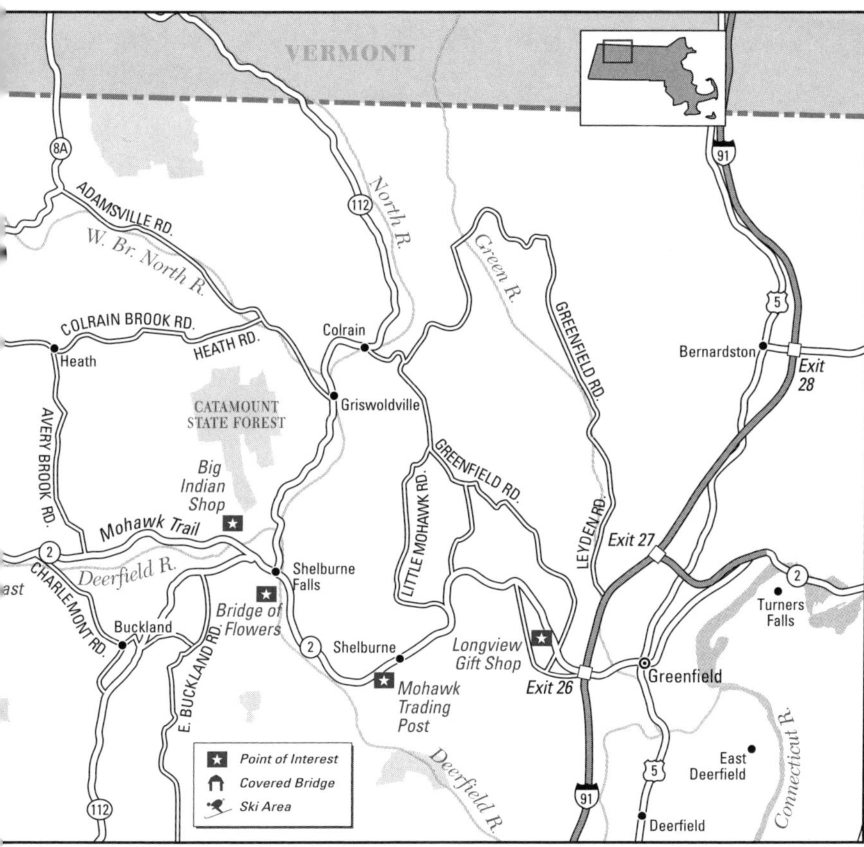

dramatically and many of the surviving trading posts were built. "Tourists" drove their first cars over the trail and returned year after year.

Over the years the road broadened and was further rerouted, and cars picked up speed. Always to some degree a day trip, the Mohawk Trail gradually lost its status as a destination, and today it's promoted primarily as a foliage route. Several of the old motor courts were replaced by motels, but most simply disappeared along with vintage restaurants and tearooms. Attractions along the Trail are small, family-owned businesses, and in many cases they have just been hanging on.

But the tourist tide is once more turning. This summer the sensitively restored vintage '30s Wigwam Cabins at the Western Summit reopen and an adjoining ridge trail further accesses views from 2,500 feet across the valley. White-water rafting on the Deerfield River now fills motels and cabins as well as a number of B&Bs and the 18th-century Charlemont Inn. The village of Shelburne Falls, known since the 1920s for its "Bridge of Flowers," is now the major dining and shopping center for the Trail, which went straight through the middle of the village until the 1950s.

LIFE'S A PICNIC ON THE MOHAWK TRAIL

Muddy River Press

THIS POSTCARD DEPICTS A VERMONT FAMILY ENJOYING A PICNIC ON WHITCOMB SUMMIT SHORTLY AFTER THE 1914 OPENING OF THE MOHAWK TRAIL.

Like the Mohawk Trail itself, this chapter links Berkshire and Franklin Counties, describing what's to be found on and just off the Trail. Our description runs from west to east, but only because that's the way the book goes. Either way, it remains one of the most scenic drives in New England.

GUIDANCE Mohawk Trail Association (413-743-8127 or 1-866-743-8127; mohawktrail.com), P.O. Box 1044, North Adams 01247, publishes a free brochure to the attractions along its length. The website is also helpful.

Also see **Shelburne Falls Village Information Center** and **Franklin Country Chamber of Commerce** in "West County."

Note: The Mohawk Trail Historic Auto Trail Guide by Clint Richmond (Muddy River Press, Brookline, $9; inquiries@muddyriverpress.com) is illustrated with many vintage postcards and photos of the Trail.

When Not to Go: All the factors that make this a glorious drive in warm weather months along the mountainous section west of Charlemont can mean white-knuckle driving in winter conditions.

✱ To See and Do

ALONG THE MOHAWK TRAIL (ROUTE 2) WEST TO EAST In 1914 the Mohawk Trail officially began in **North Adams** at the intersection (now marked by Dunkin' Donuts and McDonald's) of Union and Eagle Streets.

Natural Bridge State Park (mass.gov/dcr) is the first sight to see, marked from MA 2 westbound. Certainly worth the short detour, this is a series of waterfalls, chutes, and pools in an abandoned marble quarry, viewed from a series of bridges and stairways. There's also a visitor center with restrooms. See *Green Space* in the previous chapter for details.

The **Hairpin Turn**, the most dramatic reverse curve in all New England, zigs and zags its way up to the **Western Summit** (2,020 feet). Here the **Golden Eagle Restaurant** (413-663-9834; thegoldeneaglerestaurant.com) sits in the crook of the turn, an unlikely place to stop, but regulars tells us it's a good stop for lunch.

The **Wigwam Gift Shop and Cabins** (413-664-0400), 2350 Mohawk Trail, is the obvious turnout here. The shop with a "three-state view" dates to 1914, when a tearoom and a (long-gone) observation tower opened. As we go to press this historic complex is under restoration by Nancy Fitzpatrick, owner of The Red Lion Inn in Stockbridge and The Porches Inn in North Adams. The '30s cabins, due to reopen in the summer of 2011, are furnished comfortably with refrigerators and coffeemakers, and each has a breathtaking view of the valley below. Guests have full use of the year-round pool, hot tub, and other amenities at The Porches.

The Hoosac Range Trail. A 3-mile hiking/snowshoeing path, also due to open this summer (2011), begins at the former Wigwam Shop and continues along the ridge with spectacular views. It connects with Spruce Hill in Savoy Mountain State Forest. The trail system will ultimately connect the Florida and Savoy Mountain State Forests, part of an envisioned 100-mile Mahican–Mohawk Trail.

In **Florida,** one of the coldest towns in the state (it was named in 1805 just as the United States was purchasing Florida from Spain), the road levels out.

"FAMOUS HAIRPIN TURN" POSTCARD

Mudddy River Press

A FEW VINTAGE MOTOR COURT CABINS SURVIVE ALONG MOHAWK TRAIL.

Savoy Mountain State Forest (413-663-8469; mass.gov/dcr) is accessed by Central Shaft Road (it angles off to the right). The forest's 11,118 acres harbor some fascinating history and evocative places. A Shaker colony was among the early-19th-century settlements for which now only cellar holes exist. The most developed corner, around North and South Ponds, was later the Haskins Club, a private resort. You can swim and fish for trout in North Pond, which offers changing rooms and restrooms. There's also a boat ramp, and there are 45 campsites (open Memorial Day–Columbus Day) in a former apple orchard along with four log cabins (open year-round) by South Pond. The forest offers 24 miles of hiking trails, two ski touring loops, and a "crooked forest" of deformed trees. The waters are stocked with fish.

Whitcomb Summit, Florida, is the highest point on the trail (2,173 feet). The spectacular "100-mile view" is west over wave upon wave of hills and mountains; a steel (and lower) version of the vintage-1915 tower survives. The bronze elk, placed here by the Massachusetts Elks in 1923, is magnificent. At its dedication, speakers included Boston's Mayor Curley.

Whitcomb Summit Resort (413-662-2625 or 1-800-547-0944; whitcomb summit.com), 229 Mohawk Trail, Florida, is open year-round, but check. There is a tavern, restaurant, and 18 units in the neighboring two-story motel (currently for sale as condo units). Across the road there are also rustic, vintage cabins accommodating from three to six people; each has a heater and shower. The grounds include a pool, but the big attraction here is the view. A path leads off to **Moore's Summit** (2,250 feet), the highest point on the Mohawk Trail.

Scenic detour: **Whitcomb Hill Road/the Eastern Portal and River Road.** East of the elk statue, Whitcomb Hill Road plunges off to the north, corkscrewing downhill at a grade that vintage-1912 cars simply could not handle. This is the old road up (and down) Hoosac Mountain, the one the Mohawk Trail was designed to replace. At the bottom of the hill, turn left and drive a mile or so to the railroad tracks. Park just beyond them to see the "Eastern Portal" of the Hoosac Tunnel.

If you continue on this road a little more than 3 miles, passing a series of fishing and boating access points, you reach the Fife Brook Dam; in another mile you will see the **Bear Swamp Visitor Center** (closed at this writing; for information, call 413-424-7219). The **Dunbar Picnic Area** with restrooms and swings is another mile up the road, across from the trailheads for hiking in the **Monroe State Forest** (413-339-5504; mass.gov/dcr). You can loop back on Monroe Hill Road, past the decommissioned Yankee Rowe Nuclear Power Plant into the village of **Rowe,** and on back down the Zoar Road to MA 2.

If you return to the bottom of Whitcomb Hill, you can follow the Deerfield River east (chances are you will see trout fishers) to the lovely, pine-shaded, riverside **Zoar Picnic Area** and on through mountain-walled **Zoar Gap** to Charlemont. This makes a nice loop from the east if you only want to drive as far west as Whitcomb Summit.

The **Eastern Summit Gift Shop** (413-663-6996), 367 Mohawk Trail, is the next Mohawk Trail landmark (westbound lane, but worth the crossover). Open May–Oct. The view north and west over tier on tier of mountains is similar to that from Whitcomb Summit. The shop has been owned by the Devanney family for more than 30 years, and the complex, which began with a shop and now defunct cabins across the road, dates back at least another 40.

Dead Man's Curve is just beyond Brown's Garage ("no gas") in the village of Drury. The overhead warning sign with its flashing lights suggests many fatal accidents over the years. It marks the beginning of the descent down the eastern slope of the Hoosac Range, following the Cold River.

Detour: **Tannery Falls.** It's more difficult to catch the turnoff traveling eastbound than it is west, but just east of the bridge that marks the Florida–Savoy town line, make a right turn onto steep Black Brook Road and drive for about 2.5 miles; take a right

TANNERY FALLS IN SAVOY MOUNTAIN STATE FOREST.

Kindra Clineff/DEM

onto unpaved Tannery Road, which, after another 0.7 mile brings you to the parking area for Tannery Falls (the sign may be down—it's a local collector's item—but the path from one end of the parking area is well blazed). Just be sure not to go alone (it's steep), and don't try to climb the falls itself. It looks so tempting that people try, and several have died in the process.

The trail follows narrow Ross Brook, which rushes steeply downward beneath fir and spruce trees to a lookout at the top of the falls, fenced with wire cable. What you see below is a glorious cascade, swirling through variously shaped rock pools, a pattern repeated again and again. In spring or after a big rain, this series of cascades is replaced by a thunderous, continuous rush of water. The path continues steeply downward, but instead of shadowing the cascade it now follows another stream, Parker Brook, plunging down through a rocky gorge. New, broad steps, fashioned from rail ties, ease the descent, and more massive old granite steps lead to an island-like promontory at the confluence of the two brooks, the floor of the hollow, and the end of the trail. A circle of stone seats suggest a picnic spot fashioned by and for druids, and the view back up the waterfall is spellbinding.

✐ ♿ **Mohawk Trail State Forest** (413-339-5504; mass.gov/dcr), MA 2, Charlemont, covers 6,457 acres and offers 56 campsites and six log cabins (one wheelchair-accessible); reservations recommended. There's swimming in a man-made pool in the Cold River, a bathhouse, scattered picnic tables, and many miles of hiking trails, including a portion of the original Indian path. Camping here is permitted year-round; in winter there are snowshoeing and cross-county ski trails. The remnants of the original Mohawk Trail can be seen along Indian Trail, ascending Lookout Mountain from the west end of the camping area. *Note:* There's a $5 parking fee May–mid-Oct.

Mohawk Park in West Charlemont is the official centerpiece of the trail. A bronze statue with its arms raised, the unofficial symbol of the trail, was placed here in 1932 by the Improved Order of Red Men. The arrowhead-shaped tablet at the base of the statue reads: HAIL TO THE SUNRISE—IN MEMORY OF THE MOHAWK INDIAN. There is a wishing pool with 100 inscribed stones from the various tribes and councils from throughout the country. Note the Mohawk Park Cabins across the way, a vestige of what once was.

Note: The **Rowe Road** is a left off MA 2 here, and the next left puts you on River Road leading back along the Deerfield River to **Zoar Gap.** We have described it coming from the other direction from Whitcomb Summit. If you continue north (instead of turning left), you come to **Rowe** (see "West County").

The Shunpike Marker by the river is dedicated to the thrifty travelers of the mohawk trail who in 1797 HERE FORDED THE DEERFIELD RIVER RATHER THAN PAY THE TOLL AT THE TURNPIKE BRIDGE AND WHO IN 1810 WON THE BATTLE FOR FREE TRAVEL ON ALL MASSACHUSETTS ROADS. It's worth noting that the marker was placed here in 1957 as construction of the Massachusetts Turnpike was getting under way. The Mass Pike has substantially reduced traffic on MA 2.

✐ **Zoar Outdoor** (zoaroutdoor.com). Zoar Gap is home base for the area's oldest, most diversified white-water sports company (see *White-Water Rafting* in

Shelburne Falls Area Business Association

HAIL TO THE SUNRISE IN MOHAWK PARK.

"West County") The outfitter also offers a zip line, campsites, platform tents, and inn rooms.

Moxie Outdoor Adventures (moxie rafting.com), based at the Berkshire East ski area, also offers rafting and funyak rentals.

Berkshire East Canopy Tours (413-339-6617; berkshireeast.com), 66 Thunder Mountain Rd. at Berkshire East ski area, just off MA 2 in Charlemont. Riders fly down tensioned cable at speeds up to 50 mph, nearly 200 feet above the ground.

Charlemont Inn (413-339-5796; charlemontinn.com), Main St., Charlemont. This is the landmark inn along the Mohawk Trail and continues to offer three daily meals as well as spirits and lodging. See *Lodging* in "West County."

The **Charlemont Federated Church,** 175 Main St., has excellent acoustics and for almost 35 years has been the venue for the **Mohawk Trail Concerts** (413-625-9511 or 1-800-MTC-MUSE; mohawk trailconcerts.org).

Indian Plaza Powwow Grounds (413-339-4096), 1475 Mohawk Trail. Dating from 1933, it has been in Harold Roberts's family for 40 years, the site of periodic powwows from early May through the Columbus Day weekend.

The **East Charlemont Picnic Area** (eastbound) along the Deerfield River is a charmed spot with tables and a view of fields across the river and the venerable Hall Tavern Farm down the road. (The original Hall Tavern now serves as the reception center for Historic Deerfield.)

Several motels—the **Red Rose** (formerly cabins), the **Olde Willow Motel and Restaurant, The Oxbow** resort motel (see *Lodging* in "West

THE CHARLEMONT INN HAS BEEN WELCOMING TRAVELERS SINCE 1787.

Christina Tree

County"), and the **Hilltop Motel** (formerly Rio Vista)—are holdovers from the Trail's glory days.

Crab Apple Whitewater (crabapplewhitewater.com) has renovated and expanded what's left of a vintage cabin complex. Inquire about funyaks. See *White-Water Rafting* in "West County."

Tubing (floating downriver in rubber tire tubes) is a popular summer pastime on this stretch. Look for seasonal signs for TUBES.

Big Indian Shop, 2217 Mohawk Trail. Open seasonally, 9–5. Named for the 28-foot-tall Indian that guards its door, this is an old-fashioned souvenir shop and proud to be one. It's been in Joni Estes's family for more than 70 years, and Kim Estes is usually behind the counter to sell you a rubber drum or tomahawk, a cowboy hat, maple products, or moccasins. A must-stop for kids.

Shelburne Falls (shelburnefalls.com). The Trail no longer passes through the middle of town as it once did, but this unusual village is now the hub, offering the only visitor center (with restrooms) along the Trail and most of its places to eat. Eastbound you turn onto State Street and follow it to the **Bridge of Flowers.** Park and walk.

KIM ESTES AT THE BIG INDIAN SHOP WITH ITS 28-FOOT-TALL WOODEN INDIAN.
Christina Tree

Gould's Maple Sugarhouse (413-625-6170; goulds-sugarhouse.com), MA 2, Shelburne. Open in sugaring season (Mar.–Apr.) and during foliage (Sept.–Oct.), daily 8:30–2. A great roadside stop that's been in the family for generations; specialties include pancakes, waffles, and fritters laced with the family's maple syrup and fabulous pickles. We also recommend the BLT.

The Mahican–Mohawk Trail runs for 7.5 miles between Shelburne Falls and Deerfield. Berkshire writer and naturalist Lauren Stevens initiated the study that revealed the location of the ancient riverside path and the fact that it was still roughly maintained by the New England Power Company. Thanks to the concerted efforts of local environmental groups, this trail is accessible to sturdily shod hikers. The entire hike takes at least four hours, but the most impressive and rugged few miles are at the Shelburne Falls end. Details are in the "West County" chapter; see *Green Space.*

The Outpost (413-625-6806 or 1-800-541-5086), 1385 Mohawk Trail, Shelburne. Open year-round, daily 10–5. Looks can be deceptive. This shop (eastbound) looks both smallish and new. It was originally "Indian Park," but is now substantially expanded and specializes totally in sheepskin products (car seats, slippers, mittens, and more); also fine leather products. Beware. We left with a pair of gloves.

❀ **Mohawk Trading Post** (413-625-2412; mohawk-trading-post.com), 874 Mohawk Trail, Shelburne. Open Memorial Day through foliage season, Mon. and Wed.–Sat. 10–5, Sun. noon–5; off-season open Fri.–Mon. The easternmost Indian-themed shop on the Trail, this is less dramatic on the exterior than others (the fiberglass buffalo is smallish but big enough for a small boy to sit on), though inside there's plenty to please: a wide selection of books about Native Americans, quality soapstone carvings and pottery, sterling Indian jewelry, and moccasins. Laurie York is the current owner, and it's been in her family since 1985. Tymothy, the stuffed bear by the entrance, evokes the memory of the live bears for which the trading post was long known, York explains, and the genuine fossil by the counter was "liberated" from the Connecticut River by the son of the previous owners.

Longview Tower Specialty Shops, 497 Mohawk Trail. Opened in 1923 as the "Long Vue" by the same Misses Mansfield who also owned the Western Summit observation and gift shop. It's on the westbound side and frequently difficult to stop either way. Locals bring their picnics up (there are benches). Rebuilt in steel in 1952, this five-story observation tower is the only one left along the Trail that's still its original height. Honestly, we haven't tried to climb it lately.

Old Greenfield Village (413-774-7138), 368 Mohawk Trail. Open mid-May–mid-Oct. by appointment only (feel free to call on your cell phone from the gate). Adults $5, seniors $4, ages 6–16 $3; under age 6 free. This is a genuine, Yankee kind of phenomenon, a collection of thousands of artifacts formerly found in stores, dental offices, churches, barbershops, and tool shops around the turn of the 20th century, all collected over 30 years by retired schoolteacher Waine Morse.

THE HILLTOWNS

The rolling farm and forest between the Connecticut River Valley and Berkshire County is known, among other things, as the Hilltowns. These glacially rounded hills and river-sculpted valleys are, in topographic fact, as much a part of the Berkshire Hills as Berkshire County to the west.

Early settlers dubbed it the "Berkshire Barrier," but Native Americans knew how to traverse the region. They followed its two major rivers—the Deerfield and the Westfield—which have cut three parallel east–west valleys, now obvious traffic conduits. MA 2 (the "Mohawk Trail"), the northernmost east–west high road (*highway* would be an overstatement), shadows the ancient Mohawk Trail along the Deerfield River. MA 9 (the "Berkshire Trail") follows the main stem of the Westfield River across the middle of the state, while US 20 ("Jacob's Ladder"), now shadowed by I-90 (the Mass Pike), hugs the west branch of the Westfield. This high ground is also the watershed between the two major north–south valleys in the Northeast. It's said that raindrops falling on the western slant of the Congregational church roof in hilltop Peru ultimately flow into the Hudson, while those on the eastern slant fall into the Connecticut.

Few regions this beautiful and accessible are this unspoiled.

Much of this area looks the way Vermont did a couple of decades ago: Valleys are steep, alternately wooded and patched with open fields. In winter cross-country skiers, snowshoers, and snowmobilers drive from Boston and Hartford to take advantage of the highest, most dependably snow-covered trails south of Vermont. Early spring brings sit-down breakfasts in sugarhouses and tours of the sugarbush (there are more maple producers here than in all the rest of the state put together). In late spring white-water rafters begin converging on the Deerfield River and nationally ranked white-water canoeists compete on the Westfield. Anglers find trout in both rivers. In summer back roads beckon bicyclists, while hikers follow trails to hilltop lookouts and deep-in-the-woods waterfalls. In fall the Mohawk Trail is thronged with leaf-peepers, but back roads receive surprisingly little use.

Despite the fertile bottomland along the Deerfield and Westfield Rivers, this area was very sparsely settled until the end of the French and Indian Wars in 1756. Most towns were incorporated shortly before the Revolution, and many hill farms were deserted as early as the 1820s, when the Erie Canal opened the

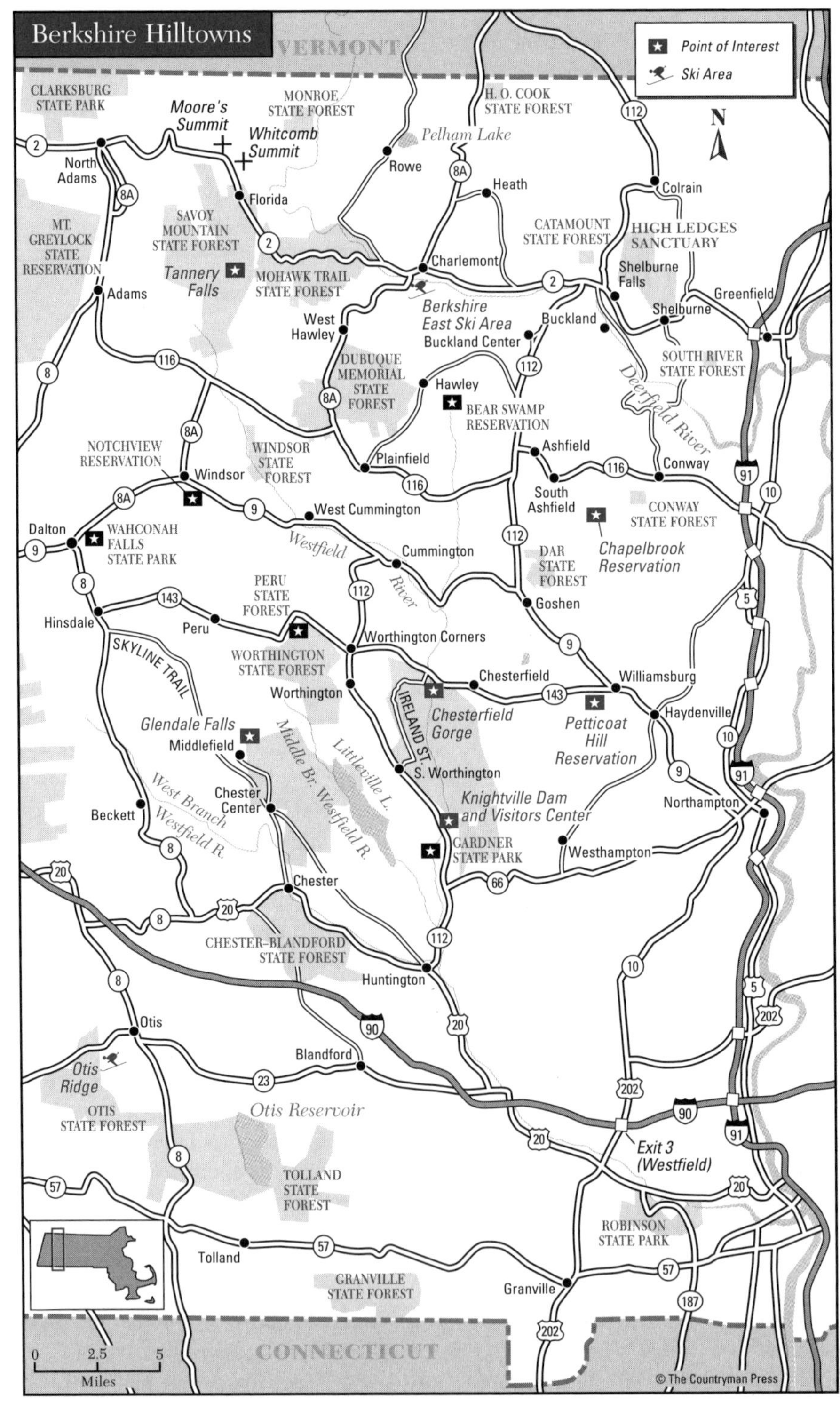
Berkshire Hilltowns
VERMONT
Point of Interest
Ski Area
N
CLARKSBURG STATE PARK
Moore's Summit
Whitcomb Summit
MONROE STATE FOREST
H. O. COOK STATE FOREST
Pelham Lake
North Adams
Rowe
Heath
Colrain
Florida
SAVOY MOUNTAIN STATE FOREST
MT. GREYLOCK STATE RESERVATION
CATAMOUNT STATE FOREST
HIGH LEDGES SANCTUARY
Charlemont
Tannery Falls
MOHAWK TRAIL STATE FOREST
Shelburne Falls
Adams
Berkshire East Ski Area
Greenfield
Shelburne
West Hawley
Buckland
Buckland Center
SOUTH RIVER STATE FOREST
DUBUQUE MEMORIAL STATE FOREST
Hawley
Deerfield River
BEAR SWAMP RESERVATION
NOTCHVIEW RESERVATION
WINDSOR STATE FOREST
Ashfield
Plainfield
Conway
Windsor
South Ashfield
West Cummington
CONWAY STATE FOREST
Dalton
WAHCONAH FALLS STATE PARK
Westfield River
Chapelbrook Reservation
Cummington
DAR STATE FOREST
PERU STATE FOREST
Goshen
Hinsdale
Peru
Worthington Corners
SKYLINE TRAIL
WORTHINGTON STATE FOREST
Chesterfield
Williamsburg
Worthington
IRELAND ST.
Chesterfield Gorge
Petticoat Hill Reservation
Haydenville
Glendale Falls
Middlefield
Middle Br. Westfield R.
Littleville L.
S. Worthington
Chester Center
West Branch Westfield R.
Knightville Dam and Visitors Center
Northampton
Beckett
GARDNER STATE PARK
Westhampton
Chester
CHESTER-BLANDFORD STATE FOREST
Huntington
Otis
Blandford
Otis Ridge
Otis Reservoir
OTIS STATE FOREST
Exit 3 (Westfield)
TOLLAND STATE FOREST
ROBINSON STATE PARK
Tolland
GRANVILLE STATE FOREST
Granville
CONNECTICUT
0 2.5 5
Miles
© The Countryman Press

way to greener, less rocky western pastures. The stone walls pioneers built now lie deep in the area's many state parks and forests. Currently the Hilltowns are home to one of the state's largest concentrations of artists, craftspeople, and musicians.

Hilltown residents cherish the elusive, firefly-like quality of the area's attractions, a quality that, admittedly, can be frustrating to casual visitors who may not be in the right place at the right time on the right day. With a little planning, however, you can hear famed musicians perform in an old church in Charlemont and a former academy in South Worthington, follow the movements of a world-acclaimed theater group from meadow to barn on a farm in Ashfield, and see legendary performers hold forth at Memorial Hall Theater in Shelburne Falls. Throughout summer and fall, hand-drawn signs steer visitors to farms offering pick-your-own berries; in August country fairs feature horse pulls, oxen draws, and local produce. In October, Conway and Ashfield hold two of the most colorful foliage festivals in New England, while November brings CiderDays and open studio tours. All these cultural and community happenings are held primarily for local residents rather than for New Yorkers or Bostonians.

Though the Hilltowns may all look much the same to visitors, locals will tell you that the region is clearly divided along county lines. Ashfield, Buckland, Charlemont, Hawley, and the towns to the north of MA 2 all fall into "West (Franklin) County," whereas Plainfield, Cummington, Worthington, and towns to the south consider themselves the "Hampshire Hills," or "Hidden Hills," both names coined by the area's bed & breakfast association. Conway seems to fall in between.

Current lodging options are widely scattered B&Bs. The region's only staffed information center is in Shelburne Falls, a lively dining and shopping town that's the hub of West County and the obvious way stop on the Mohawk Trail.

THE BRICK MEETINGHOUSE IN COLRAIN ON NOVEMBER'S CIDER DAY

Christina Tree

WEST COUNTY

INCLUDING CHARLEMONT, SHELBURNE FALLS, ASHFIELD, AND CONWAY

West Franklin County, better known as "West County," has been attracting artists, craftspeople, and musicians for many decades and now also harbors contemplative communities. Locals speak of a special creative energy emanating from this particular roll of hill and valley. It unquestionably attracts questing spirits.

"Everything that I do and make is interconnected, influenced by this view," internationally respected glass artist Josh Simpson once told us, spreading his arms to the hills that circle his studio. Simpson's deeply colored "planets" and other art pieces are featured in the Salmon Falls Artisans Showroom, a former granary in Shelburne Falls, a village formed by the centers of two towns linked by two bridges.

Nothing in Shelburne Falls works quite the way it does in other places. Its old trolley bridge is now a walkway awash with more than 500 species of colorful flowers, and its vintage-1913 iron bridge, the main thoroughfare, is the venue of an annual community banquet. An old trolley has been rehabbed and again rumbles back and forth up at the old depot, restored by volunteers.

Shelburne Falls is known for restaurants heavy on greens and grains rather than your wallet, and most galleries are artist- and artisan-owned. It is also still a mill village, with a cutlery factory dating back to 1837, an independently owned pharmacy with a soda fountain, and an old-fashioned news store.

Just north of Shelburne Falls, hills hump abruptly and roads climb steeply through Heath and Colrain. on to Vermont. West of the village the Mohawk Trail follows a stunning stretch of the Deerfield River to Charlemont, and to the south MA 112 threads Buckland's magnificent farmland to Ashfield. Back roads wind up into hills to classic clapboard villages, 50-mile views, and unexpected finds: here a farm with yaks and camels, there a woodworker's or weaver's studio, perhaps a waterfall, and always a river or brook. Hiking trails abound and lodging places, while frequently hard to find, are equally hard to leave.

"It's what you don't see here that's striking," an Ashfield resident observes. Over the past 20 years the Ashfield-based Franklin Land Trust alone has preserved many thousands of acres, just one sign of the ways local residents, few of them wealthy, feel about the look of this land.

Harry Dodson

ASHFIELD COMMON.

AREA CODE 413 applies to all of Western Massachusetts.

GUIDANCE **Shelburne Falls Village Information Center** (413-625-2544; shelburnefalls.com). The Shelburne Falls Area Business Association (413-625-2526) maintains a friendly, well-stocked information source (with restrooms) for the surrounding area as well as the village. It's housed in a former fire station at 75 Bridge St., open May–Oct., Mon.–Sat. 10–4, Sun. noon–4; catch as can the rest of the year.

Franklin County Chamber of Commerce (413-773-5463; franklincc.org) operates the Upper Pioneer Valley Visitor Information Center just off I-91 (Exit 26) at the MA 2 rotary behind Applebee's on MA 2A East. Open daily Apr. 15–Nov.1.

GETTING THERE *From Boston:* There is no bus or train service. The obvious way by car is MA 2, which technically becomes the Mohawk Trail in Orange but really begins looking like a tourist route west of Greenfield. From points north and south, take Exit 26 off I-91 at Greenfield. From Amherst, take MA 116 North; from Northampton, MA 9 North to MA 112.

GETTING AROUND A good map is a necessity because the state map and larger New England maps will leave you assuming that many of the most beautiful roads in this region don't exist. Franklin County publishes an excellent free, detailed map, and the *Rubel Western Massachusetts Bicycle and Road Map* covers the territory well.

MEDICAL EMERGENCY Dial **911.**

✷ Villages

Ashfield (population: about 1,800). This unusually spirited town publishes its own newspaper. A large, former summer hotel still stands in the middle of the village, but most traffic now stops at Ashfield Hardware and Countrypie Pizza. The pride of Ashfield remains the Christopher Wren-style steeple on its town hall (built as a church in 1814) and its unusual number of both maple producers and craftspeople, most of whom exhibit at the annual fall festival on Columbus Day weekend. Ashfield is the birthplace of movie director Cecil B. DeMille (his parents happened to be staying at the hotel) and has been home for a number of artists and writers, making for an unusually interesting **Ashfield Historical Society** (413-628-4541; ashfieldhistorical.org). Ten rooms of exhibits include the glass-plate photos of New England towns and working people taken by the two Howes brothers of Ashfield around the turn of the 20th century. It's open by appointment and during the **Ashfield Fall Foliage Festival,** always held Columbus Day weekend and one of the most colorful in New England. In summer there is swimming at the small town beach (transients discouraged) right in the village on Ashfield Lake, and there are two outstanding Trustees of Reservations properties (see *Green Space*).

Buckland (population: about 2,000). Buckland's town hall stands just across the Bridge of Flowers in the heart of Shelburne Falls (the town's northern boundary is the Deerfield River). The village center of Buckland—a gathering of a classic little church, a historical society, a small brick library, and aristocratic, 18th-century homes (one of them now a bed & breakfast), all set high on a hill—is less than 3 miles south of MA 2, off MA 112. The **Buckland Historical Society Museum** (413-625-9763; open on the second and fourth Sundays in Jul. and Aug., 2–4, as well as for special programs) is housed in a historic building near the Mary Lyon Church in Buckland Center. Inquire about special events at its **Wilder Homestead** on MA 112, a 1775 saltbox with five working fireplaces and a barn filled with equipment, weaving looms, and a shoemaker's shop. The society's collection features exhibits about Mary Lyon, the Buckland woman who pioneered education for women in the early 19th century and is remembered as the founder of both Mount Holyoke College in South Hadley and Wheaton College in Norton. It was in the ballroom of the four-square, four-chimneyed **Major Joseph Griswold House** on Upper Street that Mary Lyon opened her first academy in 1823, teaching the family and neighborhood children (open by appointment through the Mary Lyon Foundation: 413-625-2555). The way to the site of Mary Lyon's birthplace is marked from MA 112 (E. Buckland St.).

Charlemont (population: 1,386). The Deerfield River rushes down from Vermont, then slows, widens, and turns east in Charlemont, creating fertile floodplains that clearly have been farmed since the mid-18th century, judging from the age of several proud farmhouses. The 18th-century **Charlemont Inn's** tavern and restaurant mark the heart of town, along with **A. L. Avery & Son General Merchandise,** still stocking everything from cheese to hardware, boots to beef. This town is the only one in New England known for both alpine skiing (**Berkshire East**) and white-water rafting, introduced by **Zoar Outdoor.** Rafting has, in turn, introduced many visitors to the high backcountry north of MA 2.

Bissell Covered Bridge spans Mill Brook just off MA 2 on MA 8A (currently just pedestrian traffic). The **Charlemont Historical Society Museum** fills a theater-sized room in the town hall. It's open Tues. 5:30–7:30 and through the neighboring **Tyler Memorial Library,** itself worth a stop. In July and August the **Mohawk Trail Chamber Music Festival** in the Federated Church draws a sophisticated audience from throughout the Northeast. Charlemont **Yankee Doodle Days** in July commemorate the fact—perhaps apocryphal—that it was at a local muster here in the 1750s that America's first famous song was written, by a British doctor who was part of a British regiment, to poke fun at the local militia. Local historians tell us there is no basis for this story.

Colrain (population: 1,813). This hilly town boomed with sheep raising, cotton mills, and an iron foundry in the mid-19th century, all linked to the train at Shelburne Falls by trolley. The old foundry is still in Foundry Hollow, and its rebuilt covered bridge spans the North River. Catamount Hill is said to be the site of the first schoolhouse to fly the American flag, so it's appropriate that the town now harbors *Glowing Glory* (glowingglory.com), the country's largest neon American flag, designed by local artist Pacifico Palumbo and set on a hilltop across from Pine Hill Orchards on the Greenfield Road soon after 9/11 to honor U.S. veterans. The **Colrain Historical Society** (413-624-8818) is housed in the **G. William Pitt House** on Main Street. The village center, with its three churches and common, is at the junction of four scenic routes, including MA 112 north to Vermont. Colrain lists a number of sugarhouses, and **Pine Hill Orchards** showcases its own produce and apple wines from **West County Winery.** There are an exceptional number of craftsmen scattered through this sleepy town, and most hold open studios on a weekend in November (craftsofcolrain.com); many of these also exhibit at the annual village fair, held the third Saturday in September.

HELEN BAKER SERVES LUNCH, GREAT PIES, AND ALL THE LOCAL NEWS IN BAKER'S COUNTRY STORE, CONWAY VILLAGE.
Christina Tree

Conway (population: about 2,000). Turn off MA 116 and stop long enough at the triangular green to admire the domed **Marshall Field Memorial Library** (413-369-4646), gift of the native son who founded a Chicago department store. There's a marble rotunda and elaborate detailing within; the historical collection is open selected days. The heart of town is easy to miss: **Baker's Country Store** serves lunch, great pie, and all the local news you need. Note the covered bridge across the South River off MA 116. A Main Street storefront now houses the **Conway Historical Society,** open July–Labor Day, Sun. 1–4.

Heath (population: 805). Heath is worth finding just for the fun of it: a classic hill town with a common surrounded by the usual white-clapboard buildings. What's amazing (going and coming) are the long views. Heath is known for its wild blueberries, and the **Heath Fair,** held two weekends before Labor Day, features horse pulling, ox draws, music, food, and an old-time square dance in the dirt-floor cattle barn.

Shelburne Falls. Usually rivers divide towns, but in this case the Deerfield has united the 19th-century dining and shopping areas of two towns (Buckland and Shelburne) to form Shelburne Falls, one of the most unusual and lively villages in New England. Instead of a common, there's the **Bridge of Flowers** (see *To See*). An iron bridge, which the community has restored rather than replacing the way most communities do (claiming that they will be rarer than covered bridges in a couple of decades), also links the main streets on both sides of the river. An aberration from its rural setting, this totally Victorian shopping center has become a showcase for art and craft work produced in the surrounding hills. The **Glacial Potholes** at the foot of Salmon Falls (Deerfield Ave. off Bridge St.) are a many-colored and unusually shaped phenomenon, worth a look. The **Shelburne Historical Society** (413-625-6150), in the Arms Academy Building (corner of Maple and Church Sts.), is open July–Oct., Wed. 10–4 and Sun. 2–5. The second-floor Opera House in the 1897 **Memorial Hall Theater** has been restored and once more serves as the town's movie house (Pothole Pictures) as well as the stage for live entertainment and The Metropolitan Opera in HD. A **Riverwalk** runs along the Buckland side of the river. Also see the **Mahican–Mohawk Trail** along the Deerfield under *Green Space.*

Rowe (population: about 400). The **Rowe Historical Society Museum** (open July–Sept., Sun. 2–4, otherwise by appointment; 413-339-4700) showcases the town's unusual history given its position high on a ridgeline dividing Vermont

GLACIAL POTHOLES AT THE FOOT OF SALMON FALLS.

Christina Tree

and Massachusetts (elevation ranges from 1,350 to 2,140 feet). It includes construction of the Hoosac Tunnel (the Eastern Portal); power dams beginning in 1911; and New England's first atomic energy plant (1961–92) as well as the Bear Swamp Pumped Generation Station, completed in 1974. The town's population topped 800 in the 19th century; at various times there were sulfur and talc mines, several mills, a satinet factory, and some 3,000 sheep. With the arrival of train service came summer boarders. Today this is a hauntingly beautiful area with many wildflowers, including 21 species of orchids. Pick up a copy of *Wildflowers of Rowe* by Susan Alix Williams at the historical society. The **Rowe Conference Center,** originally a Unitarian Church summer camp, features workshops led by authorities on a broad spectrum of subjects. There are picnic tables in **Pelham Lake Park.**

✷ To See

The Bridge of Flowers (bridgeofflowersmass.org). The Shelburne Falls Area Women's Club began planting this last remaining five-arch concrete trolley bridge in 1929 when the trolley line was abandoned. Still meticulously tended by the club and reserved for foot traffic, it may well be the world's floweriest bridge, abloom from April through October with 500 varieties of flowering plants and trees. This all began with a local desire to do something about an eyesore in the middle of the village. It's especially beautiful at dusk with the reflections in the quiet river on its western side.

BRIDGE OF FLOWERS, SHELBURNE FALLS.

Christina Tree

Shelburne Falls Trolley Museum (413-625-9443; sftm.org), 14 Depot St., Buckland (in the railyard). Open late May–Oct., weekends and holidays 11–5; also July–Aug. Mon. 1–5. There is memorabilia in the visitor center, with model trains for "young folks" to operate. The big attraction here is a vintage-1896 trolley, which for 20 years carried passengers and freight the 7 uphill miles to Colrain and back down. It's up and running at the depot, having been restored by volunteers—after serving as Marshall Johnson's chicken coop for 70 years, which everyone agrees saved it, both because it was up off the ground and because the chicken manure kept the wood lubricated. The current ride may be short, but it's enlivened by conductor Sam Bartlett's narration. Passengers learn that they are en route to visit relatives in Colrain, having come in on the B&M (freight trains still use the adjacent tracks). They hear about passing factories, picking up schoolkids and shoppers on the way to "Colrain City" and its four-story (long since vanished) inn. There is also an old railroad handcar that vigorous visitors can help pump up and down the trolley tracks.

Glacial Potholes in Shelburne Falls. More than 50 glacial potholes—one of the largest known concentrations of these natural sculptures, scoured into the metamorphic rock layers—are clustered at the bottom of the hydro dam, best viewed from the end of Deerfield Avenue. They range in size from 6 inches to 35 feet across.

✐ Also see **Tregellys Fiber Farm** under *Farms*. The farm features a menagerie of some 200 animals, including two-humped camels, llamas, yaks, and rare and heritage breeds of many other animals.

SCENIC DRIVES **Along the Mohawk Trail.** See the previous chapter.

River Road to Whitcomb Summit is a worthwhile deviation from the Mohawk Trail. Take the road marked ROWE just west of the village of Charlemont, but bear left almost immediately at the fork (marked by a dead tree with numerous signs tacked to it) along **River Road.** Follow it along the river, by the **Zoar Picnic Area** in a pine grove. Continue along the river as the valley walls steepen, past Whitcomb Summit Road and over the railroad tracks. Look here for the Eastern Portal of the Hoosac Tunnel, opened in the 1870s by blasting through granite.

Shelburne to Conway. There are two scenic ways from Shelburne to Conway, both good bicycle routes. The first is simply to take Conway Road south along the river from the Buckland side; the second is to go south from MA 2 at the sign for Shelburne Center, where you pick up Bardwell's Ferry Road, one of the prettiest roads we know anywhere. At one high point you can see Mount Tom in Holyoke off across hills before it dips across the railroad tracks and crosses the Bardwell Ferry Bridge. Wiry and graceful, it's one of the most unusual little bridges in Massachusetts and a popular fishing spot. The Conway stretch of the road is also beautiful and joins the Shelburne Falls Road not far north of Conway Village.

Peckville Road from MA 2 up to the Apex Orchards offers a spectacular view of the hills.

Other suggested routes

Circle through Colrain. Take Greenfield Road to Colrain Center, then head back down to MA 2 on the Shelburne Falls Road, or vice versa.

MA 112 between Buckland and Ashfield threads a beautiful valley.

Get lost. There are so many beautiful roads in this area that you really can't lose—and the best way to explore them is to get lost. Again we recommend the *Rubel Western Massachusetts Bicycle and Road Map*, as well as the free map published by Franklin County.

✷ To Do

BICYCLING Zoar Outdoor (see below) in Charlemont rents both sport road and comfort bikes, suggesting routes and mapping self-guided tours. Also see **Stump Sprouts** under *Lodging* and *Cross-Country Skiing*. Trails are open to mountain bikers. Owner Lloyd Crawford is an avid bicyclist who advises on road routes and trails in local state forests. All the *Scenic Drives* described above are good for bicycling, and many more are scenic, curving, and little trafficked.

CANOEING AND KAYAKING Zoar Outdoor (1-800-532-7483; zoaroutdoor.com), MA 2 in Charlemont, rents canoes and kayaks for use on several stretches of the Deerfield. Shuttle service, canoeing and white-water clinics, and sit-on-top kayaks for the calmer reaches of the river are also offered. Inquire about "family trips."

Crab Apple (1-800-553-7238; crabapplewhitewater.com) offers inflatable kayak ("funyak") rentals with a shuttle to the put-in point.

KAYAKING ON THE DEERFIELD RIVER.

Zoar Outdoor

Moxie Outdoor Adventures (moxierafting.com), based at Berkshire East ski area, also offers funyak rentals.

FISHING The 12-mile stretch of the Deerfield River in Charlemont lures anglers from across the Northeast. There is a catch-and-release section in the village of Hoosac Tunnel. Beware the changing depth of the water throughout this area due to releases from the dam. The **Catamount State Forest** (413-339-5504) harbors a 27-acre trout-stocked lake. **Davenport's Mobil** (413-625-9544), MA 2 in Shelburne Falls, and **Avery's General Store** (413-339-4915), 127 Main St., Charlemont, stock fishing supplies. **Zoar Outdoor** (see above) offers fly casting clinics and guided float fishing.

GOLF **Edge Hill Golf Course** (413-628-6018; edgehillgolfcourse.com), 298 Barnes Rd. in Ashfield. This former dairy farm is now a nine-hole course with the golf shop, snack bar, and lounge in the former barn overlooking a pond. It will have 18 holes by this book's next edition.

Goodnow's Chip'n'Putt (413-625-6107), 1211 Mohawk Trail (MA 2), Shelburne. Open seasonally, 7:30–dusk. Fun for beginners and advanced players.

HORSEBACK RIDING **High Pocket Farm B&B** (see *Lodging*) offers trail rides to its guests, $100 for a minimum two hours, $50 thereafter; guests who bring their own horses pay only for stabling ($35 per night). This is high, beautiful country with singletrack trails through woods and fields.

Flames Stables (802-464-8329), VT 100, Wilmington, Vt. Western saddle trail rides, pony rides for young children (just over the border from Rowe).

ROCK CLIMBING **Zoar Outdoor** (zoaroutdoor.com), MA 2, Charlemont, runs a rock-climbing school that emphasizes top rope climbing with the rope anchored by an instructor; there is a low student/instructor ratio. One- and two-day novice and intermediate clinics are offered, including special parent–child clinics and climbs geared to ages 10 to 15.

SWIMMING See "Along the Mohawk Trail" for the **Mohawk Trail** and **Savoy Mountain State Forests;** ask locally about swimming holes in the Deerfield River.

TRACKING **Alan Emond** (413-624-5115; alan.emond@verizon.net), 12 Wilson Hill Rd., Colrain. A local tracker who is a naturalist, farmer, and writer, Alan offers half- and full-day guided tracking and mentoring.

WHITE-WATER RAFTING "When I first approached New England Electric, they said 'No. You can't raft the river,'" Bruce Lessels recalls, adding that over the next few years the power company became increasingly cooperative. In 1989 New England Electric began releasing water from Fife Brook Dam with a regularity that makes rafting possible on most days, April through October, on a 10-mile stretch of Class II and III whitewater—from Florida, through steep, green-walled, boulder-strewn Zoar Gap and on down to Charlemont. Admittedly not as visually and viscerally exciting as parts of Maine's Kennebec or Penobscot Rivers, it offers a great introduction to rafting. The day we ran it, a third of our group was under age 16 (minimum weight: 50 pounds). The Upper Deerfield Dryway, a stretch of Class IV whitewater above the Fife Brook Dam, is also now rafted on specific days (adding up to more than 30 each season). The lower river is great for family float trips, canoeing, and recreational kayaking and tubing.

Zoar Outdoor (1-800-532-7483; zoaroutdoor.com), based in a 1750s house with 80 acres on MA 2 in Charlemont, is headed by Bruce Lessels, a former member of the U.S. Olympic white-water team. The complex includes a bath-house with changing rooms and hot showers, an orientation pavilion, cabin tents, primitive tent sites, and **Hawk Mountain Lodge** (see *Lodging*), an attractive B&B. Trips range from challenging rides down the dryway and clinics for expert white-water kayakers to family float trips. Rates vary with the day, trip, and age of the person involved. Also see *Canoeing and Kayaking*, *Bicycling*, *Rock Climbing*, and *Zip Lines*.

ZOAR OUTDOOR OFFERS FREQUENT WHITE-WATER RAFTING ON THE DEERFIELD RIVER.
Zoar Outdoor

Crab Apple Whitewater (413-625-2288 or 1-800-553-7238; crabapple whitewater.com), MA 2, Charlemont. A well-established, family-owned outfitter with a home base on Maine's Kennebec River, Crab Apple has been offering raft trips on the Deerfield since 1989. It features the full range of rafting trips and rents "funyaks" (inflatable kayaks). Its base is a former Mohawk Trail restaurant. Inquire about two-day packages.

Moxie Outdoor Adventures (1-800-866-6943; moxierafting.com), with its home base on Maine's Kennebec, is based here at Berkshire East ski area in Charlemont. It offers both dryway (Class IV whitewater, minimum age 14) and Zoar Gap ($70 weekdays, $85 weekends) runs.

ZIP LINES AND CANOPY TOURS

Deerfield Valley Canopy Tours (1-800-532-7483; deerfieldzipline.com) at Zoar Outdoor (zoaroutdoor.com). Minimum age 10, weight 75–250 pounds. The average tour takes three hours.

Berkshire East Canopy Tours (www.berkshirezip.com), based at the ski area (see below), offers a three zip line canopy tour. Access is by chairlift.

✷ Winter Sports

CROSS-COUNTRY SKIING AND SHOWSHOEING **Stump Sprouts** (413-339-4265; stumpsprouts.com), West Hill Rd., West Hawley. High on the side of a mountain, this 450-acre tract offers some memorable cross-country skiing on wooded trails at 1,500- to 2,000-foot elevations. Snacks and rentals are available in the warming hut, which is part of Lloyd and Suzanne Crawford's home (see *Lodging*). There are more than 15 miles of trails, lessons, and guided tours.

Also see *Green Space* for trails in **Kenneth Dubuque Memorial State Forest,** "Along the Mohawk Trail" for those in the **Savoy Mountain State Forest,** and the "Central and North Berkshire" chapter for **Notchview Reservation** in Windsor.

DOWNHILL SKIING **Berkshire East** (413-339-6617; berkshireeast.com), South River Rd., Charlemont. Known affectionately as "Berkshire Beast," this is an unusually challenging mountain for its size. It's also the first in the country to generate all its own electrical power using a wind turbine.

Vertical drop: 1,180 feet.

Terrain: 45 trails, 40 percent expert, 40 percent intermediate.

Lifts: Five lifts, including a quad.

Snowmaking: 100 percent of terrain.

Facilities: Nursery, two base lodges, ski school, shop; open daily; night skiing Wed.–Sat.; snowboarding, tubing, Children's Center and Kid's Mountain Club on weekends and holidays.

Tickets: Adults $55, students $45, juniors and seniors $35; less midweek, also afternoon rates; $25 for night skiing.

SNOWMOBILING **The Snowmobiling Association of Massachusetts** (413-369-8092; sledmass.com) SAM is headquartered in Conway and, while there are no rentals in the Hilltowns, there's no doubt that this area offers some of the best sledding in the state. Snowmobilers are advised to check the website and contact local clubs.

✷ Green Space

STATE FORESTS *Note:* See mass.gov/dcr for details about all of the following:

Monroe State Forest (413-339-5504) covers 4,000 acres in the towns of Florida and Monroe. Access is on Monroe Road off MA 2 (just east of Whitcomb Summit; see **River Road** under *Scenic Drives*). Nine miles of hiking trails and several lean-to shelters are on the **Dunbar Brook Trail;** about 2 miles is in one of the last stands of old-growth forest, with a beautiful stand of red spruce and a 300-year-old hemlock. The spectacular **Roycroft Lookout** takes in a panorama of the Deerfield River Valley. Watch out for the many moose droppings.

Mohawk Trail State Forest (413-339-5504), MA 2, Charlemont. See "Along the Mohawk Trail" for details.

Catamount State Forest (413-339-5504), MA 112, Colrain. The big attraction at this 1,125-acre forest between Colrain and Charlemont is fishing in the 27-acre (stocked) **McCleod Pond**. There are also hiking and riding trails and cellar holes from abandoned farms.

H. O. Cook State Forest (413-258-4774), MA 8A, Heath. This forest has delightfully quiet hiking and riding along dirt roads. Access is off MA 8A on State Farm Rd. in northeastern Heath, 1 mile south of the Vermont line.

Kenneth Dubuque Memorial State Forest, previously known as **Hawley State Forest** (413-339-5504), northwest of Plainfield on MA 8A, offers a fine loop hike starting at Moody Spring, a genuine mineral spring with a metal pipe spouting water. A sign proclaims the legend: THIS WATER HAS PROVEN HELPFUL IN CASES OF SORE THROAT, STOMACHACHE, INTESTINAL DISORDERS, RHEUMATISM AND ALL SCROFULA DISEASES. However, this water is not tested for drinking. Not far from the spring, just off East Hawley Road, stands a well-preserved charcoal kiln. The forest's many miles of dirt roads make for fine winter ski touring and snowmobiling and summer hiking and mountain biking.

HIKING AND WALKING The **Trustees of Reservations** (413-413-532-1631; thetrustees.org) maintain:

Bear Swamp Reservation, Hawley Road, Ashfield (less than 2 miles west of the junction of MA 116 and MA 112). It has 171 acres with roads and trails and is known for wildflowers: lady's slipper, painted trillium, cowslip, marsh marigold, blue gentian, wild azalea, and flowering dogwood. Open year-round daily, sunrise to sunset. Free.

Bullitt Reservation, Bullitt Road, Ashfield, off MA 116 near the Conway line. A portion of a former gentleman's farm (William C. Bullitt served as ambassador to the Soviet Union in the 1930s), this 262 acres of field and forest offers two half-mile loop trails. The **Meadow Path,** a mown way through high grass, offers long views of hills and the **Pebble Trail,** slightly longer and steeper, threads woods and fields and skirts a beaver pond along Bullitt Road. The farmhouse houses staff on weekdays; check for periodic tours.

Chapel Brook Reservation, Williamsburg Rd., Ashfield (where MA 116 doglegs east, continue south on the Williamsburg Road for 2.25 miles). Here you'll find a series of shallow falls that spill into a deep pool, perfect for sliding down. Across the road, the Chapel Brook Ledges offer long views. Open Apr.–Nov., daily sunrise–sunset. Free.

Other

High Ledges, Shelburne. A 300-acre preserve with superb views of the surrounding countryside. From MA 2 in Shelburne, turn onto Little Mohawk Road; follow Audubon Society signs.

The stone tower on Massamett Mountain was built by the town of Shelburne. You can climb the stairs inside to some wonderful views through big open windows. The view encompasses Mount Greylock on the west, Mount Snow and Stratton Mountain in Vermont, Mount Monadnock in New Hampshire, and the Holyoke Range to the southwest. The easiest way to get there from MA 2 is up Cooper Lane behind Gould's Maple Sugarhouse, through Gould Farm to Davenport Maple Farm at the end. Be warned that although this looks like a one-way road, it definitely is not. You can park at Davenport Maple Farm and walk the fire road the mile to the tower.

The Mahican-Mohawk Trail. Based on a study and volunteer labor, a stretch of the ancient Indian path between Shelburne Falls and Deerfield is accessible to sturdily shod hikers. The entire hike takes at least four hours and entails wading the river, but the most rugged and impressive few miles are at the Shelburne Falls end—and just 1 mile can feel like a satisfying outing. The trailhead is marked on MA 2 at the pullout just east of the police station. Visitors are advised to ask directions and pick up a trail map at the Shelburne Falls Village Information Center (see *Guidance*). Another segment of this trail can be hiked in the **Mohawk State Forest** in Charlemont.

Riverwalk, Shelburne Falls. This pleasant walkway, which begins on the Buckland side of the Deerfield River opposite McCusker's Market at the end of the Bridge of Flowers, offers a view of the Salmon Falls and Potholes.

Also see **Dunbar Brook Trail,** described under **Monroe State Forest,** above.

PICNICKING

Gardner Falls, Shelburne Falls Recreation Area. Follow North Street along the river until you see the sign. The old power canal here is a great fishing spot, and it's also a fine place for a picnic (go past the picnic tables, down by the river).

South River State Forest (413-268-7098 or 413-339-5504; mass.gov/dcr), north from Conway village on the Shelburne Falls and Bardwell's Ferry Roads (see *Scenic Drives*). **South River Station** offers picnic tables and grills scattered along the gorge of the South River to its confluence with the Deerfield. Near the parking area, notice the South River Dam, once used to power the trolley line.

Malley Park on the Buckland side of the Deerfield River (near the Lamson & Goodnow factory) offers a good view of the Potholes.

Also see **High Ledges,** above.

WATERFALLS

Tannery Falls. Take Black Brook Road off MA 2 just east of the bridge that marks the Florida–Savoy line. One of the most spectacular waterfalls in the state. For directions and description, see "Along the Mohawk Trail."

Chapel Brook Reservation. See *Hiking and Walking*.

✷ Lodging

INNS AND BED & BREAKFASTS

In Ashfield 01330

Bull Frog Bed & Breakfast (413-628-4493), 1629 Conway Rd. (MA 116). Open year-round. Lucille Thibault's 200-year-old Cape sits back from MA 116 with a lovely back garden, a frog pond, and five kinds of berry bushes. The organically grown blueberries, strawberries, blackberries, several kinds of raspberries, gooseberries, and currants are the ingredients for the homemade jams that are part of a full country breakfast so special we had to take a picture. Maple syrup is also a family product. The big country kitchen with its antique, wood-fired Glenwood stove (in constant use) is the gathering place for the house; there's also an upstairs TV room. The four guest rooms share two baths, but each room has exclusive use of a bath (the other two rooms won't be rented), unless it's family or friends who share. One of our favorite rooms in the Hilltowns is the former parlor which now features a round, king-sized bed and fireplace. Lucille irons the sheets. $115 double, $85 single year-round.

The Inn at Norton Hill (413-628-4003; innatnortonhill.com), 10 Norton Hill Rd. (just off Main St.). This village house is an adjunct to Elmer's Store (see *Eating Out*) across the street. The Federal-style house offers three brightly colored, sparely furnished rooms, but there is no sitting room or sense of innkeeper. $125–150 includes breakfast at the store.

In Buckland 01338

Bird's Nest Bed & Breakfast (413-625-9523; birdsnestbnb.com), 2 Charlemont Rd., Buckland 01338. This hospitable house was built in 1797 at the head of Buckland Center's handsome street, across the road from

BREAKFAST AT THE BULL FROG BED AND BREAKFAST IN ASHFIELD.

Christina Tree

the striking Mary Lyon Church, known for its carillon. Lyon, who founded Mount Holyoke and Wheaton Colleges, taught a Winter School for Young Ladies here from 1830–32. Guests enter the house through a comfortable brick-floored room, and common space includes the original keeping room and a big, sunny dining room. Cyndy Weeks is a sculptor and painter who gives workshops, and three generations of this family are represented in the furniture, rugs, paintings, pottery, and other decorations in the house. There are three upstairs guest rooms, each with private bath. Rooms vary in size and ambience, but all are pleasant. $95–125 includes a full breakfast.

In Charlemont 01339

The Charlemont Inn (413-339-5391; charlemontinn.com), 107 Main St. (MA 2). Hospitality here dates back to a decade or so before 1787, the year Ephraim Brown formally declared his house an inn. Charlotte Dewey and Linda Shimandle continue preserving (as their brochure proclaims) "a place with character." There's a kayak above the porch and a suit of armor in the back dining room; the tavern offers local brews, a pool table, and live entertainment. The inn serves all three meals every day of the year (see *Eating Out*). The 14 clean, antique-furnished upstairs guest rooms flank a narrow hall; eight rooms share semiprivate baths, and others share two hall baths. Past guests have included Benedict Arnold, General John Burgoyne, Mark Twain, and President Calvin Coolidge. Current guests tend to be fishermen, white-water rafters, history buffs, snowmobilers, and skiers as opposed to the Jacuzzi-and-gas-fireplace crowd. From $50 for a single and hall bath; otherwise, $75 single–$100 double.

The Warfield House Inn at Valley View Farm (1-888-339-8439; warfieldhouseinn.com), 200 Warfield House Rd., off MA 2. The two guest facilities here are a white-clapboard country house with green awnings and a smaller country cottage. Together they offer nine rooms and a suite. Both buildings have living rooms and views of Berkshire East across a steep valley. The 530-acre hillside spread high above MA 2 includes a barnyard with llamas, emus, goats, and chickens, but the centerpiece of the property is a restaurant and pub (see *Dining Out*), and the complex lends itself to reunions and weddings. $99–150 for a suite, includes a full breakfast.

In Colrain 01340

High Pocket B&B (413-624-8988; highpocket.com), 38 Adams Place Rd. Sarah and Mark McKusick live down the road from this 160-year-old clapboard house with three guest rooms (all with private bath), a game room in the barn, and a hot tub on the porch with a 50-mile view. On the day we visited, dozens of goats were lazing in a neighboring field, but the specialty of this house is horseback riding. The McKusicks offer trail rides, but only to their guests. Beginners are welcome, as are more accomplished riders, and guests are invited to bring their own mounts. The adjoining properties add up to 650 acres; singletrack trails traverse surrounding fields and woods as well. This is a full house with a living room (with TV and woodstove), laundry room, full kitchen, and game room; breakfast is included in $110 per room if you stay for two nights, $10 extra for one-nighters; horses are boarded for $35 per night; pets are permitted but not in the house (there are options).

Olde Cary House (413-624-0062; oldecaryhouse.com), 7 York Rd., P.O. Box 313. Built in 1846 as a 22-room double house on 12 acres, this B&B is located up a rural road. Anneliese Zinn and her family live in the other part of the house, leaving not only the four guest rooms (two with king-sized bed) and two shared baths to guests, but also their own dining and common room with a piano and TV, and the kitchen to which they have access. It's here that Anneliese prepares a full breakfast, perhaps stuffed French toast. There's an inviting porch and a Ping-Pong table in the barn. $65–90 double. No credit cards. Children and pets are accepted by special arrangement.

In Conway 01341

House in Pumpkin Hollow (413-369-6007; pumpkinhollowhouse.com), 173 Whately Rd. Just a mile or so off MA 116 stands the town's original church and a cluster of 19th-century homes around its original, now serene green. Diane Poland has restored this 1860s house, filling it with antiques she has spent a lifetime acquiring. A fire glows in the wood-pellet stove in the parlor, the kind of place you want to linger and pick up a book you otherwise would never read. There are two guest rooms, the larger furnished with early Empire antiques including a cannonball bed; a smaller back room has a spool bed. $125–150 with private bath, $95–125 with shared. Breakfast might be perhaps a frittata with goat cheese or peach cobbler.

In Rowe 01367

Maple House Bed and Breakfast (413-339-0107; maplehousebb.com), 51 Middletown Hill Rd. A 200-year-old farmhouse that took in summer boarders a century ago, Maple House sits high on a hill surrounded by fields. Becky and Michael Bradley welcome families. Common rooms are comfortable any time of year, and the sunroom has a brick-oven fireplace. The five guest rooms feature pine floors, exposed posts and beams, and bright quilts; they range from a king with private bath to a two-room family suite. Full breakfasts feature homemade syrups (blueberry and raspberry as well as maple) and locally grown produce. Guests can swim in Pelham Lake, fish or raft, canoe or kayak on the Deerfield River, and ski downhill at nearby Berkshire East or cross-country out the back door, around the lake, and into Rowe Forest. There's also year-round trail riding 4 miles up the road in Vermont—sleigh rides, too. $60–80 single, $80–100 double; dinner is available for groups of eight or more. Inquire about special packages.

In Shelburne Falls 01370

Johnson Homestead Bed & Breakfast (413-625-6603; thejohnsonhomestead.com), 79 East Buckland Rd. Susan Grader's grandparents took in boarders for a full 40 years in this gracious 1890s farmhouse; now Susan and her husband, David, have revived the tradition. Sited on a quiet road, this is a gracious, pleasant place with a big, inviting country kitchen and two more comfortable common rooms. The two attractive guest rooms (the larger features an 1805 maple bed and hand-loomed coverlet) have private baths. Breakfast is an event, seated with a view of the garden bird feeders—and the hummingbirds, goldfinches, indigo buntings, and woodpeckers. You may feast on a mushroom and basil omelet in puff pastry, fresh fruit cup including home-grown peaches, and walnut-pumpkin muffins with homemade jam. Susan is an exceptionally hospitable host, also a writer with a flair for rhyme. $95–110 double, $20 per extra person; children 12 and older welcome. The house features an unusual outdoor fireplace and flower gardens and is set on 75 acres with a brook. A short ways off MA 112, it's on the way to nowhere except Mary Lyon's birthplace. Inquire about women's retreats.

Kenburn Orchards B&B (413-625-6116 or 1-877-KENBURN; kenburn orchards.com), 1394 Mohawk Trail (MA 2). Susan Flaccus's father and grandfather planted the apple trees in the 40-acre orchard on this 160-acre farm. Susan and her husband Larry have planted many more fruit trees as well as Christmas trees, blueberries, and raspberries (PYO), and have transformed the old homestead into a delightful B&B. The three guest rooms (with private bath), dining room, and sitting room are all sparely, nicely furnished and decorated with paintings, pottery, and other crafted work by local artisans. Nothing froufrou, but everything in keeping with the character of the house: a pencil-post canopy bed in the Isadore Pratt Room upstairs and a cherry king-sized bed in the downstairs bedroom, quilts and Oriental carpets, gas Vermont Castings stoves (air-conditioning in summer), lovely new baths, plenty of light, and exceptional views. All rooms have AC, CD clock radios, robes, ironing boards, and teakettles. There are rockers on the

THE JOHNSON HOMESTEAD BED & BREAKFAST IN SHELBURNE FALLS HAS A RICH HISTORY.
Christina Tree

porch; a gazebo lets you enjoy dusk without the bugs it brings. $139–209 per couple includes a full, candlelit breakfast featuring local ingredients served at the formal dining room table. For slightly more, the Isadore Pratt Room can be rented as a suite with a sleep sofa in an adjoining room.

Six Maple Street (413-625-6807; sixmaplestreet.com), 6 Maple St. Open weekends May–Nov. Judy Hoyt grew up in this 18th-century house, the oldest standing home in the village of Shelburne Falls. It's been in her family since the late 19th century, and the two upstairs guest rooms (sharing one and a half baths) are furnished in family antiques. The larger one retains a marble sink. There's a gracious living room with a fireplace and a big kitchen and yard. Given the superb restaurants in Shelburne Falls, it's nice to stay somewhere you can walk home to. $90–100 includes a continental breakfast.

Dancing Bear B&B (413-623-9281; dancingbearguesthouse.com), 22 Mechanic St. Remodeled by owners Phil Bragdon (former program manager of New Hampshire Public Radio) and his wife, Edith Bingham. The couple have lived many places and speak several languages. This is a vintage 1850s village house with nice detailing, and the three rooms (with private baths) are comfortably furnished. A full homegrown and homemade breakfast with eggs, pastries, fresh fruit, and espresso if so desired is included in $109–129 per couple.

OTHER LODGING **Stump Sprouts Guest Lodge** (413-339-4265; stumpsprouts.com), West Hill Rd., Hawley 01339. In 1977 Lloyd Crawford built a contemporary, hilltop lodge almost entirely with his own hands from timbers he found standing on this 450-acre spread. He also built the bunks and much of the furniture inside. Currently the Crawfords produce more electricity from their solar system than they use. There are seven rooms, sleeping from two to five, and the common spaces are on many levels (there are lofts and corners to sit in with skylights and stained glass). Windows maximize the view of tier upon tier of wooded hills. The former barn is a great rec room with table tennis, pool, and a piano; the ceiling drops down for warmth in winter and can be raised to allow even more space (the old silo is a great aerie) in summer. There's a wonderful view from the sauna, too. Vegetable gardens supply the table, which Suzanne Crawford sets family-style, or you can cook for yourself. It's possible to come singly or in couples, but it's most fun to come as a group. The repeat rate is 90 percent. In winter there are the more than 15 miles of cross-country ski trails (also used for snowshoeing) for which this place is well-known, and in summer the trails are still there to walk or bike. In winter $159 per person per weekend includes six meals; from $232 on three-day holiday weekends includes six meals. Spring through fall, a two-night weekend with three meals is $139, and if you cook and clean for yourself rates begin at $36 midweek, $72 on weekends.

Rowe Camp & Conference Center (413-339-4954; rowecenter.org), 22 Kings Highway Rd., Box 273, Rowe 01367. The Unitarian Universalist center consists of a farmhouse and assorted camp buildings on a quiet back road. There are 18 private and semiprivate rooms with a total of 125 beds, mostly dorm-style. On most weekends throughout the year there are speakers, many well-known, on topics ranging from journal-writing to tracking to overcoming insomnia and planning a garden. Seven summer weeks are also reserved for school-age, adult, and family camps. There are two costs for each conference: The first is housing, which includes six meals and ranges from $115 for two nights' camping to $335 for single occupancy in a private room; the second is the program cost, which is based on family income and runs $195–295. Bill fondly remembers his wake-up call here: "'Tis a gift to be simple" played at his door on a recorder.

((ψ)) ♿ ✐ **Hawk Mountain Lodge** (1-800-532-7483; hawkmountainlodge .com), P.O. Box 245, Charlemont 01339. This 19th-century farmhouse offers a pleasant alternative to the camping and cabin tent options at Zoar Outdoor. There are four rooms and a suite, some shared and some private baths, all comfortably furnished and sharing a living room with WiFi. Bicycle and kayak rentals as well as white-water lessons, rafting, and rock climbing are all offered here (see *To Do*). Off-season a series of tracking and historical workshop weekends is offered; this also makes a good base for skiing at Berkshire East. Breakfast is by special arrangement; otherwise the Coffee Bean (open from 6 AM), with a full breakfast menu is just down the road. May–Oct. $85–155 per room, otherwise $65–125. Inquire about discounts for groups of six to 13 and about renting the whole house.

✐ ♿ **Blue Heron Farm** (413-339-4045; blueheronfarm.com), Warner Hill Rd., Charlemont 01339. Bill and Norma Coli offer a choice of lodging options on their 140-acre organic farm with a pond and walking/ski trails. Five rentals: a self-contained cottage (two bedrooms, two baths, fireplace, sleeps up to eight), a log cabin (sleeps up to four, one bedroom), an attractive apartment attached to the sugarhouse (sleeps up to three), a bungalow (sleeps up to three), and The Maples, a post-and-beam Cape that includes a king-bedded bedroom, an upstairs bedroom with twins, a loft with a sleep sofa, two baths, plus a living room with fireplace, dining room, and full kitchen. Overall this place is great for families; pony-cart rides, berry picking, and helping with the horses and goats are encouraged.

✐ **Oxbow Resort Motel** (413-625-6011; oxbowresortmotel.com), 1741 Mohawk Trail, Charlemont 01339. A one-story, family-owned motel with 25 rooms (19 with two double beds) grouped around a swimming pool. All have air-conditioning and TV, and the property includes tennis courts with furnished balls and racquets; there's also a six-hole golf course, horseshoes, and a basketball court. Stillwaters Restaurant (see *Dining Out*) is next door, and the Deerfield River is just across MA 2. Rooms in the front have river views, but those in the rear are quieter. In summer/fall $79–95 double; from $55 off-season. No charge for children under 16. Inquire about ski packages with Berkshire East.

CAMPGROUNDS

State Parks and Forests

See mass.gov/dcr. For camping reservations, call 1-877-422-6762 or reserve online through ReserveAmerica.com.

For detailed fees, see *Camping* in "What's Where." For details on camping in the **Mohawk Trail State Forest** and **Savoy Mountain State Forest,** see "Along the Mohawk Trail."

Private

Zoar Outdoor (1-800-532-7483; zoaroutdoor.com), MA 2, Charlemont. Set in a wooded area surrounded by 80 acres of woods and offering 10 cabin tents, each with a wooden deck, four cots, a gas lantern, a gas grill, and a porch; there are also several primitive tent sites. (See *White-Water Rafting.*)Also see **Hawk Mountain Lodge** under *Other Lodging.*

Country Aire Campground (413-625-2996; countryairecampground.com), 1735 Mohawk Trail (MA 2), Shelburne Falls. Sites for trailers and tents on 45 acres of woods and fields. Amenities include a snack bar, Laundromat, swimming pool, game room, dump station and play areas.

✷ Where to Eat

DINING OUT

In Shelburne Falls

Café Martin (413-625-2795; cafemartinsf.com), 24 Bridge St. Open Tues.–Sun. from 4. This gets top local reviews. It's an informal, atmospheric storefront restaurant with a varied menu, from burgers to vegetarian. Lunch on a salade Niçoise or black bean burger. Dinner ranges from a veggie burrito to a 12-ounce Delmonico steak topped with Gorgonzola butter. Dinner entrées $11.95–24.95. Full liquor license.

Gypsy Apple (413-625-6345), 65 Bridge St. Open Wed.–Sun. for dinner. Reservation suggested. This small, atmospheric bistro garners rave reviews for the locally sourced food and beautifully prepared and presented dishes, but it tends to be overheated (poor ventilation) and service can be a bit too leisurely. Request the patio. $27 for pan-roasted chicken, $30 for rack of lamb.

West End Pub (413-625-6216), 16 State St., Shelburne Falls. Open Tues.–Sun., 11–close. Overlooking the Bridge of Flowers, this is a special spot with good food, from veggie wraps, soups, and salads at lunch to a pair of crisp-fried crabcakes in a spicy Cajun remoulade or roasted free-range chicken at dinner. Reasonably priced.

Blue Rock Restaurant and Bar (413-625-8133; thebluerockrestaurant.com), 10 Bridge St. Chef-owner Chris Ramirez characterizes the menu as "new American" and has renamed this cellar-level space (formerly Ollie's Down Under) for its blue granite walls. You might dine on pork tenderloin glazed with so, ginger, and sesame ($17) or a wild mushroom and smoky vegetable lasagna ($15) Also, soups and salads. Life music on weekends.

Elsewhere

The Warfield House (413-339-6600 or 1-888-339-VIEW; warfieldhouseinn.com), 200 Warfield Rd., off MA 2, Charlemont. Dinner Mon., Wed., and Fri.–Sun., lunch Sat.–Sun.; breakfast buffet 9–noon Sun. Set high on a hilltop with views across this steep-sided valley to Berkshire East ski area. Weddings are a specialty. Dinner might begin with pan-fried crabcakes. Entrées might range from maple-glazed chicken to filet mignon with roasted garlic mashed potatoes and fresh vegetables with thyme butter.

Check out the exotic animals in the neighboring barnyard. Dinner entrées $15–25.

In Colrain

Mike & Tony's Pizzeria at Green Emporium (413-624-5122; greenemporium.com), 4 Main Rd., Colrain. Open Thurs.–Sun.5–9. The former brick church at the heart of this gem of a village is filled with flower-decked tables, Tony Polumbo's distinctive neon art, and, frequently, live music. Chef Michael Collins's chicken soup with pasta ($5) and thin-crust pizza with locally sourced toppings ($13.95–20) are worth the short, scenic drive from MA 2. Call before coming.

EATING OUT

On and off MA 2, West to East

Charlemont Inn (413-339-5796; charlemontinn.com), 107 Main St. Open daily 6 AM through dinner; best known for live entertainment on weekends. The Full Moon Tavern is the apt name of the inn's big, informal dining room with its friendly bar and pool table; dining is also available on the sunporch, and in summer there's a patio. Anything goes here, from burgers to vegetarian dishes; specialties include homefries, Zoar steak, and BBQ ribs, and may include roast duck. There's also a children's menu.

Charlemont Pizza (413-339-4472), Main St. Open at 11 daily, noon Sun., until at least 9. Try the kielbasa pizza with extra cheese.

The Coffee Bean (413-339-4760), 90 Main St., Charlemont. Open daily 6–5. A particularly good breakfast menu, then hot and cold sandwiches, brownies.

Gould's Maple Sugarhouse (413-625-6170; goulds-sugarhouse.com), MA 2, Shelburne. Open in sugaring season (Mar.–Apr.) and during foliage (Sept.–Oct.), daily 8:30–2. If it's open, be sure to stop at this great roadside eatery that's been in the family for generations. Specialties include pan-

MIKE & TONY'S PIZZERIA AT THE GREEN EMPORIUM

Christina Tree

cakes, waffles, and fritters laced with the family's maple syrup. Try their homemade dill pickles, too. We last lunched on a memorable BLT.

Pine Hill Orchards Restaurant (413-624-3325), 248 Greenfield Rd., Colrain. Open weekdays 7–2, weekends 8–2. Closed Tues. This country oasis serves home-baked items, as well as soups and sandwiches. The property includes 75 acres with apple orchards and a duck pond. The store (open daily) sells the house cider, apples, pumpkins, and baked goods as well as local produce.

In Shelburne Falls

The Village Restaurant (413-625-6300), 43 Bridge St. Open for lunch and dinner except Tues.; breakfast, too, on weekends. An inviting place for burgers, chili, pasta, and full dinners.

McCusker's Market & Deli (413-625-9411), 3 State St. Open Sun.–Thurs. 7–7, weekends 7–8. This brightly painted (in its original colors) former Odd Fellows Hall (built in 1877) is on the Buckland side of the two bridges. Natural foods, vitamins, local cheeses, organic produce, fresh-baked breads and cookies, and much more. There are booths in back; also outdoor tables in-season. A favorite place to catch up on the news, especially if it's local.

Fox Towne Coffee Shop (413-625-6606), 25 Bridge St. Open daily 5 AM–9 PM, weekends until 6. A local gathering spot that's best for breakfast, daily specials, fresh-baked pies.

COUNTRYPIE PIZZA, ASHFIELD

Christina Tree

COFFEEHOUSES **Shelburne Falls Coffee Roasters** (413-625-0116; ibuycoffee.com), 1207 Mohawk Trail. Open 6–6 daily, this pleasant café is one of several throughout the Valley. Coffees and baked-from-scratch pastries are the draw, as well as blended frozen drinks.

OTHER **Countrypie Pizza Company** (413-628-4488), 343 Main St., Ashfield. Open Mon.–Sat. 11:30–9. Good pizza with plenty of veggie varieties, including eggplant, broccoli, artichoke hearts, feta, and Garden Delight featuring fresh spinach, mushrooms, and so forth. Also Sicilian wraps and grinders.

Elmer's Store (413-628-4003; elmersstore.com), 396 Main St., Ashfield. Open 7:30–6, weekends from 8. The heart of town since the 1830s was vacant for several years until Nan Parati arrived, a New Orleans transplant after Hurricane Katrina. It is now a destination from towns around for breakfasts (until noon) featuring local eggs and Ashfield-made syrup with "sides" that include black beans and salsa. All kinds of omelets, espressos, teas, smoothies. Drinks and pastries all day; groceries, papers, original art and crafts also sold. Dinner is served Friday at 5—recent choices were pork stew or eggplant ratatouille over polenta ($10)—and is frequently followed by live music. Check the website.

✷ Entertainment

MUSIC **Mohawk Trail Concerts** (413-625-9511 or 1-888-MTC-MUSE; mohawktrailconcerts.org). Since 1969 the acoustically fine, 225-seat (now air-conditioned) Charlemont Federated Church on MA 2 has been the summer venue for chamber and choral music from many styles, periods, and places, performed by internationally known artists. Concerts are Friday at 7 and Saturday at 7:30 in July.

Memorial Hall Theater (413-625-2896; shelburnefallsmemorialhall.org). The site of **Hilltown Folk Concerts** (413-625-2580), a series of weekend performances, as well as other live music.

Shelburne Falls Military Band. Billed as the country's oldest military band, the group performs on Wednesdays from mid-June through August at various locations in Shelburne Falls.

At **The Charlemont Inn,** Saturday-night music ranges from bluegrass and folk through jazz. Also check local listings for music at **Mocha Maya's Coffee Co.** and **The Blue Rock Restaurant** in Shelburne Falls, at **Mike & Tony's Pizzeria** in Colrain and **Elmer's Store** in Ashfield.

THEATER **Double Edge Theatre** (413-628-0277; doubleedgetheatre.org) 948 Conway Rd. (MA 116), Ashfield. Better known in the far-flung cities they tour, this highly professional company performs on its own 100-acre farm on summer nights. Performers draw their audience along in the dusk from meadow to barn to hillside to pondside, amplifying their tale with music, dance, and amazing acrobatics grounded in Eastern European traditions.

ELMER'S STORE IS *THE* GATHERING PLACE IN ASHFIELD.

Christina Tree

FILM ♿ **Pothole Pictures** (413-625-2896; shelburnefallsmemorialhall.org), Memorial Hall Theater, Shelburne Falls. A series of independent, classic, and art films, The Metropolitan Opera and National Theater of Opera Live in HD. The 425-seat restored Memorial Hall Theater is upstairs in the town hall. For the current schedule, check the website.

✷ Selective Shopping

ANTIQUE SHOPS Strawberry Fields (413-625-2039), 1204 Mohawk Trail (MA 2), on the corner of the road to Colrain. Open year-round but only Fri.–Sun. off-season.

CRAFTS SHOPS AND STUDIOS

In Shelburne Falls

Note: **Art Under the Stars** is held quarterly on a Saturday to promote village galleries and studios, 5–9 PM.

Salmon Falls Artisans Showroom (413-625-9833; salmonfallsgallery.com), 1 Ashfield St. Open Apr.–Dec., daily 10–5, Sun. noon–5; Jan.–Mar., Wed.–Sat. 10–5, Sun. noon–5. Housed in a former granary, this is an exceptional gallery showcasing more than 100 local craftspeople and artists drawn from within a radius of 65 miles. It's a prime outlet for the widely acclaimed glass orbs by Shelburne-based Josh Simpson. The quality of work displayed—notably jewelry and woodwork—is outstanding.

Shelburne Arts Cooperative (413-625-9324; shelburneartscoop.com), 26 Bridge St. Closed Mon. A shop filled with striking work by some 70 members, mostly local.

Laurie Goddard Studios (413-625-8120; lauriegoddard.com), 9 Bridge St. Open year-round. Laurie Goddard is best known for her museum-quality translucent bowls, but more recently she has been creating striking abstract designs on gessoed Masonite panels, gilded with combinations of semiprecious leaf such as copper, Dutch metal, and metallic powders, then overpainted and finally varnished.

SALMON FALLS ARTS SHOWROOM, SHELBURNE FALLS

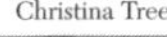

Christina Tree

Christina Tree

SHELBURNE ARTS COOPERATIVE SHOWCASES MOSTLY LOCAL ART.

Stillwater Porcelain (413-625-8250; stillwaterporcelain.com), 50 State St. Housed in a former Sunoco station and car wash, Pat Pyott's studio produces and sells professional porcelain works featuring nature designs in relief.

Vävstuga Swedish Weaving and Folks Arts (413-625-8241; vavstuga .com), 16 Water St. A showcase for the neighboring center; also Swedish looms, equipment, and yarns; two and three-day weaving classes.

Ann Brauer Quilt Studio (413-625-8605; annbrauer.com), 2 Conway St. Open Wed.–Sat. 10–5, Sun. noon–5. This nationally known quilter can usually be found in her small pink shop on the Buckland side of the river, frequently stitching away on stunning quilts, wall hangings, pot holders, shoulder bags, place mats, and other creations.

Dick Muller & Co. Leather (413-625-6205; dickmullerleather.com), 6 Bridge St. Open Thurs.–Sat. 11–5:30, Sun. 11–5. Diane and Dick Muller have been working together for more than 40 years, crafting custom sandals and lovely wallets, one-of-a-kind handbags, and belts.

Wandering Moon (413-625-9667), 59 Bridge St. Open Wed.–Sat. 10:30–5, Sun. 11–4. Since 1991 Laura and David Roberson's shop has acquired an ever-widening reputation for unusual jewelry (some made by Laura) as well as an eclectic mix of handcrafted work and books relating to nature and preindustrial history.

Young & Constantine Gallery (413-625-6866; yandcglass.com), 4 Deerfield Ave. Open daily in-season. Kathleen Young, owner of North River Glass—which was formerly blown on these premises—has revamped the former gallery here, doubling its size and now carrying jewelry, fine art, furnishings, and more.

Grow Gallery (413-625-9900; grow gallery.com), 55 Bridge St. A classy new gallery showcasing local artists in a variety of media.

J. H. Sherburne Fine Art (413-625-8306; jhsherburnefineart.com), 40 State St. A framery and gallery with changing exhibits overlooking the Bridge of Flowers.

Elsewhere

Moonshine Design at Keldaby (413-634-3090; keldaby.com), 12 Heath Rd. Cynthia Herbert is a weaver producing hand-dyed mohair yarns, throws, and wearables, both handwoven and knitted from her herd of Angora goats. Visitors are welcome at the sunflower-yellow house with its barn, fields, and shop/studio.

Mike Purington Wood Bowls (413-624-0036), 285 Thompson Rd., Colrain. Open Sun. 2–6 and by appointment. Purington turns bowls in his shop, which faces north toward the Green Mountains. Each piece of wood is turned to a shape that suits its character, then set to dry for several months before being finished with oils and beeswax.

MCCUSKER'S MARKET & DELI IN SHELBURNE FALLS.

Christina Tree

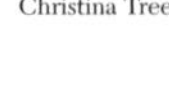

SPECIAL SHOPS

In Shelburne Falls

Lamson & Goodnow Factory Outlet Store (413-625-0201; lamsonsharp.com), 45 Conway St. Open Mon.–Sat. 10–5, Sun. noon–5. This venerable waterside complex of classic, mostly 19th-century wood and brick mill buildings dates from 1837, when it began producing Silas Lamson's invention, the curved scythe snath (handle). The company hired master cutlers from Sheffield, England, and Solingen, Germany, and grew to become the largest producer of edged tools and cutlery in the U.S. Some descendants of these early craftsmen are still employed here, some working in buildings dating from 1850. The shop features the company's products at 10 to 20 percent off, as well as a wide variety of kitchen gear and gadgets, gourmet food, cookbooks, and more.

McCusker's Market (413-625-9411), 3 State St. The hub of the Hilltowns, a combination health food store and deli/café with Internet access (see *Eating Out*), now owned by the Franklin Community Co-Operative, housed in a picturesque 1877 former Odd Fellows Hall.

Boswell's Books (413-625-9362), 10 Bridge St. A full-service independent bookshop with new and used books. Lori Pirkot also offers audio and video rentals, games, notebooks, pens, puzzles, pleasant reading corners, and Boswell the cat.

Nancy L. Dole Books & Ephemera (413-625-9850; nancydolebooks.com), 32 Bridge St., second floor. Open Tues.–Fri. from 11, Sat.–Sun. afternoons. This is a find, an upstairs cache of some 25,000 books plus old prints, photos, and postcards.

The Shelburne Falls Wine Merchant (413-825-6506; hilltownwinemerchant.com), 1 State St. (adjoining McCusker's). Open Mon.–Sat. 10–7, Sun. noon–6. A wine mecca with frequent tastings and special events.

Elsewhere

Ashfield Hardware & Supply (413-628-3299), 343 Main St., Ashfield. A store that's housed many enterprises over the years, but none more varied and useful than at present under its female owners. An exceptional independent hardware store specializing in hard-to-find items and those with natural ingredients, plus soaps and toys, hand-forged items, plants, and 50-cent ice cream cones.

Note: See "Along the Mohawk Trail" for more information on the trading posts and gift shops along MA 2.

✷ Farms

Tregellys Fiber Farm (413-625-6448; tregellysworld.com), 15 Dodge Branch Rd., Hawley. Open Wed.–Sun. 10:30–5. Turn off MA 112 at the Ashfield–Buckland line onto Clesson Brook Road, and follow the camels. Donation suggested. Spreading for some 138 acres across Hog Mountain in the Dodge Corner area of Hawley, this farm is well named. *Tregelly* means "hidden homestead" in Cornish, whence Ed Cothey originally came. Ed and wife Jody envisioned a few animals and a garden when they moved here a decade or so back, but their passion for animals and fiber arts took on a life of its own. The animals now include llamas, bactrian (two-humped) camels from Mongolia, and an assortment of birds. The farm shop sells fair trade arts and crafts from around the world. It's worth the

ASHFIELD HARDWARE & SUPPLY SELLS AN ECLECTIC ASSORTMENT OF ITEMS.

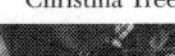

Christina Tree

drive if just for the view (there are picnic tables).

Apex Orchards (413-625-2744; apexorchards.com), 153 Pecksville Rd., Shelburne. The retail store is open Mon.–Fri. 7–2, Sat.–Sun. 8–3. PYO apples in Sept. and Oct. Also available: peaches, honey, cider vinegar, and one of the region's more amazing views. This glorious orchard has been in Tim Smith's family since 1828. This is another fabulous view.

Donovan Farm (413-339-4213), Forget Rd., Hawley. The state's largest organically certified farm, with sweeping views and five kinds of potatoes, produces its own hand-cooked, organic potato chips.

Hall Tavern Farm (413-625-9008), MA 2, East Charlemont. The state's oldest privately owned tree farm produces timbers and lumber for its sawmill and offers a variety of kiln-dried wood products, including wide pine flooring, paneling, and wainscoting as well as ash, cherry, maple, and oak flooring from its 500 acres. The property includes a 4-mile hiking and snowshoeing trail.

Burnt Hill Farm (413-337-4454), 118 Flagg Hill Rd., Heath. Pick-your-own blueberries in-season on top of a mountain with a 50-mile view.

The Benson Place (413-337-5340; bensonplace.org), 182 Flag Hill Rd., Heath. Unsprayed, wild, lowbush blueberries. PYO late July–late August; the farm stand is also open 9–5 daily.

Johnson Hill Farm (413-625-6423; lavenderland.com), 51 Hog Hollow Rd., Shelburne Falls. Guests are invited to walk the lavender labyrinth. Lavender is harvested and dried; lavender products sold. Inquire about the Lavender Festival.

SUGARHOUSES Sugaring season can begin as early as late February and extend well into April. A brochure detailing information about the sugaring process and each producer is available from the **Massachusetts Maple Producers Association** (massmaple.org), P.O. Box 6, Plainfield 01070. During sugaring season you can call the **Massachusetts Maple Phone** (413-628-3912) to get an overall view on whether the sap is flowing and producers are "boiling off." The following sugarhouses (a partial list) are geared toward visitors more than most, but it's still a good idea to call before coming. All also sell their syrup from their farms year-round.

In Ashfield

South Face Farm (413-628-3268; southfacefarm.com), Watson–Spruce Corner Rd. Tom McCrumm and Judy Haupt offer a sit-down dining room during sugaring season, as well as exhibits of antique maple-sugaring equipment. This has been a working farm for 150 years, and some of the maples along the road are probably that old. The current sugarhouse dates back 50 years, recycled from a 19th-century barn.

In Charlemont

Warfield House Inn (413-339-6600; warfieldhouseinn.com), 200 Warfield Rd., off MA 2. Call to check on whether the wood-fire evaporator is working in the sugarhouse.

In Heath

Girard's Sugarhouse (413-337-5788). Has been operating for more than 100 years.

In Shelburne

Gould's Maple Sugarhouse (413-625-6170; goulds-sugarhouse.com),

MA 2. Features locally made syrup on waffles; also homemade sausage and sugar-on-snow among a full selection of menu items (see *Eating Out*).

Davenport Maple Farm (413-625-2866), 111 Tower Rd. Set high above the valley with a splendid view, operates a restaurant on weekends during sugaring season and sells syrup from the house year-round (a good excuse to drive up).

✷ Special Events

Note: Check shelburnefalls.com for current Shelburne Falls–area events, and mafa.org for dates and details on agricultural fairs.

March: **Sugaring season** throughout the Hilltowns.

May: **Indian Powwow** at Indian Plaza, Charlemont.

May–Oct.: See farmfresh.org for details about outstanding **farmers' markets** in **Shelburne Falls** (Fri. 2–6, 53 Main St.), **Ashfield** (Sat. 8:30–12:30, 457 Main St.) and **Conway** (Wed. 4–8, in front of Field Memorial Library).

June: **Riverfest** is a daylong festival along the street and river in Shelburne Falls. **Franklin Land Trust Annual Farm and Garden Tour** (413-625-9151; franklinlandtrust.org) is a great excuse to explore back roads leading to some amazing properties.

July–mid August: **Mohawk Trail Concerts** (mohawktrailconcerts.org), Fri. and Sat. in Charlemont.

July: July 4 **Indian Powwow**, Charlemont. **July Fourth parade** in Shelburne Falls. **Rowe Old Home Day** (*first weekend*). **Charlemont Yankee Doodle Days** at the Charlemont Fairgrounds offers three days of music and games, square dancing, fireworks, and BBQ (*third weekend*).

August: **Bridge of Flowers 10K road race** and **Bridge Dinner,** Shelburne Falls. **Heath Fair** (413-337-5716) is one of the state's most colorful country fairs (*midmonth*). **Shelburne Grange Fair** (*last weekend*) and **Iron Bridge Dinner**, Shelburne Falls.

September: **Annual Shelburne Falls Wine and Cheese Festival. Colrain Fair** (*midmonth*). **Conway Festival of the Hills** (413-369-4631),

THE ANNUAL BRIDGE DINNER ON THE IRON BRIDGE IN SHELBURNE FALLS.
Shelburne Falls Area Business Association

one of New England's most colorful foliage festivals, featuring arts and crafts, skillet toss, weaving, ox driving, and more (*last weekend*).

October: **Ashfield Fall Festival** on Columbus Day weekend is not to be missed—art and crafts exhibits, music, games, antique sales, demonstrations, all kinds of food, farm products, and more.

November: **CiderDays** (ciderday.org; *first weekend*) includes tours of orchards, hard-cider-making demos, apple pie tasting, crafts fair, lunch, and supper. **Crafts of Colrain Studio Tour** (craftsofcolrain.com) opens upward of 20 studios scattered through the hills (*second weekend*). **Moonlight Madness** features tree lighting, caroling, and special sales in Shelburne Falls (*day after Thanksgiving*). **Tuba Christmas** concert in Shelburne Falls (*Sunday after Thanksgiving*).

COLRAIN IS THE SITE OF FRANKLIN COUNTY'S CIDERDAYS EVERY NOVEMBER.

Christina Tree

THE HIDDEN HILLS

INCLUDING CUMMINGTON, WORTHINGTON, CHESTER, AND WILLIAMSBURG

This 225-square-mile spread of rolling hill and woodland is so far off the tourist map that it's known as "The Hidden Hills." The Massachusetts Turnpike has passed it by. There are no exits in the 33 miles between Westfield and Lee, which suits most of its residents just fine. Along the meandering Westfield River and its branches, these fertile valleys, folded between wooded hills, remain profoundly Yankee.

During the decades before income taxes, when wealthy Americans were building themselves summer palaces in Stockbridge and Lenox, a number of farms around Worthington and Cummington were gentrified; the William Cullen Bryant Homestead is a surviving example. For much of the 20th century, however, this area was just a nameless region to pass through.

In the early 1980s, bed & breakfasts began opening throughout New England, once more offering visitors ways to explore beyond tourist routes. The Hilltown Community Development Corporation placed an ad in local papers asking people with spare rooms to consider the B&B business. A dozen or so households responded, forming the Hampshire Hills Bed & Breakfast Association and publishing a descriptive brochure—which over the years has morphed into an annual map/guide titled "The Hidden Hills of Western Massachusetts." It includes the Southern Berkshire County towns of Becket and Otis on the west, Plainfield on the north, and Williamsburg on the east (just 8 miles from Northampton). It's sparsely settled backcountry, studded with pleasant surprises.

Cultural draws include the Chester Theater Company in Chester and the Sevenars concerts in South Worthington, but most events—auctions, agricultural fairs, and town homecomings—are promoted with fliers tacked up on general store and library bulletin boards. March is the time to sample this region's true culinary specialty: maple syrup, served up on pancakes or snow right in sugarhouses. April brings fishing and one of the country's most famous white-water races. All summer is prime time, highlighted by August's old-fashioned agricultural fairs. September brings pick-your-own apples and fresh cider throughout the area, and during foliage season its high, maple-lined roads rival any in Vermont.

AREA CODE 413 applies to all of Western Massachusetts.

GUIDANCE The Hidden Hills of Western Massachusetts (hidden-hills.com) offers a visitor-friendly site and the map/guide. **The Old Creamery** (oldcreamery coop.org), 445 Berkshire Trail (MA 9) in Cummington, is a gathering spot for much of the region and a prime source of information.

GETTING THERE Part of the beauty of this area is in its approach. Few places are much more than half an hour's drive from I-91 or the Mass Pike, but you are quickly on back roads. The principal east–west roads—MA 9, US 20, and MA 23—follow the river valleys, while MA 57 to the south is a high, old byway. The major north–south routes, MA 112 and MA 8, also follow rivers. If you are coming from the east via the Mass Pike, take Exit 3 in Westfield.

MEDICAL EMERGENCY Dial **911.**

✷ Villages

Chester (population: about 1,300). Chester (chestermass.com) is a town with a split personality: Chester Village, down on US 20, and Chester Center up on Chester Hill. **Chester Village** boomed with the mining and grinding of emery (as in emery boards and sandpaper) and with the advent of the railroad, which heads northwest out of town, all uphill. It's still the way AMTRAK goes from Boston to Chicago, and it was a huge engineering feat to snake tracks up these ridges in the 1840s. The **Chester Railway Station** (413-354-7878; chesterrail waystation.org), 10 Prospect St. (off US 20), in a vintage 1841 depot, was originally built as a place to eat (dining cars had yet to be invented) midway between Springfield and Pittsfield. It's open July–Oct., Sat.–Sun. 11–4. Several vintage rail cars are parked here and overnight camping is permitted in the caboose. The **Chester Historical Society Museum** (open the first Wed. of each month and by appointment: 413-354-7829) is headquartered in the former small brick jailhouse on US 20. The town hall is seasonal home to the **Chester Theatre Company** (see *Entertainment*). On US 20 in the middle of the village, a sign for Middlefield points the way up to the **Skyline Trail.** Turn off onto Johnson Hill Road to find **Chester Center,** the picturesque 18th-century heart of town with its church and graveyard. Ask locally about how to find the **Keystone Arch**

THE CHESTER RAILWAY STATION IS HOME TO VINTAGE CARS AS WELL AS THE DEPOT
Christina Tree

Bridges off US 20. In early August, **Littleville Fair** features ox and horse draws, truck pulls, and live entertainment.

Chesterfield (population: 1,200). A white-clapboard village with an 1835 Congregational church, 1848 town hall, and the **Edward Memorial Museum** near the library. But the big attraction is **Chesterfield Gorge** (see *Green Space*). The town stages a rousing July Fourth parade. The **Bisbee Mill Museum** includes a working 19th-century gristmill as well as a rare collection of tools, equipment, and photographs of the town's past industries.

Cummington (population: 785). The **William Cullen Bryant Homestead** (see *To See*) is south of the village, up on a rise with one of the best views in the area. In the village center, posted from MA 9, the **Kingman Tavern** (413-634-5527; open July–Aug., Sat. 2–5), is a lovingly restored combination tavern, fully stocked general store, and post office. A dozen period rooms are filled with town mementos like the palm-leaf hats and cigars once made here. **The Old Creamery** (see *Eating Out*) at the junction of MA 9 and MA 112 is the town gathering place and info source. The **Cummington Fair** is one of the most colorful in the state. Cummington also harbors a number of craftspeople, musicians, and writers and is the longtime home of America's former poet laureate, Richard Wilbur.

Middlefield (population: 542). This is a town in which the main road (one of the few that's paved) is known as the Skyline Trail because it follows the edge of a 1,650-foot-high plateau and offers long views west to the Berkshires. The only specific site to visit here is **Glendale Falls,** but everywhere you walk or drive is rewarding. The **Middlefield Fair** (second week in August) is one of the oldest (since 1856) and most colorful (horse and ox draws, a sheep show, country bands, and plenty of food).

Plainfield (population: 602 year-round/2,000 in summer). Roads are lined with stone walls and avenues of maples, and the center has its mid-19th-century white Congregational church and town hall. The **Shaw-Hudson House** was built in 1833 by Dr. Samuel Shaw, medical partner and brother-in-law of William Cullen Bryant.

Williamsburg (population: 2,075). The easternmost of the Hilltowns, this is something of a bedroom town for Northampton 8 miles to the east. The village center straddles the Mill River and invites you to stroll, munching something you've bought at the **Williamsburg General Store,** the source of a *Walking Guide* published by the **Williamsburg Historical Society,** which is housed in the 1841 town hall. Exhibits include photographs of the 1874 flood that burst a dam 3 miles above the village, killing 136 residents, collapsing buildings, and wiping out most of the mills downstream in Haydenville, the town's second village. The museum also includes a collection of farm tools and equipment and the one-room Nash Hill School (the buildings are open summer Sundays). **Snow Farm** (see *Arts and Crafts Programs*) attracts participants from around the country.

Worthington (population: 1,277). The village at the heart of this town, known locally as Worthington Corners, is a classic, mid-19th-century crossroads, with its general store and surrounding old homes along roads that radiate in every direction. Note the golf course (vintage 1904), B&Bs, and hot-air ballooning. Turn off MA 112 in South Worthington to see the 19th-century academy building that now houses the **Sevenars Music Festival.** Continue on Ireland Street to farms and orchards spread along a high ridge.

✷ To See

HISTORIC HOMES **William Cullen Bryant Homestead** (413-634-2244; thetrustees.org), 207 Bryant Rd., Cummington, south of MA 9 off MA 112. Grounds: open year-round, daily, sunrise–sunset; free. House: open for guided tours late June–Columbus Day, Sat.–Sun. and Mon. holidays, 1–5; tours: adults $6, children ages 6–12 $3. This graceful mansion is filled with the spirit of an obviously tough-minded and original individual and with a sense of the era in which he was thoroughly involved. William Cullen Bryant was born in Cummington in 1794 and is remembered for his early nature poems—"Thanatopsis" and "To a Waterfowl," for example—and for his impact as editor and part owner of the *New York Evening Post* for half a century (1829–78). Bryant successfully advocated causes ranging from abolitionism to free trade to the creation of Central Park. He returned to his boyhood home at age 72, buying back the family homestead, adding another floor, and totally transforming it into a 23-room Victorian summer manse set amid 195 acres of farmland. The property has since been reduced to 189 acres, but the expansive view remains. The house has been preserved (painted in its original chocolate browns) by the Trustees of Reservations to look as it did during Bryant's last summer here, in 1878. There's a visitors center and a museum shop featuring Bryant's poetry as well as maple syrup from trees on the property.

THE INTERIOR OF THE WILLIAM CULLEN BRYANT HOMESTEAD.

Tustees of Reservations

SCENIC DRIVES In the Hilltowns, the drive that is *not* scenic is the exception. You almost can't lose, especially if you turn off the main roads in search of the waterfalls, swimming holes, craft studios, and maple producers described in this chapter. Several drives, however, are particularly noteworthy.

The Skyline Trail, accessible from MA 143 in Hinsdale and from US 20 in Chester, follows the edge of the Berkshire plateau through the middle of Middlefield. It's possible to make a loop from Chesterfield through Middlefield, stopping at Glendale Falls and the River Studio and returning via Chester Hill (another high point), but it's best to ask directions locally.

Ireland Street, Chesterfield, to South Worthington. A mile or so west of the village of Chesterfield, turn left off MA 143 at the bridge. This is Ireland Street and best known as the way to **Chesterfield Gorge** (0.8 mile from MA 143 at River Rd.). Be sure to stop. Then continue along Ireland, which is a straight, high ridge road. Stop at **Ireland Street Orchards** for the view, if for nothing else. Continue on to South Worthington. If you feel like a swim, **Gardner State Park** is just down MA 112.

Jacob's Ladder Trail Scenic Byway. The 33 miles of US 20 west from Russell to Becket are now promoted as "Jacob's Ladder," an early auto route (long since back-roaded by the Mass Pike) that takes its name from the Becket farmer who is said to have hauled autos up the steepest pitch with oxen. This route actually predated the Mohawk Trail as a motorway between the Pioneer Valley and Berkshire County. The Ladder crests in Becket at a ridge billed variously as 1,781 and 2,100 feet high. Whichever it is, the view of the Berkshire Valley is splendid. Note "Jacob's Well," the spring used to cool the radiators of early cars, still in use beside a rest area.

General Knox Trail (MA 23) forks off from US 20 in Blandford, heading west through Otis. The Otis Reservoir, with swimming and boating, is just over the line. This route derives its name (which actually applies to much of US 20, too) from Boston book dealer Henry Knox, who mounted a successful winter effort to drag the cannons captured by Benedict Arnold and Ethan Allen at Fort Ticonderoga over this path back to Boston, where they played a crucial role in liberating the city.

Route 57 from Westfield through Tolland and Granville. This route is well known to South Berkshire residents as a shortcut to Bradley International Airport in Connecticut, but it's otherwise one of the most obscure and back-roaded of the state's historic east–west highways. It's the most southerly and one of the highest, obviously the reason why the railroad chose to follow the Westfield River instead. These villages—which prospered in the late 18th and early 19th centuries, judging from the buildings along the road—were left to fade away. Tolland today is known chiefly for Tolland State Forest, with some of the best campsites in the state. West Granville is worth pausing to note its early-18th-century meetinghouse; Granville is a must-stop to buy the cheese that's been sold at the general store here since the 1850s. The road then spirals down out of the Berkshire Hills into the Connecticut River Valley at Southwick, notable for its many tobacco sheds and farm stands. Coming from the east, take Mass Pike Exit 6 to I-291 to I-91 South, and I-91 Exit 2 to MA 57.

Get lost. Seriously. This is high, largely open countryside that was far more populated a couple hundred years ago than it is now. If we try to direct you from Plainfield to Buckland via the web of back roads that begin with Union Street

Christina Tree

ONE OF THE MANY QUAINT SCENES ALONG MA 57.

north from the middle of Plainfield, you will have us to blame. So, bring a camera, a map, and a compass—and explore.

✷ To Do

ARTS AND CRAFTS PROGRAMS **Snow Farm** (413-268-3101; snowfarm.org), 5 Clary Rd., Williamsburg. A full and varied program of weekend and weeklong workshops is taught by dozens of skilled craftspeople, most of whom already have a long association with this special place. Check out the website or request a catalog for a sense of current courses, which typically include ceramics, glassblowing, silk screening, wood sculpture, basket-making, and photography. The setting is a 50-acre farm with lodging in dormitories and doubles (gender-specific shared baths), a common room, and a dining hall in which the meals are all made from scratch. A "Seconds Sale" featuring the work of craftspeople from around the country is held three weekends in November.

Also see **Becket Arts Center** (becketartscenter.org) in the "Southern Berkshire County" chapter.

BALLOONING **Worthington Ballooning** (413-238-5514; worthingtonballooning.com), Buffington Hill Rd., Worthington. Paul Sena offers champagne flights year-round. He will pick up passengers almost anywhere in the Berkshires, but prefers to fly from Worthington and neighboring Cummington, over the hills and down into the Connecticut River Valley. Request the multicolored "Thunderbuster" balloon: yellow, red, and orange on one side, blue and purple on the other.

BICYCLING Mountain bikers enthuse about the unpaved **River Road** south from Chesterfield Gorge in Worthington (see *Green Space*) to Knightville Dam. The *Rubel Western Massachusetts Bicycle and Road Map* is an excellent guide to biking throughout this area. See *Special Events* for the **Great River Ride** on the Columbus Day weekend.

CAMPING The website of the Department of Conservation and Recreation (mass.gov/dcr) describes each park. To reserve campsites in state forests, phone 1-877-422-6762 and check out what we say under Camping in "What's Where."

DAR State Forest (413-268-7098), Goshen, provides 50 campsites sited on a ridge near Highland Lake, each with a table and fireplace. Also see **Savoy Mountain State Forest** in "Along the Mohawk Trail." Both areas offer swimming.

FISHING The **Little River** and all three branches of the **Westfield River** are recognized throughout the country for the quality of their fishing.

Hilltown Wilderness Adventures (413-296-0187; hilltownwildernessadventures .com), Mount Road, West Chesterfield. Alaskan husky sled dogs are the specialty here, with both traditional and dry-land mushing on Marla BB's 18-acre properties. Marla also offers guided hiking and biking, kayaking, and fishing in nearby state forests.

GOLF The **Worthington Golf Club** (413-238-4464; worthingtongolfclub.net), designed in 1904, covers 88 acres and, at 1,700 feet in elevation, commands a view of surrounding hills and valleys. Open mid-Apr.–Oct. Just nine holes, it's a destination course with an attractive clubhouse and restaurant (see *Eating Out*). The **Beaver Brook Golf Course** (413-268-7229), 183 Main St., Haydenville, and the **Blandford Golf Club** (tennis, too), 17 North St., Blandford, are both nine holes.

SWIMMING The **West Branch, Middle Branch,** and **Westfield River** proper all weave their way through this area, offering countless swimming holes to which B&B hosts can direct you. More formal, public swimming spots like Plainfield Pond tend to be restricted to residents.

DAR State Forest (413-268-7098; mass.gov/dcr), Goshen, maintains a swimming area on Upper Highland Lake (see *Green Space*). A day-use fee is charged May–Oct.

✷ Winter Sports

CROSS-COUNTRY SKIING AND SNOWSHOEING ✪ **Notchview Reservation** (413-684-0148; notchview.org or xcskimass.com), MA 9, Windsor. Open early Dec.–early Apr., daily 8–4:30. Trail fee. The highest cross-country trails in

Massachusetts are found on this 3,100-acre Trustees of Reservations property. Technically in Berkshire County, Windsor borders Cummington and is the prime cross-cross country ski destination for this area. It takes a new snowfall to work your way up to the summit of 2,297-foot-high Judges Hill, but there are nearly 25 miles of trail to choose from, and views include the notch in the hills cut by the Westfield River, for which the preserve is named. A heated visitors lodge offers picnic tables and hot chocolate. Trails are groomed to diagonal and skating strides, and there's a separate 1.25-mile loop for "skijoring" with dogs. Thanks to the elevation, snow conditions usually persist into April.

Maple Corner Farm (413-357-8829; snow phone, 413-357-6697; xcskimass.com), Beech Hill Rd., Granville. This 500-acre working farm at an elevation of 1,400 feet offers more than 12 miles of groomed trail over varied terrain. There is a rental shop and a lodge with a fireplace and snack bar. Check the website for current hours.

Also see **Canterbury Farm** in the "Southern Berkshire County" chapter and **Stump Sprouts** in "The Hilltowns/West County."

DOWNHILL SKIING **Blandford Ski Area** (413-848-2860; snow phone, 413-568-4341; skiblandford.org), Nye Brook Road, Blandford. Call for directions. Open late Dec.–mid-Mar., Mon.–Fri. 8:30–6, Sat.–Sun. 8:30–4:30. Night skiing Mon., Wed., Fri., and Sat. Adult lift tickets $47. Billed as the oldest club-owned ski area in North America, this great family find was established by the Springfield Ski Club in 1934. The vertical is just 465 feet, but there are 22 trails and slopes and three double chairlifts to the summit. Trails at the center of the mountain are wide, but there are some narrow and steep runs. There's a 1941 lodge with a big hearth for picnicking (families can plug in slow cookers) as well as a new lodge with a cafeteria. Rentals, lessons, snowmaking.

* Green Space

STATE FORESTS *Note:* All state parks and forests are detailed at mass.gov/dcr.

DAR State Forest (413-268-7098; mass.gov/dcr), Goshen. Provides 50 campsites, each with a table and fireplace. The swimming area at Upper Highland Lake, complete with bathhouses and lifeguards, also has a boat ramp (no motors allowed). Trails lead to Moore's Hill, just 1,697 feet high but with an extensive view.

Windsor State Forest (mass.gov/dcr). Marked from MA 9 in West Cummington. **Windsor Jambs** is a 0.25-mile-long gorge with 60-foot-high sheer cliffs topped with hemlocks above the rushing water. A trail leads along the edge. Unfortunately, picnicking is not permitted at the edge of the gorge, but it's a beautiful walk (there's a railing).

East Branch State Forest (413-268-7098), River Rd., Chesterfield. Offers some good fishing.

Chester-Blandford State Forest (413-354-6347 or 413-269-6002), US 20, Chester. Offers picnicking at Boulder Park as well as extensive hiking trails, including a 1-mile easy-grade walk to 60-foot-high **Sanderson Brook Falls.**

HIKING AND WALKING Properties maintained by the **Trustees of Reservations** (413-684-0148; thetrustees.org).

Notchview Reservation, MA 9, Windsor (1 mile east of the junction with MA 8A). Open year-round, daily, sunrise–sunset. Adults $2, ages 12 and younger free. There are picnic tables and trail maps for the 25 miles of hiking on this former 3,000-acre estate maintained by the Trustees of Reservations. A long view down the valley and a good place for birding. Also see *Winter Sports.*

Chesterfield Gorge, River Road, Chesterfield. Turn off MA 143 at the West Chesterfield Bridge; the gorge turnoff is marked 1 mile south on River Rd. Open Apr.–Nov., daily, sunrise–sunset. Adults $2, under age 12 free. A deep canyon was carved by the Westfield River and walled by sheer granite cliffs topped with hemlock, ash, and yellow birch. Swimming is not allowed, but there are hiking trails and picnic tables.

Petticoat Hill Reservation, Williamsburg (up Petticoat Hill Rd. from the village). Open year-round, daily, sunrise–sunset. Free. A trail leads to the summit of Scott Hill. Stone walls and cellar holes hint that this spot was the most populated part of town in the 1700s, but it's now forested. A good spot for wildflowers.

Devil's Den Brook in Williamsburg is a rocky gorge off Old Goshen Rd. (turn right onto Hemenway Rd. at the western fringe of the center, then branch left onto Old Goshen). If you take the next left, up Brier Hill Rd., you come to 70 acres of wooded trails, good for cross-country skiing and hiking. Ask locally about **Rheena's Cave.**

WATERFALLS **Glendale Falls,** Middlefield (thetrustees.org). Turn off Skyline Trail Rd. onto Clark Wright Rd.—which is closed in winter—some 3.5 miles southeast of the village. Glendale Brook drops more than 150 feet over rocky ledges into the Westfield River and is one of the state's highest and longest waterfalls. There are 60 surrounding acres.

Salmon Brook Falls. A drop of 50 feet in the Chester-Blandford State Forest, south of Chester, marked from US 20; a good spot for a picnic.

Also see **Sanderson Brook Falls** and **Windsor Jambs** under *State Forests.*

✷ Lodging

BED & BREAKFASTS *Note:* The B&Bs described below are widely scattered. Some border Berkshire County on the west, while those on the east offer easy access to the Five-College Area. Most are pictured on the **Hampshire Hills Bed & Breakfast Association** (1-888-414-7664) website, hhbba.com, or at hidden-hills.com.

In the Cummington/Worthington area

Upland Meadows Farm (413-634-8884), 338 West Cummington Rd. (MA 112), Cummington 01026. This is a find! A beautifully restored 18th-century house on 200 acres, set at an elevation of 2,000 feet with a long view of hills and valley rolling away to the east. Owner Judy

Bogart has given her B&B an uncluttered, modern feeling while respecting the character of the house. The three bedrooms with private baths are bright, cheery, and comfortably furnished. Located in a rear wing, each has a private entrance from the porch. No extra charge for dogs. Horses are $10. Animals in residence on the farm include sheep, goats, a horse, and a llama. $80 year-round with full breakfast.

The Worthington Inn & Café (413-238-4441), at Four Corners Farm, Old North Rd. (MA 143), Worthington 01098. Debi and Joe Shaw's striking, 1780 house has wide floorboards, five fireplaces, and fine paneling. It was restored in 1942 by the architect responsible for much of the Old Deerfield restoration. There are horses in the horse barn and 60 surrounding acres on the edge of a picturesque village; it's really someplace special. The three bedrooms are sparely, tastefully furnished with antiques and down comforters; all have a private bath and wonderful light. Common space is elegant and comfortable, lived in by a real family. As appealing in winter as summer. Children and horses are welcome. The Shaws are hospitable, helpful hosts. $80–90. Inquire about dinner on Friday and Saturday.

In the Chesterfield/Williamsburg area

The Seven Hearths Bed & Breakfast (413-296-4312; seven hearths.com), 412 Main Rd., Chesterfield 01012. An 1890s Colonial Revival house set in the middle of the village historic district. Doc and Denise LeDuc serve memorable multicourse breakfasts (maybe stuffed French toast prefaced by a fruit-stuffed melon) in the formal dining room. The common rooms and three of the four guest rooms have working fireplaces; the larger guest room offers sitting and writing space and a private bath, while the fourth room is reserved for guests traveling together. Amenities include a hot tub. $80–130 double, $70–120 single.

Twin Maples Bed & Breakfast (413-268-7925; twinmaplesbnb.com), 106 South St., Williamsburg 01096. This 1806 house is set on 27 acres on a back road not far from the center of town. It's been home to Eleanor and Martin Hebert for almost 50 years and a B&B for almost 30. The three bedrooms and shared bath are clean and crisp (we like the blue room with the antique iron-and-brass bed), and the welcome is genuine. Rooms are air-conditioned and there's a screened-in sitting porch, as well as swings and a sandbox for younger guests. $85–100 includes a breakfast featuring local produce, much of it from the garden.

1886 House, Chesterfield. See "Five-College Area."

Elsewhere

Baird Tavern (413-848-2096; bairdtavern.com), 2 Old Chester Rd., Blandford 01008. This 1768 house retains its original wide paneling and floorboards, conveying a sense of comfort as well as history. Host Carolyn Taylor has carefully preserved the authentic look of the house, originally a tavern catering to travelers on the old Boston-to-Albany turnpike. (The Massachusetts Turnpike follows the same approximate route, but is out of sight of the house.) A kettle sits next to the big old fireplace in the original kitchen, and the one-time taproom is now a comfortable but

Christina Tree

TRANQUILLITY AT THE BAIRD TAVERN IN BLANDFORD.

uncluttered sitting room. Guest rooms are up the stairs built around the central chimney; one room retains its original walls and has a spinning wheel and period decor, but again nothing is cluttered. In all there are three guest rooms, the largest with a Shaker-style pencil-post canopy bed. Rooms share one and a half baths. A cot and crib are available; Persian cats (which Carolyn raises) are usually in residence. The tavern is set on 7 acres and includes a perennial flower garden. Carolyn is a local caterer, and breakfasts can as easily be quiche or omelets as blueberry pancakes, although the berry-packed latter is the house specialty. $105–140 double, $25 per extra person.

✷ Where to Eat

EATING OUT **Chef Wayne's Big Mamou Cajun Restaurant** (413-268-8901; chefwaynes-bigmamou.com), 15 Main St., Williamsburg. Open for lunch and dinner except Monday. Offshoot of a popular Springfield restaurant, this is your only chance to sample crawfish quesadillas, shrimp-n-sausage jambalaya, or alligator-n-sausage in the Hilltowns. Mixed reviews.

The Brewmaster's Tavern (413-268-7741; thebrewmasterstavern.com), 4 Main St. Open daily 11–11, until midnight Fri.–Sat. A pub and microbrewery in a great old tavern building, but very mixed reviews.

The Old Creamery (413-634-5560; oldcreamerycoop.org), 445 Berkshire Trail (corner of MA 9 and MA 112), Cummington. Open weekdays 7–7:30, Sat. 7:30–7:30, Sun. 9–7:30. This expanded general store, with its deli and hot food items, fabulous baked goods, crafts, and wine selection, is an oasis in these hills. The tables are limited but round, and strangers share—although it's true that most patrons know one another. The blackboard menu features soups and sandwiches. Bread is freshly baked. Everything possible is locally sourced. Check out the website for a sense of this special place.

Spruce Corner Restaurant (413-268-3188), 188 Berkshire Trail W. (MA 9), Goshen. Jerry Bird is the chef-owner of this cheery way stop. Open for breakfast, lunch, and dinner. This is pickup truck and Harley-Davidson country, which doesn't mean the food isn't fine. Everyone feels welcome.

THE OLD CREAMERY IN CUMMINGTON IS A GATHERING SPOT FOR FOLKS FROM MANY MILES AROUND.

Christina Tree

Liston's (413-238-5353), 324 Old North Rd. (MA 143), Worthington. Open Tues. 11:30–8, Wed.–Sat. 11:30–9, Sun. noon–8. Begun as a four-stool and candy counter in 1954, this is a classic rural family-friendly roadhouse with booths. Known for wicked good burgers and fish on weekends. Owners Diane and Steve Magargak are also known for using fresh ingredients to create plain, good cooking. Full bar.

Tavern off the Green (413-238-4492), Worthington Golf Club, 113 Ridge Rd. Open mid-Apr.–Oct., Tues.–Sun. 11:30–9, but check. Restaurants are few in this area, and this was a welcome find on a rainy summer day. The old-fashioned clubhouse is charming, and lunch was reasonably priced and good. Full bar.

ICE CREAM 🍦 **Gran-Val Scoop** (413-357-6632; gran-valscoop.com), 233 Granby Rd. (MA 189), Granville. Open mid-Apr. –mid-Oct., daily 10:30–9. This century-old family farm has a large dairy herd (along with sheep, goats, chickens, and rabbits), and makes more than two dozen flavors of gourmet ice cream using locally produced maple syrup, wild blueberries, peaches, and other fruits.

MooLicious Ice Cream (413-569-1700; mooliciousicecream.com), 214 Feeding Hills Road (MA 57), Southwick. This is usually our first stop on the scenic southerly approach to these hills.

Christina Tree

MOOLICIOUS ICE CREAM IN SOUTHWICK.

✷ Entertainment

Jacob's Pillow Dance Festival (413-243-0745; jacobspillow.org), George Carter Rd., Becket (off US 20). America's oldest dance festival and still its most prestigious, Jacob's Pillow presents a 10-week summer program of classic and experimental dance. For details, see the "Southern Berkshire County" chapter.

Sevenars Music Festival (413-238-5854; sevenars.org), the Academy, S. Ireland St. and MA 112, Worthington. Concerts are held Sunday afternoons, mid-July–late Aug. The *seven R's* are the seven Schrades, who include Robert (longtime soloist with orchestras and a member of the faculty at the Manhattan School of Music) and pianists Robelyn and Rorianne. There are also guest artists. Concerts are staged in the tongue-and-groove paneled hall of a double-porched, 19th-century academy just off MA 112 by the South Worthington Cascade. Door donation.

Chester Theatre Company (413-354-7825; chestertheatre.org), Chester Town Hall, 15 Middlefield Rd., Chester. Productions are staged late June–late Aug., Wed.–Sat. 8 PM, Sun. 2 PM. A respected theater company presenting "thought-provoking" theater. Casts are small, but these tend to be expansive shows. Worth a drive.

Dream Away Lodge (413-623-8725; thedreamawaylodge.com), 1342 County Rd., Becket. An old roadhouse that once had a funky reputation; see the "South Berkshire County" chapter.

Bel Canto Opera Concerts (413-848-2052), at the Historic White Church, North St., Blandford. Arias and ensembles held in August.

Note: Tanglewood Music Festival and the many other Lenox- and Stockbridge-area summer music and theater events are an easy drive from most parts of this region. See the "Berkshire County" chapters.

✷ Selective Shopping

Note: For a listing of dozens of area artisans, visit the website at hidden -hills.com/handcrafts.html.

CRAFTS The Basket Shop (413-296-4278), 513 Main Rd. (MA 143), Chesterfield. The shop itself is special, built by hand by Ben Higgins with an open basket-weave ceiling, woven cabinet doors, dovetailed drawers, and a variety of timeworn tools. Ben specialized in the rare art of weaving ash baskets, a skill his son-in-law, Milton Lafond, carries on using a variety of wooden molds, some of them 100 years old. The baskets are striking and unusually durable. Call before making a special trip, and inquire about Open Days.

Stonepool Pottery (413-238-5362; stonepoolpottery.com), 42 Conwell Rd., Worthington, just up Ireland St. from the old academy in South Worthington (take the next left). Open by chance or appointment year-round. Distinctive, functional work by potter Mark Shapiro and his apprentices is displayed in a small gallery above Shapiro's home, an old homestead in which the Rev. Russell Conwell was born. Conwell later added an unusual "stone pool" and built the nearby academy, but he is better known as the founder of Philadelphia's Temple University.

River Studio (413-238-7755; andrew devries.com), 42 E. River Rd., Huntington. Open by appointment. The internationally acclaimed dancing statues of Andrew DeVries are a find in their own right—especially set as they are on a meadow stage in a particularly obscure and lovely corner near Middlefield.

Quilts by Jane (413-634-5703; quilts byjane.com), 408 W. Main St. (MA 116), Plainfield. Jane Neri's eye-catching quilts festoon her front porch; visitors are welcome. Neri enjoys coming out to escort you into her studio (a.k.a. garage), hung with dozens of bright, reasonably priced quilts, all made from cast-off materials.

Snow Farm (413-268-3101; snow farm.org), 5 Clary Rd., Williamsburg. Operated by the New England Craft Program, Snow Farm offers workshops and classes year-round in a variety of crafts, including ceramics, glassblowing, silk screening, wood sculpture, basket-making, and photography. A sale featuring the work of craftspeople from around the country is held all through November.

Williamsburg Blacksmiths (413-268-731), MA 9. Wrought iron, copper, tin, brass and pewter, a third-generation business.

Noble & Cooley Drum Co. (413-357-8814; ncchp.org), 42 Water St., Granville. Gift shop open Mon.–Fri. 9–4. Housed in an impressive old mill, this company produced drums for the Northern Civil War regiments and in the early 1900s was producing 1,000 drums a day. Prized by professional drummers, the company still produces that number a year and now has a burgeoning museum here with exhibits illustrating the company's history, a sample of Yankee ingenuity.

GENERAL STORES Chesterfield General Store & Pizza (413-296-4734), 432 Min Rd. (MA 143), Chesterfield. Homemade pastries, muffins and bread, deli, package store.

The Old Creamery, Cummington. See basics under *Eating Out*. In addition to a great place to eat and gather, this community-owned store showcases local products and carries bulk and health food, CDs, and books. Check out oldcreamerycoop.org.

Granville Country Store (413-357-8555 or 1-800-356-3141; granville.stores.yahoo.net), just off MA 57, Granville. Open daily 7–8. A typical village store, but with a difference: A store cheese called Granville Cellar Aged Cheddar has been sold here since 1851. The current owners still use the original recipe and aging method, producing a cheddar that's sharper and tastier than most. They'll ship anywhere. Home-baked breads and pies, pizza and mac 'n' cheese in the slow cooker invite use of the picnic tables out front on the triangular green.

Huntington Country Store (413-667-3232; hcstore.com), MA 112 north of Huntington village. Known for its baked goods and candy; 20 flavors of ice cream and jams, mustards and herbs, also greeting cards, specialty foods, gifts, gadgets, and local crafts.

Williamsburg General Store (413-268-3036; wgstore.com), 12 Main St., Williamsburg. Local maple products, breads and pastries made daily, candy, handcrafted jewelry and many local crafts, ice cream, coffees, teas, cheese, jams, jellies, mustards, herbs, spices, and more.

Corners Grocery (413-238-5531), Worthington Center. A double-porched, extremely photogenic store in the middle of a matching village; good picnic makings.

✷ Farms

Hanging Meadow Farm (413-527-0710), 188 North Rd., Westhampton.

THE GRANVILLE COUNTRY STORE IS FAMOUS FOR ITS CHEDDAR CHEESE.

Christina Tree

SUGARHOUSES

As already noted, the Hilltowns are the prime source of Massachusetts's maple sugar. Sugaring season can begin as early as late February and extend well into April. March is Maple Month, during which sugarhouses are most likely to be open on weekends. **Massachusetts Maple Producers Association** (413-628-3912; massmaple.org) lists producers and sugarhouses open to the public and details how to get there. Check the website for current hours. Also see listings in the "West County" chapter.

The following sugarhouses offer sit-down meals, typically pancakes and French toast with new syrup:

Maple Corner Farm (413-357-8829), 794 Beech Hill Rd., Granville. Maple museum, sugarhouse tours, and a restaurant open weekends, Mar.–mid-Apr.

Norwich Lake Farm (413-667-8830), 87 Searle Rd., Huntington. A traditional, wood-burning sugarhouse with eating facilities and a menu featuring pancakes and French toast coated with freshly made syrup.

Hanging Meadow Farm (413-527-0710), 188 North Rd., Westhampton. This farm, up a country road, has been in the Aloisi family since the 1940s. They've been known since then for their maple syrup and sit-down meals in maple season. The **Strawbale Café** (Fri.–Sat. 8–1, Sun. 8–2 year-round) features straw walls—which we're assured are not flammable—as well as home-baked breads and syrup. From Northampton, take MA 66 west.

Steve's Sugar Shack (413-527-0294), 34 North Rd., Westhampton. Steve's serves breakfast weekends, Feb.–mid-Apr.

High Hopes Farm Sugar House (413-238-5919; highhopesmaple.com), 1132 Huntington Rd. (MA 112), Worthington. Displays work by local artists and

See description under *Sugarhouses.* The **Strawbale Café** is open weekends, year-round.

High Meadow Farm (413-667-3640), 410 Skyline Trail, Chester. Pick-your-own apples and blueberries in-season. Call ahead. Children welcome. Maple syrup year-round.

Ireland Street Orchards (413-296-4024), Ireland St., Chesterfield. Open daily, mid-Sept.–Nov. Wagon rides, pick-your-own. In spring and summer, visit the perennial flower gardens.

Maple Corner Farm (413-357-8829), 794 Beech Hill Rd., Granville. A working farm since 1840, Maple Corner sells maple syrup and products along with jams and jellies year-round. Pick-your-own blueberries daily, July–mid-Sept. Also see *Sugarhouses* and *Cross-Country Skiing.*

features an "all-you-can-eat" pancake buffet. Late Feb.–early Apr., stop by to savor boiling maple syrup in a wood-fired evaporator.

The Red Bucket Sugar Shack (413-238-7710), 584 Kinnebrook Road, Worthington. Features pancakes, French toast, wagon rides, and snowshoeing.

Windy Hill Farm (413-238-5869), Sam Hill Rd., Worthington. The oldest sugarhouse in town; offers a dining room with a full maple menu in-season.

Other sugarhouses that welcome visitors in-season:

Roaring Brook Farm (413-667-3692), 190 Skyline Trail, Chester. A traditional operation that still uses a wood-fired evaporator to make syrup.

Tessiers Sugarhouse (413-634-5022), 60 Fairgrounds Rd., Cummington, 0.5 mile south of MA 9, and **Maple Hollow Sugarhouse,** 337 Stage Rd., Cummington, 0.4 mile east of Plainfield Rd.

Thatcher's Sugarhouse (413-634-5582; thatcherssugarhouse.com), 12 Broom St., Plainfield. A traditional operation 0.5 mile south of MA 16 and 3.5 miles north of MA 9. Also in Plainfield: **Deer Hill Maple** (413-634-8848), 23 Mountain St. (call ahead for boiling info), and **Fournier's Sugarhouse** (413-634-0299; www.fourniers sugarhouse.com), 206 S. Central St., 1 mile south of MA 116.

Paul's Sugar House (413-268-3544), MA 9, about a mile west of Williamsburg. Antique equipment is on display, along with a maple-syrup-making video. Maple candies as well as apple, cherry, and blackberry syrups.

Lawton Family Sugar House (413-268-3145), 47 Goshen Rd., Williamsburg. A family tradition for six generations.

Dufresne's Sugar House (413-268-7509; berkshiremaple.com), 113 Goshen Rd., Williamsburg. A large-scale (4,000 maple trees) family operation. Most of the boiling is done in the late afternoon or at night. Call ahead.

Mountain Orchard (413-357-8877), 668 Main Rd., Granville. Pick-your-own apples (eight varieties), nectarines, and peaches. Open Aug.–Nov., daily 8–8.

Outlook Farm (413-529-9388), MA 66, Westhampton. Open weekdays 6–7, weekends 6–6. You can pick your own apples and find seasonal fruit and produce here, but the real specialties of the roadside store are homemade sausage, smoked hams, bacon, and ribs (although the pigs are no longer raised here the way they used to be, the USDA-certified slaughterhouse and smokehouse continue to operate). Sandwiches and daily specials are served. Hayrides available.

Christina Tree

WILLIAMSBURG GENERAL STORE

✷ Special Events

March: **Maple Month** (massmaple .org).

April: **Westfield River Whitewater Races** (westfieldriverraces.com), Huntington, is billed as the oldest continuously run white-water race in America (*third weekend*).

May: **Chester on Track** (413-354-6570; chesterrailwaystation.org) commemorates that town's railroading history with a parade, live music, and an antique car show and open house at the Railroad Museum. Always the Sat. before Memorial Day weekend.

July: **Independence Day** (413-296-4049), Chesterfield, features a parade, fireworks, and much more. **Scottish Festival** in Blandford (*third weekend*).

July–Aug: **Chester Theatre Company** and **Sevenars Concerts** season.

August: Some of the state's oldest and most colorful fairs are held in this area; visit mafa.org for exact dates. Check out the **Littleville Fair** at the Littleville Fairgrounds, Chester (*first weekend*); the **Middlefield Fair** on Bell Road (*second weekend*); and **Cummington Fair** (*last weekend*). The Cummington event is one of the best! Antique engines and tractor show, midway, circus, maybe a sheep obstacle course, trained steer classes, square dance, lumberjack championship, live music, firemen's muster, and much more; visit cummington fair.com.

September: **The Blandford Fair** (theblandfordfair.com), held since 1867 on Labor Day weekend, is big. **The Williamsburg Grange Fair** is held the following weekend.

The Pioneer Valley

2

DEERFIELD/GREENFIELD AREA

INCLUDING NORTHFIELD AND TURNERS FALLS

FIVE-COLLEGE AREA

INCLUDING AMHERST, NORTHAMPTON, AND HOLYOKE

SPRINGFIELD AREA

THE PIONEER VALLEY

The Valley seems to have been a Yankee version of the Garden of Eden: rich soil bordering a waterway to the ocean. It was farmed for thousands of years before the first English colonists arrived in the 17th century, "settling" here almost a full century before moving into the flanking hills.

Just 5 miles wide up around the Vermont–New Hampshire line, the Valley widens to 20 miles down around Springfield. It's divided by the Holyoke Range, an abrupt east–west chain of mountains, yielding views from ridge paths and from two peaks—Mount Tom and Mount Holyoke (both accessible by road)—on opposite sides of the Valley.

New England's longest river, the Connecticut, plays a far more obvious role as the boundary between New Hampshire and Vermont and is commemorated in the name of another state. Still, in its 69-mile passage through Western Massachusetts, the Connecticut has created a region as distinctive as any. The problem has always been what to call it.

In 1939 the Western Massachusetts Visitors Association sponsored a contest for a name to promote the area. The winner was *King Philip's Realm,* a reference to the 17th-century Indian chief who unquestionably visited here but received a far-from-warm welcome. Instead, *Pioneer Valley* was adopted, and the name has come to apply to the three counties—Hampden, Hampshire, and Franklin—that flank as well as include the Valley. We like the name to the extent that it underscores its early settlement. What we don't like is the way it suggests that the entire area is a flat valley when, in fact, these counties include some of the hilliest country in the state. At any rate, *Pioneer Valley* is the only name that's stuck.

Perhaps the Valley's most striking feature is the way in which its many layers of history—from dinosaurs to diners—are visible, far more than in most places. The dinosaurs left tracks, lots of them. In 1839 Amherst College geologist Edward Hitchcock was the first to identify them; his collection, the largest in the world, is displayed in the stunning new Amherst College Museum of Natural History. Many more tracks were unearthed during construction of I-91 in the 1960s and can be viewed in half a dozen places.

In the 18th and early 19th centuries, Massachusetts's communities along the Connecticut—isolated from the state's coastal capital and population centers—

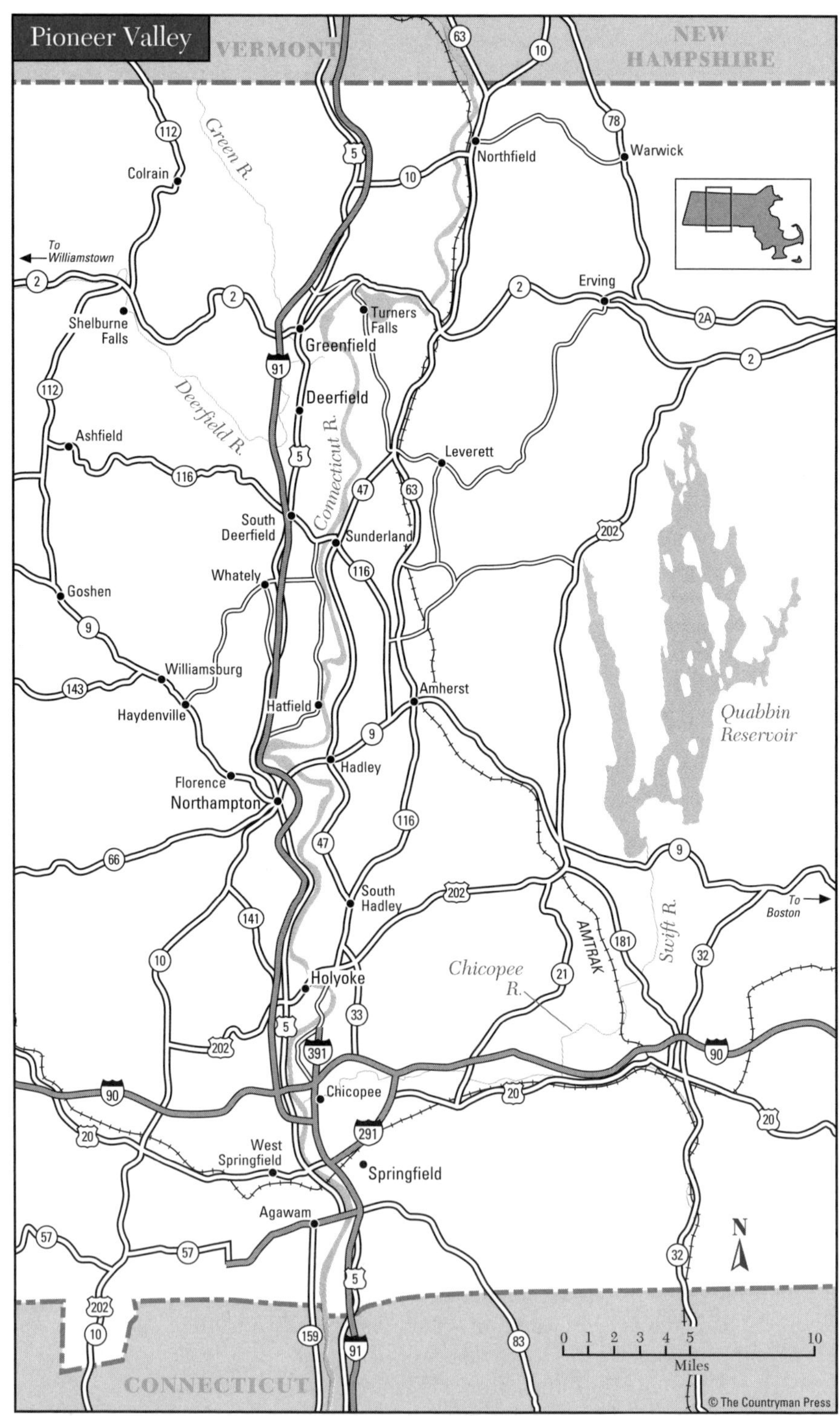
Pioneer Valley
VERMONT
NEW HAMPSHIRE
CONNECTICUT
Colrain
Green R.
Northfield
Warwick
To Williamstown
Erving
Shelburne Falls
Turners Falls
Greenfield
Deerfield
Deerfield R.
Ashfield
Connecticut R.
Leverett
South Deerfield
Sunderland
Whately
Goshen
Williamsburg
Amherst
Haydenville
Hatfield
Quabbin Reservoir
Hadley
Florence
Northampton
South Hadley
To Boston
AMTRAK
Swift R.
Chicopee R.
Holyoke
Chicopee
West Springfield
Springfield
Agawam
N
Miles
© The Countryman Press

developed their own distinctive, Valley-centered society, architecture, and religion. In the 1730s and 1740s, the Northampton-based Rev. Jonathan Edwards challenged the theology of Boston-based Congregationalism, trumpeting instead the message that everyone (not just the "elect") could be saved. Edwards's emotionally charged revival meetings launched a "Great Awakening" that rippled throughout New England.

This fire-and-brimstone brand of Calvinism lingered in the Valley well into the 19th century, long after Boston had forgotten its Puritan horror of sin and embraced a more permissive Unitarianism. Puzzling on the themes of death and eternity in Amherst in the 1850s through 1870s, the poet Emily Dickinson was more a part of her time and place than is generally understood.

The Valley's stern religion bred a concern for proper schooling. Deerfield Academy, founded in 1797, quickly attracted female as well as male students from throughout the area. Amherst College was founded in 1821 by town patriarchs, and in 1837 all-female Mount Holyoke College opened in South Hadley. Both contributed more than their share of Protestant missionaries.

Subtly but surely, education became a religion in its own right, and today it represents one of the Valley's leading industries. Its heart is the Five-College Area, home to Smith, Hampshire, Amherst, and Mount Holyoke Colleges and the University of Massachusetts at Amherst. It represents one of the country's largest rural concentrations of students and certainly one of its liveliest rural music, crafts, art, and dining scenes.

The Connecticut served as a highway on which new settlers continuously

VIEW FROM MOUNT HOLYOKE, BY WILLIAM HENRY BARTLETT.

Connecticut Valley Historical Museum

arrived and crops were exported. Flat-bottomed, square-rigged boats plied this thoroughfare, deftly negotiating half a dozen patches of "quick water." In 1794 Springfield was chosen for the site of a federal armory. Skilled workmen flocked to the spot and began turning out muskets that went downriver, too.

Today it is difficult to grasp the former importance of this waterway. In the 1790s transportation canals were built around the falls at Holyoke and Turners Falls. A number of vessels were built on West Springfield's common around 1800, and at the height of the subsequent canal-building craze, a canal system linked Northampton with New Haven.

With the dawn of the Industrial Revolution in the 1820s, the waterfalls that had been obstacles in the canal era were viewed as the Valley's biggest assets. In the 1820s Boston developers began to build textile mills at Chicopee Falls, and in the 1840s developed Holyoke from scratch—a planned, brick town, complete with factories, 4.5 miles of power canals, workers' housing, and mill owners' mansions. Meanwhile, Springfield was booming thanks to its own homegrown inventors and investors, a breed initially drawn to the area by the armory.

The 1890s through 1920s—the period to which most buildings in its towns and cities still date—was obviously the Valley's most colorful and exuberant era. Springfield's public buildings, like the magnificent City Hall and Symphony Hall, the soaring Florentine-style campanile, and the Quadrangle of museums, all conjure up this era. Trolley lines webbed the Valley, transporting mill workers to mountaintops and parks. Also during this period, volleyball was invented in Holyoke (look for exhibits in the Children's Museum at Holyoke complex), and basketball (the spectacular Naismith Memorial Basketball Hall of Fame tells the story) in Springfield.

The Valley today is distinguished by its number of extensive manicured parks, its elaborate stone and brick public buildings, and its private school and institutional buildings designed in every conceivable "Revival" style—all gifts of 19th-century philanthropists who refused to be forgotten (each bears the donor's name). Mount Holyoke itself now stands in vast Skinner Park, donated by a family that made its fortune producing satin in the country's largest silk mill. Northampton's 200-acre Look Park and 22-acre Childs Park were both donated by the industrialists whose names they bear, and Stanley Park in Westfield was created by Stanley Home Products founder Frank Stanley Beveridge. Although Springfield's 795-acre Forest Park isn't named for its principal benefactor, it does harbor New England's most elaborate mausoleum, built by ice skate tycoon Everett H. Barney.

Still linked both physically (by I-91, which superseded old north–south highways US 5/MA 10, which in turn had upstaged the railway, which had replaced the river) and culturally with Connecticut's cities and with Brattleboro, Vermont, more than with Boston, the Valley remains a place unto itself.

A case can be made that this Massachusetts stretch of the Connecticut Valley is the cultural heart of New England. The distance from Springfield's Quadrangle of art, science, and heritage museums on the south to Old Deerfield's house and town museums on the north is little more than 40 miles, a straight scenic shot up I-91. Midway between these destinations lies the Five-College Area, with its extraordinary art museums at Smith, Amherst, and Mount Holyoke Colleges; the illustrations to be seen at The Eric Carle Museum of Picture Book Art; two house museums devoted to Emily Dickinson; and the Yiddish Book Center—all within an 11-mile radius.

These cultural attractions are unusually accessible, set in one of New England's most intensely cultivated agricultural pockets, a distinctive landscape in which paved roads climb to hilltop lookouts, hiking trails follow ridgelines, and bike paths trace old trolley and rail lines.

The Connecticut itself is recapturing some of its old status as the region's focal point. It has made a dramatic comeback since the federally mandated Clean Water Act began to take effect in the 1970s. Now swimmable and fishable, it has been further improved through the protection of more than 4,000 riparian acres, the 52-mile Riverway State Park.

On summer weekends hundreds of powerboats emerge from marinas sited on the deep, lakelike stretches of the river above the power dams at Holyoke and Turners Falls, but the dozen miles below Turners Falls is too shallow for powerboating and particularly appealing to paddlers. The easiest way onto the river is aboard two snappy riverboats: The *Quinnetukut II* cruises back and forth through French King Gorge, while the *Lady Bea* is based in South Hadley. The sleepy old roads along both sides of the river are also popular with cyclists.

DEERFIELD/GREENFIELD AREA

INCLUDING NORTHFIELD AND TURNERS FALLS

Old Deerfield's single, mile-long street—lined with 18th- and early-19th-century buildings, canopied by old trees, and set against acres of cornfields—evokes the Valley's first prosperous era. It's one of those rare places in which you can genuinely step back in time through Historic Deerfield's period houses and Memorial Hall's eclectic exhibits.

With the Industrial Revolution and advent of the railroad, Greenfield replaced Deerfield as the area's commercial center. It's now a throwback to an entirely different era—the 1950s. Greenfield's century-old department store and vintage movie theater, its eateries, family-owned shops, newspaper, and community college all serve a lively community that extends west up into the surrounding hills and north up to the quietest reaches of the Valley. Neighboring Turners Falls is the smallest of the Valley's mill villages, but has its most dramatic waterfalls and a Discovery Center devoted to the region's natural history. Indeed, this area is all about discovery. Follow the winding road up Mount Sugarloaf to the summit to see the wide, shimmering ribbon of the Connecticut River far below, flanked by trees and a broad patchwork of yellow and green fields, spotted with century-old wooden tobacco sheds, and walled on the south by the magnificent east–west march of the Holyoke Range.

Bicycle or drive along river roads on either shore, through farmland in Whately, Sunderland, Montague. Find your way to the Bookmill in Montague Center and on up into Northfield along the river. Munch at farm stands selling fresh-picked produce: asparagus in May, strawberries in June, blueberries in July, apples and peaches in September, and pumpkins in October. And get out on the Connecticut. Above Turners Falls, the river itself is accessible by excursion boat as well as by rental kayaks and canoes.

AREA CODE 413 applies to all of Western Massachusetts.

GUIDANCE Franklin County Chamber of Commerce (413-773-5463; franklincc.org), 395 Main St., Greenfield. This Regional Tourism Council covers a broad area, including the West County Hilltowns as well as the northern reaches of the Valley. Request a map and guide. The chamber operates the visitors center in Greenfield (413-773-9393) off I-91 Exit 26, behind Applebee's on

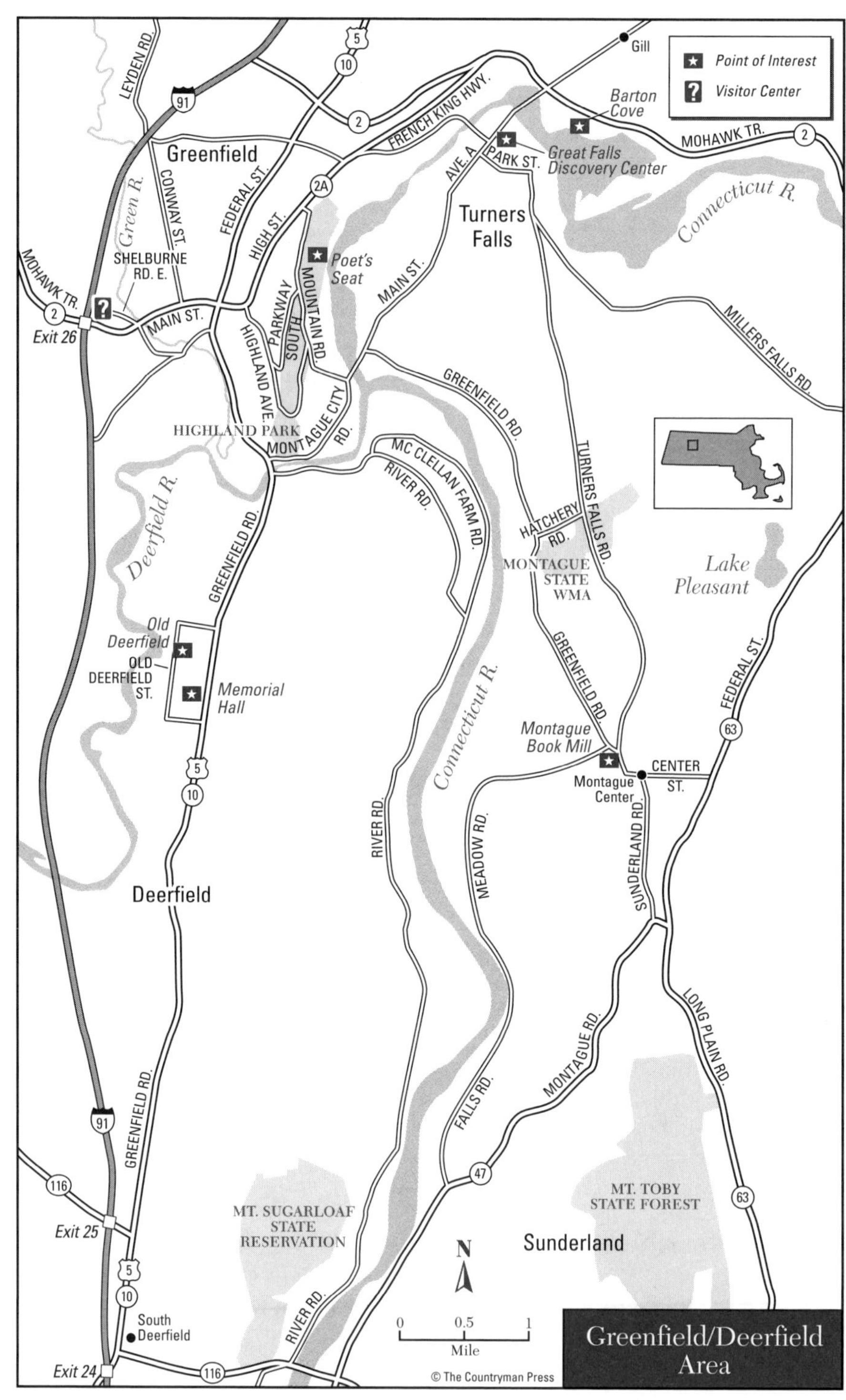
Point of Interest
Visitor Center
Greenfield
Turners Falls
Deerfield
Sunderland
Gill
Barton Cove
Great Falls Discovery Center
Poet's Seat
Old Deerfield
Memorial Hall
Montague Book Mill
Montague Center
HIGHLAND PARK
MONTAGUE STATE WMA
MT. SUGARLOAF STATE RESERVATION
MT. TOBY STATE FOREST
Lake Pleasant
Connecticut R.
Deerfield R.
Green R.
Exit 26
Exit 25
Exit 24
South Deerfield
0 0.5 1
Mile
© The Countryman Press
Greenfield/Deerfield Area

Christina Tree

SCENIC SUNDERLAND.

MA 2A east, marked from the MA 2 rotary. The center is open daily, Apr. 15–Nov. 1.

GETTING THERE *By bus:* Peter Pan–Trailways (1-800-343-9999; peterpanbus.com) connects Greenfield, Amherst, South Hadley, and Holyoke with Boston, Springfield, Bradley International Airport, and points beyond. The local departure point is town hall, Court Square, Greenfield.

By car: MA 2 is the quickest as well as the most scenic access from east or west, and I-91 is the way north and south.

PARKING *In Greenfield:* There's metered parallel and angled parking on Main Street and in the lot across from the chamber of commerce, as well as many other municipal lots.

MEDICAL EMERGENCY Dial **911.**

Franklin Medical Center (413-773-0211), 164 High St., Greenfield.

✷ Towns and Villages

Deerfield (population: 4,700). Founded on a lush plain between the Deerfield and Connecticut Rivers in 1669, Deerfield is best known for **Historic Deerfield's** museum houses lining a mile-long street of 18th- and early-19th-century homes in **Old Deerfield,** also home to prestigious **Deerfield Academy** and **Memorial Hall.** The current town center with its shops and restaurants is 6 miles south on US 5/MA10 (near **Yankee Candle**) in South Deerfield. This is

Christina Tree

MEMORIAL HALL

also the site of **Mount Sugarloaf** and the obelisk on North Main Street marking the site on which most of the town's first male settlers were killed in 1675. This region was the homeland of the Pocumtuck tribe, which had farmed the land for many centuries. Deerfield's natural as well as man-made beauty is unusually accessible: Follow River Road north along the Connecticut from MA 116 to its terminus in East Deerfield, also great for bicycling. Or hike the **Pocumtuck Ridge Trail,** the **Channing Blake Meadow Walk,** and the **Mahican-Mohawk Trail.**

Greenfield (population: 18,000). This proud and lively town is sited at the confluence of the Green and Connecticut Rivers, at the junction of MA 2 and I-91, and halfway between Northampton and Brattleboro, Vt. As noted in the chapter introduction, it has all the downtown essentials that most towns used to have but have lost since the 1950s, including people who all seem to know one another. With handsome commercial buildings around Court Square and along Main Street—and relatively low rents—it's also one of the best restaurant towns in the Valley and a venue for music. It's emerging as a recording center, attracting regional and national singers and songwriters. **Energy Park** (50 Miles St.) features solar sculptures, climbing structures, and exhibits demonstrating solar energy and transportation alternatives; the grounds and pavilion are the setting for frequent happenings. The **Poet's Seat Tower** up in the Highlands above town is also well worth finding, as is the quiet farmland along the Green and Deerfield Rivers. Several of the distinguished buildings along Main Street were designed by native son Asher Benjamin, the unsung hero responsible for the architectural look of much of rural New England. In the 1790s, a period when much of Western Massachusetts and northern New England was quickly settled,

Benjamin wrote a "do-it-yourself" architectural guide, *The Country Builder's Assistant,* followed by six more books that influenced the construction of thousands of homes and hundreds of churches that remain the pride of New England villages. The **Greenfield Public Library** (413-772-1544), 402 Main St., said to be the first building designed by Benjamin, has an exceptional children's room and an interesting historical collection. The **Historical Society of Greenfield** (413-774-3663), 43 Church St., offers eight rooms filled with furnishings, portraits, early Greenfield artifacts, and photos. You learn that Greenfield's J. Russell Company, "America's first cutlery factory," was once known for its Green River buffalo skinning knife.

Montague (population: less than 8,200). Few towns of this size encompass as many contrasting villages. By far the biggest of these is **Turners Falls,** sited at the "Great Falls" (visible from MA 2), one of the first waterfalls in the country to be circumvented by a transportation canal (begun in 1794, completed in 1800, operating until 1856). Its sophisticated power canal system functioned from 1860 to 1940, attracting cotton, silk, and cutlery factories as well as three paper mills, collectively employing between 1,200 and 1,500 in their heyday. *Note:* The Montague–Gill bridge linking MA 2 with Turners Falls is currently under construction and only has one lane open until 2014.

The original 1860s building of Montague Paper (once a 15-building complex covering 5 acres) now houses the **Great Falls Discovery Center,** with outstanding displays focusing on the natural history of the Connecticut River

THE MONTAGUE MILL.

Christina Tree

watershed. The **Shea Theater** stages frequent music and drama. Turners Falls sits at a bend in the Connecticut River, which surrounds it on three sides—wide and placid as it enters town at **Barton Cove** (which offers camping, paddling, and nesting eagles), then dividing into two strips, the narrow old power canal and the wide river, magnificently wild as it plunges over the dam beneath the bridge linking the town with MA 2. The brick commercial buildings and blocks of mill housing flanking the town's wide, grandly conceived Avenue A (down which trolleys once ran to Amherst and Northampton) are beginning to fill with studios and galleries. The **Hallmark Museum of Contemporary Photography** (413-863-0009) 85 Avenue A, is open Thurs.–Sun. 1–5. It displays work by well-known photographers and members of the 250-member student body at the nearby **Hallmark Institute of Photography** (hallmark.edu). **Unity Park,** overlooking Barton Cove, is a great picnic site; a **fish ladder** at the dam is staffed by naturalists late May–mid-June, when the fish are running upstream (call 1-800-859-2960). Events are listed at **turnersfallsriverculture.org.** The town's many churches served German, French Canadian, Italian, Lithuanian, Bohemian, Irish, and Polish immigrants. In **Our Lady of Czestochowa Catholic Church** (413-863-4748), 84 K St. (turn off Avenue A onto Seventh and then left up K; open Sat. 7–4 and otherwise 3–6:30), the painting of the Black Madonna, the famous Polish icon, is an object of special veneration, a 1920s copy of the original embellished with the jewelry of parishioners. The village is named for Captain William Turner, whose company massacred virtually all the local Indians (the Pocumtucks) near the falls in 1617. This brick mill town was, however, designed and built in the 1860s by Colonel Alvah Crocker.

Montague Center, south of Turners Falls (best accessed from MA 2 via MA 63 south) has a classic New England green, the site of Montague Old Home Days and the town's Independence Day activities. Nearby, **The Bookmill** is an early-19th-century gristmill on the Sawmill River, now housing crafts studios, a large antiquarian bookshop, café, and restaurant. The town's other hidden gem is **Lake Pleasant,** off MA 63 north of Montague Center, a pristine lake (the town's drinking supply) rimmed by gingerbread cottages built as a spiritualist camp in the late 19th century. It's still the site of frequent "psychic fairs" (call 413-774-4705). North and west of Lake Pleasant lies one of the state's most extensive pine barrens. The town also includes Millers Falls, another small mill town just off MA 2, bisected by the Millers Falls River.

Northfield (population: about 1,145). Flanking both sides of the Connecticut River, Northfield is bounded on the north by both Vermont and New Hampshire, making it the only town accessing both those states. Its unusually wide and long Main Street is lined with many houses built during the 19th century heyday of river traffic and sheep farming. The prestigious **Northfield Mount Hermon** prep school, founded by the evangelist minister Dwight Moody in the late 19th century, has consolidated its two formerly separate (male and female) schools west of the river. The original college-sized Northfield campus, north of the village, will open as the C. S. Lewis Great Books College in the fall of 2012. South of the village, **Northfield Mountain,** an unusual hydroelectric facility hidden inside the mountain, is webbed with public hiking trails maintained for snowshoeing and cross-country skiing in winter. In-season it also offers naturalist-narrated river cruises on excursion boat *Quinnetukut II,* as well as a visitor center with historical displays and nature-geared programs.

Sunderland (population: 3,777). Settled as "Swampfield" at the turn of the 18th century, this riverside town represents some of the richest and best-protected farmland in the state, much of it still planted in shade-grown tobacco. Early industries included covered buttons, and the big sight to see in town is the **Buttonwood Tree,** said to be the largest of its kind (a variety of sycamore) east of the Mississippi and dating to the 18th century. It's on Main Street (MA 47), which is lined with handsome old homes. The brick town hall here, built in 1867 to double as the school, houses the **Blue Heron,** one of the area's leading restaurants. MA 47 and MA 116 meet in the middle of town and then diverge again, both heading south through farmland. Follow MA 47 north and fork onto Falls Road for a scenic route along the river to Greenfield, or follow it northeast, turning down Reservation Road to find the access to trails up **Mount Toby** (1,269 feet), which offers an observation tower and fine view across the Valley.

Whately (population: 1,573). Motorists from Canada to Florida know Whately's "Fillin' Station," a 24-hour diner just off I-91, but the town itself is blessedly little touristed, from the farm stands along River Road by the Connecticut River in "East Whately" to the steep hillside and ridgetop roads radiating from the tiny village of West Whately. Whately Center, a classic old town center with two general stores, an old town hall, library, post office, church, and inn, is just off US 5.

✷ Also See

FOR FAMILIES 🏵 ✐ **Great Falls Discovery Center at the Silvio O. Conte National Fish and Wildlife Refuge** (413-863-3221; greatfallsma.org), 2 Avenue A, Turners Falls. Open Memorial Day weekend–Columbus Day, daily 10–4, Fri. and Sat. other months of the year. A free, publicly funded must-see showcase for the entire Connecticut River watershed featuring superbly painted and constructed displays. Check out the time line and "Tales of Tourists and Timber" exhibit as well as those on the local environmental history (great sound effects) of the Valley and upland habitats. There is also an aquarium of indigenous fish. A full schedule of nature-geared programs is offered. Nearby Unity Park offers picnicking facilities and a playground.

NATURE TAKES CENTER STAGE AT THE GREAT FALLS DISCOVERY CENTER.

Christina Tree

✐ **Magic Wings Butterfly Conservancy and Gardens** (413-665-2805;

OLD DEERFIELD

Marked from US 5; 6 miles north of Exit 24 off I-91, or 3.5 miles south of Greenfield (I-91 Exit 26). Also see the shortcut from MA 2 to Old Deerfield under *Scenic Drives*.

Old Deerfield's serene good looks belie its ups and downs during the 19th and 20th, as well as the 17th and 18th, centuries. Founded in 1669, the first settlement here was deserted in 1675 after Native Americans, led by the young Wampanoag chief known as "King Philip," burned the town and killed most of its young men in an ambush that's remembered as the Bloody Brook Massacre. Seven years later, however, the settlers were back, harvesting crops and listening to Sunday sermons in the square, tower-topped meetinghouse (reconstructed on a smaller scale as the current village post office). In all there were 30 attacks in the community's first 50 years, the most famous one on a blustery February night in 1704, when more than 100 villagers were marched off to Montreal. Today visitors are amazed by the richness and sophistication of life as it was lived here during and after the Revolution—as judged from the quality of the architectural detailing, furniture, silver, and furnishings on view. Ironically, after all those early struggles, Old Deerfield survives today as a unique sampling of life in the late 18th and early 19th centuries.

By the 1820s, however, Deerfield had been upstaged by Greenfield as the local commercial center. Already it had become a place to attend school (Deerfield Academy was founded in 1797) and to visit "historic" sites. In 1830 an elaborate granite obelisk replaced the 1720s wooden marker at the site of the Bloody Brook Massacre in South Deerfield; the original is believed to be the first historic monument in what became the United States. In 1848 a campaign was mounted to save the Indian House, which still bore the mark of the hatchet implanted in its door during the 1704 raid. Though the campaign failed, it is now cited as the first effort in this country to save a historic house. The door was acquired by a Boston antiquarian, which so outraged local residents that he had to return it. For some time it was displayed in the Pocumtuck House, a hotel that stood on the village common.

Deerfield's zeal for self-preservation was fanned in the 19th century by George Sheldon, a self-appointed town historian given to raiding his neighbors' attics. Sheldon organized the Pocumtuck Valley Memorial Association in 1870 and a decade later acquired a striking, three-story brick building designed by Asher Benjamin (it had been the original Deerfield Academy building). The society filled this Memorial Hall with local relics ranging from the Indian House door to colonial-era cooking utensils, displayed in what is now recognized as the first "period room" to be seen in any American museum.

Sheldon also enticed his cousin, C. Alice Baker, back to town. Born in Deerfield, Baker had become a teacher and noted preservationist in the Boston area (she was involved in the campaign to preserve the Old South Meeting House), and was familiar with the then-current attempts to restore colonial buildings in and around the village of York, Maine. Back in Deerfield, Baker acquired the Frary House and restored it. At this time two societies were also founded to revive colonial-era crafts such as weaving, hearth cookery, pottery, and basketry. Visitors came. They came by rail and later by rural trolley, stayed in local farms and several now-vanished hotels (including Jewitt House atop Mount Sugarloaf), and shopped for arts and crafts in local homes and studios.

By the 1930s Deerfield was again forgotten. The 1937 *WPA Guide to Massachusetts* described it as "the ghost of a town, its dimness almost transparent, its quiet almost a cessation, but it is essential to add that it is probably quite the most beautiful ghost of its kind, and with the deepest poetic and historic significance to be found in America."

Following World War II, Deerfield Academy headmaster Frank Boyden came to the rescue of the old houses, persuading Deerfield Academy alumnus and parent Henry Flynt and his wife, Helen, to buy a number of decaying Old Deerfield properties. The Flynts subsequently restored many of these buildings, incorporating them as the nonprofit Heritage Foundation (now Historic Deerfield) in 1952. The entire town of Deerfield has been remarkably lucky in preserving some 5,900 acres of cultivated land. Although tract housing sprouted in several fields in the late 1980s, a Deerfield Land Trust was subsequently established and is now dedicated to preserving local farmland.

The largest property holder in Old Deerfield is Deerfield Academy, and there are two more private schools—Eaglebrook up on a hill and Bement School—in the village. Also in Old Deerfield is the Brick Church, built in 1824, which has arched doorways and a closed wooden cupola. It's the scene of frequent special events as well as regular services. The Old Burying Ground (walk along Albany Road) has many 18th-century stones and the mass grave of the English colonists killed in 1704. The big attraction here is Historic Deerfield; see the accompanying sidebar.

HOUSING HISTORY

Historic Deerfield (413-774-5581; www.historic-deerfield.org). In Old Deerfield, marked from US 5/MA 10; 6 miles north of Exit 24 off I-91 or 3.5 miles south of Greenfield, I-91 Exit 26 and MA 2. Open mid-Apr.–late Nov., daily 9:30–4:30. Closed Thanksgiving, Christmas Eve, and Christmas Day. Adults $12, ages 6–17 $5. Tickets are sold in the **Hall Tavern** (be sure to see the upstairs ballroom). Guided tours (on the hour) are currently offered through a dozen buildings displaying a total of some 25,000 objects made or used in America between 1650 and 1850. **The Flynt Center of Early New England Life** (open, in addition to the usual museum season, weekends Dec.–mid-Apr. except Christmas Eve and Christmas Day) houses objects not on display, a "visible storage gallery" featuring some 2,500 historic household furnishings, and an outstanding collection of colonial-era powderhorns. Also inquire about special exhibitions, antiques forums, and frequent programs on traditional crafts and the decorative arts.

HISTORIC DEERFIELD HOUSES OPEN TO THE PUBLIC

The Wells-Thorn House (sections built in 1717 and 1751) shows the dramatic changes in Deerfield lifestyles through two centuries. The **Ashley House** (1733), with its elegantly carved cupboards and furnishings, depicts the lifestyle of the village's Tory minister (note his 1730s Yale diploma). The **Asa Stebbins House** (1799/1810) is the first brick home in town, grandly furnished with French wallpaper, Chinese porcelain, and Federal-era pieces (self-guided). **The Wright House** (1824), another brick mansion, is a mini museum of high-style furniture and ceramics. The **Sheldon-Hawks House** (1743), a self-guided tour, is still filled with the spirit of George Sheldon, the town's colorful first historian. The **Frary House** is a mid-18th century house restored in the 1890s by pioneering preservationist Charlotte Alice Baker. The **Barnard Tavern** (1795) was the center of village life at the end of the 18th century. **Dwight House,** built in the mid-18th century, was moved to Deerfield from Springfield to save it from demolition; it now houses the **Apprentice's Workshop,** where there are daily demonstrations of how 18th-century products such as furniture, ceramics, and cloth were made. The **Hinsdale and Anna Williams House** (1750s, rebuilt 1816–20), furnished from an 1838 inventory, is surprisingly airy and modern, with touches like the light-toned rag stair rug, "glass curtains," venetian blinds, and exceptionally beautiful patterned wallpapers and floorcloths. Children's workshops are offered weekend afternoons in July. Inquire about walking tours.

♿ **Memorial Hall** (413-774-7476; old-deerfield.org), Memorial St., Old Deerfield. Open May–Oct., daily 11–5. Adults $6, ages 6–21 $3. In addition to the Indian House door and the country's first period room (see the "Old Deerfield" sidebar), this beautiful old building houses the Pocumtuck Valley Memorial Association's wonderfully eclectic collection. You learn about the Pocomtuck tribe, caught between the English who had settled in the lower Valley and the Mohawks to the west. In 1675, you learn, the Pocumtucks reclaimed the land they had been tilling for centuries, replanting their cornfields until they were again dislodged by settlers, from whom they again attempted to wrest their ancestral homeland in 1704. Among "The Many Stories of 1704" you hear the Rev. John Williams describe the massacre in which his wife and children were murdered and a son and daughter kidnapped; the son was ransomed but the daughter refused to return, visiting 40 years later but remaining in a Mohawk community near Montreal until her death at age 81. There is also an exhibit on the history of African Americans in this village. Old Deerfield's 1890s–1920s era as an artistic center is illustrated in paintings by the Fuller family, among others, and by an extensive collection of work by the Deerfield Society of Blue and White Needlework. The **Indian House Memorial** (open Aug.–Labor Day, daily 11–5, then weekends through Columbus Day), a 1929 reproduction of the Sheldon House (demolished in 1848), houses activities geared to young visitors. Also see *Special Events.*

HISTORIC DEERFIELD AMID VIBRANT FALL FOLIAGE.
Historic Deerfield

magicwings.com), 281 Greenfield Rd. (US 5/MA 10), South Deerfield. Open daily, spring and summer 9–6, fall and winter 9–5. Adults $12, seniors $10, ages 3–17 $8. Some 4,000 butterflies flit though this vast glass conservatory filled with bright flowers and lush vegetation. A glassed display also reveals the evolution of butterflies. There's the bright Monarch's Restaurant (closed Mon.–Tues.) and, of course, an extensive gift shop.

Northfield Mountain Recreational and Environmental Center (1-800-859-2960; firstlightpower.com/northfield), MA 63 in Northfield. Trails are open except during mud season; the visitor center is open June–Aug., Wed.–Sun. 9–5. The project draws water from the Connecticut River up into an artificially created lake on top of the mountain, using it to generate power during high-use periods. The visitors center houses displays dramatizing the story of the river's 18th- and early-19th-century flat-bottomed sailing barges for which canals were constructed in the 1790s. The story of steamboating and the advent of the railroad is also told, along with subsequent industrialization, logging, and the current hydro uses of the river's "white gold." See *To Do* for late-June through mid-October cruises on the Connecticut aboard the *Quinnetukut II* as well as snowshoeing and cross-country skiing opportunities. The website has information on current programs.

Yankee Candle Company (413-665-2929; yankeecandle.com), US 5/MA 10, 0.25 mile north of I-91, Exit 24, South Deerfield. Open daily 10–6, except Thanksgiving and Christmas. Now billed as "the world's largest candle store"—400 kinds of candles and 200 different scents—Yankee Candle is a huge complex that includes a Bavarian Village complete with year-round falling snow, a make-your-own-country-candles kitchen, and Santa's Enchanted Toy Shop complete with elves, a live Santa in his workshop, and a countdown-to-Christmas clock.

CANDLES ARE JUST ONE OF THE ATTRACTIONS AT YANKEE CANDLE COMPANY IN SOUTH DEERFIELD.

William A. Davis

Attractions also include a castle courtyard and waterfall; nutcracker castle; a Candle Making Museum; Yankee Candle Home with home furnishings for the bath, kitchen, and garden; and Chandler's Restaurant (see *Dining Out*).

✐ **Old Greenfield Village** (413-774-7138), 368 Mohawk Trail (MA 2). Open mid-May–mid-Oct. by appointment only (feel free to call on your cell phone from the gate). Adults $5, seniors $4, ages 6–16 $3, free for children under age 6. This is a genuine, Yankee kind of phenomenon: a collection of thousands of artifacts formerly found in stores, dental offices, churches, barbershops, and tool shops around the turn of the 20th century, all collected over 30 years by retired schoolteacher Waine Morse. Morse also constructed the buildings himself. Raising the church steeple alone, he admits, was a bit tricky.

✷ To Do

BICYCLING The river roads described under *Scenic Drives* are all suited to bicycle touring. River Road in Northfield, dating to the 1600s, passes under the French King Bridge (on a bicycle bridge) leading to Cabot Camp, a glorious spot for a picnic at the confluence of the Connecticut and Millers Rivers. The 3.5-mile **Canalside Rail Trail** runs from the Great Falls Discovery Center in Turners Falls south along the river. Mountain biking is also popular in summer on the 40 miles of trails at **Northfield Mountain.**

Basically Bicycles (413-863-3556) in Turners Falls and both **Bicycle World** (413-774-3701) and **Bicycles Unlimited** (413-772-2700) in Greenfield are knowledgeable about local routes. Bikeway maps are available at the Franklin County Chamber of Commerce office and the visitors center (see *Guidance*).

BOATING EXCURSION **The *Quinnetukut II*** (1-800-859-2960; firstlightpower.com/northfield) offers seasonal cruises (Fri.–Sun., conditions permitting) on the Connecticut. Call for reservations. The narrated cruise (12 miles round-trip) is through French King Gorge to Barton Cove, home to nesting eagles. Departures are three times per day from late June–mid-Oct.

CAMPING **Barton Cove Nature and Camping Area** (413-659-3714 beginning early Apr.; firstlightpower.com/northfield), MA 2, Gill. Open Memorial Day–Labor Day. This is an unusual facility maintained by Northfield Mountain on a peninsula that juts into the Connecticut River. Wooded tent sites are available; no hook-ups, showers at ranger station. Also see *Canoeing and Kayaking*.

CANOEING AND KAYAKING **Northfield Mountain's Barton Cove facility** (413-863-9300), on MA 2 in Gill, offers rental kayaks and canoes and shuttle service as far north along the Connecticut as Vernon Dam (20 miles). This is also a source of information about canoeing sites Northfield Mountain maintains for public access: **Munn's Ferry Campground** (with Adirondack shelters and tent sites, accessible only by boat), and **River View,** which has a float dock, picnic tables, and sanitary facilities on the river across from the entrance to Northfield Mountain. Also note **Bennett Meadow Wildlife Management Area,** with parking and river access at the MA 10 bridge in Northfield, and the launch area at **Paucaug Brook,** MA 63 beyond Northfield Center.

FISHING The **Connecticut River** offers outstanding fishing for bass, shad, yellow perch, all kinds of sunfish, carp, walleye, and trout (check out the mouths of feeder streams). The most user-friendly put-in place for visitors is **Barton Cove.**

Trout-stocked fishing spots include **Cranberry Pond** on Reservation Rd. between MA 63 and US 7 in Sunderland, and the **Green River** on its way down from Leyden to Greenfield. The Division of Fisheries and Wildlife maintains the **Bitzer Fish Hatchery** (413-367-2377) in Montague (open 9–3) between Greenfield and Montague Roads. In Sunderland on East Plumtree Rd. near the Amherst town line, the **Richard Cronin National Salmon Station** (413-548-9010) is responsible for capturing Atlantic salmon that swim up the Connecticut River to spawn in spring. They remain here in hatcheries all summer and their eggs are distributed to hatcheries throughout the watershed as part of the salmon restoration program. The public is welcome to view the fish in an outdoor raceway system.

A Massachusetts fishing license is required, available from town clerks.

Pipione's Sport Shop (413-863-4246), 101 Avenue A (the main drag), Turners Falls, is a source of advice as well as equipment and licenses. Open daily from 7 AM.

Note: The nearby **Quabbin Reservoir** is the state's premier fishing hole, and the Deerfield, West, and Millers Rivers are nationally famed among anglers for fly-fishing.

GOLF **Crumpin Fox Golf Club** (413-648-9101), MA 10, Bernardston. Eighteen holes. The front nine were designed by Robert Trent Jones himself, and the back nine by his firm.

Northfield Golf Club (413-498-2432), 31 Holton St., Northfield. A nine-hole, par-36 course.

Oak Ridge Golf Club (413-863-9693), 231 W. Gill Rd., Gill. Nine holes, par 36.

Thomas Memorial Golf Club & Country Club (413-863-8003), 29 Country Club Lane, Turners Falls. Nine holes, par 35.

HIKING AND WALKING **Barton Cove Nature and Camping Area** (413-863-9300; off-season, 1-800-859-2960), MA 2 just east of Turners Falls in Gill. An interpretive nature trail meanders along a rocky ridge overlooking the Connecticut River, and there's a picnic area in addition to tent sites. During nesting season, eagles are usually in residence. Canoe and kayak rentals available.

Along Route 2, Millers Falls, Gill, and Erving

French King Bridge (MA 2 west of Millers Falls) spans a dramatically steep, banked, narrow stretch of the Connecticut, 140 feet above the water. Park at the rest area and walk back onto the bridge (there's a pedestrian walk) for the view. Note the mouth of the Millers River just downstream. The bridge is named for

French King Rock, 0.5 mile upriver. No one seems to knows why the rock was so named.

Erving Castle/Hermit Cave. In Erving, turn at the sign onto Mountain Road, which climbs steadily for 1.8 miles. The trail sign is on your left before a gated access road. Park here (don't block the gate) and follow the blazes into the woods. After about 1.5 miles, turn left, following blue blazes or the sign down a steep pitch to the crevice cave in an impressive cliff. Hermit John Smith lived in a shack near the cave for 30 years. Allow more than an hour for the hike.

In Deerfield

Channing Blake Meadow Walk. A 0.5-mile path through Old Deerfield's north meadows and a working 700-acre farm begins at the northern end of Deerfield Street; inquire at Historic Deerfield about special family tours and nature activities.

Pocumtuck Ridge Trail, South Deerfield. Take North Main Street to Hillside Drive (across from Pelican Industries) to Stage Road. Turn left at the top of the hill onto Ridge Road for the trailhead for paths through Deerfield Land Trust's 120-acre preserve.

Mahican-Mohawk Trail. The first 1.5 miles of this 7.5-mile trail, said to be the actual 10,000-year-old route along the Lower Deerfield, is accessible from Deerfield. Drive south on Deerfield Street, but instead of turning back onto US 5, jog right and then south along Mill Village Road. Turn right at the small stone building at the corner of Stillwater Road; after 0.9 mile take Hoosac Road and you will see the trailhead 0.2 mile later. The trail follows an abandoned railbed to the South River. For a description of the rest of the trail, see the "Along the Mohawk Trail" chapter.

THE FRENCH KING BRIDGE SPANS THE CONNECTICUT RIVER.

Christina Tree

VIEWS Mount Sugarloaf State Reservation, off MA 116, South Deerfield. A road winds up this red sandstone mountain (said to resemble the old loaves into which sugar was shaped) to a modern observation tower on the summit, supposedly the site from which King Philip surveyed his prey before the mid-17th-century Bloody Brook Massacre. There are picnic tables, restrooms, and great views down the Valley.

Poet's Seat Tower and Rocky Mountain Trails, off High St. in Greenfield. This medieval-looking

William A. Davis

AN EXPANSIVE VIEW FROM MOUNT SUGARLOAF.

sandstone tower on Rocky Mountain honors local 19th-century poet Frederick Goddard Tuckerman, who liked to sit near this spot. You can understand why. The Ridge Trail (blue blazes) loops along the top of the hill.

Mount Toby, at 1,269 feet, offers great views plus caves and waterfalls. As is the case with Mount Holyoke and Mount Sugarloaf, a hotel once capped its summit, but now there is just a fire tower. Access is off MA 47, 4 miles south of Sunderland Center. It's a three-hour round-trip hike, but you can go just as far as the cascades. From MA 47 in North Sunderland, turn right onto Reservation Road; the parking area is in 0.5 mile.

ON TOP OF MOUNT SUGARLOAF

Christina Tree

Crag Mountain, off MA 63, Northfield. This 1,500-foot summit offers sweeping views east, south, and west. Ask directions at the Northfield Mountain Environmental and Recreation Center, 99 Millers Falls Road.

CROSS-COUNTRY SKIING/SNOWSHOEING **Northfield Mountain Ski Touring Center** (1-800-859-2960; xcskimass.com or firstlightpower.com/northfield), MA 63, Northfield. Open Dec.–Mar.,

Wed.–Sun. The center offers cross-country and snowshoe rentals for use on its 25 miles of doubletrack trail, designed for both single stride and Nordic, including an 800-meter vertical climb. Exceptional grooming, a range of rentals including pucks. More than 6 miles of dedicated snowshoeing trails. Heated lounge with fireplace for picnicking; cocoa on weekends. Trail fee.

SCENIC DRIVES Along the western shore of the Connecticut all the way from Hatfield north to its confluence with the Deerfield, River Road is lined with farms, tobacco sheds, and fields. It's flat except for Mount Sugarloaf, which thrusts up all alone; be sure to drive to the top. Note the old headstones in Pine Nook Cemetery some 4 miles north of MA 116. Also see *Views* and *Farms and Farm Stands.*

Along the eastern side of the Connecticut, follow Falls Road, forking left off MA 47 a short way beyond the Buttonwood Tree. This becomes Meadow Street, shadowing the river and threading its way through farm country. At the junction with Ferry Road, turn right onto Meadow Road, right again on Bridge Street, and into the Montague Mill (see below).

Route 2 to Montague Center to either Greenfield or Deerfield. Turn off MA 2 at MA 63 south to Swamp Road (a right). Stop at the Montague Mill with its crafts, bookstore, shops, and restaurants. You might also want to detour less than a mile south to Montague Center, a classic village with a Congregational church designed by Asher Benjamin and a brick town hall on its common. Otherwise continue west (Swamp changes to Ferry Road at the mill) and turn right (north) onto Greenfield Road; then take a left onto Montague City Road and cross the river. To reach the Poet's Seat, turn right onto Mountain Road. For Old Deerfield, continue to US 5/MA 10 and turn left; Old Deerfield is a mile or so south on your right.

River Road in Northfield runs south from the landing (off MA 63) at Northfield Mountain to MA 2. It's beautiful.

Mohawk Trail. The stretch of MA 2 designated in 1914 as the Mohawk Trail, New England's first official tourist trail, begins in Greenfield and heads west, abruptly uphill. Shelburne Falls, the hub of the Mohawk Trail, is just 8 miles west of downtown Greenfield. (See the "Along the Mohawk Trail" chapter.)

Deerfield to Greenfield, the scenic route. From "The Street" in Old Deerfield, head south, continuing as the village ends and the street becomes Mill Village Road, flanked by farmland. Turn right onto Stillwater Road and follow it along the Deerfield River. Turn right on the bridge across the river (this section of the Deerfield is popular with tubers) and follow the West Deerfield Upper Road through more beautiful farmland. Note Clarkdale Fruit Farms (303 Upper Rd.), a fourth-generation family farm. Route 116 west from South Deerfield climbs steeply and quickly out of the Valley and into Conway. (See the "Hilltowns" chapter.)

Route 47 North from Sunderland runs through farmlands, past the turnoff (Reservation Rd.) for Mount Toby, farm stands, and sugarhouses.

✷ Lodging

INNS (ψ) ♿ **Deerfield Inn** (413-774-5587 or 1-800-926-3865; deerfieldinn.com), 81 Main St., Deerfield 01342. Open year-round, except Christmas. A newcomer by Old Deerfield standards (it opened in 1884), the antiques-filled inn is dignified but not stiff. It is the place to stay when visiting Historic Deerfield, enabling you to steep and sleep in the full atmosphere of the village after other visitors have gone. There are 24 rooms, each with private bath, 13 in an annex added since a 1979 fire (from which townspeople and Deerfield Academy students heroically rescued most of the antiques). Rooms feature period wallpaper and fabrics, and furnishings are either antiques or reproduction antiques; some canopy beds. There is a definite attention to detail, and some annex rooms are quite spacious. $170–250 includes breakfast, afternoon tea, and passes to Historic Deerfield museum houses. Rooms vary in size and feel, and come with and without ghosts. Also see **Champney's Restaurant & Tavern** under *Dining Out*.

THE DEERFIELD INN, OLD DEERFIELD.

William A. Davis

BED & BREAKFASTS

In Greenfield

(ψ) **The Brandt House** (413-774-3329 or 1-800-235-3329; brandthouse.com), 29 Highland Ave., Greenfield 01301. This expansive, centrally air-conditioned, 16-room Georgian Revival house is set on more than 3 acres and offers nine guest rooms, seven with private bath. Common rooms include a tastefully comfortable, plant-filled living room, a dining room with large sash windows overlooking the garden, a wicker-furnished porch and patio, and an upstairs sunroom stocked with local menus and a microwave. Most guest rooms are relatively small but tastefully furnished; two have a working fireplace, and there's a two-room suite on the top floor. $95–295 includes a full breakfast. Extra guests, children, or well-behaved dogs: $25 fee. Inquire about corporate rates.

(ψ) **Poetry Ridge Bed & Breakfast** (413-773-5143; rkotours.com), 55 Stone Ridge Lane, Greenfield 01310. One of the showplaces of Greenfield, a town with many imposing houses. Built in 1910 as a summer home for a New York doctor, it sits high on the wooded ridge above town that's now primarily parkland, webbed with walking trails leading to the Poet's Seat Tower (see *Views*). Errol and Mary Sorensen came from California to buy this gem, which has seven working fireplaces. All rooms have private baths and are furnished with a mix of reproduction and genuine antiques. The two high-end rooms both have a large deck and a king-sized bed. Children are welcome (there's a two-room family suite). Breakfast is served in the formal dining room. Allow time here to hike or at least take advantage of the game room. $125–295 in-season includes a full breakfast; from $105 off-season.

House on the Hill B&B (413-774-2070; www.thehouseonthehillbnb.com), 330 Leyden Rd., Greenfield 01301. Donna and Alain Mollard's big, old, white, 1920s farmhouse is minutes from MA 2 and downtown Greenfield, but high on a quiet green shoulder of the Valley, overlooking a wide spread of green fields. There are three second-floor air-conditioned guest rooms (two queens, one king), all with private bath, TV, and DVD player. Shared space includes an attractive living/dining area with a large fireplace and a big, comfortable front porch. Another ground-level guest room with private bath is available on request. $145 double, from $105 single, includes a full breakfast.

Hillside House (413-665-5515; hillsidehousebb.com), P.O. Box 183, 60 Masterson Rd., Whately 01093. Julia and Ed Berman searched the country before picking this hillside home as their B&B. A modern home wasn't what they had in mind, but when you step into its airy, glass-walled spaces and out onto the deck, you understand why anyone would like to spend much of their life here. Furnishings are comfortable and tasteful, with some exceptional pieces, art, and mementos from their far-flung travels. The Pink Guest Room is what you want here, spacious and bright with a Valley view—but the Yellow Guest Room also has its charm, and both have a private bath. There is also a Spa Room, and a swimming pool is set below the house in landscaped gardens. The Bermans dine out around the Valley and share with guests their critiques of local restaurants. Children older than 12 are welcome. $95–175 includes a generous breakfast.

Old Tavern Farm Bed & Breakfast (413-772-0474; oldtavernfarm.com), 817 Colrain Rd., Greenfield 01301. A quiet byway today in the lush Green River part of town, this was a main road between Boston and Albany when the tavern was first licensed in 1746. Current hosts Gary and Joanne Sanderson are devoted to preserving the feel of this very special place, which retains its classic old ballroom (still a great place for a dance). Common space includes the sunny, low-ceilinged dining room, warmed by a soapstone woodstove; a pleasant former "ladies parlor"; and the old taproom with fireplaces and attractive but authentic antiques, some rather rare and special. The master bedroom is warmed by a Rumford fireplace and features a vintage-1814 Sheridan bird's-eye maple four-poster. There is also a smaller upstairs bedroom and a downstairs suite with a genuine feather bed. Bathrooms are private and breakfast is full. Gary is a local sportscaster and also a licensed fishing and hunting guide. $150 May–Oct., $135 off-season. The house and ballroom can be rented for small weddings.

West Winds Inn (413-774-4025; westwindsinn.com), 151 Smead Hill Rd., Greenfield 01301. Sandi Richardson designed this contemporary dream house with cathedral ceilings and great spaces. There are seven guest rooms, all with private bath. Several feature a patio or balcony overlooking a sweep of valley and hills beyond, and some are fitted with Jacuzzis and fireplaces. Breakfast is served in the light-filled dining area with a fieldstone fireplace off the open kitchen or on the deck. $105–195 includes a continental breakfast weekdays, full on weekends.

The Greenfield Lion House (413-774-1732; greenfieldlionhouse.com), 81 High St., Greenfield 01301. Joyce and Steve Lanciani have created a delightful self-contained three-room unit in the back of their elegant Victorian home. There's a bedroom with twin beds, a full kitchen stocked with breakfast food and snacks, and a small den with TV. $115 per night, two-night minimum in May and June. Guests have access to the flowery grounds.

Elsewhere

The Centennial House (413-498-5921 or 1-877-977-5950; thecentennialhouse.com), 94 Main St., Northfield 01360. Built handsomely in 1811 for a local magistrate who heard cases in the parlor—explaining why Calvin Stearns (the town's premier builder) included so many Greek and Roman motifs on the mantels and woodwork in the front two rooms. Later it was home to the headmaster of the Northfield Seminary for Girls. There are six guest rooms, including the two-room Deerfield Suite on the second floor with a whirlpool tub and electric fireplace. All guest rooms are furnished in antiques; three have a fireplace. Common space includes a pine-paneled living room with a hearth, a gracious parlor, and, best of all, a glassed sunroom, which serves as a venue (weather permitting) for breakfast. It overlooks the 2-acre "back

THE CENTENNIAL HOUSE, NORTHFIELD, BUILT IN 1811.

Christina Tree

meadow," with its sunset views. The house sits on Northfield's long, wide Main Street, which invites strolling. $117–209 (for the king suite) includes breakfast. Innkeepers Joan and Steve Stoia offer numerous "specials," including tickets to local museums and attractions. The inn is a popular venue for meetings, seminars, and weddings.

The Ashley Graves House (413-665-6656; ashleygraveshouse.com), 121 N. Main St., Sunderland 01375. One of the finest houses around, proudly built in 1830 and lovingly preserved by Carole and Mike Skibiski. Guests enter through the Barn Room, a large, comfortably furnished common space with guest fridge and adjoining dining and breakfast rooms. The King Philip Suite is a beauty, with skylights in a post-and-beam ceiling and a "Vermont crazy window" in the wall. It's huge, with a king-sized bed, private entrance, and private bath with whirlpool tub. (There is also a room with twins, another with a lovely antique double bed and a balcony, and a second-floor suite with a queen bed and a pullout sofa in the adjoining sitting room.) All rooms have private bath and are tastefully furnished with antiques, as is a front parlor with a brick fireplace. Centrally air-conditioned, too. From $185 including a full breakfast.

Sunnyside Farm (413-665-3113), 21 River Rd., Whately 01093. Mary Lou Green welcomes visitors to her big, yellow, turn-of-the-20th-century farmhouse 5 miles south of Deerfield. It's been in her family since it was built and stands on 50 acres of farmland that grew tobacco and is now leased in part to the neighboring berry farm. All three guest rooms overlook fields. Two spacious front rooms with TVs face River Road. There's a small but appealing corner double, and a back room has a king-sized bed; baths are shared. Guests have access to a comfortable living room and a dining room in which everyone gathers around a long table for breakfast. Don't miss the porch swing. $95–110. Also see "West County."

MOTELS **The Inn at Crumpin Fox** (413-648-9131 or 1-800-436-9466), 71 Northfield Rd. (MA 10), Bernardston 01337. An unusually attractive, recently renovated 29-room motel just off I-91 Exit 28, but with an out-in-the-country feel. Request a room overlooking greenery. Under the same ownership as Crumpin Fox Golf Club and Bella Notte Restaurant; inquire about stay-and-play packages and wedding receptions. $99–125.

♿ **Hampton Inn & Suites** (413-773-0057), 184 Shelburne Rd., Greenfield. Just off I-91. Clean, comfortable, and predictable, this 69-room motor inn has a heated indoor pool and fitness room. Breakfast is included in the rates, which vary with the date.

✱ Where to Eat

DINING OUT **Blue Heron Restaurant** (413-665-2102; blueherondining.com), 112 N. Main St., Sunderland. Open year-round, Tues.–Sun. from 5 PM. Reservations advised. The dimly lit, melon-colored rooms of a handsome former town hall are a country-elegant setting for one of the Valley's top restaurants. The produce is local, but chef and co-owner Deborah Snow's preparation certainly isn't. Entrées ($13–26) may range from

William A. Davis

THE BLUE HERON RESTAURANT, SUNDERLAND.

pan-roasted breast of Peking duck with grape gastrique to grilled swordfish or Provencal vegetable tian with cannellini bean ragout.

The Whately Inn (413-665-3044; whatelyinn.com), 193 Chester Plain Rd., Whately Center. The boast here is that you "eat greatly at the Whately," and the menu certainly supports it. House specialties include rack of lamb Dijonais, broiled jumbo shrimp Francoise, and roast crisp duckling Bigarde. Entrées $18.95–29.95. The dining area is large, taking up most of the ground floor of the old inn, but this is a popular place and reservations are recommended. Open Mon.–Sat. at 5, Sun. at 1.

The Night Kitchen (413-367-9580; montaguenightkitchen.com), 440 Greenfield Rd., Montague. Open most of the year, Thurs.–Sun. 5:30–9. A must. Housed in the picturesque Montague Mill, this is a small gem with a chef-owner named Max, the son of a cookbook author who has trained in kitchens in Italy and Asia. On a hot summer night there's no better place to dine than on the terrace here with the brook racing down below. It's an ambitious menu with starters that might include broiled honey goat cheese parfait with sliced almonds, or crab fritters with horse radish sour cream. Main dishes range from Parmesan and pine nut–crusted rack of lamb to maple-bourbon glazed duck breast. Entrées $21–24.

Ristorante DiPaolo (413-863-4441; ristorantedipaolo.com), 166 Avenue A, Turners Falls. Open Wed.–Sat. from 5 PM. Reservations advised. Steps from the Shea Theater, this attractive place is worth seeking out in its own right. Denise DiPaolo's menu features all the Italian classics but with style: A calamari appetizer is lightly floured and flash-fried, served with sweet potato, leeks, and a citrus crème fraîche sauce; Rollatini de Pollo is a chicken breast wrapped around asparagus, spinach, prosciutto, and smoked Gouda, drizzled with a sun-dried tomato and Dijon mustard sauce, served with fettuccine. Pasta sauces are all house-made. Entrées $21–30.

Champney's (413-774-2359; champneysrestaurant.com), the Deerfield Inn, Main Street, Old Deerfield. Open daily for lunch, dinner nightly. Reservations advised. This is a formal dining room with white tablecloths, Chippendale chairs, and a moderately expensive lunch menu. At dinner you might begin with cornmeal-crusted Maine lobster cakes with fennel remoulade and heirloom tomato aioli ($13); then dine on pan-seared scallops with coconut curry sauce ($23) or grilled heritage breed Berkshire pork chop with mead-glazed apples and sweet onion marmalade ($25). Wine is available by the glass, and the wine list is extensive.

Alina's Ristorante (413-397-2190; myalinas.com) Elm Street, South. Open Tues.–Sun. 5–10. A cozy, white tablecloth restaurant, Alina's serves Italian cuisine with Mediterranean flair. The extensive menu includes dishes such as osso buco and saltimbocca; fish crusted with black sesame seeds and served over Parmesan polenta; and a choice of beef filet, sirloin chicken, or veal served with a rich marsala wine sauce. Entrees $13–29. Specials include a Wednesday night chef's tasting with free samples of appetizers, new dishes, desserts or specialty drinks; a pasta night on Sunday with a choice of three pastas along with a salad for $15; and couples' night on Tuesdays with dinner for two and a bottle of wine for $75.

Goten of Japan (413-665-3628; gotenofjapan.com), 104 Old Amherst Rd. (MA 116), Sunderland. Open for dinner, also lunch on Sat. Closed Mon. Set back from the road on its own grounds, this long-established Valley favorite offers a varied menu of traditional teriyaki, hibachi, and sukiyaki dishes. Prices range from $15–38 including soup, salad, green tea, and dessert. A special "Delight Dinner Menu" features lobster and seafood; there's also a kids' menu.

Chandler's Restaurant at Yankee Candle (413-665-5089), US 5/MA 10, South Deerfield. Open for lunch and dinner. The decor is both rustic and romantic, lit by candles of course, some 200 of them. Dine on Asian barbecue duck breast, rib-eye steak, or grilled scallops. Lunch entrées $11–16, dinner $26–29.

Bella Notte Ristorante (413-648-9107; foxinnmass.com), 199 Huckle Hill Rd., Bernardston, off MA 10, minutes from I-91 Exit 28. Open nightly for dinner May–Dec.; Wed.–Sun. the rest of the year. Reservations advised. A glass-faced, hilltop building with the best views of any restaurant in the Valley and a comfortable summer terrace. The extensive menu features northern Italian dishes: many appetizers, pastas, and veal, chicken, and seafood dishes. Entrées $16.98–29.99.

Rooster's Bistro (413-498-0006), 74 Main St., Northfield. Open Tues.–Sat., 5:30–8, Sun. breakfast 6–noon. This is a find. An attractive, reasonably priced dining spot with a menu that might include bourbon pork medallions or chicken saltimbocca stuffed with prosciutto, sage, and a blend of cheeses. Everything from scratch. Homemade breads, soup, daily specials, wine, and beer. Entrées: $11.95–13.95.

EATING OUT

In and around Greenfield

❀ **Hope & Olive** (413-774-3150; hopeandolive.com), 44 Hope St., Greenfield. Lunch Tues.–Fri. 11:30–2:30; dinner Tues.–Sat. 5–9, Sun. 5–8; Sun. brunch: 10–2. No reservations for less than six. The local favorite. Changing art exhibits, occasional musical entertainment, and comfortable booths. A nice mix of comfort, locally grown food, and specialty drinks. Dining favorites include Maryland-style crabcakes with collard greens and corn pudding, and Italian seafood stew with polenta. Also, vegetarian dishes, burgers, steak, and pasta. The best meat loaf anywhere!

Thai Blue Ginger (413-772-0921; thaiblueginger s.com), 298 Main St. Open for lunch and dinner daily; dinner reservations advised. Classic Thai dishes get great reviews for flavor and freshness. Brick-walled, white tablecloth atmosphere, reasonable prices. Try the glass noodle soup and Siam seafood (shrimp, squid, and scallions sautéed with cashew nuts, mushrooms, and celery in a mild chili sauce).

The People's Pint (413-773-0333; thepeoplespint.com). 24 Federal St. Open daily at 11, but call to check; dinner 4–10; light menu until midnight. No reservations. All ages welcome. A first-rate brew pub that's also a great people place; good food, too. Specialties include soups, breads, and "The Ploughman Classic" (crusty sourdough topped with sharp cheddar, a pickle, and mustard). Ingredients are as local as possible. Reasonably priced entrées like New Orleans red beans and rice or grilled chicken salad. Chess, board games, and darts weekday evenings, live music Saturday night, Celtic music Sunday. Check the website for current entertainment schedule.

Pete's Seafood (413-772-2153), 54 School St. Closed Sun. and Mon. Call ahead for hours. Great fried whole belly clams, scallop rolls, fried fish sandwiches, chowder and onion rings, daily specials, pasta, and burgers. Seasonal outdoor tables.

Hattaporn's Kitchen (423-774-5304), 221 Main St. Fresh and flavorful Thai food with seating for around 20. Try the spring rolls and the fried tofu. Ample servings.

China Gourmet (413-774-2299), 78 Mohawk Trail (MA 2A). Open for lunch and dinner, until 10 most nights and until 11 Fri. and Sat. A local favorite, light on the MSG, a reasonably priced menu, and new sushi bar. Szechuan and Hunan specialties include hot-and-sour seafood soup, General Tso's chicken, and "Hot Lover's Triple Treat."

Magpie Woodfired Pizzeria (413-475-3570; magpiepizza.com), 21 Bank Row. Open daily except Tues. from 4. An offshoot of Hope & Olive (*Dining Out*), this is all about not-your-basic pizzas: potato and garlic; house-made sausage and broccoli; and fennel, arugula and goat cheese. Some pasta, salads, tiramisu. Outside seating, weather permitting.

Brad's Place (413-773-9567), 353 Main St. Open Mon.–Fri. 6–3, Sat. 6–2, and Sun. for breakfast. "Serving downtown for 30 years," this is the kind of place where everyone knows everybody—but visitors are also served quickly and well. Daily specials, burgers, soups, and sandwiches, a long counter and booths.

Green Fields Market (413-773-9567), 144 Main St. This natural foods cooperative occupies a former JCPenney building and includes a tempting deli and "from scratch" bakery with attractive seating space near the windows and outside.

Manna House (413-774-5955), 205 Main St. Open daily except Sun. for lunch and dinner. Not much from the outside, but bright and inviting within, this Korean restaurant offers tantalizing vegetarian dishes as well as noodle soups, rice, and meat dishes.

Greenfield Grille (413-376-4777), 30 Federal St. Open daily 11:30. Breakfast on Sat. and Sun. from 7 AM. Once the home of Famous Bill's and its much-sought-after lobster pie, the Grille now features American cuisine with daily specials.

Taylor's Tavern (413-773-8313; taylorstavernandrestaurant.com), 283 Main St. Open Mon.–Wed. 11–10, until 11 Thurs.–Sat.; Sun. noon–10; breakfast Sat.–Sun. from 8. A long-established local gathering place, Taylor's has a pub atmosphere with dark wood paneling, booths, and a large menu offering everything from pizza and pasta to steaks.

Elsewhere

Wolfie's (413-665-7068), 52 S. Main St., South Deerfield. Open Mon.–Sat. 11–10. This is our kind of place: an appealing family restaurant with wooden booths, a bowl of popcorn, and fast, friendly service. The menu features a blackened Wolfieburger (a charbroiled, 5-ounce, ground round Cajun burger with melted cheddar, etc.), a "Big Bad Wolfburger" (8-ounce ground round with melted cheese, etc.), many sandwiches, grinders, and salads. Also, dinner specials starting at $11.95, draft beer, mixed drinks, and wine.

Go Nomad Café (413-665-5005; gonomadcafe.com), 4A Sugarloaf St., South Deerfield. A small, pleasant café with WiFi and an extensive breakfast and sandwich menu. Grilled sandwiches are served on extra-thick bread and you can design your own panini. It's billed as "A Traveler's Café," and the walls are decorated with photos of scenes from around the world. Open Mon.–Fri. 6:30–5, Sat.–Sun. 8–4.

Lady Killigrew Café (413-367-9666), 440 Greenfield Rd., Montague Center. Open Wed.–Sat. for lunch and dinner, until midnight on weekends when there is usually live music. Located in the Montague Bookmill, this is an attractive space with windows overlooking the brook and a feel and menu that's a cross between a café and pub. The atmosphere is literary, with patrons often reading while they're eating. The "Bill of Fare" includes a warm brown rice salad and unusual sandwiches such as Brie with apricot jam and marinated apples. Tea, coffee, wine, and beer are also served.

2nd Street Baking Company (413-863-4455; 2ndstreetbakingco.com), 69 Second St., Turners Falls. Open Tues.–Sat. 7–6, Sun. 8–1. Soups, sandwiches, breads. A find! The breads are made daily, and patrons lunch on from-scratch-soups, salads, paninis, and wraps with plenty of vegetarian choices. We feasted on a

GO NOMAD CAFÉ, SOUTH DEERFIELD

Sandy Ward

William A.Davis

LADY KILLIGREW CAFÉ, MONTAGUE CENTER.

veggie wrap with homemade sun-dried tomato and basil white bean hummus, avocado, and plenty of fresh greens. Cakes and pastries are special. Check the website for special events.

Bub's Bar BQ (413-548-9630; bubsbbq.com), MA 116, Sunderland. Open at 4 weekdays, noon Sat.–Sun. Rated "best barbecue joint in New England" by *Yankee,* this place offers great variety: kielbasa and blackened fish, "spicy dirty rice," and "orange-glazed sweet potatoes," as well as pulled-pork back ribs.

Smiarowski Farm Stand and Creamery (413-665-3830), 320 River Rd. (MA 47), Sunderland. Open May–Nov., daily 8–6. The thing to order here is Karen Smiarowski's "Polish Power Plate": a *golabki,* a "lazy cabbage pierogi," and a chunk of kielbasa, plus homemade potato salad, baked beans, and rye bread. Desserts change with what's in season, beginning in June with rhubarb pie, then strawberry shortcake, then crisps—blueberry, peach, and finally apple in September and October. Fruit toppings for the Snow's ice cream are also homemade. The self-serve snack bar, with seating at picnic tables, is attached to the family's post-and-beam farm stand.

ROAD FOOD

Along Route 2

Wagon Wheel Restaurant (413-863-8210), 39 French King Hwy., Gill. Open seasonally for all three meals. Homestyle cooking, seasonal outside dining. Great food and great value. Memorabilia galore.

♿ **Shady Glen Restaurant** (413-863-9636), 7 Avenue A, Turners Falls. Open Mon.–Sat. 5 AM–9 PM. No credit cards. A step back to the 1950s, this diner, with its L-shaped counter and eight cozy booths, is just off MA 2 and over the bridge. Not the way it was under previous longtime owners, but still a pleasant place with decent, reasonably priced food. (*Note:* The bridge is one-way south until 2014.)

French King Restaurant (413-659-3328), handy to MA 2, Millers Falls. A family restaurant, open (except Mon.) for lunch and dinner.

Off I-91

Tom's Hot Dog, US 5/MA 10 south of I-91 Exit 23 in North Hatfield. Legendary steamed hot dogs and lots more.

Fillin' Station (413-665-3696), US 5/MA 10 just off I-91, Exit 24. The best we can say is that this classic chrome diner is open 24 hours, adjacent to a gas station–truck stop. The flashy decor is great.

The Four Leaf Clover Restaurant (413-648-9514), US 5, Bernardston. Open daily for lunch and dinner, until 9 Fri. and Sat. Just off I-91 Exit 28, a family restaurant that's a local favorite, good for chicken potpie, baked haddock, lobster rolls, and liver and onions as well as homemade soups, pies, and bread pudding.

7 South Bakery (413-648-0070), 7 South St. (US 5), Bernardston. Open 6:30 AM–5 PM, closed Sun. The moment you walk into Kay and Mike Dougherty's small shop, you know you've struck gold. There's an irresistible aroma of freshly baked breads and coffee; pastries, too.

ICE CREAM Northfield Creamie (northfieldcreamie.com), 62 Main St., Northfield. Open seasonally, Tues.–Sun. noonish–9. An institution for more than 50 years: yummy soft-serve, shakes, floats, local hard scoop.

Also see Smiarowski Farm Stand and Creamery in *Eating Out*.

✷ Entertainment

Shea Theater (413-863-2281; the shea.org), 71 Avenue. A, Turners Falls. Call Tues.–Fri. noon–3 to inquire about year-round plays and musicals staged by three local community theater organizations. This is also home to the Shea Young Stage Company for actors ages 11–18.

1794 New Salem Meetinghouse (978-544-5200), off US 202, New Salem. A beautiful setting for music—choral, folk, and jazz—and an assortment of live performances.

Full Moon Coffee House (978-544-2086), Wendell. Monthly concerts held in the town hall on the Saturday night closest to the full moon.

Pioneer Valley Symphony Orchestra and Chorus (413-773-3664; pvso .org) based in Greenfield. One of the oldest symphony orchestras in the country.

In Greenfield

Frequent evening music venues include **Hope & Olive, People's Pint,** and **Greenfield Grille** (see *Eating Out*). Also check out the recently opened **Arts Block Café** (theartsblock.com), 289 Main St., and **Pushkin Gallery** (thepushkin.com), 4 Federal St.

FILM Northfield Drive-In (603-239-4054; northfielddrivein.com), MA 63 north of Northfield. Weekends, Apr.–Oct. Half in New Hampshire and half in Massachusetts, a vintage 1948 drive-in showing new releases.

Greenfield Garden Cinemas (413-774-4881; gardencinemas.net), 361 Main St., Greenfield. No longer the movie palace it once was, but still a place to see first-run films.

✷ Selective Shopping

AUCTIONS Auction houses include **Douglas** (413-665-2877; douglas

Ed Wierzbowski

ARTS BLOCK, GREENFIELD, FEATURES LIVE MUSIC SEVERAL NIGHTS A WEEK.

auctioneers.com), 241 Greenfield Rd. (US 5), Deerfield, and **Northfield Auctions** (413-498-4420; www.northfieldauctions.com), 105 Main St., Northfield. Monday nights as scheduled; previews at 4 PM.

ART AND CRAFTS GALLERIES At **The Montague Bookmill** (montaguebookmill.com), 440 Greenfield Rd., Montague. Also at the Montague Mill, **Louise Minks Millworks Studio** (413-367-2885; louiseminks.com) features the artist's outstanding paintings, prints, and cards depicting mostly local landscapes.

Artspace Community Arts Center (413-772-6811), 15 Mill St., Greenfield. Changing two-dimensional and crafts shows represent area artists and artisans.

Hallmark Museum of Contemporary Photography (413-863-0009), 84 Avenue A, Turners Falls. Open Thurs.–Sun. 1–5. Displays work by well-known photographers and students at the nearby Hallmark Institute of Photography.

Green Trees Gallery (413-498-0283; greentreesgallery.com), 105 Main St., Northfield. A very attractive consignment gallery featuring handmade pottery, weaving, paintings, sculpture, and the Media Arts Café, which shows art movies Fri. and Sat.

11 South Gallery/Workshop (413-648-5484; 11southgallery.com), US 5/MA 10, Bernardston. Open Wed.–Sat. 11–5. This is a magical space on the southern fringe of the village. Featuring painted local and Maine landscapes by Elice Davis Pieropan and pottery by her daughter, Pamela. There are also exceptional woodcarvings and decorative weavings from the Pacific atoll of Kapingamarangi, where the family lived for many years.

BOOKSTORES **World Eye Bookshop** (413-772-2186; worldeyebook shop.com), 156 Main St., Greenfield. Open daily. This well-stocked book and gift store serves a wide upcountry area.

Raven Used Books (413-772-1968; ravenusedbooks.com), 5 Bank Row, Greenfield. Open daily for casual browsing. Housed in a restored turn-of-the-century building, it offers a wide variety of books for all interests.

((ᵠ)) **Northfield Coffee and Books** (413-624-7119; coffeeandbooks.net), 105 Main St., Northfield. David Pontius has created an inviting oasis; new/old books, coffee, comfortable seating.

Meetinghouse Books (413-665-0500; meetinghousebooks.com), 70 N. Main St., South Deerfield. Open Wed.–Fri. 10–6, weekends noon–6 and at other times if the flag is flying outside. A destination for browsers and book lovers since 1996. Judith Tingley and Ken Haverly have filled a former church with their eclectic selection of more than 25,000 used and out-of-print books that include literature, history, the arts, children's books, and much more, "priced to every budget."

The Montague Bookmill (413-367-9206; montaguebookmill.com) in the Montague Mill, Greenfield, and on Depot Rd., Montague. Open daily 10–6. True to its slogan, "Books you don't need in a place you can't find," this bookworm's mecca offers thousands of used and discounted books with plenty of reading corners and frequent concerts and readings. It's housed in a picturesque old mill by a rushing stream, along with The Lady Killigrew Café (see *Eating Out*) and The Night Kitchen (see *Dining Out*).

Whately Antiquarian Book Center (413-247-3272), US 5/MA 10, Whately. Open Mon.–Sat. 10–5:30, Sun. noon–5; closed Wed., Sept.–June. A group shop with 40 dealers and 40,000 good used and rare books.

SPECIAL STORES

Greenfield and North

Wilson's Department Store (413-774-4326; wilsonsdepartmentstore.com), 258 Main St., Greenfield. Open Mon.–Thurs. 10–5:30, Fri. 10–8, Sat. 9:30–5:30. In business since 1882, one of New England's few surviving independently owned downtown department stores: four floors with everything from appliances, bedspreads, and cosmetics to toys, cards, and clothing.

Magical Child (413-773-5721; magical-child.com), 134 Main St.,

THE MONTAGUE BOOKMILL, ONE OF SEVERAL ATTRACTIONS AT MONTAGUE MILL.

William A. Davis

Greenfield. A first-rate toy and children's clothing store.

Kringle Candle Company (413-648-3077; kringlecandle.com), 220 South St. (US 5, just over the Greenfield line), Bernardston. Open daily, 10–6. In 1969 Michael Kittredge used his mother's kitchen to make his first candles. And now the founder of Yankee Candle is observing his son, Mike Kittredge III, launch another large and serious candle store not many miles up US 5. Nowhere near as elaborate as the destination emporium dad created in South Deerfield, it differs from other such stores in that all the candles are white, most distinguished from each other by their distinctive scents. Thirty-six different fragrances are available, but there is also a line of scent-free dinner candles. Crafted largely by hand, the candles are all dye-free, made of pure paraffin wax, and have an attractive luminous glow. There is also a year-round Christmas shop and restaurant.

The Textile Co., Inc. (413-773-7516), 21 Power Square, Greenfield. Open Mon.–Sat. 9–5:20, Fri. until 8:20. Closed Mon., June–Aug. Customers come from far and wide to this old-fashioned, quality fabric store for good cottons, silks, polyesters, vinyls, linens, acetates, calicos, notions, and patterns. Specializes in all colors and designs for quilters.

Mim's Market (413-498-9900), 60 Main St., Northfield. Open Mon.–Sat., 6 AM–11 PM, Sun. 7–10. The heart of Northfield, a general store and full-service deli with fresh-baked muffins and bagels, coffees, tables.

In Deerfield/Sunderland

Richardson's Candy Kitchen (413-772-0443 or 1-800-817-9338; richardsonscandy.com), US 5/MA 10, Deerfield. Open daily 10–5:30. Handmade and specialty candies with a wide and enthusiastic following. Nationally recognized for their "Dixies."

KRINGLE IS THE HOT NEW CANDLE COMPANY IN THE AREA.

William A. Davis

Pekarski's Sausage (413-665-4537), MA 116, South Deerfield. Homemade Polish kielbasa, breakfast sausage, smoked ham, and bacon.

Millstone Farm Market (413-665-0543), 22 S. Main St. (MA 47), Sunderland. The store's name and design, both featuring genuine millstones, date to 1929. Known for its meat, this is an exceptionally friendly store featuring local produce as well.

✷ Farms and Farm Stands

Also see **Smiarowski Farm Stand and Creamy** under *Eating Out*.

Hamilton Orchards (978-544-6867; hamiltonorchards.com), 22 West St. (just off US 202), New Salem. Open July–Aug., daily 9–5; Sept.–Oct., weekends 9–5. The Hamilton family has been welcoming visitors to their 100-acre hilltop farm since 1943. In fall, with four kinds of apples to pick and tables piled with apple pies and dumplings, the place is hopping. In summer there are PYO raspberries and blueberries. Picnic tables overlook the hills.

Upinngil (413-863-2297; upinngil.com), 411 Main Rd., Gill. Open daily year-round. Organically grown asparagus, melons, sweet corn, potatoes (many varieties), pumpkins, winter squash, honey, hay, maple products, and baked goods. Strawberries picked and U-pick.

Riverland Farm (413-687-5781; riverlandfarm.com), 197 River Rd. (MA 47), Sunderland. Open early June–late Oct., daily. A large selection of farm-grown organic vegetables, plus other local milk, cheese, eggs, goat cheese, fruit, and maple syrup.

Warner Farm (413-665-8331; warnerfarm.com), 159 Old Amherst Rd., Sunderland. Open May–Oct., daily 10–6. Farm-grown produce: asparagus, strawberries, peas, beans, peppers, sweet corn, pumpkins, and squash. Pick-your-own strawberries in June. In Sept.–Oct. visit "Mike's Amazing Maze," the area's first and only corn maze, 9–5 at 23 S. Main St. (MA 47).

Golonka Farm (413-247-3256; golonkafarm.com), 6 State Rd., Whately. Open June 15–Oct., daily 9–6. Specializing in sweet corn, but has a variety of other homegrown vegetables.

Long Plain Farm (413-665-1210), 149 Christian Lane, Whately. Open May–Dec., daily 9–5. Onions, potatoes, cabbage, eggplant, summer and winter squash, pickle and salad cucumbers, sweet corn, Halloween and sugar pumpkins.

Songline Emu Farm (413-863-2700 or 1-866-539-2996; allaboutemu.com), 66 French King Hwy. (MA 2), Gill. Open Apr.–Sept. 15, Thurs.–Sat. noon–6. A working emu farm offering tours and selling lean emu burgers and steak. Adults $3, children ages 12 and younger $2.

Chee Chee Mamook Farm (413-498-2160), 341 Caldwell Rd., Northfield. Open year-round. Hours by appointment. This is a visitor-geared alpaca farm with a store selling homespun alpaca-fleece yarn and clothing.

FLOWERS **Baystate Perennial Farm** (413-665-3525; baystateperennial.com), 36 State Rd. (US 5/MA 10), Whately. Open mid-Apr.–Sept., daily 9–6. New and unusual as well as proven classic perennials, shrubs, and vines. Free gardening workshops and informal garden walks/talks.

Mill River Farm (413-665-3034), US 5 and MA 116, South Deerfield,

Christina Tree

FARM STANDS ARE PLENTIFUL THROUGHOUT THE VALLEY.

across from the fire station. Open Apr.–late June, Sept.–Oct., and Thanksgiving weekend–Christmas. Annuals, herbs, hanging baskets, mums, asters, pumpkins, Christmas trees, and perennials.

Five Acre Farm (413-498-2208; faf growers.com), 108 Hinsdale Rd. (MA 63), Northfield. An extensive garden center. Outstanding.

PICK-YOUR-OWN Clarkdale Fruit Farms (413-772-6797; clark dalefruitfarm.com), 303 Upper Rd., Deerfield. A fourth-generation farm that has PYO apples, pumpkins, peaches, pears, and great cider, including pear if you're lucky.

Nourse Farms (413-665-2658; noursefarms.com), 41 River Rd., South Deerfield. This 400-acre riverside farm ships some 15 million "virus-free plants" throughout the world. While most business is through its catalog and website, it also welcomes PYO customers June–Oct., daily 8–4, for whatever is in-season: strawberries (24 varieties) and several kinds and colors of raspberries.

Quonquont Farm (413-575-4680; quonquont.com), 9 North St., Whately. Open mid-July–early Nov., 10–6. Closed Mon. and holidays. Pick-your-own blueberries, peaches, and apples. Farm stand with fruit, cider, and preserves. A blueberry maze.

SUGARHOUSES Maple producers who welcome visitors include **Williams Farm Sugarhouse** (413-773-5186; williamsfarmsugarhouse .com), US 5/MA 10 in Deerfield, open mid-Feb.–mid-Apr., 8:30–5, with pancake breakfasts served daily and sugarhouse tours; products available year-round. Also, **Brookledge Sugarhouse** (413-665-3837; brook ledgesugarhouse.com), 159 Haydenville Rd. (2 miles from Whately Center), Whately; **River Maple Farm**

(413-648-9767), US 5, Bernardston; and **Ripley's Sugarhouse** (413-367-2031), 195 Chestnut Hill Rd., Montague.

✷ Special Events

February: **Greenfield Winter Carnival** (413-772-1553) at Highland Pond, Beacon Field, and all around town, includes an ice sculpture contest, ice skating, cross-country skiing, and sledding (*first weekend*).

March: **Sugaring**—local sugarhouses invite the public; check the listings above or visit massmaple.org.

May: **Gas and Steam Engine Show,** MA 10, Bernardston.

Mid-May–June: The **fish ladder** behind town hall in Turners Falls, operated by Northfield Mountain (1-800-859-2960), offers views through a window behind the falls of shad and occasional Atlantic salmon finding their way up the Connecticut River.

Spring–fall: **Farmers' markets** are held in Greenfield, Sat. 8–12:30; in Northfield, Thurs. 4–7; and in Turners Falls, Wed. 3–6.

June: **Old Deerfield Summer Crafts Fair at Memorial Hall** (413-774-7476; deerfield-craft.org) includes more than 200 exhibitors (*last weekend*).

July: **Old-Fashioned Independence Day** (413-774-3768) in Old Deerfield. **The Green River Festival** (413-773-5463; greenriverfestival.com) features nationally known musicians, a craft fair, and hot air balloon launches. **Old Deerfield Sunday Afternoon Concert Series** (413-774-3768) celebrates chamber music.

Late August: **Montague Old Home Days** (413-367-9467) has games, an auction, food, music, and a footrace in Montague Village and Montague Center.

September: **Franklin County Fair** (413-774-4282; fcas.com), held at the county fairgrounds in Greenfield, includes livestock, crafts, music, a midway, and food (*first weekend after Labor Day*). **Old Deerfield Fall Craft Fair** (413-774-3768; deerfield-craft.org) features traditional crafts by more than 200 juried exhibitors from throughout the country. **Garlic and Arts Festival,** New Salem.

October: Antiques Dealers Association of America's **Historic Deerfield Antiques Show** (*Columbus Day weekend;* adadealers.com). **Friends of Gill Fall Crafts Fair** (413-863-9708; friendsofgill.org) has crafts and music (*third weekend*). **Fiber Twist** (413-773-5463; fibertwist.com) features open farms and a marketplace for fiber farmers, weavers, and spinners throughout Franklin County (*Sept. or Oct.*). **Pumpkin Fest** in Turners Falls (*mid-month*).

November: Annual Franklin County **CiderDays** (413-773-5463; ciderday.org), with open farms, studios, and winery; tasting salon, marketplace, and more (*first weekend*).

FIVE-COLLEGE AREA

INCLUDING AMHERST, NORTHAMPTON, AND HOLYOKE

The "Five Colleges" are the University of Massachusetts as well as four small, prestigious private colleges: Amherst, Mount Holyoke, Hampshire, and Smith. Together these very different campuses are home to a total of 30,000 students within an 11-mile radius.

In cities, such academic concentrations are less noticeable. Here, against a backdrop of cornfields, apple orchards, and small towns, the visible and cultural impact of academia is dramatic. Art collections in seven college museums are exceptional. For families, the dinosaur tracks and remains in the Amherst College Museum of Natural History and the exhibits in The Eric Carle Museum of Picture Book Art are worth the trip. The area's galleries, shops, and restaurants are numerous and appealing.

Still, the Five-College Area is one of the state's better-kept secrets. This stretch of the Connecticut River was better known as a destination more than a century ago. As early as the 1820s, sophisticated visitors came to view the Valley's peculiar mix of factory and farmscape, bottomland and abrupt mountains. In 1836 Thomas Cole, one of America's most celebrated landscape artists, painted the mammoth work, *The Oxbow: View from Mt. Holyoke, Northampton, Massachusetts, after a Thunderstorm,* now owned by New York's Metropolitan Museum. The Oxbow subsequently became the "motif number one" of Western Massachusetts, and the small Mountain House on the summit of Mount Holyoke was soon replaced with a more elaborate hotel (a portion of which survives), accessed from riverboats and a riverside train station by a perpendicular cog-and-cable-driven railway. There was also a hotel on Mount Tom and a mineral spa in Northampton. During the academic year, buses circulate among the five campuses (residents and visitors welcome). Thousands of students annually take courses at the other institutions, and all share a lively "Five-College" calendar of plays, concerts, and lectures. Many graduates have opted to stay on in the Valley, establishing the crafts and art galleries, restaurants, shops, and coffeehouses for which the area is now known.

Northampton, the Valley's focal point for both students and visitors, is known for the quantity and quality of its restaurants, galleries, and evening music venues. It's an architecturally interesting old county seat, with an outstanding art

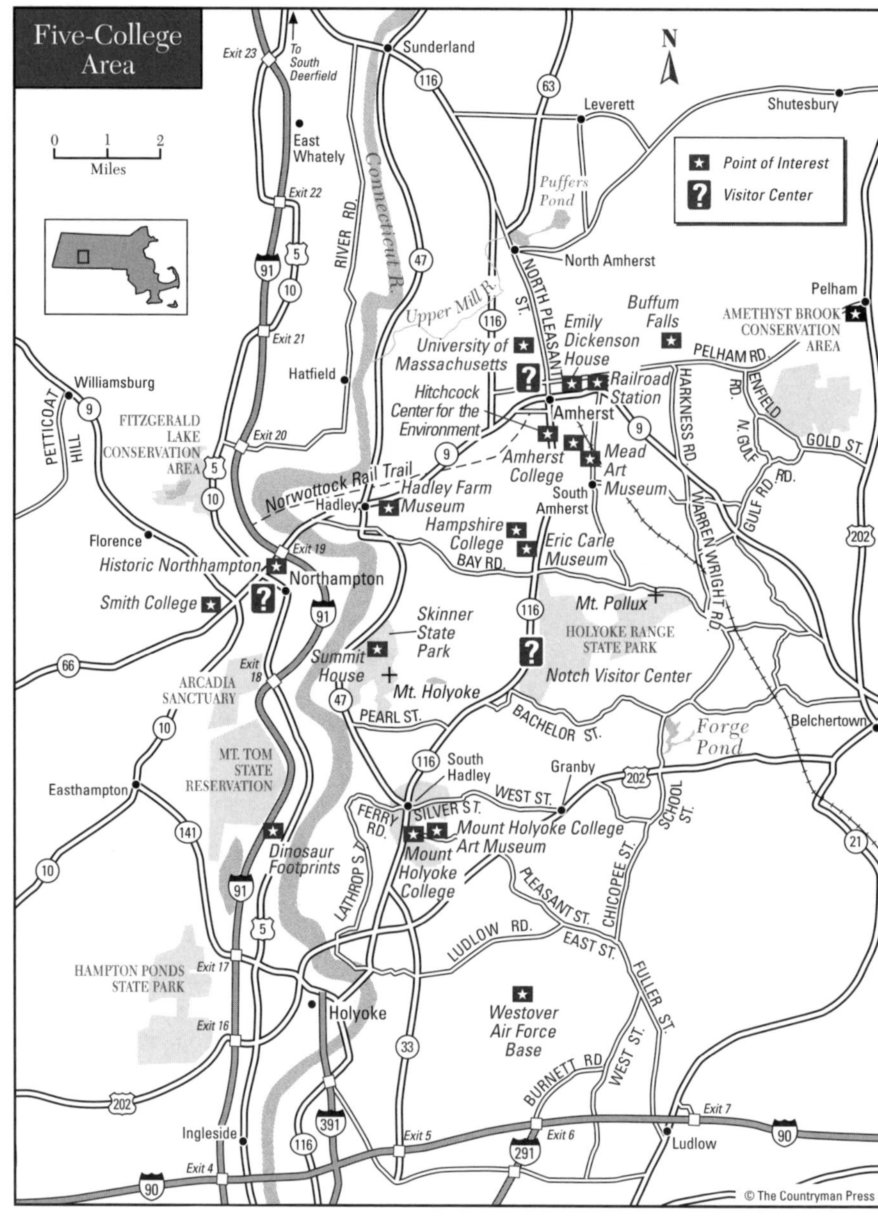

museum at Smith College and the country's oldest municipal theater, the Academy of Music.

Amherst is a classic, increasingly lively college town. The large, shaded common, framed by the Amherst College campus and 19th-century shops, remains its centerpiece, connected to the UMass campus (curiously invisible, despite its high-rise dormitories and library, unless you go looking for it) by one long street of shops and restaurants. The evolving Amherst Cinema Arts Center just off the common will complement the wide choice of good, inexpensive places to eat or simply sit and sip while working on your computer (downtown is virtually all WiFi).

Innovative Hampshire College is a few minutes' drive south of downtown Amherst. Mount Holyoke, a few more miles south in the village of South Hadley, is the country's oldest women's college and arguably the most beautiful of the five campuses, an 800-acre spread designed by the firm of Frederick Law Olmsted with two lakes and majestic trees.

The fact that each of the five is so different contributes to the beauty of their mix—a phenomenon that can be experienced year-round. Entertainment options include concerts in venues like the garden at Forty Acres in Hadley, as well as several theaters. Hiking trails run east–west across the Valley, along the ridge of the Holyoke Range, and through many miles of conservation land.

We include the small brick-mill city of Holyoke in the Five-College Area. Designed from scratch by Boston developers in the 1840s and '50s, it's a sharp contrast to the nearby ivy-covered communities. Industrial-architecture buffs will be intrigued by canalside mill buildings, and families will appreciate the attractions conveniently grouped around the Holyoke Heritage State Park—the Children's Museum at Holyoke and a working antique merry-go-round. Mount Tom offers great views.

THE VALLEY IS HOME TO 30,000 STUDENTS, INCLUDING THOSE FAMILIAR WITH THIS SPOT ON THE CAMPUS OF MOUNT HOLYOKE COLLEGE.

Christina Tree

Thanks to AMTRAK from New York City and frequent buses from Boston and among the campuses, the Five-College Area is almost accessible without a car, especially if you bring your bicycle.

GUIDANCE **Amherst Area Chamber of Commerce** (413-253-0700; amherst area.com), 28 Amity St. Open Mon.–Fri. 8:30–4:30. This friendly, well-stocked storefront in the Amherst Cinema Arts Center Building is worth a stop. A volunteer-dependent information booth on the common is also open summer weekends.

Greater Northampton Chamber of Commerce (413-584-1900; explore northampton.com), 99 Pleasant St. (US 5 South), Northampton. Open Mon.–Fri. 9–5, also weekends May–Oct., noon–4.

For area museums, visit **museums10.org.**

GETTING THERE *By air:* Bradley International Airport; see "Springfield Area."

By bus: **Peter Pan–Trailways** (1-800-343-9999; peterpanbus.com) connects Greenfield, Amherst, South Hadley, and Holyoke with Boston, Springfield, Bradley International Airport, and points beyond. The departure point in Amherst is 79 S. Pleasant St. (but buy tickets in Amherst Books); the Northampton terminal is at 1 Round House Place (413-586-1030) behind City Hall.

By train: **AMTRAK** (1-800-872-7245; amtrak.com).

By car: The Mass Pike and MA 2 offer east–west access, and I-91 runs north–south. From MA 2, the quickest and most scenic way to the Amherst area is via US 202 (Exit 16), the Daniel Shays Highway, running down along the Quabbin Reservoir; turn west at the Pelham Town Hall.

For Northampton the quickest access is via I-91.

GETTING AROUND **The Pioneer Valley Transit Authority,** or PVTA (413-586-5806), connecting Northampton, Amherst, and South Hadley, is free and frequent. It circles among the five campuses from 6:45 AM until 11:35 PM weekdays during the academic year, less frequently on weekends and in summer.

PARKING *In Northampton:* The parking garage (Hampton Ave. behind Thornes Market) offers the first hour free. Scattered through town, lots are heavily patrolled. Some streets and lots have a two-hour limit. Meters are free after 6 PM.

In Amherst: In addition to metered street parking, there are four downtown lots. The Boltwood lot (access from Main St.) is the handiest, with access to N. Pleasant St. shops. Behind the CVS on N. Pleasant St. is another lot, and there are also small lots on Spring St. (adjacent to the common) and Amity St. (across from the Jones Library). All are closely monitored. *Note:* Parking on side streets is by permit during the academic year.

In Holyoke: The downtown parking garage is on Dwight St., one block from the Heritage State Park.

Christina Tree

A PIONEER VALLEY TRANSIT AUTHORITY BUS IN NORTHAMPTON.

MEDICAL EMERGENCY Dial **911.**

Cooley Dickinson Hospital (413-582-2000), 30 Locust St. (MA 9), Northampton.

✱ Villages, Towns, and Cities

Amherst. With significantly more students than Northampton (the town's population of some 35,000 includes a percentage of the 24,000 undergraduates and 5,500 graduate students at UMass, 1,600 at Amherst, and 1,200 at Hampshire College), Amherst is a lively college town. It's also walkable, with intriguing shops and restaurants lining two sides of its common as well as North Pleasant Street. More restaurants cluster around Boltwood Walk, squirreled away between North Pleasant and Main. As noted in the introduction, the vast and high-rise UMass campus, north of downtown Amherst, is curiously invisible. The far smaller Amherst College campus, just off the common, also eludes visitors but is well worth finding, both for the treasures in its **Mead Art Museum** and the dinosaurs in its **Amherst College Museum of Natural History.** Emily Dickinson buffs should visit not only the **Emily Dickinson Museum,** but also the exhibits devoted to the poet's life in the **Jones Library** just off the common. The Special Collections here form the literary heart of town, with exhibits and material devoted to Emily Dickinson, but also an 11,000-item collection relating to poet Robert Frost. Portraits depict Frost not as the shaggy poet laureate we usually see but as the strikingly handsome young man who lived in Amherst from 1931 to 1938 and returned in the 1940s to teach at Amherst College. As noted in the introduction, Amherst enjoys direct train service to Manhattan and

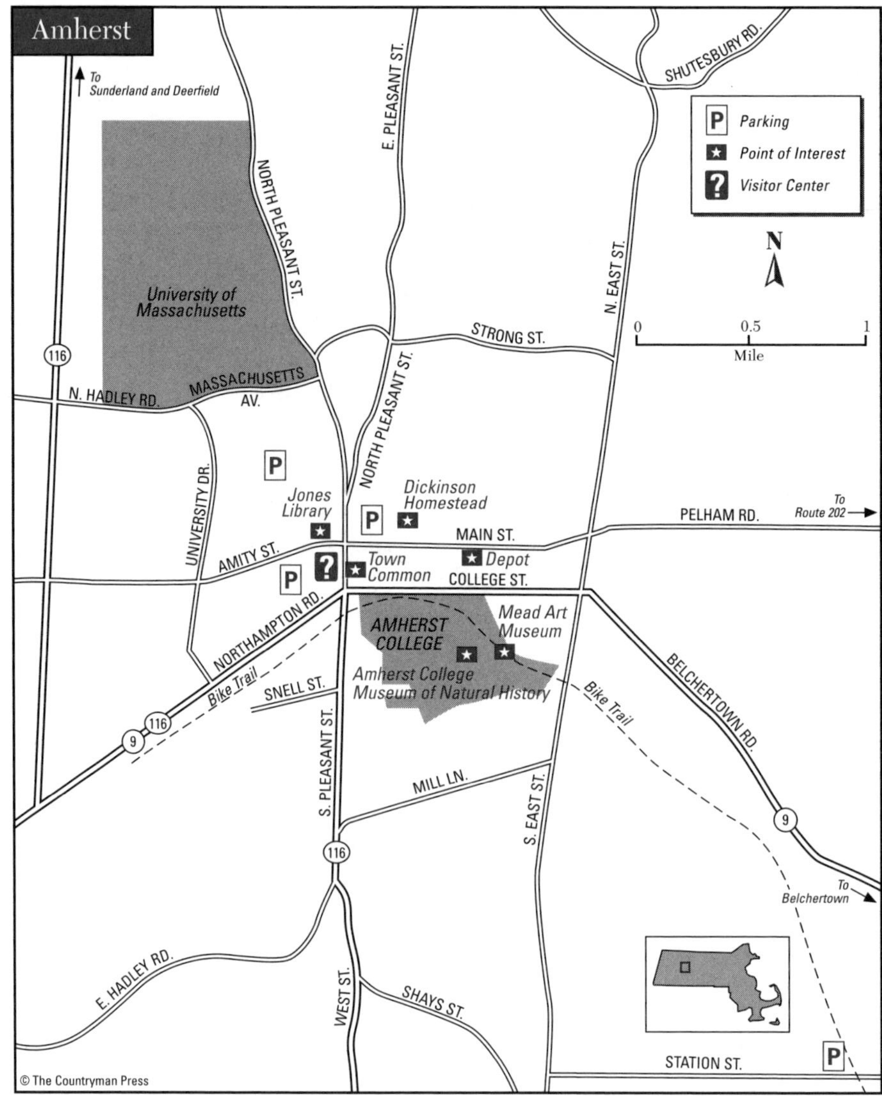

a direct bus from Boston, as well as excellent local public transportation and a bike trail to Northampton. It also offers a surprising amount of very accessible natural beauty, if you know where to look.

Northampton. Despite a population of less than 30,000, this is a city, one with more art and music, film and drama, shopping and dining than most urban centers a dozen times its size. Thanks to Round Hill, an 1840s–1860 mineral water spa, Northampton loomed large on New England's pre–Civil War tourist map. In 1852 Jenny Lind, the Swedish Nightingale, spent a three-month honeymoon at Round Hill and called Northampton "Paradise City," a name that's stuck (current local listings include Paradise City Travel, Paradise Copies, etc.). The brick hotel itself survives as part of the Clarke School for the Deaf (established in 1867) on Round Hill Road, off Elm Street. Northampton is home to **Smith College** as well as to historical figures as different as the fiery 18th-century preacher Jonathan Edwards, the 19th-century former slave and advocate for justice Sojourner Truth, food faddist Sylvester Graham (as in *graham cracker*), and the 1920s Northampton mayor and U.S. president Calvin Coolidge. The city's unusual history is nicely depicted in the **Historic Northampton Museum.**

Northampton has reinvented itself several times over the centuries; the current Main Street lineup of restaurants, art galleries, and boutiques is relatively recent. Now known as Noho, Northampton continues to evolve, having a long tradition of tolerating people with dissenting religious and political views and nontraditional lifestyles. The town has a vibrant gay and lesbian community, the latter especially active in local cultural life. Civic pride runs as high as it did during the years the city's former mayor was sitting in the Oval Office (1923–29), a brief era in which the **Hotel Northampton** (which opened with a mini museum village attached, to serve as an auto touring destination) and several handsome art deco buildings appeared. These include a jewel box of a building featuring a stained-glass skylight that now appropriately houses Silverscape Designs; another splendid former bank is the setting for sculpture and prints (R. Michelson Galleries), and the fabulous **Calvin Theatre** serves regularly as a venue for stellar live performances.

DOWNTOWN NORTHAMPTON

Christina Tree

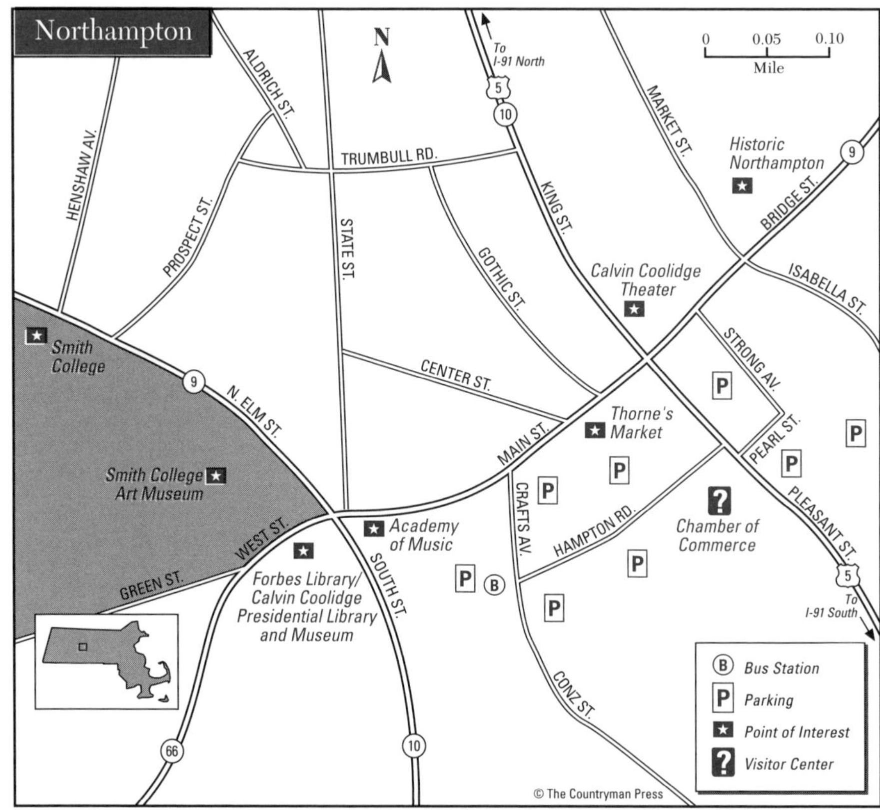

Northampton these days has a synergy all its own. It's not unusual to find the city's internationally famed **Young at Heart Chorus** of senior citizens sharing a stage with the Northampton **Gay Men's Chorus,** or for visitors to view a Matisse or Picasso in the **Smith College Museum of Art** and then stroll down the street to see a concert or a locally produced film at the municipally owned (since 1890) **Academy of Music.** Live music is a nightly given in several venues. Restaurants are so plentiful that patrons know they can always find a table within a block or two.

Don't overlook the village of **Florence,** still in Northampton, west on MA 9. Once known for silk mills, today its landmarks are the **Miss Florence Diner** and **Look Park.** Florence was also home to **Sojourner Truth;** her statue stands in a triangular park on Pine Street.

Hadley. Sandwiched between Northampton and Amherst, Hadley is easy to miss because it's still predominantly tobacco, onion, and asparagus fields beyond the MA 9 shops and malls. Settled in 1659, it is the mother town of Amherst, South Hadley, Sunderland, Granby, and Hatfield, and was originally known as Norwottuck, a name resurrected for the bike path that threads its fields. In 1675 a white-bearded recluse, reputedly William Goffe (a Charles I regicide), saved the town from an Indian attack and has ever since been known as the Angel of Hadley. Turn off MA 9 at Middle Street to see the pillared **town hall** (1841), the **Hadley Farm Museum,** and the **First Congregational Church** (1808). The **Porter-Phelps-Huntington House** (1742) hidden away on the river (MA 47, north from MA 9) is a jewel.

Holyoke (holyoke.org). In 1847 Boston investors formed the Hadley Falls Company, buying 1,000 acres with the idea of utilizing the water power from the magnificent falls here. The company—and its dam—went bust, but were soon replaced by the Holyoke Water Power Company, until recently the city's major political and economic force. Holyoke is a classic planned mill city. Its 4.5 miles of canals flow in tiers past dozens of mills; the commercial area is set in a neat grid above the mills. Housing changes with the altitude—from 1840s brick workers' housing on "The Flats" near the river, through hundreds of hastily built late-19th- and early-20th-century tenements, to the mill owners' mansions above, and above that the parkland on Mount Tom. In the visitors center at **Holyoke Heritage State Park,** a film conveys a sense of the city's late-19th-century vitality, of the era in which immigrants turned neighborhoods into "Little" Ireland, Poland, France, and half a dozen more ethnic bastions. If the film were remade today, it would note the last two decades' influx of Puerto Ricans, a group first drawn to work in the nearby tobacco fields in the 1960s. Specialty papers, from college bluebooks to hospital johnnies, remain Holyoke's most notable product, but its mills incubate artistic, high-tech, and a variety of fledgling endeavors. Inquire about guided and leaflet walking tours and frequent special events. Mill

A MURAL DEPICTS NORTHAMPTON'S RICH HISTORY.

Christina Tree

architecture buffs will appreciate the beauty of the canalside Graham Mill (Second Level Canal near the MA 116 bridge).

✷ Must See

Smith College Museum of Art (413-585-2760; smith.edu/artmuseum), Elm St. (MA 9, just beyond College Hall), Northampton. Open Tues.–Sat. 10–4, Sun. noon–4. On the second Friday of each month it's open until 8 (free after 4) for Northampton's Arts Night Out. Adults $5; less for students, seniors, children. This world-class art collection is second in Western Massachusetts only to the Clark Art Institute in Williamstown. The third-floor, naturally lit gallery is hung with works by Picasso, Degas, Winslow Homer, Rockwell Kent, Marsden Hartley, Seurat, and Whistler, and sculpture by Rodin and Leonard Baskin. American primitives and impressionists, such as the starkly realistic oils by Edwin Romanzo Elmer evoking 19th-century scenes from the nearby Hilltowns, also are displayed. From its 1870s beginnings, the college's art collecting focused on "contemporary American art," and by the 1920s included European "modern art." Curator Jere Abbott, who had served on the founding staff of New York's Museum of Modern Art, was instrumental in acquiring works like Picasso's cubist piece, *La Table.* The museum's second floor houses its European collection and a remarkable print room; the first floor is devoted to special exhibits and includes a gift store and what are undoubtedly the most artistic restrooms in any museum.

MAN WALKING BY VINCENT VAN GOGH, PART OF THE SMITH COLLEGE MUSEUM OF ART COLLECTION.

Smith College Museum of Art

The Emily Dickinson Museum: The Homestead and The Evergreens (413-542-8161; emilydickinsonmuseum.org), 280 Main St., Amherst. Open Mar.–Dec., Wed.–Sun. 11–4; June–Aug. 28, Wed.–Sun. 10–5. Call to reserve a place. Two tours are offered: "Emily Dickinson's World," an in-depth tour of the Homestead and The Evergreens (adults $10, seniors and students $9, ages 6–18 $5); and "This Was a Poet," an introduction to Dickinson and her poetry (adults $8, seniors and students $7). Be sure to see "Voice of the Valley," (page 298).

Christina Tree

AN EXHIBIT AT THE AMHERST COLLEGE MUSEUM OF NATURAL HISTORY.

Amherst College Museum of Natural History (413-542-2165; amherst.edu/museumofnatural history). Open Tues.–Sun. 11–4 (from noon in summer), Thurs. 6–10. This is one of the country's outstanding collections of paleontology (dinosaurs), minerals and other geological specimens, and anthropological material. While the mammoth dinosaur skeletons aren't themselves native to the Valley, the fact that Amherst scholars were collecting them from the ends of the earth in the 19th century is directly related to Amherst College geologist Edward Hitchcock's identification of a local dinosaur track in 1836. Hitchcock's famous collection of 21,000 dinosaur tracks (on 1,200 slabs) is beautifully displayed. The story of the evolution of the Valley over the past 200 million years is dramatized in numerous fascinating exhibits. Free.

The Eric Carle Museum of Picture Book Art (413-658-1100; carle museum.org.), 125 W. Bay Rd. (off MA 116), Amherst. Open Tues.–Fri. 10–4, Sat. 10–5, Sun. noon–5. Adults $9, children and students $6, $22.50 for family of four. Opened in 2003 adjacent to the Hampshire College campus, this independently funded museum showcases the work of

A CAT AND A GIRL FROM ERIC CARLE'S FAMOUS *HEAD TO TOE*.

© 1997 Eric Carle

VOICE OF THE VALLEY: EMILY DICKINSON

Emily Dickinson (1830–86) was born in the staid, 1813 Dickinson Homestead not far from Amherst College. After attending Mount Holyoke Female Seminary for one year, she returned to her father's house, rarely leaving between 1855 and 1886, consumed with writing her honest puzzlings on the grand themes of love and nature, God and death, ragged-edged lines like:

"Hope" is the thing with feathers,
That perches in the soul,
And sings the tune without the words
And never stops—at all.

One of the most phenomenal aspects of Dickinson's story is that only 10 of these poems were published during her lifetime. The poet's work did not achieve widespread fame until well after her death.

The quality of the tour at the Emily Dickinson Museum is excellent. Dickinson's own room in the Homestead looks much as she knew it. The house itself was sold out of the family in 1916, but by 1965, when Dickinson's work was known worldwide, the house was purchased by Amherst College and opened to the public.

Though changes were made to the house, the small world in which Dickinson moved so intensely has been uncannily well preserved. The garden she tended remains a pleasant place to sit, and a path still leads next door to The Evergreens, an Italianate villa built in 1856 on the occasion of her brother Austin's marriage.

Emily and Austin's wife, Susan, were close friends, and Emily was a frequent visitor and present at social events with intimate friends and family. She was very much a part of this family, attached to their children, first a son and daughter and then, 10 years later, another little boy. When "Gib," the much-loved third child, died from typhoid fever, Emily grieved so deeply that she is said to have never fully recovered; she died herself two years later. Austin began an affair that is still the talk of the town, and many of his meetings with Mabel Loomis Todd, the lively wife of an Amherst College professor (she also founded the Amherst History Museum), were at the Dickinson Homestead, where Austin's two sisters, Emily and Lavinia, still lived.

A DAGUERREOTYPE PORTRAIT OF EMILY DICKINSON.

Amherst College and Special Collections

After Emily's death, Lavinia first approached her sister-in-law, Susan, to edit Emily's poetry, but Lavinia later turned to Mabel Todd.

Christina Tree

THE EVERGREENS, NEXT DOOR TO THE DICKINSON HOMESTEAD.

Austin Dickinson died in 1895, and subsequent bitterness between the Todd and Dickinson families clouded publication of Dickinson's poetry for many decades after her death as competing versions of her verses appeared.

After Susan Dickinson died in 1913, her daughter, Martha Dickinson Bianchi, dedicated herself to publishing the Emily Dickinson poems she had inherited from her mother, and to writing about her memories of her Aunt Emily. After the Homestead was sold out of the family in 1916, Bianchi began to establish The Evergreens as a destination for admirers of the poet's work, and she set up a room with her aunt's belongings that people could visit. Although some of these artifacts were subsequently transferred to the Houghton Library at Harvard University, The Evergreens retains its own original furnishings and interiors as well the feel of the house that Emily Dickinson knew so well. The quality of this experience is due in large part to Bianchi's heirs and to the work of the Martha Dickinson Bianchi Trust, established in 1988 to ensure the preservation of the house.

The Homestead and The Evergreens recently joined forces as the **Emily Dickinson Museum** (see *Must See*). Both houses are now owned by Amherst College. The Dickinson Homestead—with its formal displays about Emily Dickinson and her second-floor bedroom—and the magic of The Evergreens next door complement each other nicely.

For more about Emily Dickinson, visit the Special Collections rooms upstairs in the nearby Jones Library. Here panels depict the poet's life in Amherst. Several of her handwritten poems are among the collection of 8,000 items related to the history of Amherst.

Dickinson buffs might want to continue on to **West Cemetery** on Triangle Street. It's not difficult to find the Dickinson family plot, which is bounded by an ornate black iron fence. Here Emily lies surrounded by her grandparents, parents, and sister. Note that on the Saturday nearest May 15 (the anniversary of her death), visitors are invited to meet at the Emily Dickinson Museum and walk to the cemetery. The museum offers other special events throughout the year. Also note the profile sculptures of Dickinson and Robert Frost in the small neighboring park across from the puzzlingly grandiose Amherst Police Station (site of an apartment in which Frost wrote "Fire and Ice").

world-acclaimed illustrators and is aimed at "children of all ages." Local artist Eric Carle, author of *The Very Hungry Caterpillar* among many other books, contributed a founding gift and is often but not necessarily always represented in the frequently changing exhibits—which are hung at child's-eye level. Facilities include a library of children's books, a hands-on painting room, a family-friendly café, and a big museum store.

MORE ART MUSEUMS **Mead Art Museum** (413-542-2335; amherst.edu/mead), on the campus of Amherst College, Amherst. Open Tues.–Sun. 9–5 during summer and academic recess, until midnight Tues.–Thurs. and Sun. during the academic year. Free. The building, designed by McKim, Mead & Whitte, has been totally revamped within the past few years. The well-rounded permanent collection includes paintings by Thomas Eakins, Winslow Homer, Marsden Hartley, and Childe Hassam. The stunning *Salome* by Robert Henri and *Morning on the Seine* by Claude Monet are usually on display; special exhibits are frequently contemporary and provocative. Totally unexpected is the Rotherwas Room, an ornately paneled, vintage-1611 English hall, a setting for furniture, portraits, and silver.

Mount Holyoke College Art Museum (413-538-2245; mtholyoke.edu/go/art museum), Lower Lake Rd., South Hadley. Open Tues.–Fri. 11–5, weekends 1–5. Free. One of the oldest collegiate art collections in the country, but housed in a modern building with 10 spacious galleries. Permanent holdings number 14,000 objects ranging from ancient Asian and Egyptian works and Pompeiian frescoes, through Roman and medieval statuary, to some outstanding 19th-century landscapes by Albert Bierstadt and George Inness. Also, works by William Glackens, Robert Henri, and Milton Avery. Special exhibits.

Note: Art lovers should also visit Northampton's major art galleries (see *Selective Shopping*), which represent current artists whose works hang in many of the world's major museums.

A CHILD ADMIRES *FAUSTINA*, A SCULPTURE OF EMPRESS FAUSTINA THE ELDER AT THE MOUNT HOLYOKE COLLEGE ART MUSEUM.

Mount Holyoke College Art Museum

✷ Also See

HISTORIC HOUSES AND MUSEUMS **The Amherst Historical Society and Museum** (413-256-0678; amhersthistory.org), 67 Amity St., Amherst. Open mid-May through Oct. or by appointment; check for current hours. Small admission. This circa-1750 gambrel-roofed house largely reflects several periods, including one in which it was a home and a "Young Ladies School." In addition to period rooms there are pictures and products (like palm-leaf hats) of Amherst past, along with changing exhibits. The garden is 18th century. In 1899 it was the Amherst Historical Society's colorful founder, Mabel Loomis Todd, who secured this property. A room dedicated to her includes her paintings and souvenirs from world travels. Todd was Austin Dickinson's mistress and was responsible for editing and publishing early volumes of Emily Dickinson's poetry (see *Voice of the Valley*). Inquire about special events.

Porter-Phelps-Huntington House Museum (413-584-4699; pphmuseum.org), 130 River Dr. (MA 47, 2 miles north of the junction of MA 9 and MA 47), Hadley. Open May 15–Oct. 15 for hour-long guided tours, Sat.–Wed. 1–4:30. $5 per adult, $1 per child. "Wednesday Folk Traditions" (ethnic folk music) at 6:30 in June, July, and August are staged in the garden, weather permitting (adults $10, children $2; picnickers welcome before concerts). "A Perfect Spot of Tea" (pastries and music) at 2:30 and 3:30 Saturdays in July and August; $10. Also known as Forty Acres, this aristocratic old farm was built near the banks of the Connecticut River in 1752, and there have been no structural changes since 1799. The furnishings have accumulated over six generations of one extended family.

The Hadley Farm Museum (413-586-1160; hadleyfarmmuseum.org), MA 9 and MA 47, Hadley. Open May 15–Oct., Fri.–Sat. 11–4, Sun. 1–4. Adults $5, seniors $3, children under 12 $1; families negotiable. The 1782 barn from Forty Acres (see above) was moved to its current site near the First Congregational Church and white-pillared town hall in 1930. It houses old broom-making machines (broom corn was once the town's chief crop) and other old farm implements, pottery, an old stagecoach from Hardwick, and other assorted mementos of life in the Valley.

THE PORTER-PHELPS-HUNTINGTON HOUSE MUSEUM IN HADLEY.

Christina Tree

In Holyoke

Wistariahurst Museum (413-332-5660; wistariahurst.org), 238 Cabot St. Open Sat.–Mon. noon–4. Nominal admission. Check for frequent lectures, workshops, children's programs, concerts, and exhibits. An opulent 19th-century, 26-room mansion with leather wall coverings, elaborate woodwork, and etched glass, the home was built for the Skinner family, owners of the world's largest silk mill. It evokes the expansive spirit of Belle Skinner, the socialite who added a

Christina Tree

THE HADLEY FARM MUSEUM

marble lobby, grand staircase, and great hall. Inquire about changing exhibits, concerts, and other events. The 3 acres of landscaped grounds include dinosaur footprints and fossil marks. Check the website for a lively program of art exhibits, concerts, and lectures. This is also a popular venue for weddings.

Holyoke Heritage State Park (413-534-1723), 221 Appleton St. (follow the signs for downtown). Open Tues.–Sun. 10–4. Free. A short film conveys a sense of the city's late-19th-century vitality (see Holyoke under *Villages, Towns, and Cities*). Inquire about guided tours; also see *For Families* for more about the merry-go-round, Children's Museum at Holyoke, and Volleyball Hall of Fame here.

In Northampton

Historic Northampton (413-584-6011; historic-northampton.org), 46 Bridge St. (MA 9 between I-91 and downtown). Open year-round, Tues.–Fri. 10–5; Sat.–Sun. noon–5. $3 per individual, $6 per family. There is also a gift shop. This is a major research facility as well as a fascinating museum with a permanent exhibit dramatizing the city's many-layered history. Display topics range from extensive Indian artifacts to Jonathan Edwards, industrial products to the Coolidge years. There are also changing special exhibits. Three historic houses reflecting lifestyles over three generations—the **Parsons House** (1719), the **Damon House** (1813, home of architect Isaac Damon), and the **Shepherd House** (1796)—are on their original sites, set in landscaped grounds. Inquire about special programs and events.

Calvin Coolidge Presidential Library and Museum at the Forbes Library (413-587-1014 or 413-587-1012; forbeslibrary.org), 20 West St. Open Mon. and Wed. 3–9, Tues. and Thurs. 1–5, Sat. by appointment. The only presidential library in a public library, this recently renovated area contains all of Calvin Coolidge's papers from his years as governor, vice president, and president. The Amherst College graduate (1895) studied law and first hung out his shingle in Northampton. He became city solicitor, met his wife (Grace Goodhue was teaching at the Clarke School for the Deaf in Northampton when she met fellow Vermonter Cal), was elected a state representative, and then served two terms as mayor of Northampton. He became state senator, then governor, then vice president, and, when Warren G. Harding died suddenly on August 3, 1923, president for six years. The Coolidges had remained Northampton residents, and they returned to their Northampton house from Washington; Calvin died here in 1933. Personal belongings on display range from a replica of Coolidge's Northampton office, fitted with all its original furnishings, to an elaborate headdress presented by the Sioux nation, to an electric horse.

In South Hadley

Skinner Museum (413-538-2085), MA 116. Open mid-May through Oct., Wed. and Sun. 2–5. Housed in the 1821 First Congregational Church that once stood in the town of Prescott (flooded by Quabbin Reservoir), this is a classic "cabinet of curiosities," some 4,000 items collected by Joseph Allen Skinner (1862–1946). The Skinner family owned major silk mills in Holyoke (see **Wistariahurst Museum,** above) and built The Orchards, a summer "cottage" across MA 116. Skinner's wealth permitted him to indulge his passion for collecting, which he did in his own world travels as well as those of his friends. To preserve it all, he acquired the once famous resort atop Mount Holyoke in 1916, and in 1930 he rescued this church and its surrounding buildings (a school and carriage house) with the idea of creating his own small museum village. Exhibits in the basement re-create a colonial hearth and early crafts, but the real wonder of this place is the eclectic mix of the collection, much of it displayed in high, old-fashioned glass cabinets—with and without labels: shells and fossils, scrimshaw, glass and china, here a huge old key to the Northampton jail, there two medieval sets of armor (one real and one fake—see if you can guess which is which).

MORE TO SEE **The Jones Library** (413-256-4090), 43 Amity St., Amherst. Open Mon.–Sat. 9–8:30, Tues. and Thurs. until 9:30. The Special Collections rooms with exhibits on Emily Dickinson and Robert Frost are open Mon. 1–5, Tues.–Fri. 10–5, Sat. 2–5, but call to check.

Yiddish Book Center (413-256-4900; yiddishbookcenter.org), 1021 West St., Amherst, off MA 116 adjacent to the Hampshire College campus. Visitor center open Sun.–Fri. 10–3:30; closed Shabbat and Jewish and legal holidays. This handsome wooden complex of work, exhibition, and performance spaces is designed to resemble an Eastern European *shtetl.* Credit for the very idea of rescuing Yiddish literature (roughly a century's worth of works in the Yiddish language, beginning in the 1860s) goes to the cultural center's director, Hampshire College graduate Aaron Lansky. This is a clearinghouse for books of a genre presumed almost dead when the center was founded in 1980; at the opening of the current facility in 1997 it had collected 1.3 million works, with an average 1,000 arriving weekly. Volumes are distributed to shops and libraries throughout the world. Exhibits change, but the quality of the artwork on display alone would have been worth our trip; also inquire about frequent lectures and performances.

FOR FAMILIES ✐ **Dinosaurs.** The Pioneer Valley is a treasure-trove of dinosaur prints, said to range in age from 65,000 to 200,000 years old. The Valley's dramatic topographic and climatic history is told in the **Amherst College Museum of Natural History** (see *Must See*), the **Springfield Science Museum** (Springfield Area Chapter), and **Nash Dinosaur Track Site and Rock Shop** (413-467-9566; nashdinosaurtracks.com), off MA 116 north of the village of South Hadley. Open Mon.–Sat. 10–4, Sun. noon–4. The sign on Dino Land's door at the Nash facility reads PLEASE SOUND HORN. That fetches Kornell Nash from his house to this shop, which has been in the Nash family for more than 60 years. Billed as "the world's largest dinosaur footprint quarry," Dino Land is the source of more than 3,000 dinosaur tracks sold ($50–1,000 apiece) over the years, clearly embedded in shale. Admission: adults $2.50, children $1.50. **Trustees of Reservations** (thetrustees.org) maintains a property studded with dinosaur footprints across the river north of Holyoke. On US 5 near Mount Tom, Holyoke, look for a well-marked turnout on the river side of the road. A path leads down to smooth rocks in which you can look for three-toed tracks, each 15 inches long and belonging to a 20-foot-long dinosaur (*Eubrontes giganteus*) that lumbered by 200 million years ago. Smaller tracks and other fossils have also been preserved. Also note the dinosaur footprints in the garden at Wistariahurst Museum in Holyoke.

✐ **Merry-Go-Round** (413-538-9838; holyokemerrygoround.org) at the Holyoke Heritage State Park Visitor Center. Open Sept.–June, weekends noon–4; July–Aug., Tues.–Sun. 10:30–4 and Sun. noon–4.This vintage-1929 carousel with 48 hand-carved steeds, two chariots, and 800 lights was built for Mountain Park, an old-fashioned amusement park that closed in 1987. It was restored and moved to this handsome pavilion at a total cost of $2 million. Rides are $1 (or six for $5); there's popcorn and a snack bar. Also available for private parties.

NASH DINOUSAUR TRACK SITE AND ROCK SHOP BILLS ITSELF AS "THE WORLD'S LARGEST DINOSAUR FOOTPRINT QUARRY."
Christina Tree

✐ **Children's Museum at Holyoke** (413-536-KIDS; childrensmuseumholyoke.org), 444 Dwight St. (across from the Heritage State Park Visitor Center), Holyoke. Open Wed.–Sat. 10–4, Sun. noon–4. Hours vary. Adults and children $6, seniors $3, children under 1 year free. A stimulating space with a Main Street that simulates downtown Holyoke's shops and enterprises. Also, a kids' TV studio and "body of water" exhibit.

✐ **Robert Barrett Fishway,** Holyoke Dam, Holyoke, just off MA 116 at the

Christina Tree

THE MERRY-GO-ROUND AT HOLYOKE HERITAGE STATE PARK.

South Hadley Falls Bridge. Open May and June only. For details contact Northfield Mountain (1-800-859-2960). Viewing windows and an observation platform overlook American shad and Atlantic salmon as elevators help them bypass the falls on their trip upriver to spawn.

✐ **Volleyball Hall of Fame** (413-536-0926; volleyhall.org), 444 Dwight St., Holyoke. Housed in the Children's Museum at Holyoke complex (see above). Open Thurs.–Sun. noon–4:30. Volleyball, invented in Holyoke in 1895, is commemorated here in a series of interpretive panels, an interactive video presentation, and a model half-court.

✐ **McCray's Farm** (413-533-3714; mccrays-farm.com), 55 Alvord St., South Hadley. Open daily except Nov. and Mar., with a seasonal dairy selling homemade ice cream, a petting zoo, mini golf, wagon rides, and (in-season) PYO pumpkins.

✐ **Flayvors of Cook Farm** (413-584-2224; cookfarm.com), 129 S. Maple St., Hadley. Open weekdays 8–7, weekends 10–8. Great ice cream (see *Snacks*) made from the cows in residence.

✐ **Look Memorial Park** (413-584-5457; lookpark.org), 300 N. Main St. (MA 9), Florence. Open weekends Apr., May, Sept.–Columbus Day (check hours); Memorial Day–Labor Day, Sat.–Sun. 10–6. The many attractions of this 150-acre park include swimming and wading pools; pedal boating and canoeing on Willow Lake; bumper boats around "the lagoon"; a playground; the small **Christenson Zoo** with native deer, peacocks, pheasants, and raccoons; the **Pines Outdoor Theater** (summer concerts and children's entertainment); and a miniature replica of an 1863 train that circles the zoo. Also, fishing in the Mill

Christina Tree

PATRONS AT FLAYVORS OF COOK FARM THANK THE COWS THAT MADE THE MILK THAT MADE THEIR ICE CREAM.

River (perch and small trout), an 18-hole miniature golf course, six all-weather tennis courts, a Picnic Store where you can rent horseshoes, volleyballs, and other sports equipment, and plenty of places to picnic. Admission is free on foot or bike, but cars are $4 on weekends, $3 midweek, and there are charges for rides and rentals—though not for the zoo.

✐ **Western Massachusetts Family Golf Center** (413-586-2311; wmassfamily golf.com), 294 Russsell St. (MA 9), Hadley. Open daily in-season, but check hours. Facilities include an 18-hole mini golf course, open field batting range, pedal cars, and ice cream parlor.

THE COLLEGES For an overview and current programs, see fivecolleges.edu.

Amherst College (413-542-2000; amherst.edu), Amherst. Founded in 1821 to educate "promising but needy youths who wished to enter the ministry," Amherst is today one of the country's most selective liberal arts colleges, with 1,700 students. The campus is handsome and nicely sited, its oldest buildings grouped around a common overlooking the Valley to the south and the Holyoke Range beyond. The Mead Art Museum is well worth a look.

Hampshire College (413-549-4600; hampshirecollege.edu), 893 West St. (MA 116), Amherst. Opened in 1970, this liberal arts college is predicated on cooperative programming with the other four colleges. Its 1,400 students design their own programs of study. Inquire about current exhibits at the College Art Gallery in the Johnson Library Center and events at the Performing Arts Center. A "cultural village" has evolved in the former apple orchard adjacent to the campus. To date it includes the Yiddish Book Center and The Eric Carle Museum of Picture Book Art.

Mount Holyoke College (413-538-2000; mtholyoke.edu), MA 116, South Hadley. Founded in 1837, Mount Holyoke is the country's oldest women's college. The 800-acre campus, with its Upper and Lower Ponds and ivied buildings in a number of Revival styles, is home to some 2,200 women drawn from throughout the country and the world. The adjacent Village Commons, a complex of restaurants, shops, and a theater, was designed by Graham Gund. Spend some time in the Talcott Arboretum (413-538-2116), open weekdays 9–4, weekends 1–4. This exquisite little Victorian-style greenhouse is filled with a jungle of exotic flora and features special late-winter and spring flower shows. *Note:* Prospective students, parents, and others with an MHC affiliation are welcome to stay at the attractive, on-campus Willits-Hallowell Center (413-538-2217). Be sure to see the Mount Holyoke College Art Museum, marked from the South Hadley common.

Smith College (413-584-2700; smith.edu), Northampton. Founded in 1875 for "the education of the intelligent gentlewoman," the 125-acre campus for 2,600 students now includes 97 buildings of an eclectic mix of ages and styles. Don't miss Paradise Pond. The newly renovated Lyman Plant House (413-585-2740), open daily 8:30–4, is known for its spring and fall flower shows; adjacent are an arboretum and gardens. Definitely don't miss the Smith College Museum of Art.

University of Massachusetts (413-545-0111; umass.edu), Amherst. Founded in the mid-19th century as the state's agricultural college, "UMass" now includes 10 undergraduate schools and colleges as well as graduate schools in more than

THE GATES OF MOUNT HOLYOKE COLLEGE IN SOUTH HADLEY.

Christina Tree

150 buildings on a 1,200-acre campus. Some 5,500 courses are offered by 1,000 faculty members to 22,000 undergraduates and 6,000 graduate students. Sights to see at UMass include the Fine Arts Center and Gallery (413-545-3670) with its changing exhibits. Also, the William Smith Clark Memorial, a 0.5-acre memorial at the eastern entrance to the campus (off N. Pleasant St.) dedicated to the first president of the university and his work in Japan, where he founded Sapporo Agricultural College, now Hokkaido University. The unusual memorial encompasses two circles linked by a spiral walk and twin steel walls depicting Clark's Amherst home and the Agricultural Hall at Hokkaido. Clark is widely revered in Japan, and many youth clubs are still dedicated to his memory. The memorial garden is sited on a hill with views extending across the campus to the river and hills. The Durfee Gardens and Durfee Conservatory (413-545-5234), open weekdays 8:30–4:30, are also worth a visit. The conservatory dates from 1867 and houses tropical plants such as banana, coffee, and papaya divided by a 40-foot pool with an ornamental bridge and fountain. Five interlocking garden spaces offer benches, paths, and trellised wisteria and morning glories.

SCENIC DRIVES **MA 47, South Hadley to Hadley.** This beautiful road runs along the Connecticut River and through its floodplain, below Mount Holyoke. Be sure to turn in and follow the road through Skinner State Park to the summit.

MA 47, Hadley to Sunderland. The 9 miles from MA 9 in Hadley to the village of Sunderland shadow the river, passing through cultivated fields spotted with distinctive long tobacco sheds and some of the best farm stands in the Valley.

Bay Road. For a quick sense of the beautiful farm country still surviving in Hadley at the heart of the Valley, cut across Bay Road from MA 47 to MA 116. It runs along the southern foot of the Holyoke Range.

Also see *Views*.

✷ To Do

BICYCLING Given the number of young and young-in-spirit residents of this Valley, combined with relatively level, quiet, unusually scenic rural roads, it's not surprising that bicycle touring is big here. More than 30 miles of contiguous bike paths include the **Norwottuck Rail Trail,** a bike path linking Northampton, Hadley, and Amherst along the former Boston & Maine Railroad right-of-way, and the **Northampton Bikeway** (fntg.net), running west to Look Park. A good access option is the bike path entrance behind Stop & Shop on King Street. It's a great ride to do with kids; bring a picnic and explore Look Park (see *For Families*). Free bikes can be borrowed from **Pedal to Properties** (413-584-1885), 14 Strong Ave., Northampton. See also **Laughing Dog Bicycles** (413-253-7722), 63 S. Pleasant St., Amherst (closed Sun.). Other access points to the rail-trail are at Mountain Farms Mall on MA 9 in Hadley and at **Elwell Recreation Area** on Damon Road, just north of the MA 9 bridge in Northampton. The trail crosses the Connecticut on an old rail bridge and passes through open farmland, with views to the Holyoke Range to the south and Mount Toby and Mount Sugarloaf to the north. **Northampton Bikeway** runs from State Street west 2.6 miles to Look Park. It's a great ride to do with kids; bring a picnic and explore Look Park (see *For Families*). *Note:* The bikeway begins in a residential neighborhood without parking. Your best access option is the bike path entrance behind Stop & Shop on King Street. The **Manhan Rail Trail** (manhanrailtrail.org) connects Northampton with Easthampton to the south, with the best access from Flaherty Park on Ferry Street it Easthampton. The scenic drives outlined in this book lend themselves to bike touring, but there are many more loops. Inquire at local bike shops. For mountain biking trails, see **Northfield Mountain** in "Deerfield/Greenfield Area."

BIRDING **Arcadia Wildlife Sanctuary in Easthampton** (see *Hiking and Walking*) is the area's most obvious birding center, but there are others.

Hawk-watching. The Valley represents a major migratory flyway and is known especially for its many soaring hawks in fall. In September prime watching spots include Goat Peak on Mount Tom and Prospect House on Mount Holyoke.

The Hitchcock Center for the Environment (see *Hiking and Walking*) offers some birding workshops and is the base for the Hampshire Bird Club. An excellent guide, *Birding Western Massachusetts: The Central Connecticut River Valley,* edited by Peter Westover for the Kestrel Trust and Hampshire Bird Club, is available in local bookstores. *Birding in Massachusetts* by Robert Tougias (New England Cartographics) describes 26 prime birding sites. Check out **Backyard Birds** (413-586-3155), 15 Strong Ave., Northampton, the store for the Valley's birdwatchers.

BOATING ♿ **Elwell** Recreation **Area,** just north of MA 9 at the Northampton end of the Coolidge Bridge, is a handicapped-accessible state-of-the-art boat dock.

For river information, the **Connecticut River Watershed Council** (413-529-9500; ctriver.org), publishes a canoe guide to the entire river and offers periodic guided canoe trips. **The Great Falls Discovery Center** (413-863-3221; greatfallsma.org), 2 Avenue A, Turners Falls, is also a source of river information. At **Barton Cove** (413-863-9300 or 1-800-859-2960), Northfield Mountain maintains tent sites, rents canoes and rowboats, and offers shuttle service to put-in places in Northfield. See "Deerfield/Greenfield Area."

BOAT RENTALS **Sportsman's Marina** (413-586-2426), 1 Russell St. (MA 9 at the Coolidge Bridge), Hadley, rents boats Apr.–Oct. (weather permitting): canoes, aluminum outboards, and pontoon boats. Bring a picnic and head for an island. **Brunelle's Marina** (413-536-3132; brunelles.com) in South Hadley has a restaurant and launch area. There is also a state access ramp almost 1.5 miles north of Hatfield Center, and another off US 5 at the Oxbow in Easthampton. The 16-mile stretch of the Connecticut River above the Holyoke Dam is heavily used on summer weekends by water-skiers, fishermen, and powerboat owners as well as canoeists. **Oxbow Marina** (413-584-2775; oxbow-marina.com), Island Road off US 5 south of I-91 in Northampton, is the largest marina in the area, offering a boat launch, sales, a picnic area, and a beach.

Christina Tree

TAKING A BREAK AT BRUNELLE'S MARINA IN SOUTH HADLEY.

BOAT EXCURSIONS ***Lady Bea*** (413-315-6342; brunelles.com), an excursion boat based at Brunelle's Landing in South Hadley, offers seasonal 75-minute narrated tours up and down the Connecticut River daily at 1, 4, and 7 (weather permitting); inquire about special evening cruises. See also ***Quinnektikut II*** in "Deerfield/Greenfield Area."

CANOEING AND KAYAKING **Arcadia Nature Center and Wildlife Sanctuary** (see *Hiking and Walking*), 127 Combs Rd., marked from US 5, Easthampton, but on the Northampton–Easthampton line in Northampton. This Massachusetts Audubon sanctuary is a great place for novice canoeists to explore quiet waters. Inquire about guided canoe trips.

THE *LADY BEA*

Christina Tree

♿ The **Connecticut River Greenway State Park** (see "Deerfield/Greenfield Area") includes a 12-mile Connecticut River Water Trail that runs from the Turners Falls Dam in Montague to the Hatfield state boat ramp. The water along this trail is too shallow for powerboating, so the area is limited to small boats and canoes and to low-impact recreation. A detailed brochure guide to the trail is available from the Department of Conservation and Recreation (413-586-8706), 136 Damon Rd. near the **Elwell Recreation Area** (access for paddlers only) on the river in Northampton.

Fitzgerald Lake off North Farms Rd. (in Florence, turn off MA 9 onto Maple), Northampton. An oasis of quiet roughly 1 mile long and 0.25 mile wide; look for a wooden dock about 100 yards off North Farms Road.

Puffers Pond, North Amherst (see *Swimming*). No powerboats allowed.

FISHING For licensing, see "What's Where."

Quabbin Reservoir is open for fishing mid-Apr.–mid-Oct., 6 am to one hour before sunset. To rent a boat you must be 16 years or older and have a Massachusetts fishing license; licenses and bait are available from such local shops as Bill and Kathy Martell's **Gate 8 Boat & Bait Co.** (413-323-7117) in Pelham. Much of the reservoir is off-limits, but Gate 8 (US 202 in Pelham) accesses cold salmon- and trout-filled water. For detailed information, contact the **Quabbin Visitor Center** (413-323-7221). The **Charles L. McGlaughlin Trout Hatchery** (413-323-7671) in Belchertown (open daily 9–3:45) adjoins the Swift River Wildlife Management Area, which offers good fishing in the Swift River as well as fields and woodlands webbed with trails.

The Connecticut River

Dave's Pioneer Sporting Center (413-584-9944), 137E Damon Rd. (next door to the Department of Conservation and Recreation offices), Northampton, is a source of advice as well as equipment. During migrating shad and salmon season in mid-June, the **Robert E. Barrett Fishway** at the Holyoke Dam, just off MA 116 at the South Hadley Falls Bridge, is staffed by naturalists from Northfield Mountain (1-800-859-2960); viewing windows and an observation platform overlook the two elevators that hoist more than a million migrating fish over the falls.

GOLF **Hickory Ridge Country Club** (413-253-7094; hickoryridgecc.com), 191 W. Pomeroy Lane, Amherst, is an 18-hole championship course with a clubhouse and snack bar/restaurant. **Pine Grove Golf Course** (413-584-4570), 254 Wilson Rd., Northampton, has 18 holes. Town-owned **Ledges Golf Course** (413-532-2307; ledgesgc.com), 18 Mulligan Dr., South Hadley, is handicapped accessible, with 18 holes, a pro shop, and restaurant. **Beaver Brook Golf Club** (413-568-1636), 183 Main St. (MA 9), Haydenville, offers nine holes. **Orchards Golf Club** (413-533-4653; orchardsgolf.com), 18 Silverwood Terrace in South Hadley, is a private 18-hole course.

HIKING AND WALKING

In Amherst and Pelham

The Amherst Conservation Department (413-256-4045) maintains some 1,450 acres scattered in 45 distinct holdings, with 60 miles of trails for walking, birding, and ski touring. It's worth stopping by the town hall or local bookstore to pick up printed maps or guides.

♿ The most popular (and most heavily used) areas include **Upper Mill River** and **Puffers Pond,** State Street off Pine in North Amherst, both good for swimming and picnicking. Trails—including one designed for handicapped access and blind walkers—lead upstream from the pond along the Cushman Brook cascades.

Hitchcock Center for the Environment (413-256-6006; hitchcockcenter.org), at the Larch Hill Conservation Area, 1 mile south of Amherst Center on MA 116. The 25 acres include hiking trails, formal gardens, and ponds. The center offers a variety of lectures and workshops; it also exhibits local artwork.

Mount Pollux, Amherst, is a favorite spot from which to watch the sunset—a gentle slope to climb through old apple orchards to a summit with a 365-degree view. The entrance is just off South East Street in South Amherst (turn left heading south). It's a very small sign and then a short way to the parking area, plus a brief walk to the top of a hill with the memorable view.

Amethyst Brook Conservation Area, Pelham Rd., Pelham, is a great spot to walk or ski through woods and fields.

Buffum Falls, Amherst Rd., Pelham. Heading east, turn left onto North Valley Road (almost a mile west of Amethyst Brook); look for a parking area on your left. Not particularly well marked, but well used and an unusually beautiful spot. A one-hour hike.

Between Amherst and South Hadley

Holyoke Range State Park (413-253-2883), MA 116. Trail maps are available at the Notch Visitor Center (staffed and with restrooms), which is open daily 9–4 except Tues. and Wed. in winter. Inquire about guided hikes. This dramatic east–west range rises from the Valley's floor. It is the most striking feature of the area, visible everywhere from Belchertown to Northampton. Mount Holyoke at its western tip (see **Skinner State Park** under *Views*) is the only summit accessible by road, but a trail traverses the entire 9-mile-long ridgeline. From the visitor center, a trail leads east to Mount Norwottuck (connecting with trails to Mount Toby in Sunderland and Mount Monadnock in New Hampshire). Ask about the Horse Caves below Mount Norwottuck in which Daniel Shays and his men supposedly sheltered after raiding the Springfield Armory (the caves are actually so shallow that two Boy Scouts and a pony would have trouble fitting in).

In Northampton

Fitzgerald Lake, in the Broad Brook Conservation Area, North Farms Rd. A 550-acre, town-owned preserve with 5 miles of well-marked trails, including a self-guided nature trail geared to kids. Much of the trail is right along the lake under tall pines. Allow two hours. Maps are at the trailhead. No restrooms. From MA 9 in Florence, take Maple Street, which turns into North Farms Road.

🐾 **Northampton Dog Park,** Burts Pit Rd. The 7-acre grounds of a former state mental hospital (*Cider House Rules* was filmed here) now offers a circular loop through fields and woods, the one off-the-leash area in town.

In Easthampton

♿ **Arcadia Wildlife Sanctuary** (413-584-3009; massaudubon.org), 127 Combs Rd., on the Northampton–Easthampton line. Trails and restrooms open Tues.–Sun. and Mon. holidays, dawn to dusk. Nature Center open Mon.–Fri. 1–3, closed holidays. Adults $4, children and seniors $3. Five miles of trail meander through meadows, marsh, and wetlands. Inquire about the many programs, including canoe trips.

Also see *Green Space.*

SWIMMING In Amherst the swimming hole is **Puffers Pond** (413-256-4045), off Pine St. in North Amherst. Open June–Sept., dawn to dusk. It's a beauty, with a small beach and wooded area; no lifeguards.

Carroll A. Holmes Recreation Area (413-367-0317) in Shutesbury, better known as **Lake Wyola,** is a sandy public beach with changing rooms on a wooded lake, maintained by the Department of Conservation and Recreation ($5 parking fee).

Musante Beach (413-587-1040), off Reservation Rd., Leeds. Open June 30–Labor Day, 10–7. Nominal admission. Lifeguards and bathrooms.

ICE SKATING **Mullins Center Ice Rink** (413-545-3001; mullinscenter.com), 200 Commonwealth Ave., UMass campus, Amherst. Olympic-sized skating rink open to the public. Rentals; call for hours.

✷ Green Space

VIEWS What sets off this Massachusetts stretch from the rest of the Connecticut River Valley is the number of abrupt mountains thrusting from its floor and the fact that so many old carriage roads, built to serve long-vanished 19th-century hotels, access their summits. Only by taking advantage of these amazing vantage points can you appreciate the Valley's unusual mix of farmland and villages, cities and woods—a mix that has not altered essentially since Thomas Cole painted the Oxbow from the top of Mount Holyoke in 1836.

Mount Tom State Reservation (413-527-4805; off-season, 413-534-1186), access from US 5 in Holyoke or from MA 141 in Easthampton. This 1,800-acre mountaintop woodland contains 20 miles of trails, picnic tables, lookout towers, and a visitors center (May–late Oct.). Inquire about programs. Midweek, even in midsummer, the road out to Goat Peak is eerily empty; chances are you will be alone with the spectacular view north to Easthampton and off across the Valley. This is one of the outstanding places in the state for hawk-watching from mid-August through late October. In winter the road isn't plowed, but you can ski or snowshoe in. Lake Bray near the US 5 entrance offers fishing.

Skinner State Park (413-586-0350), MA 47, Hadley. Summit Road is open mid-Apr.–mid-Nov. "The Paradise of America" is the way Swedish singer Jenny Lind described the view from the top of Mount Holyoke in 1850—the same view of the Connecticut River Oxbow, surrounding towns, and distant hills that Thomas Cole popularized in his 1836 painting. One of the first mountaintop inns

Christina Tree

PROSPECT HOUSE ON TOP OF MOUNT HOLYOKE IN SKINNER STATE PARK.

to be built in New England (the first inn opened in 1821) and the only one preserved in any shape today, the surviving part of the Summit House (also known as Prospect House) is currently closed. In 1938 Joseph Skinner donated the Summit House and the surrounding 390 acres to the state. The park is webbed with hiking trails, one of which—the Seven Sisters Trail—leads back along the ridgeline of the Holyoke Range to the Notch Visitor Center (see Holyoke Range State Park under *Hiking and Walking*).

✷ Lodging

Note: "High" and "low" season rates tend to be pinned to the academic season. There are crunch periods in late May and early June during graduation, for instance; midweek in summer is relatively low season, while fall is high.

HOTELS AND INNS 🐾 ♿ **The Lord Jeffery Inn** (413-256-8200 or 1-800-742-0358; lordjefferyinn.com), 30 Boltwood Ave., Amherst 01002. Built in 1926 by the same architect who designed the matching Colonial Revival Jones Library across the common, this Amherst College–owned and –geared inn is a comfortable rendezvous for locals and visitors alike. You can picture Robert Frost rocking on the porch, but in 2011 the Lord Jeff reopened after extensive renovations. There are 49 rooms, all newly furnished, and the renovations incorporate numerous energy-efficient and sustainable features. The inn's full-service restaurant (unnamed at this writing) offers three meals featuring farm-to-table menus, as well as a full bar. Groups meet here all week, and on weekends there are frequently wedding receptions in the brick courtyard. From $140–250. There's an elevator and handicapped access.

The Hotel Northampton (413-584-3100 or 1-800-547-3529; hotelnorthampton.com), 36 King St., Northampton 01060. Built in 1927, this is a proud, five-story, redbrick hotel with guest cottages, handy to all of downtown's shops and restaurants. The lobby has a hearth, wing chairs, and a soaring ceiling. There are 106 rooms, including 13 suites, all tastefully furnished with reproduction antiques. The glass-fronted Coolidge Park Café serves breakfast, lunch, and dinner. Note also the vintage-1786 Wiggins Tavern restaurant, a Valley landmark that was moved here from Hopkinton, New Hampshire, and incorporated into the hotel as part of a mini museum village. It once enhanced the hotel's appeal as a "motoring objective" in an era when auto touring was largely restricted to the wealthy. $165–195 per couple, low season; "deluxe" rooms and suites are $210–350. Packages available. Amenities include valet and full room service. Four handicapped-accessible suites.

BED & BREAKFASTS *Note:* The **Five** College **Area Bed & Breakfast Association** (fivecollegebb.com) details a number of area B&Bs, and the **Hampshire Hills B&B Association** (hhbba.com) offers more listings within easy striking distance of Northampton. What follows is our selection.

In Amherst/Hadley

Ivory Creek Bed & Breakfast Inn (413-587-3115 or 1-866-331-3115; ivorycreek.com), 31 Chmura Rd., Hadley 01035. Judy Loebel grew up on a farm in Hadley and graduated from Mount Holyoke College ('65), then went on to live in many places before returning with her husband, Tod, to build this gracious retreat on 24 acres beside Skinner State Park. At first glance you assume the house is vintage 1890s, but the comforts include central air-conditioning, luxurious baths, gas fireplaces, and WiFi in all the unusually spacious guest rooms. An attractive, totally handicapped-accessible first-floor room features a private deck. Each room is different, but furnishings throughout are tasteful. There's comfortable common space, a guest pantry, and an aviary with finches, parakeets, and parrots. Judy and Tod have nine grown and two at-home adopted children and 26 grandchildren. Children are welcome and dogs can be accommodated in a garden-level Bronze Suite. A nicely designed and landscaped pool and a hot tub are available to guests. A stair chair is available for accessing upper- and ground-level rooms. $150–259 includes a full breakfast with yogurt, granola, and perhaps lemon soufflé pancakes or Tod's "Red Pepper Surprise."

Wilbur Homestead (413-253-2281; wilburhomestead.com), 126 Northampton Rd. (MA 9), Amherst 01002. Within walking distance of the Amherst College campus and downtown, this is a big, gracious, exquisitely crafted 1880s house that Al and Barbara Wilbur purchased in the 1970s but have only recently restored as a B&B. A retired state trooper, Al is an enthusiastic host. He presides over the state-of-the-art country kitchen in which the cookie and muffin jar is always full. The three

Christina Tree

THE POOL AT IVORY CREEK BED & BREAKFAST INN IN HADLEY.

upstairs rooms (each with private bath) are all nicely furnished, and the two-room Shannon Suite (comfortably sleeping three or four) is definitely worth the top dollar. There's a pleasant garden to sit in and a small but elaborate fish pond. A full breakfast—maybe apple cinnamon pancakes or an asparagus and feta cheese omelet—is included in the cost of $95–160.

Amherst Inn and **Allen House Inn** (413-253-5000; allenhouse.com), 599 and 257 Main St., Amherst 01002. These two Victorian houses have been lovingly restored by Ann and Alan Zieminski, and both are inviting, genuine "painted ladies," painstakingly furnished to period with Eastlake chairs and mantels, but also with amenities like personal computers and WiFi. If we have to pick we would choose Amherst Inn because of its location across from the Emily Dickinson Museum and because it's the lighter and airier of the two, with a pleasant garden behind. There are eight rooms, all with private bath, phone, central air-conditioning, and WiFi. Some rooms are papered in hand-silk-screened William Morris paper and hand-stenciled by Ann. Breakfast is full. There's a sense of caring here: hot water and munchies on the sideboards, genuine attention to guests' needs. Well-behaved children older than 8 are welcome. From $75 in low season to $195 on graduation weekends.

Horace Kellogg Homestead (413-253-4988; hkhbb.com), 459 S. Pleasant St., Amherst 01002. This 1828 clapboard house is on the southern edge of town, but still an easy walk from the Amherst College campus. Steve and Sue Mallett offer two attractive but very different guest rooms (one with a formal four-poster, the second with a queen and twin) with in-room cable, DVD/VCR, and shared bath. $95–115 includes a full breakfast served in the dining room off a pleasant, wicker-furnished screened porch.

✐ **Stone House Farm Bed & Breakfast** (413-549-4455; stonehouse farmbb.com), 695 E. Pleasant St., Amherst 01002. On the northern edge of town just beyond the UMass campus, this great spot for families offers two suites in a pretty clapboard house. There's an inviting central dining/eating area with microwave and fridge, and two country-fresh bedrooms share a bath. Innkeeper Candace Tulley maintains an extensive commercial flower garden in the rear of the house and the barn, in which she also offers children's craft programs. Resident animals include ducks, chickens, and goats. The grounds include shade perennial gardens with paths and scattered benches. $175–250 includes a full breakfast featuring the inn's own eggs, fruits, and vegetables.

In Northampton/Easthampton

Park Street Bed and Breakfast (413-527-7861; parkstreetbb.com), 238 Park St., Easthampton 01207. A bit out of the way but worth it, this striking 19th-century brick home has been nicely renovated. The three guest rooms are furnished with antiques and an eye to comfort, each with a TV/VCR and small fridge. There's plenty of common space, inside and out; $80 (shared bath) and $120 (private) includes a very full breakfast on weekends, continental on weekdays. Innkeeper Sue Lehman is knowledgeable and helpful with local sights and dining.

Sugar Maple Trailside Inn (413-585-8559; sugar-maple-inn.com), 62 Chestnut St., Florence 01062. Kathy and Craig Della Penna's 1860s bicyclist-geared house is sited beside the Northampton Bikeway, no coincidence since Craig is a rail-trail activist who has written three books on rail-trails. The two guest rooms with private bath are $80–120 per night with breakfast. High-speed wireless available. Common space is attractive; the library features a large collection of antique rail maps and information. Amenities include a couple of retro cruiser bikes.

The Knoll (413-584-8164; theknollbedandbreakfast.com), 230 N. Main St., Florence 01020. An English

THE AMHERST INN.

Christina Tree

Tudor–style home set well back from MA 9 on 17 acres 3 miles west of downtown Northampton, handy to the Northampton Bikeway and adjacent to Look Memorial Park. This has been Lee and Ed Lesko's home since 1963, when their former home by the Connecticut River was moved to make way for I-91. The house itself is quite grand, but decor is homey. The three guest rooms (two with a double bed and one with twin beds) are furnished simply and comfortably, sharing two baths. Breakfast is included in $90; no smokers and no children under 12.

(((ψ))) **Mount Tom River Bed & Breakfast** (413-584-4884), 4 Symansky Ave., Mount Tom 01207. Open May until early Nov., weekends only during spring and fall. Sited 2 miles south of Northampton, just off US 5, this big Victorian house was built as a lodging place in 1902. Beverly Wodick, the fourth generation of her family to live here, is a graphic-design professor, and rooms are tastefully, minimally decorated (nice prints, no fluff). The Yellow Room, a two-room suite with a sleep sofa, and the Rose Room (with a double sleigh bed) share a bath. The small, sunny White Room has its own. A full breakfast is served in the big, old-fashioned dining room. Common space includes a wraparound porch with a view of the Connecticut River as well as an attractive, antique-furnished living room. $90–100.

Elsewhere

The 1886 House (413-296-0223 or 1-800-893-2425, ext. 44; 1886house.com), 202 East St., Chesterfield 01012. This farmhouse isn't far west of the Northampton line, but it has a way-out-in-the-country feel. The three second-floor rooms all have central air. The Rose Room and the spacious Chelsea Room (TV/VCR) both have queen beds and private baths. There's a general air of hospitality here. $85–130 with full breakfast; no minimum-stay requirement.

MOTELS AND MOTOR INNS (((ψ)))

Autumn Inn (413-584-7660), 259 Elm St., Northampton 01060. This is a splendidly built and maintained two-story, 31-unit motel geared to the parents of Smith students. The 29 rooms are large with varied bed arrangements, TV, phone, WiFi, and private bath; a couple of one-bedroom suites have cooking facilities, and a third has a microwave. Breakfast and lunch are served in the coffee shop with a hearth, and there's a landscaped pool. $110–120 weekdays, $130–180 weekends, $30 more for efficiencies or suites and more than two guests.

Note: We don't pretend to have checked the following chain motels, but to omit them would be wrong, too. Rates vary by the day at the following:

Country Inn and Suites by Carlson (413-533-2100), 1 Country Club Rd. (US 5 at Smith's Ferry), Holyoke 01040. Sited between I-91 and the Connecticut River, this 61-room "inn" features luxurious rooms and suites with gas fireplace, two phones, and dataport. Facilities include a pool and exercise room. The Delaney House restaurant (see *Dining Out*) is next door.

🖍 **Clarion Hotel & Conference Center** (413-586-1211), junction of US 5 and I-91, Northampton 01060. A good bet if you have children along: 124 rooms, an indoor and an outdoor pool, sauna, game room, lighted tennis court. Also, a restaurant and lounge.

✐ **Holiday Inn** (413-534-3311 or 1-800-465-4329), Holidome and Conference Center, junction of I-91 and the Mass Pike at Ingleside, Holyoke 01040. A 219-room, four-story complex featuring a tropical recreation area with 18-foot-high palm trees, a pool, a full spa, and, of course, a volleyball court.

✐ **Holiday Inn Express Hotel & Suites** (413-582-0002; HIExpress .com/Amherst-Hadley), MA 9, Hadley 01035. Offers 78 rooms, 22 suites, and an indoor pool.

✐ **Econo Lodge** (413-582-7707; hampshirehospitality.com), 329 Russell St. (MA 9), Hadley 01035. Offers 63 rooms and an indoor pool.

✐ 🐾 **Howard Johnson** (413-586-0014; hampshirehospitality.com), 401 Russell St. (MA 9), Hadley 01035. One hundred rooms, outdoor pool.

✐ 🐾 **Quality Inn** (413-584-9816), 237 Russell St. (MA 9), Hadley 01035. Seventy rooms, indoor pool.

✐ **Best Western** (413-586-1500), 117 Conz St., Northampton 01060. Sixty-five rooms, outdoor pool.

✐ ♿ **Hampton Inn** (413-586-4851; hamptoninn.com), 24 Bay Rd., Hadley 01035. Offers 73 rooms and suites and an indoor pool.

✱ Where to Eat

DINING OUT This is recognized as one of the liveliest dining areas in New England. Because the largely academic clientele is unusually sophisticated but not particularly flush, many of the top restaurants aren't that expensive.

In Amherst

Chez Albert (413-253-3811; chez albert.net), 27 S. Pleasant St. Open for lunch Wed.–Fri., dinner Tues.–Sat., Sunday brunch 11:30–2:30. Reservations a must. An intimate (less than 30 seats), warmly painted, dimly lit bistro ambience complements a menu featuring "tartines" and tuna Niçoise salad for a summer lunch. Dinner hors d'oeuvres include a vegetable napoleon, escargots, and duck confit. For an entrée, you might select sweet corn risotto or bouillabaisse. Chef-owner Paul Hathaway has worked closely with several of the country's top chefs and in many places. There's a sense of caring here and a good wine list.

♿ **Judie's** (413-253-3491; judies restaurant.com), 51 N. Pleasant St. Open daily, 11:30–10 (until 11 Fri.–Sat.). This cheerful, glass-fronted restaurant seems to be everyone's favorite: casual, friendly, and specializing in oversized, overstuffed popovers; we recommend the gumbo and basil chicken. The menu is extensive, with many salads and veggie dishes at lunch. Dinner entrées ($17.25–19.25) include a salad and popover or bread. Full bar.

Bistro 63 at the Monkey Bar (413-259-1600; mymonkeybar.com), 63 N. Pleasant St. Open daily 11:30–10. This sleek bistro offers a menu as hip as its decor. Lunch on coconut-breaded shrimp, blackened scallops, or a salad Niçoise. Dine on sesame charred tuna, jambalaya, or iron steak Gorgonzola. Outdoor seating in-season. Dinner entrées $12.95–19.95.

Moti Persian Mediterranean Restaurant (413-259-2150; motiamherst .com), 25 N. Pleasant St. Open daily 11–10, until 2 AM weekends. Daily specials include "Famous NY Chicken and Lamb" ($7.95), a delicious bowl of basmati rice topped with pieces of juicy lamb, grilled chicken, chopped lettuce, and a yogurt sauce. Try the energy drink, a sweet combination of fresh-squeezed fruit juices flavored with rosewater. Dinner entrées $10-34. Wine, beer, and cocktails.

In Northampton

Green Street Café (413-586-5650; greenstreetcafenorthampton.com), 64 Green St. Open for lunch Mon.–Sat., dinner nightly from 5, Sun. brunch 10–2. Owner-chef John Sielski is a Valley native who operated a restaurant in Brooklyn before opening this elegant storefront bistro. The plum-colored rooms are hung with original art and the menu is handwritten. A blackboard lists local sources (much of it grown on Sielski's farm) for the day's food. A mural depicts the restaurant's run-in with Smith a half-dozen years ago when the college threatened to expand along Green Street. Since then the café has expanded and also opened seasonal dining in its garden. On a summer evening you might you might dine on duck breast with lemon, whiskey, and polenta, or striped bass with sorrel beurre blanc and mashed potatoes ($22–26). Liquor is served. Inquire about evening jazz.

Mulino's Restaurant (413-586-8900; mulinosrestaurant.com), 41 Strong Ave. Open nightly for dinner. Under new ownership, this trattoria remains as popular as ever. Antipasti are large, as is the choice of freshly made pasta dishes like ziti zuccala (julienned chicken sautéed with prosciutto, zucchini, onions, garlic, and tomatoes, tossed with ziti and ricotta cheese). Pastas $13.95–16.95; entrées $16.95–26.95. *Warning:* Portions are large. Try the veal balsamico (scaloppine sautéed with olive oil in a balsamic vinegar, butter, and wine sauce). There's music nightly in the third-floor Bishop's Lounge. The first floor houses another very popular restaurant, Sierra Grille (413-584-

A MURAL AT THE THE GREEN STREET CAFÉ IN NORTHAMPTON.

Christina Tree

1180; sierragrille.net), with creative American fare; design your own entrée ($14–29) by choosing a protein, a sauce, and two sides. Excellent food, beer, and wine choices.

Spoleto (413-586-6313; spoleto restaurants.com), 50 Main St. Open for dinner nightly. Featuring Spoleto Festival posters and creative "Fine Italian" dishes like eggplant terrine (layers of eggplant, roasted red peppers, spinach, ricotta, mozzarella, and mascarpone cheese) or hazelnut-crusted veal. Entrées run $15.95–26.95.

Bistro Les Gras (413-320-4666; bistrolesgras.com), 2 West St. Open Mon.–Thurs. 5–9, Fri.–Sat. 5–10, Sun. 5–8:30. This attractive place is dedicated to "sustainable French cuisine" and aims for high-quality, organic, locally sourced ingredients. The menu changes frequently, but you might begin with a vol-au-vent, a light pastry stuffed with mushrooms and "cellared roots," then dine on bouillabaisse à la Marseille. Entrées $25–30.

♿ **Eastside Grill** (413-586-33; east sidegrill.com), 19 Strong Ave. Open for dinner weekdays from 5, weekends from 4. A popular place with a pleasant, multilevel dining room (try for a booth) as well as a big, reasonably priced menu with something for everyone. No reservations, so come early if you don't want to wait at dinner. A raw bar features shrimp and oysters. Start with gumbo of the day, then maybe try a blackened steak salad or sesame scallops with lobster and sake. Dinner entrées $11.95–19.95.

Osaka Japanese Sushi and Steak House (413-587-9548; osakanorth ampton.com), 7 Old South St. Open for lunch and dinner (until 11 most nights, midnight Fri. and Sat.). The menu is large, with a wide choice of hibachi dinners as well as sushi and chef's specials such as tuna steak, grilled eel, and grilled chicken rolled with avocado. Dinner entrées $10.95–25.95. Lunch specials.

Eclipse (413-584-6006; eclipse186 .com), 186 Main St. Open Wed.–Sun. 5–midnight. Reservations suggested. A sleek new restaurant with a mouthwatering menu. You might begin with a kale and scallop salad, and dine on eggplant napoleon. Entrées $15–26. Live jazz Fri. and Sat.

Elsewhere

Apollo Grill (413-517-0031), Eastworks Building, 116 Pleasant St., Easthampton. Open Tues.–Fri. for lunch 11:30–2, dinner Tues.–Sat. Chef-owner Casey Douglas has created a hip dining spot in the Valley. The decor is zany, the locale offbeat (the ground floor of a vast mill, with tenants ranging from the Registry of Motor Vehicles to several galleries). The reasonable menu is varied and the food, fabulous. Lunch on a hummus plate with eggplant, caviar, sun-dried tomato purée, grilled onion, and red pepper in a fried tortilla; dine on fried catfish with smoked shrimp cream sauce, sautéed greens, and polenta fries. Dinner entrées $13–22.

Tavern on the Hill (413-493-1700), 100 Mountain Rd. (MA 41), Easthampton. Open nightly for dinner. Across from the entrance to the Mount Tom Reservation, this restaurant has been through many incarnations, and for all the big draw has been the view. We hear good things about the food this time. The menu might include smoked Gouda–stuffed chicken breast wrapped in bacon with spinach, blackened beef tips, and a fresh herb crêpe. Entrées come with salad: $13.95–23.95.

✐ **The Delaney House** (413-535-5077; www.logcabin-delaney.com), MA 5 at Smith's Ferry, Holyoke. Open nightly for dinner. Options include Delaney's Grill (featuring steak and ribs; entrées $20–35) and The Mick ("lighten up" casual dining with entertainment some nights; entrées $8–20).

EATING OUT

Amherst (unless otherwise specified)

✐ **Esselon Café** (413-585-1515), 99 Russell St. (MA 9), Hadley. Open Mon.–Fri. 11–3 for lunch and weekends 8–3 for brunch; also open 7–6 weekdays and 8–5 weekends for coffee and munchies. A former auto parts store has been transformed into an open-sided (weather permitting) café with terrace seating overlooking a garden and a large round table for singles who simply want to sit with their laptops (there is WiFi). Patrons order at the deli counter from a menu and blackboard daily specials. We lunched on a Mediterranean salad that included hummus, roasted red pepper, eggplant, feta, tomatoes, and more. Many people just come for the coffee, reputedly the best in the Valley. There's wine, too.

✐ **Crazy Noodles Café** (413-253-3287), 36 Main St. Open daily lunch through dinner. This is an attractive, casual Asian café with wine and WiFi, good for some interesting salads (like peanut noodle and crispy wonton) and noodle soups. Free ice cream for kids.

Fresh Side (413-256-0296), 39 S. Pleasant St. Open daily 11–10. A delightful eatery and teahouse serving healthy wraps filled with warm sea vegetables, spicy bean concoctions,

ESSELON CAFÉ, A FORMER AUTO PARTS STORE IN HADLEY, IS KNOWN FOR ITS COFFEE AND MUNCHIES.

Christina Tree

ginger tofu, and the like, plus a similar selection of salads, noodle soups, rice, and pasta dishes.

Baku's African Restaurant (413-253-7202), 197 N. Pleasant St. Open Mon.–Sat. for lunch and dinner, Sun. from 4 PM. Colorful, authentic, and reasonably priced, this inviting eatery offers a gluten- and lactose-free menu. House specialties include black-eyed pea fritters, roasted plantain with peanut sauce, pounded yams, and a choice of vegetarian or meat-based West African melon seed soup.

Antonio's (413-253-0808), 31 N. Pleasant St. Ask any student around: This is simply the best pizza, conveniently sold by the slice so you can sample several.

Amherst Brewing Company (413-253-4400; amherstbrewing.com), 24 N. Pleasant St. Open daily for lunch and dinner; live entertainment Thurs.–Sat. 10 PM–1 AM. The town's first microbrewery, with a reasonably priced menu that includes traditional pub food like Irish stew, shepherd's pie, and cock-a-leekie pie. Tell us what you think of the brew.

Amherst Chinese (413-253-7835), 62 Main St. Open daily for lunch and dinner. A mural in the dining room depicts the restaurant's nearby farm, source of the vegetables in its dishes. Known fondly as AmChi, this is a local favorite. Note the daily specials; no MSG.

La Veracruzana (413-253-6900), 63 S. Pleasant St. Reasonably priced Mexican specialties.

Pasta e Basta (413-256-3550), 26 Main St. Open 11–11, Thurs.–Sun. until midnight. An unusually attractive little trattoria with a wide selection of homemade pastas. Specialties include penne chicken and broccoli cream and spinach linguine. The reasonably priced menu also includes grilled and skewered seafood and chicken.

Panda East Restaurant (413-256-8923), 103 N. Pleasant St. Open 11:30–10 daily, Fri. and Sat. until 11. This is part of an excellent local chain specializing in traditional Hunan-style Chinese food and Japanese staples (sushi, tempura, and teriyaki). Full bar.

The Black Sheep (413-253-3442; blacksheepdeli.com), 79 Main St. Open Mon.–Thurs. 7–7, Fri.–Sat. 7–8, Sun. 7–6. A genuine coffeehouse-deli since 1986, with exceptional pastries made daily with natural ingredients and real butter. Also deli sandwiches, pasta, salads, and hot entrées. Good picnic makings.

Bueno y Sano (413-253-4000; buenoysano.com), 1 Boltwood Walk. Open daily lunch through dinner. An old-timer in a new location with reasonably priced, authentic Mexican food.

Atkins Farms Fruit Bowl (413-253-9528), corner of MA 116 and Bay Rd., South Amherst. Open daily; hours vary. Probably the fanciest farm stand in New England, this handsome redwood building sits amid thousands of fruit trees on the 190 acres that have been farmed for generations. There is a first-rate deli, but for some reason it's on the opposite side of the building from the bakery, where there's seating.

Cushman Market and Café (413-549-0100), 491 Pine St., North Amherst. Open Mon.–Sat. 7–7, Sun. 8–4. This is a neighborhood crossroads store that's so good it's become

Christina Tree

AT AMHERST CHINESE, A MURAL DEPICTS THE FAMILY'S FARM, SOURCE OF MUCH OF THE PRODUCE AT ITS POPULAR TABLES.

a local icon and has added tables in the rear. Baked breads and pastry, local produce and products are the attraction. There are plenty of breakfast rolls, sandwiches, burgers, and panini.

In Northampton

Sylvester's Restaurant, Cafe & Bakery (413-586-5343; sylvestersrestaurant.com), 111 Pleasant St. Open daily 7 AM–3 PM. Named for and housed in the one-time home of pioneer vegetarian and whole-wheat advocate Dr. Sylvester Graham of graham cracker fame. The long, well-lit dining room and adjoining café are cheery, perfect for breakfast (try the Lox-Ness omelet). There's also a large choice of soups, salads, sandwiches, wraps, burgers, and hot entrées at lunch, from a Mango Tango Salada to a "West of Woostah" (sliced avocado and veggies on homemade toast) to shrimp sautéed with spinach, garlic butter, white wine, artichoke hearts, and mushrooms served over grilled polenta. Tea isn't from a bag, and coffees are from the café. The food is so good here, in fact, that we lament the fact dinner is no longer served. Come early for lunch. There's a specials menu and trivia cards for kids. Beer and wine served.

Amanouz Café (413-585-9128; amanouz.com), 44 Main St. Open for breakfast, lunch, and dinner. A narrow but deep and rewarding Moroccan oasis to which we keep returning. Specialties include tabbouleh salad, great falafel, salads, kebobs, a selection of couscous dishes (including chicken or lamb), and both vegetarian and meat sandwiches like *shawerma* (marinated lamb and beef, vegetables, and tahini). Wine and beer.

Paul and Elizabeth's (413-584-4832; paulandelizabeths.com), entrances from Thornes Market (150 Main St.) and Old South St. Open Sun.–Thurs. 11:30–9:15, Fri.–Sat. 11:30–9:45. The town's oldest natural foods restaurant, a great space with big second-story plate-glass windows overhung with fanciful stained glass and a high tin ceiling, plenty of plants, and wood. The extensive menu specializes in but is not limited to vegetarian dishes, soups and salads, tempura, and noodle dishes; also seafood, home-baked breads, and pastries. Sides of baked brown rice, deep-fried tofu, sea vegetables, and more. Daily specials. Dinner entrées average $10.25–14.50. Beer and wine.

Spoleto Express (413-586-8646), 225 King St. Open daily from 11 AM, until 9:30 Sun.–Wed. and until 10:30 Thurs.–Sat. This offshoot of the popular Main Street dining spot (see *Dining Out*) is good for wraps in a tomato-basil tortilla or on grilled rosemary focaccia; also soups, pizzas, salads, and pastas. Eat in or take out.

No. 40 Green Street (413-586-2443; 40green.com), 40 Green St. Open Mon.–Fri. 6–8, Sun. 6–6. The ambiance is that of a self-consciously French café, a bakery and wine bar with persimmon walls, a chandelier, tables inside and (seasonally) out. The madeleines and French tarts are outstanding, croissants vary. The charcuterie, fish, and meat plates to go with wine by the glass seem overpriced.

Fitzwilly's (413-584-8666), 23 Main St. Open daily 11:30–midnight. One of New England's first fern bars: brick walls, plenty of copper, antiques, hanging plants. It all works, including the immense menu with blue plate luncheon specials like chicken potpie and sandwiches; burgers are a specialty, along with "lotsa pasta."

Northampton Brewery (413-584-9903), 11 Brewer Court. Open Mon.–Sat. 11:30–1 AM, Sun. noon–1 AM. Housed in a 19th-century livery stable, this is a pleasant, multilevel space with a popular roof deck, serving sandwiches, pizza, burgers, steaks, seafood, and stir fries. Beer changes daily.

Pizzeria Paradiso (413-586-1468; fundining.com), 12 Crafts Ave. Open nightly. This is all about wood-fired, brick-oven, very-thin-crust pizza, both white and red, in unusual varieties such as Chèvre Delight—goat cheese, sun-dried tomatoes, and roasted garlic cloves with mozzarella and Parmesan. Beer is served, along with kids-only pizza, finger food, and salads.

Bela Vegetarian Restaurant (413-586-8011), 68 Masonic St. Open Tues.–Sat. noon–8:45. A small, bright eatery with a full vegetarian menu: soups, pasta and tofu entrées, and polenta. Try the butternut bisque and tempeh with zucchini in red wine rosemary butter, served with salad and brown rice.

Mosaic Café (413-585-1155; mosaiccafemed.com), 78 Masonic St. Open daily 8–10, Fri.–Sat. until 11. Mediterranean cuisine featuring fresh fish, authentic stews, and many vegetarian/vegan options. Enjoy sweet desserts and the outdoor patios.

Viva Fresh Pasta Co. (413-586-5875; vivafreshpasta.com), 249 Main St. A cheerful corner storefront with white brick walls and a varied menu that includes focaccia, pizza, pasta, and chicken specialties. Try the grilled eggplant with fresh basil and goat cheese. Wine and beer served.

Teapot (413-585-0880 or 413-585-9308; teapotusa.com), 116 Main St. Open from lunch through 11 PM, until midnight on weekends. Said by many to be the Valley's best Asian restaurant, with a wide selection of reasonably priced meat and vegetarian dishes. Specialties include tea-smoked duck, and chicken, shrimp, and eggplant with scallions and garlic.

Side Street Café (413-587-8900; sidestcafe.com), 42 Maple St., Florence. Open lunch through dinner except Sunday. A pleasant café, good for some imaginative sandwiches and salads plus a serious dinner menu ranging from grilled vegetable risotto to honey bourbon glazed flatiron steak. Wine and beer are served.

Karma (413-727-8143), 48 Main St. Juice bar: 8 AM–9 PM; café 10:30–9. Closed Sun. The focus here is raw vegan and a few cooked vegan options. The juicebar features wheatgrass shots, green drinks, smoothies, and teas. Try a red pepper and avocado wrap stuffed with corn, cabbage and bell pepper, and sprouted wheat berries topped with a chili tropical fruit salsa. The menu includes papaya filet, sprouted nut loaf, and a variety of soups and salads.

Local (413-586-5857; localnorthampton.com), 16 Main St. Farm to table isn't just for vegans. The aim here is good food fast (as opposed to fast food). Locally sourced burgers, fries, and shakes are the specialty, but the Cap'n Crunch chicken gets raves, too.

In Holyoke

Gramps Restaurant (413-534-1996), 216 Lyman St. Open daily for breakfast and lunch. An attractive, easy-to-find Polish restaurant that's as genuine as they come, operated by Danuta and Krzysztof Wojick, longtime owners of the neighboring Polish deli. Pierogi and blintzes are made fresh each day. It's definitely the place for *golabki* (stuffed cabbage).

Fernandez Family Restaurant (413-532-1139), 161 High St. Open Mon.–Fri. 10–5:30. A Puerto Rican eatery with some 20 dishes on display so that you can point rather than having to pronounce *surullitos* (sweet cornmeal with cheese), *boquito* (crabmeat fritter), or *mofongo* (plantains, garlic, and bacon).

Elsewhere

Yarde House Food & Spirits (413-315-4339), 3 Hadley St., South Hadley. Open daily for lunch and dinner. This big, friendly, old tavern (booths on the bar side, tables on the other) on the common has a large menu of burgers, sandwiches, salads, and dinner entrées ($11–18).

Dockside at Brunelle's (413-536-2342; dock-side.com), 1 Alvord St., South Hadley. Open daily for lunch and dinner (until 9); the lounge is open until midnight. A local favorite with a large, reasonably priced menu and nightly specials, located on a scenic stretch of the river. This is the departure point for the *Lady Bea.*

Zoe's Fish House (413-527-0313; zoesfish.com), 195 Russell Street (MA 9), Hadley. Open Mon.–Thurs. 4–9, Fri.–Sat. 4–9:30, Sun. brunch 10:30–2, Sun. dinner 4–8. Basic American restaurant featuring shellfish and fried fish. Dinner entrées $15–26.

DINERING OUT **Miss Florence Diner** (413-584-3179), 99 Main St., Florence (Northampton). Open for early breakfast through late dinner, 3 miles west of downtown Northampton. Known locally as Miss Flo's, this is the most famous diner in Western Massachusetts, and it's been in the same family since the 1940s. Forget the banquet addition and stick to the stools or booths. Unexpected specialties like clam and oyster stew or baked stuffed lobster casserole, a soup and salad bar, and full liquor license. Good beef barley soup and coconut and macaroon cream pudding.

Bluebonnet Diner (413-584-3333; bluebonnetdiner.net), 324 King St., Northampton. Open Mon.–Fri. 5:30 AM–midnight, Sat. 6 AM–midnight. A classic diner with "home cooking." Full bar. Dinners $8–14.

Look Restaurant (413-584-9850), 410 N. Main St., Leeds (Northampton). A landmark with a 1950s look and menu, "homestyle cooking," breakfast available all day. Fresh-made breads, muffins, and pies.

Easthampton Diner & Restaurant (413-527-0855; easthamptondiner .com), 117 Union St., Easthampton. Open 24 hours on weekends, otherwise from 6:30 AM until 11 PM (closes Sun. at 10). This is the real deal, with a huge menu; seafood, Italian, and Greek specialties; and homefries with bacon or gravy. Beer and wine. Early-bird specials.

SNACKS AND BREWS **Bart's Homemade** (413-253-2278; barts homemade.com), 103 N. Pleasant St., Amherst. Open Sun.–Thurs. noon–11, Fri. and Sat. until midnight. Since 1976, milk from local cows has been used for great ice cream in 100 flavors, including mud pie, blueberry cheesecake, and orange Dutch chocolate.

La Fiorentina Pastry Shop (413-586-7693), 25 Armory St., Northampton. A hidden jewel of a coffee shop with delectable desserts like sfogliatelle and tiramisu as well as coffees, Italian soft drinks and juices, gelati, and memorable biscotti. For the story of the original Fiorentina, see "Springfield Area."

Flayvors of Cook Farm (413-584-2224; cookfarm.com), 129 S. Maple St., Hadley. Open daily year-round,

THE VENERABLE MISS FLORENCE DINER.
Kim Grant

seasonal hours. Milk from the resident cows is used to make outstanding ice cream (try the ginger!). Also available: turkey pie, chili, soups, and salads. The setting is one of the most beautiful in the Valley, surrounded by fields at the foot of the Holyoke Range. Plenty of outdoor tables and plenty of cows, both behind the fence and in the neighboring meadow. Sunday music 2–5, the kind to please both kids and cows.

Amherst Coffee (413-256-8987), 28 Amity St. This has quickly become the center of town. It's a casual café with espresso, loose-leaf tea, wine, spirits, and WiFi. The Noho version is Northampton Coffee, 269 Pleasant St.

Cup and Top Café (413 585-0445; cupandtop.com), 1 N. Main St., Florence. Open weekdays 6–6, weekends 8–3. A family-friendly café with play space and yummy food.

McCray Farm (413-533-3714), 55 Alvord St., South Hadley. The dairy bar, open spring through fall, features homemade ice cream. This working dairy farm, located near the river, has a small petting zoo and maple breakfasts during sugaring season.

Woodstar Café (413-585-9777), 60 Masonic St., Northampton. Be prepared for a wait; it's a very popular place.

The Moan and Dove (413-256-1710; themoananddove.com), 460 West St. (MA 116 south), Amherst. A serious pub with 20 beers on tap, several casks, and some 125 bottled brands to choose from. It's been so successful that owner Daniel Lanigan has opened a similar watering hole, **The Dirty Truth** (413-585-5999; dirtytruthbeerhall.com), 29 Main St., Northampton.

Paper City Brewery (413-535-1588; papercity.com), 108 Cabot St., Holyoke, offers Thursday and Friday evening "tastings" from 6–8. A microbrewery serving amber ale, Cabot Street Summer Wheat, and Irish stout, among many others.

✱ Entertainment

For the academic year consult the *Five College Calendar of Events,* published monthly and available at all campuses as well as at calendar.five colleges.edu. A typical month lists more than 25 films, 30 lectures, 20 concerts, and 30 theatrical performances. Visitors welcome.

The Valley Advocate, with weekly arts listings, is published Thursday. It's free and can be found everywhere in Northampton/Amherst; also online at valleyadvocate.com.

Academy of Music (413-584-9032; academyofmusictheatre.com), 274 Main St., Northampton. This Renaissance-style, century-old, municipally owned, 300-seat theater features a balcony and a baby grand in the women's lounge. It schedules live entertainment as well as films.

The Calvin Theatre (413-584-1444), 19 King St. First opened in 1924 as a 1,300-seat vaudeville house, it's now the splendidly restored venue for stellar live performances three to six nights a week during the academic season, less frequently in summer. Check out Bar 19 after the show.

Mullins Center (413-545-0505), UMass campus, Amherst. A 10,500-seat sports and entertainment arena with a year-round schedule of theater and concerts as well as sports.

Fine Arts Center (413-545-2511; fineartscenter.com), UMass campus,

Christina Tree

NORTHAMPTON'S ACADEMY OF MUSIC.

Amherst. Performing arts series of theater, music, and dance.

Commonwealth Opera (413-586-5026; commonwealthopera.org), 4 Old South St., Suite #3, Northampton, stages a fall opera, a December *Messiah,* a March Broadway musical, and other performances at local venues.

Northampton Center for the Arts (413-584-7327; nohoarts.org), 17 New South St., Northampton. Theater, dance, and art exhibits.

MUSIC **Northampton Box Office** (413-586-8686 or 1-800-THE-TICK; nbotickets.com) serves the Calvin Theater, the Iron Horse, and Pearl Street.

The Iron Horse (413-584-0610), 20 Center St., Northampton. This is only open when there's a performance, but that tends to be nightly. Live folk, jazz, and comedy, plus 50 brands of imported beer; dinner served. According to *Billboard* magazine, The Iron Horse "boasts one of the richest musical traditions in the country."

Pearl Street (413-584-7771), 10 Pearl St., Northampton. Dancing on Fri. and Sat., live music several nights a week. DJ.

Jazz in July at UMass (413-545-3530) a series of summer concerts and workshops in Amherst celebrating jazz music.

Look Memorial Park Sunday Concerts are held at 4 PM Sundays, late June to mid-August, in Look Park, MA 9, Northampton.

THEATER *Note:* For on-campus performances during the academic year, check fivecolleges.edu/theater.

Pioneer Valley Summer Theatre (413-529-3434) at Williston Northampton School (P.O. Box 53), Easthampton 01027. The theater is in Scott Hall on Payson Avenue. Performances late June to mid-August. Inquire about Theater for Young Audiences, Wed.–Sat. at 10 AM during the company's season.

New Century Theatre (413-585-3220; newcenturytheatre.org). Over the past decade this regional company has developed a reputation for quality performances, staged late June to mid-August at the air-conditioned Hallie Flanagan Studio Theatre within the Mendenhall Center for Performing Arts at Smith College on Green Street, Northampton.

Hampshire Shakespeare Company (413-548-8118; hampshireshakespeare.org). Summer Shakespeare plays and varied performances in other months—but no permanent home, so check the website or call.

New World Theater (413-545-1972; newworldtheater.org), based at UMass, presents works by people of color.

FILM **Amherst Cinema** (413-253-CLIP; amherstcinema.org), 28 Amity St., Amherst. A nonprofit, three-screen theater offers nightly showings of independent, art, and foreign films. It replaces the old Amity Cinema, which occupied the front of this complex from 1926 until 1999. This historic building now also houses the Amherst Chamber of Commerce Visitor Center.

Academy of Music (413-584-9032), 274 Main St., Northampton. Art films and general releases alternate with live performances (see above).

Cinemark at Hampshire Mall (for movie times, 1-800-326-3264), Café Square, Hampshire Mall, 367 Russell St. (MA 9), Hadley. Has 12 theaters.

Pleasant Street Theatre (413-584-5848), 27 Pleasant St., Northampton. First-run and art films, one theater upstairs and the well-named Little Theater in the basement.

Tower Theaters (413-533-2663), 19 College St., South Hadley. First-run and art films; seats may be reserved.

* Selective Shopping

ANTIQUES **Collector Galleries** (413-584-6734), 11 Bridge St. Open Mon.–Sat. 11–5, Sun. noon–5. This is one of the oldest and biggest shops around, a good bet for furniture.

ART GALLERIES *Note:* **Northampton** is an arts center in its own right, a place where aspiring artists gather to study with established names. Many restaurants and coffeehouses also mount constantly changing work (for sale) by local artists. There's even a distinctive Northampton school of realism. **Amherst,** too, has its share of galleries; an **Amherst (Gallery) Art Walk** is held the first Thursday of each month, when many nongallery businesses also open their space to artists. In Northampton it's the second Friday of each month. The Easthampton Arts Walk is held the second Saturday of each month.

R. Michelson Galleries (413-586-3964; rmichelson.com), 132 Main St., Northampton, and 25 S. Pleasant St., Amherst. Open Mon.–Wed. 10–6, Thurs.–Sat. 10–9, Sun. noon–5. Richard Michelson has maintained galleries at various locations since 1976, moving in 1995 into the huge and handsome two-story-high space designed in 1913 for the Northampton Savings Bank. The gallery showcases work by 50 local artists, including Leonard Baskin, one of America's most respected sculptors, painters, and printmakers, with works selling here from $100 to $100,000. Other well-known artists whose work is usually on view include Barry Moser, Gregory Gillespie, Linda Post, and Lewis Bryden. Note the special gallery devoted to original children's book illustrations by nationally known local artists.

Leverett Crafts and Arts Center (413-548-9070), 13 Montague Rd., Leverett. Open Wed.–Fri. 2–5, Sat. 1–4. Off the beaten track, this is a long-established nonprofit gallery with changing exhibits, talks, classes, and workshops.

CRAFTS Some 1,500 craftspeople work in the Valley and nearby Hilltowns, and Northampton is their major showcase, known particularly for handcrafted jewelry, pottery, and furniture. **One Cottage Street** in Easthampton, the **Cutlery Building** in Northampton, and the **Pro-Brush Building** in Florence all house artisans. For periodic tours and open houses, check with the Greater Northampton Chamber of Commerce (see *Guidance*).

The Valley is also the venue for several major craft and fine art happenings: The **Paradise City Arts Festivals** (413-527-8994; paradisecityarts.com)—held Memorial Day weekend and Columbus Day weekend at Northampton's Three-County Fairgrounds—are rated as the state's premier showcases for fine, contemporary, juried crafts and art.

Also see **Snow Farm** in "Hampshire Hilltowns."

In Northampton

Pinch (413-586-4509; pinchgallery.com), 179 Main St. A variety of artistic, functional pottery and decorative accessories.

Skera Gallery (413-586-4563; skera.com), 221 Main St. Open daily, Sun. from noon, Thurs. until 8. Longtime owners Harriet and Steve Rogers specialize more and more in stunning handcrafted clothing, "wearable art."

Silverscape Designs (413-586-3324; silverscapedesigns.com), 1 King St., Northampton; also (413-253-3324), 264 N. Pleasant St., Amherst. The Northampton store (open weekdays 10–6, Sat. until 9, Sun. noon–5) is a beauty, the Tiffany's of the Valley—a former bank building with art deco detailing and a glorious stained-glass skylight. The old tellers' windows are still in place; there's also a cascading fountain. A wide variety of jewelry and accessories, plus Tiffany-style lamps.

Don Muller Gallery (413-586-1119; donmullergallery.com), 40 Main St. An outstanding store displaying a wide variety of crafted items, specializing in art glass, always exhibiting the deeply colored signature orbs created by local artist Josh Simpson.

The Artisan Gallery (413-586-1942; theartisangallery.com), 162 Main St. A quality selection of jewelry, pottery, woodwork, glass, and clothing.

Bill Brough Jewelry Designs (413-586-8985; drusydesigns.com), 104 Main St. Original jewelry designs in gold, diamonds, pearls, and special stones.

Ten Thousand Villages (413-582-9338), 82 Main St. Open Mon.–Wed.

10–6, Thurs.–Sat. until 8. Fairly traded handicrafts from around the world.

BOOKSTORES Book browsing is a major pastime in this area.

In South Hadley

The Odyssey Bookshop (413-534-7307 or 1-800-540-7307; odysseybks.com), Village Commons, 9 College St. Open Mon.–Sat. 10–8, Sun. noon–5. An independent bookstore across from Mount Holyoke College. Large children's books and poetry sections, author readings, and other special events.

FOOD FOR THOUGHT BOOKSTORE IN AMHERST FEATURES ALTERNATIVE AND PROGESSIVE TITLES . . . AND BUMPER STICKERS.

Christina Tree

In Northampton

Broadside Bookshop (413-586-4235), 247 Main St. A general trade bookstore with a strong emphasis on fiction and literature as well as personal advice.

Booklink (413-585-9955), 150 Main St., in Thornes Marketplace. Specialties include travel and local books.

Bookends (413-585-8667), 80 Maple St., Florence. Nine rooms of quality used books. Raven Used Books (413-584-9868), 4 Old South St. Specializes in scholarly titles, women's studies, and philosophy.

In Amherst

Amherst Books (413-256-1547; amherstbooks.com), 8 Main St. A locally owned, independent bookstore specializing in poetry, literature, and philosophy. New and used books.

Food for Thought Books (413-253-5432), 106 N. Pleasant St. Features gay and lesbian, progressive political, and African American titles.

CLOTHING

In Amherst

Rural chic is the look at **Zanna** (413-253-2563), 187 N. Pleasant St., and **Clay's** (413-256-4200), 32 Main St.

In Northampton

Talbots (413-858-5985) is at 34 Bridge St.; **Cathy Cross** (413-596-9398), 151 Main St.; **Country Comfort, Ltd.** (413-584-0042), 153 Main St.; and **Eileen Fisher Store** (413-585-1118), 24 Pleasant St. Also: **J Rich Clothing for Men** (413-586-6336), 22 Masonic St.

OTHER SPECIAL STORES AND ENTERPRISES **Northampton Wools** (413-586-4331), 11 Pleasant

Christina Tree

SHOPPING IN NORTHAMPTON.

St., Northampton. Linda Daniels's small shop just off Main Street is crammed with bright wools and knitting gear; workshops offered.

WEBS (413-584-2225; yarn.com), 75 Service Center Rd., Northampton. A warehouse-sized, family-owned shop, said to be the largest yarn store in America.

Faces (413-584-4081), 175 Main St., Northampton. Open daily. A hip, student-geared department store with toys, clothing, furniture and furnishings, cards, and much more.

The Mountain Goat (413-586-0803), 189 Main St., Northampton. The area's premier outdoor "funfitters"; mostly clothing, some hiking and camping equipment, a great selection of shoes.

SHOPPING CENTERS **Thornes Marketplace,** 150 Main St., Northampton. An incubator for many Northampton stores: a five-story, 30-shop complex with high ceilings and wood floors.

The Village Commons (413-532-3600; thevillagecommons.com), College Street, South Hadley. A whimsical, white-clapboard complex of shops designed by Boston architect Graham Gund to house shops, restaurants, and a movie theater (two screens).

Holyoke Mall (413-536-1440; holyokemall.com) at Ingleside (I-91 Exit 15 or Mass Pike Exit 4). Open Mon.–Sat. 10–9:30 and Sun. 11–6. The single biggest mall in Western Massachusetts, second largest in all of New England, with Sears, Macy's, and JCPenney anchors.

Hampshire Mall (413-586-5700; hampshiremall.com), 367 Russell St. (MA 9), Hadley. Open Mon.–Sat. 10–9, Sun. 11–6. A major mall with a multiscreen Cinemark Theater, Target, Best Buy, JCPenney, and Dick's as the anchors.

Mountain Farms Mall (mountainfarmshadley.com), 335 Russell St. (MA 9), Hadley. Open Mon.–Sat. 10–8, Sun. noon–6. Anchors include Walmart, Whole Foods, Eastern Mountain Sports, Barnes & Noble, and Marshall's.

✷ Farmers' Markets, Farms, and Farm Stands

Farmers' Markets are held in **Amherst** on Spring Street, May–Oct., Sat. 7:30–1:30; Winter Market at Amherst Regional Middle School, Oct.–May, Sat. 10–2; in **North Amherst** on Sunderland Road,

May–Oct., Sat. 9–2; Winter Market at Swartz Family Farm on Meadow Street, Sat. 10–2; in **Northampton** behind Thornes Marketplace on Gothic Street, late Apr.–mid-Nov., Sat. 7–12:30 and May–Nov., Tues. 1:30–6; in **South Hadley** on the village green, June–Oct., Thurs. 1–6; and in **Holyoke** on High Street by City Hall, May–Oct., Thurs. 11:30–3:30.

This area also represents one of New England's richest concentrations of farm stands, PYO farms, and organic farms; see buylocalfood.org and farmfresh.org for an interactive map to members of CISA (Community Involved in Sustaining Agriculture).

✷ Special Events

Year-round: **Arts Night Out, Northampton,** a gallery walk with openings and lectures in many galleries, is held the second Friday of each month. **Art Walk** is held the first Thursday of each month in Amherst and the second Saturday in Easthampton.

See the town websites listed under *Guidance* for details of these and all of the following events. Also see *The Valley Advocate,* published Thursdays, for current entertainment and events.

Spring–fall: **Farmers' markets** are held in **Amherst, Northampton,** and **Holyoke.**

March: **Annual Bulb Show,** Smith College (*first two weeks*). **St. Patrick's Day Parade,** Holyoke (*Sunday after St. Patrick's Day*).

May: **Emily Dickinson's World Weekend,** Amherst. **Western Massachusetts Appaloosa Horse Show,** Three-County Fairgrounds, Northampton.

Memorial Day weekend: **Paradise City Arts Festivals** (paradisecityarts.com).

June: **Taste of Amherst,** third weekend.

July: **Fireworks,** Amherst (*July 4*). **Amherst Crafts Fair** (*weekend after Independence Day*). **Morgan Horse Show,** Northampton.

August: **Three-County Fair** at the Three-County Fairgrounds, Northampton.

September: **The Great Holyoke Block Party** (*Sunday of Labor Day weekend*).

November: **Northampton Independent Film Festival** (niff.org).

December: **Open crafts studios** at Eastworks in Easthampton (*first weekend*). **First Night,** Northampton (*New Year's Eve*).

SPRINGFIELD AREA

One of the oldest cities in the country—it was founded in 1636 on the east bank of the Connecticut River between two waterfalls—Springfield has known booms and busts over three centuries. Unlike many other old New England industrial communities, it has tried hard to adapt creatively to change, although with mixed success. Today a city that once based its prosperity on manufacturing firearms is a tourist destination thanks to its central location, the worldwide craze for basketball, and the endearing characters created by local boy Theodor Geisel, better known as Dr. Seuss.

With a population of more than 150,000, Springfield is the third-largest city in Massachusetts and the metropolis of the Pioneer Valley. Although 33 square miles in area, most of its attractions—shops, restaurants, stately Court Square, the Springfield Museums at the Quadrangle, the Dr. Seuss National Memorial Sculpture Garden, and the MassMutual Center—are within a few blocks of one another in the compact downtown area known as Springfield Center. The Naismith Memorial Basketball Hall of Fame, the city's most popular attraction, is just a few minutes' drive away, as is the Springfield Armory National Historic Site. Both Springfield Center and the Basketball Hall of Fame are well marked from I-91 and I-391.

The Springfield you see today is largely the result of the young federal government's decision in 1794 to establish a national armory to manufacture muskets for the U.S. Army in the then-small riverside village. The armory attracted skilled workers and developed machinery and manufacturing techniques that made Springfield one of the engines of the Industrial Revolution in America. Machine shops and factories utilizing tools and methods developed at the armory were established up and down the Connecticut Valley, which in time became known as Precision Valley.

With the War of 1812 Springfield became an overnight boomtown, but it was the Civil War that really transformed the city, which doubled in population as it became the chief arsenal of the Union army. The armory produced more than half the rifled muskets used by Northern troops, while nearby Smith & Wesson turned out 110,000 revolvers and the Ames Sword Company in neighboring Chicopee made 150,000 cavalry sabers.

After the Civil War, Springfield evolved into a prosperous, diversified

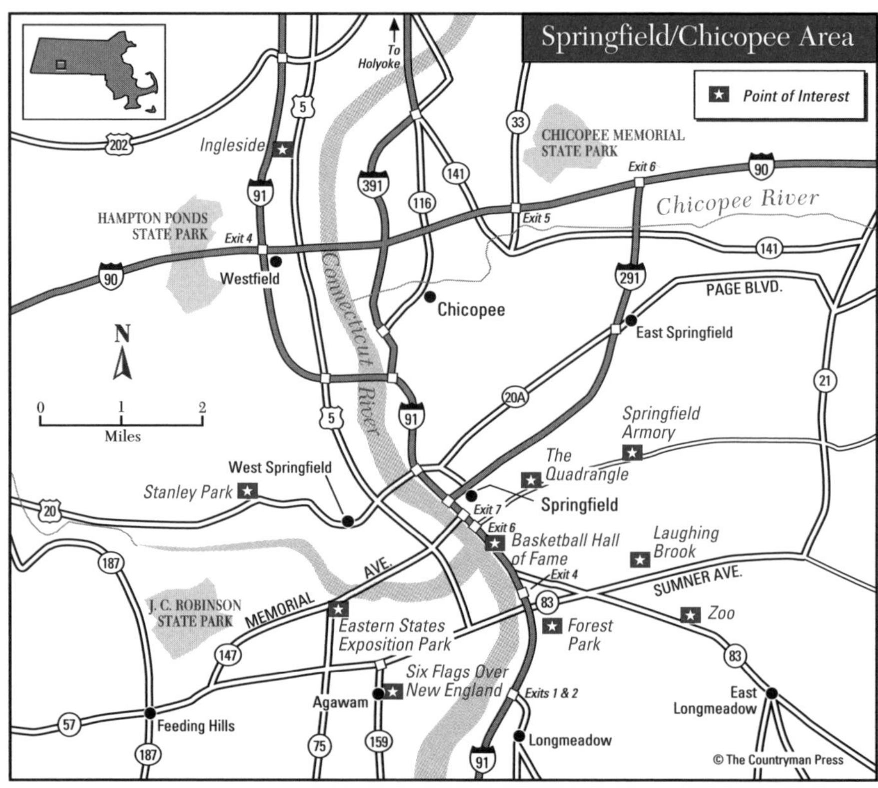

manufacturing city known for an impressive variety of inventions, including the first gas-powered car and the first motorcycle, along with pioneering versions of airplanes and vacuum cleaners. The city was also home to manufacturers of household-word products such as Breck shampoo and Milton Bradley board games.

Most workers were well-paid craftsmen who could afford to buy their own houses, rather than live in rented tenement flats as in most New England cities, and as a result Springfield boasted it was "the City of Homes." Wealthy industrialists built themselves grand mansions, of course, but also supported the arts, endowing the Springfield Museums at the Quadrangle—an extraordinary civic amenity—and creating grand public spaces like Forest Park with its delightful zoo.

Geisel, born in Springfield in 1904, spent his childhood following his father, the city's superintendent of parks, around Forest Park. The zoo provided the inspiration for Dr. Seuss's whimsical creatures, his father was the model for the kindly zookeeper, and the park was the setting for many of his stories. A visit to Forest Park is particularly rewarding after seeing the sculptures in the Dr. Seuss Memorial in the Quadrangle.

Well-to-do local businessmen were also major supporters of self-improvement organizations such as the Young Men's Christian Association. It was at a YMCA training school for physical education instructors in Springfield in 1891 that Dr. James Naismith took a soccer ball and two peach baskets and created the game of "basket ball." His students and other graduates of the school took the game around the world.

In 1968 the closure of the Springfield Armory, which at the height of production in World War II employed some 13,000 people, marked the end of an era for the already economically troubled city, which saw its industrial base continue to shrink and its population decline. Many formerly pleasant neighborhoods deteriorated into near slums, and once-busy downtown department stores, hotels, theaters, and restaurants were forced to close.

Impressive but rather sterile urban renewal projects such as the MassMutual Center and the Tower Square complex (a 29-story office tower and hotel with a shopping arcade and large parking garage) have brought some life back to downtown, particularly after dark. However, many handsome 19th- and early-20th-century buildings that gave the city its distinctive character were bulldozed to create them. Efforts are now being made to preserve landmark buildings, restore historic older neighborhoods, and revitalize downtown, which these days has more entertainment options and is much livelier at night.

More recent projects, such as Riverfront Park between I-91 and the Connecticut River, have a more human dimension than their predecessors. The park includes a 3.5-mile-long bicycle path and is also home to the Naismith Basketball Hall of Fame.

Built at a cost of $45 million, the Hall of Fame is an architecturally striking building: shaped like a basketball with a 15-story spire topped by an illuminated 14-foot basketball. At night, when it's illuminated in changing colors, the Hall of Fame looks like something from outer space and definitely brightens the Springfield skyline.

One local institution that has endured through Springfield's vicissitudes is the Eastern States Exposition—always referred to locally as "The Big E"—founded in 1917 and still going strong. Held for 17 days starting in mid-September at its vast fairgrounds in West Springfield, The Big E is the only annual event of its kind encompassing all six New England states. A huge and still basically agricultural fair, it also includes big-name entertainment and the Avenue of States, replicas of the various New England state capitol buildings, each housing exhibits.

Also a survivor is the large amusement park just across the river in Agawam. Now called Six Flags New England and operated by the giant Six Flags national theme park corporation, it was originally Riverside Park, founded at the turn of the 20th century to provide inexpensive entertainment for Springfield factory workers and their families. The park was famous for its roller coaster and other scary rides back then—and still is.

AREA CODE 413 applies to all of Western Massachusetts.

GUIDANCE Greater Springfield Convention and Visitors Bureau (413-787-1548 or 1-800-723-1548; valleyvisitor.com), 1441 Main St., Springfield

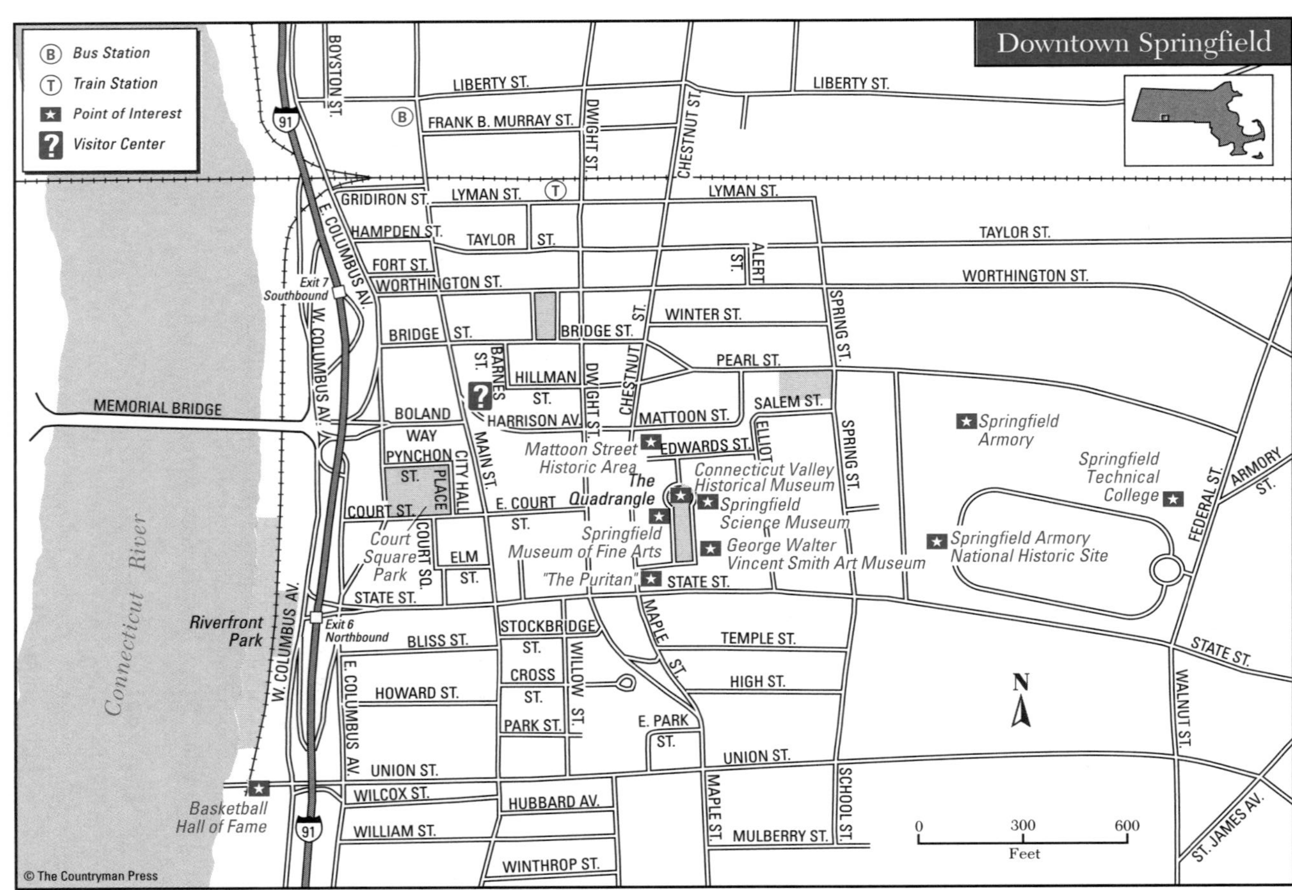
Downtown Springfield
Bus Station
Train Station
Point of Interest
Visitor Center
Springfield Armory
Springfield Technical College
Springfield Armory National Historic Site
Connecticut Valley Historical Museum
Springfield Science Museum
George Walter Vincent Smith Art Museum
Springfield Museum of Fine Arts
The Quadrangle
Mattoon Street Historic Area
"The Puritan"
Court Square Park
Riverfront Park
Basketball Hall of Fame
Connecticut River
MEMORIAL BRIDGE
Exit 7 Southbound
Exit 6 Northbound
LIBERTY ST.
FRANK B. MURRAY ST.
BOYSTON ST.
LYMAN ST.
GRIDIRON ST.
HAMPDEN ST.
TAYLOR ST.
FORT ST.
WORTHINGTON ST.
BRIDGE ST.
WINTER ST.
PEARL ST.
HILLMAN ST.
BARNES ST.
HARRISON AV.
MATTOON ST.
SALEM ST.
ELLIOT
EDWARDS ST.
BOLAND WAY
PYNCHON ST.
CITY HALL PLACE
MAIN ST.
COURT ST.
E. COURT ST.
COURT SQ.
ELM ST.
STATE ST.
BLISS ST.
STOCKBRIDGE ST.
CROSS ST.
PARK ST.
WILLOW ST.
E. PARK ST.
MAPLE ST.
TEMPLE ST.
HIGH ST.
HOWARD ST.
UNION ST.
WILCOX ST.
HUBBARD AV.
WILLIAM ST.
WINTHROP ST.
MULBERRY ST.
SCHOOL ST.
SPRING ST.
CHESTNUT ST.
DWIGHT ST.
ALERT ST.
E. COLUMBUS AV.
W. COLUMBUS AV.
91
FEDERAL ST.
ARMORY ST.
WALNUT ST.
ST. JAMES AV.
N
0 300 600 Feet
© The Countryman Press

01103. The well-stocked and -staffed visitor center is open 10–4 weekdays. **William C. Sullivan Tourist Information Center,** 1000 Hall of Fame Ave., Springfield 01103. Open year-round, Mon.–Sat. 10–6; Sun. 10–5. A walk-in, self-service visitor center next to the **Basketball Hall of Fame,** it offers information about the Pioneer Valley as well as Springfield.

GETTING THERE *By air:* **Bradley International Airport** (860-292-2000; bradleyairport.com). Eighteen miles south of Springfield in Windsor Locks, Conn., served by most national and regional carriers and major car rental companies. See *Getting Around* for taxis.

By train: **AMTRAK** (1-800-USA-RAIL; amtrak.com), 66 Lyman St., connects Springfield with Hartford, New Haven, New York City, Philadelphia, Baltimore, Washington, D.C., and Chicago. There is frequent service from New York (change in New Haven). The bus depot is right around the corner from the train station.

By bus: **Peter Pan** (413-781-2900 or 1-800-237-8747; peterpanbus.com), based in Springfield with its own terminal at 1776 Main St., connects with the airport, Boston, Hartford, Cape Cod, Albany, and New York City. Greyhound (1-800-552-8737) stops en route from New York and Albany to Vermont, New Hampshire, and Montreal.

By car: From points north take I-91 to Exit 7, and from points south to Exit 6. From Boston, take the Mass Pike to Exit 6 to I-291 to I-91 north to Exit 2B (Dwight Street), which parallels Main; take it to State Street and turn left for the Quadrangle complex; from Holyoke, I-391 is another connector.

GETTING AROUND **Pioneer Valley Transit Authority** (413-781-7882) serves the Springfield/Holyoke area.

By taxi: **Yellow Cab** (413-739-9999).

PARKING The Quadrangle museums, Springfield Armory National Historic Site, and the Basketball Hall of Fame all offer free parking (see map on p. 336), and downtown parking lots are reasonably priced.

MEDICAL EMERGENCY Dial **911.**

Baystate Medical Center (413-794-0000), Chestnut at Spring St.

* To See

MUSEUMS **Naismith Memorial Basketball Hall of Fame** (413-781-6500; hoophall.com), 1000 Hall of Fame Ave. (Just off I-91 and well marked: Look for the 15-story-high spire with the basketball on top.) Open 10–6 Mon.–Sat, 10–5 Sun. mid-June to mid-Sept.; 10–4 Mon.–Sat., 10–5 Sun. rest of the year. Admission: adults $16.99, seniors (65 plus) $13.99, ages 5–15 $11.99. Dr. James Naismith invented basketball at a YMCA college in Springfield in 1891, and the Hall of Fame has been housed at various locations around the city since 1968. The current $45 million museum is Springfield's pride, its most visible landmark (it's shaped like a giant basketball and illuminated in different colors at night), and its biggest tourist attraction. A combination history museum, shrine, computer game arcade, and gymnasium—there's nothing else quite like it.

Basketball is anything but static, and neither is the Hall of Fame, which has 41 interactive computer stations where visitors can, among other things, try their hand at basketball trivia questions and virtual reality basketball games. Some 70 TV screens are going all the time, showing interviews with players and coaches and highlights of championship games. There are also plenty of opportunities to toss basketballs around. The Hall of Fame gallery, the game's Valhalla, displays photos and mementos of basketball's greatest players, coaches, managers, and teams. Among the museum artifacts on display are Milwaukee Buck Bob Lanier's size 22 sneakers, a pair of gym bloomers worn by a member of the first women's basketball team (Smith College), and Naismith's not-very-well-typed 13 original rules of the game. The heart of the building is a regulation basketball court—pickup games are encouraged—directly under the 90-foot-high basketball-shaped dome.

Springfield Museums at the Quadrangle (413-263-6800, springfieldmuseums .org), 21 Edwards St. At this unique cultural common, four museums—a science, history, and two art museums—and the city's main library are all assembled around a grassy green. The Quadrangle green is the site of a sculpture garden memorializing the work of children's book author and illustrator Dr. Seuss, nom de plume of native son Theodor Geisel. The museums are open Mon.–Sat. 10–5, Sun. 11–5. A ticket good for admission to all four museums is $12.50 for adults, $9 for seniors and college students, $6.50 for ages 3–17, and free for children under 3. Inquire about frequent special events. The museum welcome center adjacent to the Springfield Science Museum contains the ticket office, a large gift shop, and a snack area with vending machines.

Dr. Seuss National Memorial (413-263-6800; catinthehat.org), the Quadrangle. Open daily 9–8 spring and summer, 9–5 fall and winter. Free. This imaginative sculpture garden is the kind of humorous, fantastical tribute Theodor Geisel would have appreciated. The 22 bronze figures range in size from a tiny Lorax (a gnome with a walrus mustache) to a 14-foot-high trunk-waving Horton the Elephant, depicted stepping out of a giant book with Thidwick the Big Hearted Moose, Sam I Am, and other beloved Dr. Seuss characters. All the sculptures are the work of Lark Grey Diamond-Cates, Geisel's stepdaughter. The man himself is depicted sitting at his drawing board—and standing beside him, grinning mischievously, is Dr. Seuss's muse: the Cat in the Hat. As you might imagine, this sculpture garden is kid-friendly and there is even a bronze "storyteller chair" where parents can sit and read a favorite Dr. Seuss story to their child.

The Michele & Donald D'Amour Museum of Fine Arts (413-263-6800; springfieldmuseums.org), the Quadrangle. A 1930s art deco building with a central court, the museum houses a surprisingly superb collection. You might expect the 18th- and 19th-century portraits and Hudson River landscapes (be sure to locate *New England Scenery* by Frederic Church), some memorable Winslow Homers and Frederick Remingtons, but what you don't expect is the wealth of early-20th-century paintings by Georgia O'Keeffe, Charles Sheeler, Charles

William A. Davis

DR. SEUSS CHARACTERS IN HORTON COURT AT THE DR. SEUSS NATIONAL MEMORIAL IN SPRINGFIELD.

Demuth, Reginald Marsh, and others. Paul Sample's *Church Supper* alone is worth a trip. The modern art collection is also far more than token. The museum's paintings and sculpture are complemented in an interesting way by period furnishings and decorative art. Another surprise: Erastus Field's *Historical Monument of the American Republic,* a huge, absorbing fantasy depicting 300 scenes on 10 elaborate towers, a visual saga culminating with the triumph over slavery (note Abraham Lincoln rising to heaven in a fiery chariot near the top of the central tower). *The Newsboy,* a moment in 1889 captured by George Newhall, Springfield's leading late-19th-century artist, is also worth noting. The museum has the country's only permanent gallery devoted to Currier & Ives prints. There are also frequent changing exhibits.

George Walter Vincent Smith Art Museum (413-263-6800; springfieldmuseums.org), the Quadrangle. The first museum on the Quadrangle (1896), this is a one-man collection housed in a magnificent palazzo. G. W. V. Smith (always called by his full name locally) amassed a fortune in New York and married Springfield's Belle Townsley, retiring here at age 35. The couple devoted the next five decades to collecting ancient Japanese swords, armor, and art; Middle Eastern rugs; the largest Western collection of Chinese cloisonné; and 19th-century landscape paintings. The Art Discovery Center, an interactive, colorfully decorated gallery, is designed to introduce children and families to the museum's collection. Like Boston's Isabella Stewart Gardner, the Smiths stipulated that the collection not be altered after their deaths, and their ashes are interred in the museum. The couple's portraits are just off the entry hall, surrounded by those of stern past captains of Valley industry.

Springfield Museum of Fine Arts

HISTORICAL MONUMENT OF THE AMERICAN REPUBLIC, AN 1876 WORK BY ERASTUS SALISBURY AT THE MUSEUM OF FINE ARTS IN SPRINGFIELD.

Lyman & Merrie Wood Museum of Springfield History (413-263-2800; springfieldmuseums.org), the Quadrangle. The newest museum in the complex, the Museum of Springfield History was built at a cost of $10 million and opened in the fall of 2009. The emphasis is on Springfield's development as a diversified manufacturing center after the Civil War, with exhibits on products invented and made in Springfield such as Indian motorcycles, Breck shampoo, Smith & Wesson handguns, Milton Bradley board games, and Gee Bee airplanes, two of which hang from the museum ceiling. In the infancy of the automobile industry, Springfield even had several car makers. One exhibit is devoted to locally made Rolls-Royces. The Indian motorcycle collection is the country's largest. The museum also contains the Springfield History Library and Archives, which includes 2.5 million manuscripts, 50,000 photographs, 30,000 books, thousands of reels of microfilm, and computer databases with information of interest to historical researchers and genealogists. The Springfield History Theater here shows documentary films and presents educational programs. *Note:* At this writing the museum also contains exhibits from the Connecticut Valley Historical Museum, which is currently closed for renovation.

Springfield Science Museum (413-263-6800; springfieldmuseums.org), the Quadrangle. Dinosaur buffs will find a 20-foot-high model of *Tyrannosaurus rex* and the tracks of much smaller dinosaurs. Exhibits also include a 1937 Gee Bee monoplane made in Springfield, a hands-on Exploration Center, an impressive African Hall full of animals, some great old-fashioned dioramas, Native American artifacts, and a new Eco-Center featuring live animals in realistic habitats—lifelike vegetation, fish that walk on land, turtles that look like leaves, and an

Springfield Museums

THIS 20-FOOT-HIGH *TYRANNOSAURUS REX* RESIDES AT THE SPRINGFIELD SCIENCE MUSEUM.

Amazon rain forest. Planetarium shows daily. Adults $3, children $2.

Springfield Armory National Historic Site (413-734-8551; nps.gov/spar), Armory Square (1 mile east on State St. from the Quadrangle; enter from Federal St. near the corner of State). Open daily 9–5 year-round except holidays. Free. It was the presence of this federal armory, established in 1794 to manufacture muskets for the U.S. Army, which transformed Springfield from a sleepy village into a vibrant industrial city. The museum in the Main Arsenal building, which dates to 1850, contains one of the world's largest and most comprehensive collections of firearms. Exhibits include an array of weapons, from flintlock muskets to M16 rifles, used in every American war since the Revolution. There are also film presentations, displays of innovative machinery invented at the armory, special exhibits on firearms development, and weapons firing demonstrations. Only about 20 percent of the armory's vast firearms collection is on view in the public galleries at any time. There are daily ranger-guided interpretive tours at 2 PM. The imposing brick armory complex, which occupies more

DISPLAYS AT THE LYMAN & MERRIE WOOD MUSEUM OF SPRINGFIELD HISTORY.

William A. Davis

than 15 acres along a bluff above the city, is now largely occupied by Springfield Technical Community College.

The Titanic Museum (413-543-4770; titanichistoricalsociety.org), rear of Henry's Jewelry Store, 208 Main St., Indian Orchard. Open weekdays 10–4, Sat. 10–3. A large collection of thousands of objects about or recovered from the RMS *Titanic,* which sank on April 15, 1912, with a loss of 1,517 lives in the world's most famous maritime disaster. The society's founder and president, Edward Kamuda, was inspired to begin the collection after seeing the 1953 film, *A Night to Remember.* There is an online gift shop.

Storrowton Village Museum (413-205-5051; thebige.com/sv), 1305 Memorial Ave., West Springfield, at the Eastern States Exposition grounds (MA 147). Open mid-June to late Aug., Tues.–Sat. 11–3. Admission $5, children under 6 free. The gift shop is open year-round (closed Sun.). Donated to the exposition in 1929 by Mrs. James Storrow of Boston (the same family for whom Storrow Drive is named), this grouping of restored 18th- and early-19th-century buildings makes up one of the first museum villages in the country. The buildings, all of which were moved here from their original locations, include an 1834 meetinghouse, an 1810 brick school, a huge and handsome 1776 mansion, and a genuine 1789 tavern that would now be deep in Quabbin Reservoir if it hadn't been rescued.

HISTORIC HOMES AND SITES **Court Square,** bounded by Court and Elm Sts. Springfield's "Municipal Group" recalls the city's golden era. Completed in 1913, the monumental, many-columned, Greek Revival City Hall and Symphony Hall buildings are separated by a soaring, 300-foot Italianate campanile. The City Hall interior is graced by 27 kinds of marble and fine wood paneling, and includes an auditorium that can seat 3,000. Symphony Hall is equally elegant and known for its acoustics.

Historic Springfield neighborhoods. In the late 19th century Springfield became known as the City of Homes, reflecting the quality of the thousands of wooden homes—single- and two-family houses instead of the usual tenements and triple-deckers for the working class, and truly splendid houses for the middle and upper classes. Unfortunately, with the flight of families to the suburbs, several once-proud neighborhoods are now shabby, but still well worth driving through. Forest Park, developed almost entirely between the 1890s and 1920, is filled with turreted, shingled Victorian homes, many built by the McKnight brothers (for whom the McKnight District, boasting some 900 of these homes, is named). Some of the city's stateliest houses, a number on the National Register of Historic Places, are found in the Maple Hill District. Right downtown, the Mattoon Street Historic District is a street of 19th-century brick row houses leading to the 1870s Grace Baptist Church designed by Henry Hobson Richardson.

FOR FAMILIES ✐ **Six Flags New England** (413-786-9300 or 1-877-4-SIXFLAGS; sixflags.com/parks/newengland), 1623 Main St. (MA 159), Agawam. Open weekends mid-Apr.–May, daily June through Labor Day, weekends in

Sept. and Oct.; call for hours. Season pass $59.99; otherwise, adults $42.99, under 54 inches high $32.99, children 2 and younger free. The largest theme and water park in New England, with more than 160 rides (including eight roller coasters) and an 8-acre water park with more than two dozen water slides. Also, a midway, arcades, food, and live entertainment. Day parking $15, season parking $50.

The Zoo in Forest Park (413-733-2251; forestparkzoo.org). Off Summer Ave./MA 83 (I-91 North, Exit 2; I-91 South, Exit 4). Open Apr.–early Oct., daily 10–5, weather permitting. Adults $6, seniors and children 5–12 $4, under 5 $2. A small wild-animal zoo (deer, bears, woodland and exotic animals) and a petting zoo.

Eastern States Exposition. See *Special Events*.

✷ Green Space

Forest Park (413-787-6434), 3 miles south of the center of Springfield (see directions to the zoo under *For Families*). Open year-round. Free for walk-ins, nominal charge for cars. The 735 acres include two small zoos. The park also offers paddleboats, 21 miles of nature trails, tennis courts, picnic groves, swimming pools, and summer concerts at the Barney Amphitheater. A magnificent, columned mausoleum built by ice skate tycoon Everett H. Barney (his mansion was destroyed to make way for I-91) commands a great view of the Connecticut.

Riverfront Park, foot of State St., Springfield. This 6-acre riverfront park offers a 3.5-mile-long bicycle path and a view of the Connecticut River, which is otherwise walled from the city by railroad tracks and interstate highway.

FOREST PARK OFFERS TWO SMALL ZOOS FOR CHILDREN.

Kim Grant

Stanley Park (413-568-9312; stanleypark.org), 400 Western Ave., Westfield. Open mid-May–mid-Oct., 8 AM–dusk. Endowed by the founder of Stanley Home Products, the 300-acre park is known for its extensive rose garden (more than 50 varieties), mini New England village, 96-foot-high carillon tower, Japanese garden with teahouse, arboretum, and large fountain. Sunday evening concerts range from singing groups to the Springfield Symphony Pops.

Laughing Brook Education Center & Wildlife Sanctuary (413-566-8034), 789 Main St., Hampden. From I-91 in Springfield, take Exit 4 (MA 83) to Sumner Ave., then go 3.6 miles. Open dawn to dusk. Adults $3, children and seniors $2. Off any main route to anywhere, this is a popular destination for families drawn by the one-time home of beloved children's author Thornton Burgess. The house is now part of a 356-acre preserve owned by the Massachusetts Audubon Society; it includes hiking trails, fields, streams, a pond, caged animals, a picnic pavilion, and a "touch-and-see" trail.

✷ Lodging

The downtown convention hotels include the 265-room high-rise **Springfield-Marriott Hotel** (413-781-7111) and the 325-room **Sheraton Springfield Monarch Place** (413-781-1010), both right at the downtown I-91 exit, both with indoor heated pools and full health clubs.

NAOMI'S INN, A DELIGHTFUL B&B ON SPRING STREET.

William A. Davis

Marriott rates are $119–199 and the Sheraton's are $99–159. A 12-story, 242-room **City Place Inn and Suites** (413-781-0900), 711 Dwight St. (I-291, Exit 2A), has an indoor pool and rooftop restaurant. $89–129 double. The **Hilton Garden Inn** (413-886-8000 or 1-800-234-3744; hiltongarden inn.com) is an attractive, 143-room hotel adjacent to the Basketball Hall of Fame (they share a parking lot) with a large indoor pool. $109–159.

BED & BREAKFASTS

Naomi's Inn (413-433-6019 or 1-888-762-6647; naomisinn.net), 20 Spring St. Innkeeper Marci Webber (Naomi is her young daughter) has completely restored this handsome 1846 house across from Bayside Medical Center. She rents three units, all with private baths, separate sleeping and sitting areas, central air-conditioning, WiFi, and television. Each has a distinctive décor, with furniture, wallpaper, and paintings reflecting a specific period. We liked the eclectically furnished British Travel Suite, decorated to reflect different corners of the British Empire in its heyday. The inn is about a 10-minute drive from downtown and easily accessed from I-91. There is ample off-street parking. Rates are $115–135 with full breakfast. Inquire about hospital stays and other packages.

Lathrop House B&B (413-736-6414; dianamarahenry.com/lathrop), 188 Sumner Ave. An imposing, white-pillared, Gilded Age mansion across from 735-acre Forest Park, home of the city's s zoo. This was Springfield's first kosher B&B and remains its only one. There are three air-conditioned guest rooms with shared bathroom and a Victorian decor reflecting the house's era; it was built in 1899 by the well-to-do Lathrop family. All faiths are welcome and Lathrop House is also gay friendly. Rates are $80–175 with continental breakfast. Innkeeper Diana Henry notes that the dairy products and baked goods served at breakfast are all certified kosher. There is a two-day minimum for guests arriving on Friday.

✷ Where to Eat

DINING OUT **The Student Prince Cafe & The Fort Dining Room** (413-734-7475; studentprince.com), 8 Fort St. (off Main). Open Mon.–Sat. 11–11, Sun. noon–10. A downtown Springfield institution, The Student Prince was founded in 1935 by German immigrants, and its decor and menu are still thoroughly Germanic. The place is festooned with decorative beer steins—one of the largest collections in the country—and the extensive menu offers diners a choice of hearty Middle European dishes such as sauerbraten, Wiener schnitzel, Hungarian goulash, bratwurst, and chicken paprika along with steak and seafood. Specials change with the seasons. Lunch runs $8.95–20.95, dinner $10.50–27.50.

Storrowton Tavern & Carriage House (413-732-4188; storrowton .com), 1305 Memorial Ave., West Springfield. Located in Storrowton Village Museum on the grounds of the Eastern States Exposition, the tavern occupies two antique buildings that were moved to the site. It serves traditional New England fare such as Yankee pot roast and baked Boston scrod, along with some Italian specialties. Open Tues.–Sun. for lunch and dinner (daily 10–10 during the 17-day Eastern States Exposition in mid-Sept.). Reservations recommended. Luncheon entrées $10–16; dinner $17–26.

Hofbräuhaus (413-737-4905; hofbrauhaus.org), 1105 Main St., West Springfield. The dining room features murals of German landscapes, and the atmosphere is quite formal but fun. Try deep-fried sauerkraut balls or goulash soup, a selection of good veal dishes, and a sparkling German wine among a choice of 300 vintages. Be sure to leave room for a torte. Dinner entrées are $16–32.

Bottega Cucina (413-732-2500; bcucina.com) 46 Morgan Rd., West Springfield. Open for lunch Tues.–Sat. 11–3; dinner Tues.–Wed. 4:30–9, Thurs.–Fri. 4:30–10, Sat. 3–10. Popular neighborhood restaurant that emphasizes fresh local ingredients and authentic Italian cuisine. Menu items include shrimp scampi, chicken Picatta, cotoletta (beer-battered white fish with a caper remoulade), and porchetta (pan-seared pork chop topped with an apple, honey, walnut, and Gorgonzola crumble). Entrées $16–18.50.

Red Rose Pizzeria (413-739-8510), 1060 Main St. Open Tues.–Sun. for lunch and dinner. A full-service restaurant despite the name, Red Rose is one of Springfield's most popular dining spots. The cavernous dining room seats 400, but there is often a line to get in, particularly on weekends. (Reservations are taken only for parties of 10 or more.) The food is authentically Italian and the portions, including the pizzas, are famously outsized. Pizza $12–22, entrées $10.50–17.

Onyx Fusion Bar & Restaurant (413-730-6699; onyxfusion.com), 1150 Hall of Fame Ave. Located next to the Basketball Hall of Fame, this is a three-level restaurant, lounge, and function venue with a fusion menu that includes pasta and other Italian specialties along with a raw bar, steak, and seafood. Entrées $10–31.

EATING OUT **Cafe Lebanon** (413-737-7373; cafelebanon.com), 1390 Main St. Traditional Middle Eastern cuisine at its flavorful best. Full liquor license. Live belly dancing every Fri. and Sat.

Chef Wayne's Big Mamou (413-732-1011; chefwaynes-bigmamou.com), 68 Liberty St. Open for lunch Mon.–Sat., dinner nightly. Chef Wayne's Louisiana fried oysters, crabcakes, crawfish, and jerked beef get rave reviews. Atmosphere is minimal and there is no liquor at this, the mother location (there is at the Williamsburg restaurant), but the food and prices draw patrons from many miles around.

Theodore's–Booze, Blues and BBQ (413-736-6000; theobbq.com), 201 Worthington St. Voted Number One blues club in the country by The Blues Foundation. Open daily. Famous for BBQ, but quesadilla, nachos, Buffalo wings, and Cajun fried fish are also on the menu along with popcorn shrimp and gumbo. Local, regional, and national blues groups perform on Friday and Saturday nights. Dinner entrées $11.99–18.99.

Two Eagles (413-737-6135), 110 Island Pond Rd. Open daily 11:30–9. This popular place has a loyal local following. The menu is large, ranging from a BLT to surf and turf, lamb shish kebob to fried seafood dinners.

Mom & Rico's Market (413-732-8941), 899 Main St. Open Mon.–Fri. 8–5. A great Italian deli and grocery with a self-service buffet that usually includes lasagna, sausage and peppers, and eggplant parmigiana (better than your mother's). Pay $5.49 a pound for the buffet or order from the large choice of grinders. For cappuccino and a cannoli, step next door to the La Fiorentina Pastry Shop (883 Main St.; see *Snacks*).

Frigo's (413-731-7797), 1244 Main St. Open Mon.–Fri. 8–5, until 6 in summer. The blackboard menu features take-out specialties like pizza rustica, veal parmigiana, and large and interesting sandwich combinations, favorites with the downtown lunch crowd. If you have time, step around to Frigo's Gourmet Foods at 90 Williams St., a cheese lover's mecca that also offers Italian cold cuts and take-out.

Lido (413-736-9433), 555 Worthington. Open Tues.–Sat. 11–11. Drive (don't walk) to this Italian favorite, good for the basics like lasagna, eggplant parmigiana, and hot or sweet sausage. Best garlic bread in town.

Sitar (413-732-8011), 1688 Main St. Open Mon.–Sat. for lunch and dinner,

Sun. for dinner. Sampler platters and luncheon specials help the uninitiated choose from a large menu of Indian and Pakistani dishes.

Uno's Chicago Bar & Grill (413-733-1300), 820 Hall of Fame Ave. Open daily for lunch and dinner. A large, moderately priced family restaurant next to the Basketball Hall of Fame. Deep-dish pizza is the specialty, but there is a full menu. Live music nightly in the garden courtyard.

Hot Table (413-782-1200; hottable .com), Tower Square, 1500 Main St. Paninis made to order and grilled the way you want them. Also salads, wraps, and desserts. Free WiFi.

Abudanza Ristorante (413-737-1000), 613 Belmont Ave. Open Mon. 8–3, Tues.–Sat. 8–10. Pleasant, reasonably priced restaurant in the historic Forest Park neighborhood. Extensive menu includes a variety of traditional Italian dishes.

SNACKS **La Fiorentina Pastry Shop** (413-732-3151), 883 Main St. Open Mon.–Sat. 8–6, Sun. 8–2. The real thing. Mauro and Clara Daniele first opened La Fiorentina in 1947, using recipes for which Mauro's father, Giuseppe, had won awards for baking in Florence. Try the tiramisu (espresso, liqueur, mascarpone cheese, and cocoa powder layered between ladyfingers). Gelati, coffees, biscotti, and many pastries; known for rum cake layered with custard and chocolate.

✷ Entertainment

City Stage (413-788-7033), 1 Columbus Center. Professional theater, Sept.–May.

MassMutual Center (413-787-6600; massmutualcenter.com), Main at E. Court St. Contains a 6,677-seat arena and hosts concerts, conventions, trade shows, and sporting events, including home games of the Springfield Falcons hockey team.

Symphony Hall (413-788-7033), Court Square. The classic, columned music hall is the home of the Springfield Symphony Orchestra. It also hosts top-name performers, Broadway shows, and children's theater.

The Hippodrome (413-787-0600), 1700 Main St. A former 1920s movie palace, now the largest nightclub in Western Massachusetts, featuring live (frequently Latin) entertainment.

Showcase Cinemas (413-733-5131), 864 Riverdale Rd., West Springfield. A multiplex showing first-run films.

Majestic Theater (413-747-7797; majestictheater.com), 131 Elm St., West Springfield. Live theater Sept.–May. Children's theater, open mic nights, music and comedy shows in summer.

✷ Selective Shopping

Tower Square (413-733-2171; visit towersquare.com), 1500 Main St., Springfield. This downtown indoor mall has restaurants and a variety of shops and services.

Springfield Museums Gift Shop (413-263-6800; springfieldmuseums .org), 220 State St., Springfield. Located in the welcome center of the four-museum complex (adjacent to the Science Museum). Besides the usual museum store items, this attractive shop has all the Dr. Seuss books and a wide assortment of Dr. Seuss–themed toys, stuffed animals, lunchboxes, and other gifts.

Holyoke Mall (413-536-1440; hol yokemall.com) in the Ingleside section of Holyoke (I-91 Exit 15, and

Mass Pike Exit 4). Open Mon.–Sat. 10–9:30, Sun. 11–6. The biggest mall in Western Massachusetts and one of the largest in New England. There are nearly 200 stores, with Macy's, JCPenney, and Sears among the anchors. Also a dozen food outlets.

✷ Farms

Fini's Plant Farm (1-800-342-2205; finiplants.com), 217 James St., Feeding Hills. Open May–Oct., weekdays 8–6, weekends 9–5. A large selection of perennials, annuals, and herbs. There are wagon rides, corn and hay mazes, and a perennial garden.

Birdhaven Blueberry Farm (413-527-4671; birdhavenblueberry.info), 55 Gunn Rd., Southampton. Open year-round, Tues.–Sat. 9–6, Sun. 9–3. Homemade pies, jams, and jellies sold at the farm store. Pick-your-own flowers, blueberries, and raspberries in-season.

Calabrese Farms (413-569-6417), 257 Feeding Hills Rd. (MA 57), Southwick. Open Apr.–Sept., daily 8:30–7. Has bedding plants, hangers, geraniums, and perennials in spring; its own corn, tomatoes, melons, peaches, and other produce in summer.

Coward Farms (413-569-6724), College Hwy. (US 202), Southwick. Open from the day after Thanksgiving through the Christmas season. Cut-your-own Christmas trees (four kinds of fir trees and blue spruce) as well as wreaths, swags, and kissing balls.

Ray's Family Farm (413-569-3366), 723 College Hwy. (US 202 and MA 10), Southwick. Open mid-Apr.–Dec., daily 8–8. Annual bedding plants and farm-grown produce.

Kosinski Farms/North Country Harvest (413-562-4643; kosinskifarms.com), 420 Russellville Rd., Westfield. Open Jan.–Mar., Tues.–Sun. 8–5; Apr.–Dec., daily 6–8. Plants, flowers, apples, berries, sweet corn, pumpkins, and other produce. The farm store sells bread, muffins, mulled cider, and fresh fruit sundaes. There is a corn maze. Daily hayrides Sept.–Nov.

Pomeroy Farm and Sugar House (413-568-0049 or 413-568-3484), Russellville Rd., Westfield. Sugarhouse open mid-Feb.–early Apr.; farm stand open seasonally, selling fresh produce. Maple syrup, candy, and gift baskets are available year-round. B&B accommodation is available (413-568-3783).

✷ Special Events

Note: For event information, call 413-755-1351 or visit valleyvisitor.com.

May: **World's Largest Pancake Breakfast** (413-733-3800), Eastfield Mall, Boston Road, Springfield.

June: **West Side's Taste of the Valley** (413-734-1118), Town Common, West Springfield. More than 25 restaurants participate.

June–September: **Downtown Farmers' Market,** held every Friday 11–2 at Tower Square Park.

July: **Star Spangled Springfield** (413-733-3800) is a Fourth of July celebration with live music, food, an arts festival, and fireworks in Court Square.

July–August: Sunday performances by **Springfield Pops** in Stanley Park, Westfield. **Theatrical and musical performances** in Forest Park, Sunday evenings.

July–September: **Bike Night, free concerts** in Springfield's Stearns Square on Thursday evenings.

September: **Harambee Festival of Black Culture,** Winchester Square, Springfield. **Eastern States Exposition** (413-737-2443), West Springfield. "The Big E" is the biggest annual fair in the East, with livestock shows, horse shows, a giant midway, and entertainment. Always runs 17 days, including the third week in September. **Quadrangle Weekend** (413-737-1750) features outdoor festivities, films, lectures, and craft demonstrations. **Mattoon Street Arts Festival** (mattoonfestival.org) is an outdoor fair on a downtown Springfield street lined with brownstones and gaslights.

October: **Fright Fest** (413-786-9300), Six Flags New England, Agawam.

November: **Parade of the Big Balloons** (413-733-3800), downtown Springfield (*day after Thanksgiving*).

Late November–mid-January: **Bright Nights at Forest Park** (413-733-3800) is New England's largest Christmas light display, with themes like Seuss Land, Victorian Village, and North Pole Village. Evenings from 6 o'clock.

INDEX

C

N

O

T

U

V

W